AMERICAN PUBLIC OPINION:
ITS ORIGINS, CONTENT, AND IMPACT

AMERICAN PUBLIC OPINION:
ITS ORIGINS, CONTENT, AND IMPACT

Robert S. Erikson
Assistant Professor of Government,
Florida State University

Norman R. Luttbeg
Professor of Government,
Florida State University

JOHN WILEY & SONS, INC.
New York • London • Sydney • Toronto

Library of Congress Cataloging in Publication Data:

Erikson, Robert S.
  American public opinion.

  Includes bibliographical references.
  1. Public opinion—United States.   I. Luttbeg,
Norman R., joint author.   II. Title.
HM261.E67   301.15′4′0973   72-13498
ISBN 0-471-24425-2   ISBN 471 24426 0

Printed in the United States of America

10 9 8 7 6 5 4 3 2

PREFACE

Our work obviously benefits from the efforts of others. Two classic studies of the American electorate—Campbell, Converse, Miller, and Stokes's *The American Voter* and Key's *Public Opinion and American Democracy*—stand as the scholarly heritage most valuable to our thinking. In many ways our efforts here are an updating of their thoughts and data to include findings as late as the 1970 congressional elections. To this understanding of American political behavior we add evidence of the origins of public opinion gleaned from the studies of political socialization and media impact and especially studies of the interactions between the public and their representatives that act to achieve congruence between public opinion and public policy.

In writing we sought to reach the college student with the best available data in the belief that our disciplinary understanding of these phenomena merits the attention of future practitioners—citizens or politicians. The body of knowledge that permits this effort relies not only on the research and thoughts of others but, most importantly, on the existence of data conscientiously gathered by the Survey Research Center of the University of Michigan (made available to scholars through the Inter-University Consortium for Political Research) and the long experience of the Gallup poll. Without such data our conclusions would be far more tenuous.

Not only is the book dependent on the thoughts, writing, and data of others, it is vastly improved by the kind personal efforts of others. We particularly thank John L. Sullivan, James Q. Wilson, and Harmon Zeigler for their most valuable comments and criticisms. Our colleagues at Florida State University, especially Brian Silver, receive our gratitude for enduring our preliminary drafts and developing ideas. We also acknowledge the efforts of Stanley Freedman who helped with the data analysis and the secretaries of the Department of Government and the Institute for Social Research whose efforts helped us to avoid missing our deadlines.

Robert Erikson
Norman Luttbeg

CONTENTS

ONE

PARTICIPATION IN DEMOCRATIC POLITICS

"No matter how you vote, vote!"; "Make your beliefs count, send your contributions to Save Our Schools today!"; "Give a damn!"; Write your Congressman to tell him you oppose the gun registration bill. We are continually exhorted to be active in governing our city, school, county, state, and nation. In a typical year we could express ourselves politically six times just in our choice for various public offices up for election.[1] And voting is not the sole possible political act —the utilities commission calls public meetings; candidates seek both workers and contributions; friends cajole our participation in political causes; groups call for public outcries; and late in the evening, our anger may urge us to write a letter to what's his name, our Congressman. In short, political activities continually beckon our attention and participation. A person who feels strongly about political candidates and issues could clearly participate in politics to the point of precluding his earning a living, raising a family, or enjoying leisure. Political participation seems more limited by the time and energies people wish to commit to it than by the opportunities to do so.

CITIZEN POLITICAL PARTICIPATION

Although continually urged to be politically concerned, Americans, like people everywhere, are more involved in personal concerns. On several occasions since 1959, researchers have asked Americans about their personal hopes and fears.[2] These surveys show that concern with family and personal health and with personal living standards preoccupy Americans' thoughts about the future. In 1971, for example, 28 percent said they feared a loss of personal health; 18 percent feared a lower standard of living; 16 percent, ill health in the family; and 13 percent unemployment.[3] But all of these percentages had declined since 1958 and 1964. The public in 1971 expressed greater concern about drug problems in the family (7 percent), pollution (7 percent), political instability (5 percent), and crime (5 percent). Although the researchers were not concerned with the question of whether the public looked to government for help with these hopes and fears, a reading of the actual responses of a representative sampling on the standard of living responses found no mention of turning to the government or expectation that government is responsible.

Also distinctly political fears such as a Communist takeover, corruption in government, or a loss of personal freedoms troubled very few Americans. Finally, many social problems around which most political controversy presently rages, such as crime, pollution, and drugs, seem not to be among the concerns of typical Americans. Personal hopes and fears center largely on family well-being, and even these concerns are not perceived to involve the government.

Even when specifically asked to focus on fears and hopes of national significance, only the fear of war and the hope for peace greatly concern Americans. Fifty-one percent hope for peace. Inflation, communism, lack of law and order, pollution, drugs, racial tensions, unemployment, lack of public morality, and loss of personal freedoms each concern no more than 17 percent of the public. But a most dramatic change between 1964 and 1971 came in the increase from 8 to 26 percent fearing national disunity.[4] The protest activity of the late 1960s and early 1970s over civil rights and the war in Vietnam seems largely at the root of this anxiety. Considering the scale of the protests, the coverage they received on television, and the controversy surrounding them, we get a strong impression that public concern will focus on political matters only in the most extraordinary circumstances. Only 5 percent of Americans report this concern among their personal fears and only 26 percent see it as a national danger. Apart from war with its Herculean investment of human resources and clear personal significance, few if any other actions by government seem to concern Americans.

When Gallup polls ask national samples to name "the most important problem facing this country," typically almost all will name some problem, such as crime, pollution, or unemployment. But since few of these problems are personal hopes or fears, one might question whether the public is greatly preoccupied with the political concerns they are able to mention or demand particular solutions. Americans are seldom asked what they would do were they government officials, but the responses to such a question in 1943 suggest that Americans are not preoccupied with government matters. When asked, "If you were elected to Congress this fall what laws would you want to have passed?" more than 47 percent answered that they had no opinions. Furthermore, when asked, "Can you think of any problem which you feel a congressional committee should investigate?", only 38 percent could think of any such problem.[5] More recent surveys suggest little change in this pattern. In 1970, just prior to the congressional election, 54 percent of a national sample claimed that candidates' stands on the issues were the most important reasons for their voting decision, but only 22 percent could name an issue that motivated their vote choice in their local Congressional race.[6]

The 1959 study of hopes and fears included samples from 12

countries. For each country, the researchers defined national political fears to include all mentions of the quality of government, losses of freedoms, and concerns with law and order. The 23 percent of Americans who expressed national political fears proved quite typical of political concerns in most of the countries untroubled by unrest at the time.[7] Other data also confirm the fact that the average American is not unusually apolitical or insensitive to government actions. Compared with the people in four other Western democracies, Americans express the most concern for the potential impact of government on their day-to-day lives. While in 1960 less than a majority of Americans (41 percent) said national government has a great effect on them, even fewer Britons (33 percent), Germans (38 percent), Italians (23 percent), and Mexicans (7 percent) agreed.[8] In fact, an amazing 66 percent of the Mexicans said their national government had no effect on their lives. Moreover, most people in all countries felt that whatever the impact of government, it would improve conditions.

Not surprisingly, this public indifference to government proves insufficient to motivate their rapt attention to, and participation in, political and governmental affairs. Tables 1-1 and 1-2 show the majority in most democracies professing to the very minimal political acts of following accounts of political and governmental affairs from time to time and paying a little attention to political campaigns. But substantial minorities do not participate even to this limited extent, and Americans prove to be high rather than low participators.

TABLE 1-1 **Following Accounts of Political and Governmental Affairs, by Nation (in Percent)**[a]

Percent Who Report They Follow Accounts	United States	United Kingdom	Germany	Italy	Mexico
Regularly	27	23	34	11	15
From time to time	53	45	38	26	40
Never	19	32	25	62	44
Other and don't know	1	1	3	1	1
Total percent	100	100	100	100	100
Total number	970	963	955	995	1,007

Source. The Civic Culture: Political Attitudes and Democracy in Five Nations, by Gabriel A. Almond and Sidney Verba (Copyright © 1963 by Princeton University Press), published for the Center of International Studies, Princeton University: Tables 6 and 7, p. 89.
[a] Actual question: "Do you follow the accounts of political and governmental affairs? Would you say you follow them regularly, from time to time, or never?"

TABLE 1-2 **Paying Attention to Political Campaigns, by Nation (in Percent)**[a]

Percent Who Say They:	United States	United Kingdom	Germany	Italy	Mexico
Pay much attention	43	25	34	17	15
Pay little attention	44	47	34	25	38
Pay no attention	12	29	27	54	45
Other and don't know	1	0	5	4	2
Total percent	100	101	100	100	100
Total number	970	963	955	995	1,007

Source. Gabriel A. Almond and Sidney Verba, *The Civic Culture* (Princeton, New Jersey: Princeton University Press, 1963), p. 89.
[a] Actual text of the question: "What about the campaigning that goes on at the time of a national election—do you pay much attention to what goes on, just a little, or none at all?"

Sense of Civic Duty

Even if politics is of little concern to most people, Americans apparently do feel obligated to participate when called upon to vote. Summed over three presidential election surveys, 89 percent said that regardless of whether or not others voted, they should.[9] As Table 1-3 shows, a person's sense of civic duty is a good predictor

TABLE 1-3 **Relationship between Voting and Sense of Civic Duty, 1956**

	Sense of Civic Duty				
	Low				High
Percent voting	13	42	52	74	85
Percent of sample	5	4	8	36	46

Source. Angus Campbell, et al., *The American Voter* (New York: John Wiley and Sons, Inc., 1960), p. 106.

of whether he will vote. Civic duty, in fact, appears to be the most important motivation for voting.[10] However, even though Americans feel more obligated to participate than do citizens of other democracies,[11] America fails to match the 85 to 90 percent voting rate of many democracies. Other factors, such as difficult registration procedures, bad timing of elections, or even the tiresome frequency of American elections, must explain our relatively low voter turnout.

Levels of Public Participation

Few political activities other than voting attract the typical American, as Table 1-4 indicates. Apart from voting and giving opinions, one study shows 63 percent participate in no other political activity which would put the citizen in closer contact with political parties or candidates. And only 15 percent engage in more than one of these minimally time consuming acts.[12]

TABLE 1-4　**Percent of Americans Professing to Having Been Active in Various Political Actions, 1952-1970**

Activity	1952	1956	1960	1964	1968	1970
Belong to political club	2	3	3	4	3	5
Work for political party	3	3	6	5	5	7
Attend political rally or meeting	7	10	8	9	9	9
Contribute money to campaign	4	10	12	11	9	a
Use political sticker or button	a	16	21	16	15	9
Give political opinions	27	28	33	31	30	27
Vote in election	73	73	74	78	75	59[b]

Sources. John P. Robinson, Jerrold G. Rusk, and Kendra B. Head, *Measures of Political Attitudes* (Ann Arbor: Survey Research Center, 1968), p. 591 and (for 1968 and 1970) Survey Research Center data.
[a] Not asked.
[b] The 1970 election is a midterm congressional-only election, resulting in a typically lower turnout.

Although the information is less than complete, Americans seem to be about as politically active as citizens of other democracies. For example, 2 percent of Norwegians report taking a personal part in campaigns, as compared with the 3 to 6 percent of Americans who report having worked for the party. Similarly, 7 percent of the Norwegians sampled have attended one or more election meetings, compared with 7 to 10 percent of Americans.[13] The figure for the British is 8 percent, with 3 percent having taken an active part in the campaign.[14] Finally, the French seem somewhat more politically active as 30 percent report attending public meetings, and 20 percent claim to having contributed money.[15]

Apparently the citizens of democracies do not perceive the happenings of the government and politics around them as demanding their attention. These happenings are thought generally to be benign; and to fulfill totally one's civic duty, one need only vote. Also, in surveys most people say that if it were ever needed, they could use the available channels for communicating with their government officials, and that they would be successful in getting the situation changed to their liking.[16] Whether the ordinary citizen of a large country is justified in feeling he can personally correct government policies seems most dubious, but this confidence certainly must be comforting to persons who feel they must, and can, ignore politics to devote their time and energies to the other demands in their lives.

Despite the apparent low level of time and energy necessary to wear a campaign button or to engage in other political activities, conceivably such low participation is the result of obstacles to individual participation, such as restrictive election laws, inopportune scheduling of public meetings, and inaccessibility of public officials. Noting the lower American national voting turnout as compared with the turnout in West European countries, several political scientists have severely criticized the use of personal voting registration here, which requires the voter not only to remember to vote but also to register several weeks or months prior to the election.[17] Moreover, this procedure more severely affects the poor and the black.[18]

Who Participates?

Table 1-5 shows that persons most likely to vote have high education and income and are older, up to retirement age (65). Better than three quarters of such people voted in the presidential elections of 1964 and 1968. In contrast, the most recently eligible voters prove least likely to vote, with only 33 percent of the 18 to 20-year-olds actually taking advantage of this opportunity. The 21 to 24-year-old group is next least likely to vote. Other groups with very low voting rates are the unemployed and very poor.

Combinations of these attributes distinguish active from inactive voters more than do single attributes. Thus, less-educated young voters and better-educated oldsters differ even more than just the young and old or the better-educated and less-educated. Figure 1-1 shows this to be the case. Less than 20 percent of the least-educated 21 to 24-year-olds vote, in sharp contrast to the nearly 95 percent vote of 45 to 64-year-olds with 16 years of education or more.

The importance of education and measures of economic success persists when we move to consider the other acts of political par-

TABLE 1-5 Percent of Different Groups Voting in Presidential Elections, 1964 and 1968

Voters	Percentage voting
More than 12 years education	81%
Family income: $10,000 and over	80
Age: 45-64 years	75
Family income: $7500-9999	73
Employed	71
Residence in North or West	71
Age: 35-44 years	71
Male	70
White	69
Education: 9-12 years	69
Residence in metropolitan area	68
Residence in non-metropolitan area	67
Female	66
Age: 65 years and over	66
Family income: $5000-7499	66
Age: 25-34 years	63
Residence in the South	60
Family income: $3000-4999	58
Negro	58
Education: 8 years or less	55
Family income: under $3000	54
Unemployed	52
Age: 21-24 years	51
Age: 18-20 years	33

Scale: 25   50   75   Percentage voting

Source. U.S. Census, 1970.

Citizen Political Participation   7

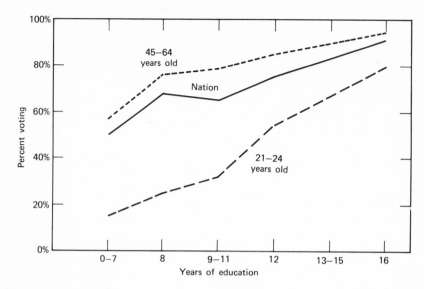

Figure 1-1. Turnout in the 1964 Presidential Election According to Age and Education. (*Source.* U.S. Bureau of the Census, *Current Population Reports,* Series P-20, No. 143, "Voter Participation in the National Election: November 1964," U.S. Government Printing Office, Washington, D.C., 1965, p. 16. Reprinted from William H. Flanigan, *Political Behavior of the American Electorate,* 2nd ed., © Copyright 1972 by Allyn and Bacon, Inc. Used by permission.)

ticipation. Higher-educated and wealthier persons are consistently more likely to express their political opinions to others, contribute money to campaigns, attend meetings, and display stickers and buttons.[19]

Inasmuch as all people do not have the same political attitudes and values, the attitudes of voters, as distinct from nonvoters, may distort the political opinions that are brought to the attention of government because voters tend to be educated, wealthy, employed, white, and males.

Party Identification

We have thus far found the public to be rather inattentive to its government and to be rather inactive in attempting to shape government policies. Although the average citizen perceives few government actions as having personal significance for him, his sense of duty nevertheless prods him to vote. Many voters approach elections with the decision-making guide of a long-standing loyalty to either the Republican or the Democratic party—what political scientists call "party identification." Since an individual's party identification is generally one of the most central and stable elements of his political beliefs, we refer to it extensively in subsequent chapters. As Table 1-6 shows, the distribution of party identification within the electorate has been very stable since at least 1940, with Democrats clearly outnumbering Republicans.

Figure 1-2 strongly illustrates the pattern of people voting for their political party for four presidential elections. We find that in none of these elections had more than 15 percent of the strong Democrats ever been sufficiently tempted to vote Republican by that party's candidate or program, even in 1952 and 1956 with the strong attraction of General Eisenhower. Similarly, only in 1964 when the Republican candidate was Goldwater, did the Democrats get more than 3 percent of the strong Republicans' vote. The only noticeable change over this 16 year period is the large jump in nonvoting at all levels of party identification in 1968, suggesting perhaps that supporters of neither party found much satisfaction with their candidate. The stability of party identification, and the consistency of the patterns of voting suggest that most people continually vote for the same party, and, indeed, this is the case. Yet party voting may be declining. In 1968 people were asked, "Have you always voted for the same party or have you voted for different parties for President?" Better than 45 percent claimed that they have always or mostly voted for the same party. But this is down considerably from 1956 when 62 percent gave this answer; and among the strong party identifiers, this percentage declined to 73 percent, down from 82 percent in 1956.[20] While the parties seem to be getting more successful in attracting members of the opposition, many remain entirely loyal, especially the strong identifiers. Furthermore, about half the voters vote a straight ticket for the same party in all races.[21]

Finally, noting the time when the voter decided on his presidential choice as shown in Table 1-7, we find that less than one person in three admits to deciding on his presidential choice during the campaign. Clearly, most people have a standing decision—to vote for the candidates of their political party.

EXPLAINING WHO WINS ELECTIONS

Although party identification remains very stable over the years as shown in Table 1-7, the Democratic percentage of Presidential and Congressional elections, as shown in Figure 1-3, varies greatly. While the Democratic candidate, Lyndon Johnson, received 60 percent of the vote in 1964, the Democratic candidate for President in

TABLE 1-6 **The Party Identification of the Electorate, 1940-1970**

	1940	1944	1947	1952	1954	1956	1958	1960	1962	1964	1966	1968	1970
Democrats	41%	41%	46%	47%	47%	44%	47%	46%	47%	51%	45%	45%	43%
Independents	20	20	21	22	22	24	19	23	23	22	28	29	31
Republicans	38	39	27	27	27	29	29	27	27	24	25	24	24
Nothing, other don't know	1	*	7	4	4	3	5	4	3	2	2	2	1
Total	100%	100%	101%	100%	100%	100%	100%	100%	100%	99%	100%	100%	99%
n =[a]	?	?	1287	1614	1139	1772	1269	3021	1317	1571	1291	1557	1507
	(Gallup)		(NORC)					(Survey Research Center)					

Sources. National Opinion Research Center; Survey Research Center; George Gallup, *The Political Almanac, 1952* (New York: Forbes, 1952), p. 37; Angus Campbell, et al., *Elections and the Political Order,* (New York: Wiley, 1966) p. 13. The 1940–1968 data is presented in: William H. Flanigan, *Political Behavior of the American Electorate* 2nd ed. (Boston: Allyn and Bacon, Inc., 1972), p. 33. The 1964–1970 data are from the Survey Research Center.
[a] In this table and most of those that follow, the number of individuals interviewed is given underneath the total percentage for the column. In each table, the n's give the number of individuals who are represented by the percentages in the column above. In this table, the n's represent the total sample sizes of many studies, but in most tables the n's will represent subsets of a single sample.

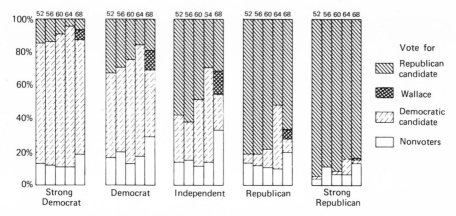

Figure 1-2. Vote for President by Partisans and Independents in 1952, 1956, 1960, 1964, and 1968. (*Source.* Survey Research Center. Reprinted from William H. Flanigan, *Political Behavior of the American Electorate,* 2nd ed., © Copyright 1972 by Allyn and Bacon, Inc. Used by permission.)

1968, Hubert Humphrey, found only 43 percent of the electorate supporting him, a drop of 17 percent or approximately 12 million voters! If most people's voting is explainable in terms of their party identification, which is quite stable, how is it that Democrats do not always win?[22]

TABLE 1-7   **Distribution of Time of Decision on Vote Choice for President in 1948, 1952, 1956, 1960, 1964, and 1968**

	1948	1952	1956	1960	1964	1968
Decided:						
Before conventions	37%	35%	57%	30%	40%	33%
During conventions	22	39	18	30	25	22
During campaign	26	31	21	36	33	38
Don't remember, NA	9	4	4	4	3	7
Total	100%	101%	100%	100%	101%	100%
n =	421	1251	1285	1445	1126	1039

Source. Survey Research Center; and William H. Flanigan, *Political Behavior of the American Electorate* 2nd ed. (Boston: Allyn and Bacon, Inc., 1972), p. 109.

The answer lies in the difference between how most people vote, and how those crucial to victory vote. In a partisan election, the majority of voters will support the party with which they identify, thus assuring both parties a substantial block of voters whose relative size will depend on the popularity of the parties in the area. At the national level, as we saw in Table 1-6, the Democrats are assured of a substantial advantage. The additional votes necessary for victory, then, must be found among the partisans who temporarily defect to the opposition candidate and the independent voters. As Table 1-8 dramatically illustrates, only once since 1940 (in 1960)

TABLE 1-8 **The Distribution of Votes for President by Independents from 1940 to 1968**

	1940	1944	1948	1952	1956	1960	1964	1968
Democratic	61%	62%	57%	33%	27%	46%	66%	32%
Republican	39	38	43	67	73	54	34	47
Wallace (1968)								21
Total	100%	100%	100%	100%	100%	100%	100%	100%
n =	?	?	?	263	309	298	219	228
		(Gallup Poll)			(Survey Research Center)			

Sources. George Gallup, *The Political Almanac, 1952*, p. 38; Survey Research Center; and William H. Flanigan, *Political Behavior of the American Electorate,* 2nd ed. (Boston: Allyn and Bacon Inc., 1972), p. 44.

has a presidential candidate been victorious without dominant support by the 20 percent of the electorate calling themselves independents. But this should not be taken to mean that elections are decided by concerned and informed voters who eschew the simple solution of voting for a political party, rather than for the best man judged by his stand on the issues. Table 1-9, indeed, finds the independents indistinguishable from the partisans in their interest in government and politics.[23] To gain the support of independents is not to gain a mandate for one's issue positions from the most informed and concerned element of the electorate.

A study of the 1952, 1956, 1960, and 1964 presidential elections centering on the attractions voters found in the Democratic and Republican parties and their presidential candidates, found the greatest change between the elections derived from voter reaction to the images of the candidates—their personalities and leadership

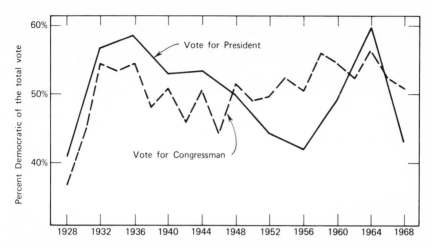

Figure 1-3. Democratic Presidential and Congressional Votes, 1928-1968.

Sources: U.S. Bureau of the Census, *Statistical Abstract of the United States: 1969* (90th edition), Washington, D.C., 1969; U.S. Bureau of the Census, *Historical Statistics of the United States, Colonial Times to 1957: Continuation to 1962 and Revisions* (U.S. Government Printing Office, Washington, D.C., 1965); *Congressional Quarterly Weekly Report,* Vol. XXIV (1966), no. 45, p. 2809.

Note. While presenting these data I have not bothered to draw attention to the wide range of errors that may exist. There are errors in collecting and recording data as well as errors in computation. The Presidential election of 1960 provides an illustration of another form of uncertainty that enters into these data —choices made among alternative ways of presenting the data. It is customary to list the popular vote in such a way that Kennedy appears a narrow winner over Nixon in 1960. Actually in order to reach this distribution of the total vote it is necessary to exaggerate the Kennedy vote from Alabama, since on the slate of Democratic electors in Alabama there were uncommitted electors. Eventually six of the uncommitted electors voted for Harry Byrd; five electors voted for Kennedy. If the Kennedy popular vote in Alabama is reduced to a proportion, say 5/11 in this case, of the vote for Democratic electors and if only this reduced popular vote is added to his national total, Nixon, not Kennedy, has the larger popular vote total nationally in 1960. In percentages these are negligible changes, but symbolically such differences can become important. In these tables I have followed the usual practice of presenting the augmented Kennedy total.

Reprinted from William H. Flanigan, *Political Behavior of the American Electorate,* 2nd ed., © Copyright 1972 by Allyn and Bacon, Inc. Used by permission.

TABLE 1-9 **Distribution of Interest in Government and Politics Generally according to Partisanship, 1968**

Interested	Strong Democrat	Weak Democrat	Independent	Weak Republican	Strong Republican
All the time	29%	23%	32%	29%	34%
Some of the time	28	25	27	26	30
Only now and then	14	16	17	19	16
Hardly at all	15	21	10	14	11
NA	13	15	14	12	9
Total	99%	100%	100%	100%	100%
n =	312	394	452	224	148

Sources. The Survey Research Center; and William H. Flanigan, *Political Behavior of the American Electorate,* 2nd ed. (Boston: Allyn and Bacon, Inc., 1972), p. 47.

capabilities as the voters saw them.[24] Although Eisenhower's image garnered some 4.8 million voters for the Republican party in 1956, Goldwater lost the normal Republican advantage of having the most attractive candidate, losing some 3.8 million votes to his opponent as a result. Since mentions of domestic and foreign issues are also assessed in this study, and proved considerably less varied, one cannot help but be suspicious of the basis of these images seen by the public. Are they easily manipulated by impressions of sincerity, courage, and integrity, or by overall impressions accurately generalizing his success in coping with the pressures of the campaign and its issues to his likely performance as President? No definitive assessment of this important question has been made.

STANDARDS OF DEMOCRATIC PARTICIPATION

Were the public to show such low interest in nonpolitical social activities such as bird watching, we would conclude that further inquiry into the motives and quality of this behavior merited little interest. But politics is not like other activities. The relationship between the public and its leaders is crucial both to the quality of life and to the existence of democracy. Two potential problems confront a democratic society. One is that if the public majority abuses its political rights by demanding immediate government satisfaction of all its wants, a state of anarchy and civil strife may result. The other problem centers on the possible excesses of leaders who control the devices of government. What is to keep the leaders and other influentials from ignoring the public and using government to further their own interests? We first consider the importance of forcing representatives to be accountable to the public.

Accountability and Responsibility

Lincoln captured the standard for judging democracies when he spoke of government of, by, and for the people. Somehow the policies enacted by government must satisfy the public. The unique characteristics of a democracy, one democratic theorist argues, rest primarily on (1) popular control of policymakers, but also on (2) all citizens being politically equal, (3) elections being meaningful, and (4) divisions of opinion being decided by majority rule.[25] As long as all men do not share the same opinion as to what the best government actions to cope with social problems are, this standard stresses the importance of the representatives' accountability to the public to assure responsible government. The public's role in assuring this accountability is not a small one, even though the public's behavior falls dismally short of expectations. What must the public do to achieve control?

Probably the most broadly accepted basis of achieving popular control is captured in what might be called the *Rational-Activist Model*. Assuming equality of votes, meaningful elections, and decision-making by majority rule, this model sees control achieved by voters rationally choosing among candidates, and being at least active enough to vote for them. A voter's rational choice of candidates rests on his being informed, having well-conceived opinions on the issues, accurately knowing the positions of the candidates, and supporting those whose positions most closely resemble his personal positions.

An alternative but somewhat more complex *Political Parties Model* greatly reduces the number of political choices required of the citizen. This model depends on the political parties' desire to win elections to achieve popular control. As a whole, the party states its position on the various issues of the day in its party platform. The rational and active voter then selects only among platforms, giving his support to the candidates of the party whose platform most conforms to his personal preferences. Rather than facing multiple decisions for all offices up for election, thanks to the political parties the voter need only make a single decision among the available party platforms. In the interest of victory at the polls, the parties force their elected representatives to honor the platform promises in the hope that satisfying these promises will assure continuing public support.

For most of the American public, political participation falls far short of either of the two models we have considered. Neither voting for a candidate out of lifelong loyalty to a political party, nor voting for him because he seems sincere satisfies the critical public evaluation demanded in both models. Indeed, any continuing process of public monitoring of elected officials seems improbable with a public preoccupied with other activities and confident that government actions will be appropriate. For those who urge accountability, four conclusions are possible: (1) that America is not a democracy; (2) that extensive public involvement is not really necessary; (3) that remedial action is urgently needed; or (4) that the findings are no longer true. Except for the second conclusion listed, each is critical of democracy in America, at least as it existed in the 1960s. If persons with influence on what government does do not share opinions with the general populace, government may well be serving minorities' interests and not those of the public. Some fear that public apathy allows the wealth and business interests of those controlling government to affect their decisions to the disadvantage of the general public. Such actions as government officials or their friends buying land with the knowledge that it will soon be in the path of a new interstate highway (so its value will increase tenfold), or Congress failing to pass a broadly supported government medical insurance program because of opposition by doctors who fear its economic impact on them, exemplify the concerns of those who desire more public controls.

The overall pessimism with public performance among those advocating this standard of democracy buoys only with a change seen in very recent years. The rise of protest over Vietnam, the retirement of President Johnson, the strength of the Wallace vote, the defeat of the Supersonic Transport, and a myriad of other happenings, perhaps suggest a growing public concern with public events, and even some success in opposing the dominant economic interests in the country. The rise in the number of independents, the decrease in party loyalty, a modest increase in "ideological awareness" (see Chapter Three), and the increase in public expression of distrust for government may be symptoms of greater political responsiveness. Time will tell whether these small changes only mark an episode of public concern soon to be followed by more indifference and inactivity, or represent the beginning of a change in American political behavior.

Political Communication

Communication between leaders and followers is essential to achieve democratic accountability. For representatives in a democracy to respond to public demands, they need to know what these demands are, and for the public to achieve accountability from their representatives, it needs to know what the representatives have done, and what alternatives were available. The representative faces innumerable difficulties in getting public opinion and weighing its importance in deciding how he will act. Each of the assessments he might use—his personal mail, opinion polls, or conversations with friends and constituents—convey different opinions. Some measures yield the opinions of the conservative parts of society, some include the opinions of those who are marginally involved, and the one communication that cannot be ignored—votes in elections—may communicate only the popularity of his party in his constituency, how attractive he is personally to the voters, or an opinion on only a single issue of crucial importance at the time of the election, but irrelevant to other issues on which he must vote. If a representative is elected because of his position on the busing of children to achieve integration, how does he use this knowledge to decide how to vote on whether to accept the new treaty with the Soviet Union on control of missiles?

Various organized groups in society claim to speak for that part of the electorate they claim to represent. While many of these groups were formed for nonpolitical purposes, they also serve as a communication link between the people and their representatives. Because they pressure government for their particular interests, they are called pressure groups (or interest groups). At one extreme, such groups could be so inclusive of all individuals in our society, and could so accurately represent their members' opinions that representatives could achieve accountability merely by recording the choice of each group, weighing them by the numbers of voters they represent, and voting with the strongest pressure. This would be in accord with what might be called the *Pressure Group Model* of popular control.

The representative who fails to be responsive under this *Pressure Group Model* would lose the support of dissatisfied groups when he comes up for reelection. At another extreme, pressure groups may merely give expression to the opinions of the wealthy and influential.

Just as there can be substantial error in the information communicated from the public to the representatives, so can communication downward be distorted (deliberately or not). If members of the public are to monitor their representatives properly, they must be supplied with adequate information. The news media (radio, television, newspapers, and magazines) carry a heavy load in getting this information to the public. Although public ignorance on political issues may often be blamed on inadequate coverage by the news media, their audience may simply not want more political information. Even more ominously, information available to the public may be manipulated. In any situation of communication between politically active persons, such as holders of public offices, and the general public, the activists have several advantages in getting public compliance to and acceptance of their positions. The political leader can use the respect people have for his office to gain respect for himself and his opinions. By holding the rostrum at a meeting, one can direct the area and flow of discussion, evade questions, and generally say only what one wants to say. Also, a good part of the communication between activists and the public travels one way only—from the activists to the public—since one can hardly talk back to the radio or television. Symbols too may be used to manipulate public opinion. The widespread acceptance by Americans of such symbols as the American flag, desires for unity and peace, the impartiality represented by the judge's black robe, efficiency as an unquestioned standard for government performance, and the assumption that people in charge know best can be manipulated by political leaders to mobilize public support. Advertising firms manipulate symbols to sell toothpaste, perhaps they can also sell political candidates and policy positions. Thus it becomes unclear whether public policy reflects public opinion, or whether both are the creation of bright advertising executives and the more amateur practitioners of the same skills—politicians.

If the public were this readily manipulated, activists would merely need to decide what they wished as policy, and then manipulate public opinion by using available symbols. Even more cynically, democracy itself becomes a symbol, used to convince the people that they should comply with decisions of government because they had a say in them, and the majority has ruled.

Stability and Balance

If those who value accountability as a standard are anxious about the quality of American public participation in politics, others who stress the political stability enjoyed by the United States in an otherwise troubled world find little with which to be concerned. Perhaps the goal of extensive public participation in politics would detract from stability, which for many is equally, if not more, desirable. The principal theorists taking this position argue that accountability is not to be sacrificed in the interests of stability, but instead, is adequately achieved in existing developed and stable democracies, such as the United States.[26] A balance is necessary between the public actions that would assure accountability, and the latitude the government needs for coping with social problems to the satisfaction of its public. With such a balance, the United States skirts the dangers of both mob control and control by an elite insensitive to public opinion.

If public inattentiveness permits the system to be harmonious, the threat of the citizens becoming active forces the leader to respect public opinion. From this perspective, a trend toward greater public participation may be a bad omen for the system, since the extensive demands and the intensity of opinion may overtax the system's ability to satisfy.

Sense of Community and Consensus

In addition to the importance of a system's stability, and of a low level of public demands, several theorists also stress that some broadly held attitudes might condition and insulate government from pressures that otherwise might fracture it into warring camps. These broadly held and conditioning attitudes are frequently called a sense of community. They include a sense of trust in government leaders, because they too share the community's interest and are not alien forces. Other accepted beliefs may also be crucial to a developed state of democracy, such as a broad public acceptance of minority rights, and willingness to accept outcomes made by accepted procedures, even when those outcomes are personally unpleasant.

Although the principle of community is not always applied to the question of accountability, shared values can supply congruence between public opinion and policy via two additional models of political linkage. These models are the *Role Playing Model* and the *Sharing Model*. Notably, both play down the importance of broad public participation to force leadership responsibility.

The *Sharing Model* simply states that since many attitudes are broadly held throughout the public, elected leaders cannot help but satisfy public opinion even if the public is totally apathetic. Americans surrendering to the will of the Soviet Union, total government management of the economy, a termination of public education, and complete disregard for preserving the environment are all actions so contrary to broadly held American attitudes, as to be rejected by any government, even given the great apathy of the American public. Of course, it would be possible to assemble a group of men who would enact each of these policies, but other sources of linkage are sufficient to preclude this happening.

The *Role Playing Model* relies on leaders in government sharing with the public the belief that representatives should be responsive to the public. Because of this orientation, representatives will anticipate public opinion and respond quickly to public protest. To the degree that elected officials act on the belief that a good representative should respond to public opinion, and to the degree that they know what the public wants, public opinion will be reflected in public policy. Accountability occurs without coercion of officials by the electorate. But the main concern given this criterion for assessing democracy is not accountability but stability. If a low level of public participation can be taken as an indication of satisfaction with the system and its performance, this criterion leads to pleasure with our earlier findings, not alarm.

THE PLAN OF THIS BOOK

Interest in public opinion arises from the belief that the public is important in a democracy. But as we have seen, observers differ in precisely what role for the public they see as vital to democracy. Very important questions are involved in the interplay among these vital standards. Is it really important to have accountability of representatives in a democracy, or is it sufficient to have public policy reflect public opinion even without accountability? How do accountability and stability interplay? Can a society be stable only if its leaders are accountable or does extensive public participation actually threaten stability? Is a strong sense of community vital, or can democracy function in an atmosphere of heated societal conflict?

Because many will select answers to these questions on the basis of their personal value preferences, these "larger" issues cannot be easily resolved. But to evaluate the role of public opinion by any standard, it is necessary to have facts about public opinion. Our goal is to present the best available information on contemporary American public opinion. Much of what masquerades as public opinion distorts reality, thus fostering actions and conclusions that will prove incorrect. Tentative conclusions, we will find, are justifiable, but the findings to date do not support any overall characterization of public opinion. Any heated attempt to exhort large-scale remedial change, or any retrenchment against public opinion, rests more on passions about the standards we discussed above than on the facts of public opinion.

Necessarily, we order these facts into various chapters that strike us as convenient. Chapter Two discusses the difficulty in assessing public opinion and its content from opinion polls. Chapter Three continues the concern with the content of public opinion, focusing on the limited role of "ideology" in shaping peoples' political beliefs. Chapter Four evaluates available information on broad public acceptance of certain attitudes that seemingly might stabilize government. Chapters Five and Six discuss the origins of political opinions. In the fifth chapter, we consider the sources of a person's opinions

—whether they be part of childhood learning or influence in adult life. The sixth chapter focuses on the opinion differences between the various types of people that comprise the public. The next three chapters turn to the important questions of the impact of public opinion on government policy. Chapter Seven evaluates the effectiveness of the public's policy role in elections. Chapter Eight examines the opposite aspect of political linkage—how elected officials respond to the views of their constituents. Finally, Chapter Nine considers the importance of political parties and pressure groups in achieving a correspondence between public opinion and public policy. The chapter finishes with tentative findings about the impact of linkage failure.

FOOTNOTES FOR CHAPTER 1

[1] This is figured for a person living in a municipality and state having the typical number of city and state officials. The average state has nine statewide elected officials, and one state senator and representative serving any given citizen. At the municipal level, one mayor and six councilmen need to be elected, and at the national level, a Senator, Congressman, and President are elected. Thus, 11 state, seven municipal, and three national officials are elected. Adjusting for those typically having only two year terms, over a 12 year period, a total of 70 officials need to be elected, averaging six each year.

[2] Albert H. Cantril and Charles W. Roll, Jr., *Hopes and Fears of the American People* (New York: Universe Books, 1971) and Lloyd A. Free and Hadley Cantril, *The Political Beliefs of Americans* (New York: Simon and Schuster, 1968), pp. 94–112.

[3] Ibid., p. 19.

[4] Ibid., pp. 23–36.

[5] John C. Wahlke, "Public Policy and Representative Government: The Role of the Represented," a paper prepared for the Seventh World Congress of the International Political Science Association, Brussels, Belgium, September 20–31, 1967.

[6] *The CBS News Poll,* 3, (October 30, 1970), p. 7.

[7] Hadley Cantril, *The Pattern of Human Concerns* (New Brunswick: Rutgers University Press, 1965), p. 175.

[8] Gabriel A. Almond and Sidney Verba, *The Civic Culture* (Princeton, New Jersey: Princeton University Press, 1963), pp. 80–82.

[9] John P. Robinson, Jerrold G. Rusk, and Kendra B. Head, *Measures of Political Attitudes* (Survey Research Center, Institute of Social Research, 1968), p. 639.

[10] Angus Campbell, et al., *The American Voter* (New York and London: John Wiley and Sons, Inc., 1960), p. 106.

[11] Almond and Verba, loc. cit., p. 171.

[12] Robinson, Rusk, and Head, loc. cit., p. 594.

[13] Stein Rokkan, *Citizens Elections and Parties* (New York: David McKay Company, Inc., 1970), p. 355.

[14] David Butler and Donald Stokes, *Political Change in Britain* (New York: St. Martin's Press, 1969), p. 25.

[15] Duncan MacRae, Jr. *Parliament, Parties, and Society in France, 1946–1958* (New York: St. Martin's Press, 1967), p. 51.

[16] Almond and Verba, loc. cit., Chapter 15.

[17] Stanley Kelley et al., "Registration and Voting: Putting First Things First," *American Political Science Review 61,* (June, 1967), pp. 359–379.

[18] Walter Dean Burnham, *Critical Elections and the Mainsprings of American Politics* (New York: Norton, 1970), p. 90.

[19] Robinson, *loc. cit.,* p. 593.

[20] Campbell et al., loc. cit., p. 125. 1968 data comes from the 1968 Survey Research Election study.

[21] Ibid., p. 407.

[22] After a careful evaluation, Converse found that apart from the short-term effects on any presidential election, such as topical issues and the attractiveness of specific candidates, the Democratic candidate would get 54 percent of the popular vote. Philip E. Converse, "The Concept of a Normal Vote," *Elections and the Political Order,* ed., Angus Campbell, Philip E. Converse, Warren E. Miller, and Donald E. Stokes (New York: John Wiley and Sons, Inc., 1966), pp. 9–39.

[23] William H. Flanigan, *Political Behavior of the American Electorate,* 2nd ed., (Boston: Allyn and Bacon, Inc., 1972), pp. 44–47.

[24] Donald Stokes, "Dynamic Elements of Contests for the Presidency," *American Political Science Review,* (March, 1966), pp. 22–23.

[25] H. B. Mayo, *An Introduction to Democratic Theory* (New York: Oxford University Press, 1960), pp. 61–67.

[26] Almond and Verba, loc. cit., Chapter 15.

TWO

OPINION POLLS AND PUBLIC OPINION:
AN INTRODUCTORY VIEW

Before the advent of the public opinion polls in the early 1930s, one had to rely on much more inexact measures of what the public was thinking. To understand his constituency's concerns, the political leader of the prepoll era had to choose from among several intuitive indicators of public opinion. He could consult his friends and assume that their thinking was representative of his constituency; he could have his staff make a count of the pro and con letters on given issues received in his office; he could make a similar count from letters to the editor in various newspapers; or he could try to assess the relative enthusiasm of a crowd for different ideas during his speech. But the most relied on method of assessing public opinion prior to the opinion poll was the interpretation of election outcomes and the occasional referendum that managed to find its way onto the ballot.

Until the development of scientific polling techniques, both practitioners and theorists of politics could not know the error in assessing public opinion in these manners. We now know that most informal methods of assessing public opinion, such as those listed above, have a substantial bias built into them. For example, people who write letters to editors or congressmen on public issues tend to be more "extreme" in their opinion—and, on the whole, more conservative—than the bulk of the public.[1] Taking this in combination with the fact that liberals tend to communicate with liberal politicians and conservatives with conservative politicians, we can expect that the impressions of public opinion that politicians receive are often greatly distorted. The development of public opinion polls forced our attention to the fact that the various devices of public expression available in a democracy were not channeling an accurate reflection of public opinion to public decision makers. Furthermore, the development of the polls uncovered various properties of how people reacted to the political world that contradicted the normal role that public opinion is expected to play in a democracy.

Today, the results of numerous opinion polls continually inform interested politicians, scholars, and concerned citizens about the "pulse" of public opinion. On the basis of about 1500 carefully selected interviews, polling organizations can predict with remarkable accuracy how the American public as a whole would divide on the questions they ask. But polls can tell more than just the breakdown of mass opinion on a question at a given moment. For example, they can reveal important opinion differences between various groups within society. They can be analyzed to discover the interrelations among the political attitudes that individuals hold. Data from polls can be examined to locate the extent to which voters are influenced by certain issues in election campaigns. Moreover, historians have begun to ransack the data archives of polling organizations in order to discover historical trends.

In short, most of the information we now have about public opinion comes from the analysis of opinion poll data. In this and several of the following chapters, poll data will be employed extensively to illustrate findings about public opinion. In the present chapter, we will take a preliminary look at some of the characteristics of American public opinion as revealed by the commercial polls, such as the Gallup and Harris polls, and academic polls such as the periodic surveys by the Survey Research Center of the University of Michigan. Our first task in this chapter is an examination of the extent to which people hold meaningful opinions and beliefs on political issues. Second, we will look at how the American public has distributed itself—both recently and in the more distant past—on important political questions.

THE DEPTH OF OPINION HOLDING

We have already seen, in Chapter One, that the participation level of most Americans rarely extends beyond the act of voting. It is also true that most Americans are not very attentive *observers* of the political world. From the occasional information "quizzes" given the public in opinion surveys, we find that the citizen typically has little political information at his disposal. Indeed, careful analysis of data from opinion surveys indicates that many opinions people express are so shallow that extreme caution must be exercised in extracting significance from the tabulation of opinion breakdowns. Thus, before we attempt to find out what the public is thinking about political issues, we must first examine the extent of political inattentiveness and the problems this creates for the proper analysis of the findings from opinion surveys.

How Politically Informed Is the Public?

First, we will examine the level of political information held by the mass public. In Table 2-1, an information scale is presented, which gives the percentage of adults who could give the "correct" answer to various political information questions. The information

TABLE 2-1 **The Level of Political Information Among the Adult Public**

	Year	Source
95% know that Russia has tested atomic weapons	1964	(Robinson)[a]
94% know the capital city of U.S.	1945	(AIPO)
94% know the President's term is four years	1951	(AIPO)
93% recognize photograph of the current President	1948	(AIPO)
90% know name of governor in home state	1961	(Matthews and Prothro)[b]
87% know Franklin Delano Roosevelt was a Democrat	1961	(Matthews and Prothro)[b]
80% know meaning of term "veto"	1947	(AIPO)
78% know what initials "FBI" stand for	1949	(AIPO)
74% know meaning of term "wiretapping"	1969	(AIPO)
72% know China to be "Communist"	1964	(SRC)
70% can name their mayor	1967	(AIPO)
69% can name the current Vice President	1952	(AIPO)
68% know President limited to two terms	1970	(SRC)
65% know Spain to be "non-Communist"	1964	(Robinson)*
65% can identify Secretary of State	1966	(AIPO)
63% have some understanding of term "conservative"	1960	(SRC)
58% know meaning of term "open housing"	1967	(AIPO)
53% can name their Congressman	1970	(AIPO)
49% know there are two U.S. senators from each state	1954	(AIPO)
38% know Russia is not a NATO member	1964	(AIPO)
36% know the meaning of term "welfare state"	1950	(AIPO)
34% can name *both* U.S. Senators from their state	1967	(ORC)
28% can name their *state* senator	1967	(AIPO)
19% know meaning of "no fault" insurance	1971	(AIPO)

Sources. American Institute of Public Opinion (Gallup); Survey Research Center; Opinion Research Corporation; Donald R. Matthews and James D. Prothro, *Negroes and the New Southern Politics* (New York: Harcourt, Brace and World, 1966); John P. Robinson, *Public Information about World Affairs* (Ann Arbor, Mich.: Survey Research Center, 1967).
[a] Detroit sample: [b] southern white sample; all other items are based on national adult samples.

varies from civics book knowledge to simple information about foreign governments. Although the results are for various years and some are based on regional or local samples rather than national ones, it is reasonable to assume that the data are a fairly accurate representation of the public's information level at the present time. Since the lack of an adequate benchmark of what exactly is a passing grade creates the danger of making too severe a judgment about the political capabilities of the average American, we merely suggest that many people are rather inattentive to the political world that dominates the front pages of the daily newspapers. One must, however, also notice that some people are, in fact, fairly knowledgeable.

The Frequency of Opinion Holding

One implication from the public's low level of political information is that many Americans do not follow current events closely enough to develop concrete opinions on topical political issues. Typically, people are less able to offer opinions on specific government proposals than on broad issues. Occasionally a public opinion poll will reveal a striking example of this lack of opinion. One instance was the lack of opinion crystallizing over the complicated, but well-publicized, 1969 Senate battle over President Nixon's controversial ABM program. Informed observers generally agreed that the Senate vote over appropriations for Nixon's Antiballistic Missile program would vitally structure American defense policy and expenditure priorities for years to follow. When the showdown Senate vote came, Nixon's ABM program was approved by a margin of one vote. If we ask the question whether this outcome reflected the will of the majority of public opinion, the answer is difficult to determine for the simple reason that a sizeable majority of American adults apparently did not even have an opinion on the issue. Shortly before the Senate vote, Gallup asked this question: "Have you read or heard anything about the Antiballistic Missile program as submitted to Congress by President Nixon?" The 69 percent who indicated that they had read or heard something about it were then asked if they had an opinion on the program and, if so, whether they favored or opposed it. One quarter of these "informed" respondents indicated that they were "undecided" on the issue. The breakdown of the results, which indicates that only 41 percent held opinions on the ABM issue at the peak of the controversy, were:[2]

Aware of program and favor
ABM program   23%
                                      } 41% with opinion
Aware of program and oppose
ABM program   18%

Aware of ABM program but undecided	28%	
Unaware of ABM Program	31%	59% without opinion
	100%	

The extremely low rate of opinion holding on ABM was largely because of the extreme complexity of the issue. But in public opinion polling, the number of respondents who fall in the "no opinion" category is not caused by the nature of the issue alone. One factor that can often influence the frequency of "no opinion" responses is the question format itself. Notice that, in the ABM survey, respondents were first asked if they were familiar with the issue and then whether they had opinions on it. Only those who indicated familiarity and also that they held an opinion were then asked for their opinions. This filtering device gave respondents considerable opportunity to place themselves in the category without opinions. Most likely, very few would have failed to offer an opinion if all respondents were simply asked one question in which a "no opinion" response would have to be volunteered, such as: "Do you favor or oppose the Antiballistic Missile program that was submitted to Congress by President Nixon?" The use of filter questions to screen out some of the haphazard "doorstep opinions" that might be offered by the disinterested and undecided is a frequent practice in public opinion research. One type of filter question is the information filter. The "read or heard . . ." question in the ABM survey is an example. Sometimes it is possible to eliminate respondents who are too ignorant to have a meaningful opinion by means of a simple quiz. For example, in the fall of 1964 the Survey Research Center surveyed attitudes toward admission of Communist China to the United Nations, but asked opinions of only those respondents who, in earlier questions, correctly identified mainland China as having a Communist form of government and as a nonmember of the UN. The breakdown of responses to the question, "Do you think Communist China should be admitted to the United Nations or do you think it should not?" was:

China should be admitted	15%	
China should not be admitted	45%	60% with opinions
Don't know	10%	
China not known to be Communist and non-member of UN	29%	40% without opinions

On broad questions of policy (for example, school integration, foreign aid) information filters are usually inappropriate. However, by offering the right encouragement, some respondents can still be induced to say they have no opinion when they have none. For example, in recent Survey Research Center polls, respondents are generally asked "have you been interested enough in this [question] to favor one side over the other?" Only respondents who answer affirmatively are then asked for their opinions. Generally about 20% of the respondents are found to be without opinions using this technique. Some examples of nonopinion rates on selected issues from the SRC's 1968 survey are given in Table 2-2.

TABLE 2-2 **Rates of opinion holding on selected issues, 1968**

Issue	Percent With Opinions	Percent Without Opinions
Should the government in Washington "support the right of Negroes to go to any hotel or restaurant they can afford?"	86	14
Should the government in Washington "see to it that white and Negro children go to the same schools?"	82	18
Should the government in Washington "help people get doctors and hospital care at low cost?"	79	21
Should the government "see to it that every person has a job and a good standard of living?"	78	22
Is the government in Washington "getting too strong for the good of the country?"	71	29
Should our farmers and businessmen "be allowed to do business with Communist countries?"	70	30
Should the United States "give aid to other countries if they need help?"	68	32

Source. Survey Research Center 1968 election data. For the full questions, see the Appendix. The percentage without opinions includes "don't know," "no interest," and "depends" responses.

From Table 2-2, some differences in the rate of opinion holding from issue to issue can be noticed. In large part, these differences reflect the degree of difficulty in reacting to the particular issue in terms of direct personal experience, perceived self-interest, or group-related attitudes. For example, most respondents have a ready opinion on civil rights issues such as school integration because their racial attitudes provide the necessary cues for a response. At the other extreme, relatively few respondents offer opinions on foreign aid or trading with Communist nations for the reason that these foreign policy questions are remote from everyday experience. Two social welfare issues—guaranteed jobs and medicare—evoke opinion rates that are in between these two extremes. But on the question of whether the Federal Government is getting too powerful, a relatively low rate of opinion holding is found, even though this question gets at the "core" of the ideological differences between domestic conservatives and liberals. Perhaps it is *because* a basic liberal or conservative predisposition is required in order to have a meaningful opinion on the proper role of the Federal Government that the opinion rate on this issue is so low.

Despite the precautions taken to assure respondents that they are under no obligation to offer opinions when they have none, the fear of appearing uninformed causes many respondents to conjure up opinions even when they had not given the particular issue any thought prior to the interview. It is unavoidable that a large share of "opinions" that get counted in survey tabulations are of this "doorstep" variety. In fact, a surprisingly large percentage of respondents give opinions that are so weak to nonexistent that they will give one opinion in one interview and its opposite at a later time. Philip Converse has pinpointed the extent to which this occurs in his report of the findings from an ambitious "panel study" by the Survey Research Center where the same group of respondents was interviewed in 1956, 1958, and again in 1960.[3] In each of the three years, the panel of respondents was asked the extent of their agreement or disagreement with the statements shown in Figure 2-1 below. Converse reports that when these questions were asked twice over a two-year interval, only about 13 out of 20 respondents would locate themselves on the same side of a given issue both times.[4] This frequency of consistency is remarkably low when we consider that about half would answer consistently on the basis of chance alone. In sharp contrast, the respondents were consistent in their party identification, since under 5 percent of the sample made a complete switch from Democratic to Republican identification or vice versa[5] between 1956 and 1960. Figure 2-1 ranks the opinion items (and the "party identification" question) according to the correlation or consistency of opinions over the 1958 to 1960 period.

One might be tempted to argue that the high degree of opinion turnover is evidence that voters are frequently changing their political opinions in a meaningful fashion, just like open-minded concerned citizens ought to be doing. However, a more acceptable interpretation is that most respondents who appear to be changing their minds are actually people who give little or no thought to the particular issue. One reason for this statement is that although many

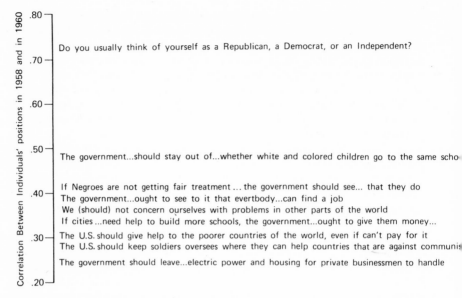

Figure 2-1. Temporal stability of different belief elements for individuals, 1958-1960. [*Source.* Reprinted with the permission of the Macmillan Company from Philip E. Converse, "The Nature of Belief Systems in Mass Publics," in David Apter (ed.), *Ideology and Discontent,* p. 240. Copyright © 1964 by The Free Press of Glencoe, a Division of the Macmillan Company.]

"conversions" were found in the 1956 to 1960 study, the various pro to con changes cancelled out those in the opposite direction, so that the distributions of opinions on the issues were quite stable over the time period. If, in fact, the high rate of opinion turnover had represented meaningful opinion change, the shift would most likely have been largely in one direction or the other. A second reason for this interpretation is that turnover was found to be greatest on issues, such as the "power and housing" question, which were rather quiet at the time, and least on the more hotly debated issues such as school integration. This could hardly have been the pattern if most of the opinion "conversions" were provoked by highly visible political debates on the issues.

After analyzing the pattern of responses, Converse suggests that most of the "opinion change" detected in this 1956–1960 survey may have been the result of respondents answering in random fashion rather than of meaningful opinion conversion. Converse argues that if people who changed the direction of their opinion between 1956 and 1958 had undergone a real conversion, then their 1958 opinions should be reasonably good predictors of their opinions in 1960. But, in fact, Converse found that the 1956–1958 "converts" were only slightly more likely to repeat their 1958 opinion in 1960 than they were to revert back to their earlier 1956 opinion. On the foreign aid issue, for example, people who "switched" from anti-aid to pro-aid over the 1956–1958 period were only slightly more likely to respond favorably to foreign aid in 1960 than those who supported aid in 1956 but opposed it in 1958.

On the "power and housing" question, Converse found that the pattern of responses fit very closely with the results that would be expected if *every* opinion "changer" had actually been "guessing" or answering "randomly": for example, the two groups who "switched" in opposite directions over one time interval responded virtually alike at a third time. Thus Converse assumed that the portion of the sample who failed to respond consistently in the same direction over the three interviews were actually answering randomly. Moreover, this assumption that all "change" was actually random allowed Converse to calculate the additional percentage of the sample who answered "consistently" but randomly. Just as three tosses of a coin will yield all "heads" or all "tails" one quarter of the time, about one-fourth of the people who answered randomly and without real opinions would appear "consistent" on the basis of chance alone. Calculating on the basis of this logic, Converse estimated that less than 20 percent of the adult public held meaningful opinions on the abstract issue of whether the government should leave things like housing and power plants to private enterprise, even though about two-thirds would venture a viewpoint on the matter when asked in a survey.[6]

No panel study of the scope of the SRC's 1956–1960 effort has been done since then. However, the Survey Research Center's 1968 survey reveals the existence of a high degree of opinion turnover on the war in Vietnam. The SRC's 1968 voter survey included questions about the war in both the preelection survey and the followup postelection survey of the same respondents. The two questions, asked from one to four months apart, were slightly different. In the first survey, respondents were asked whether we should "pull out of Vietnam entirely," "keep our soldiers in Vietnam, but try to end the fighting," or "take a stronger stand even if it means invading North Vietnam." In the followup survey, the respondents were asked to rank their positions on the Vietnam war on a seven point scale from one (immediate withdrawal) to seven (an all out effort for military victory.) Response categories to the two questions can be made roughly equivalent by assuming that the "dovish" self rankings of "one" or "two" on the second question are equivalent to the "withdraw all troops" response to the first; that hawkish responses of "six" or "seven" on the second question are equivalent to the proescalation response on the first; and that responses of "three", "four," and "five" on the second question are equivalent to the status quo response to question one.

TABLE 2-3 **Consistency of Opinion on the Vietnam War**[a]

		Preelection Response, 1968			
		Withdraw	Status Quo	Escalate	No Opinion, Other
Postelection Response, 1968	Withdraw	10	7	3	2
	Status Quo	6	22	13	5
	Escalate	2	6	16	2
	No Opinion, Other	1	2	2	1

Source. Survey Research Center 1968 election data.
[a] Cell entries represent percentages of the entire sample.

The frequencies of the various response patterns are shown in Table 2-3. Of all the respondents who were interviewed twice, only 48 percent were consistent—either "withdrawal-withdrawal" (10 percent); "status quo-status quo" (22 percent); or "escalation-escalation" (16 percent). Fifteen percent did not produce an opinion to at least one of the two questions, while 2 percent appeared to switch from dove to hawk and 3 percent appeared to move from hawk to dove. The remaining 32 percent switched back or forth between the status-quo response and one of the more extreme alternatives. Moreover, examination of the earlier responses by those who picked the extreme categories of "one" and "seven" in the latter interviews reveals the following results: only 55 percent of those who chose the most extreme dovish alternative (of immediate withdrawal) in the second question had claimed to favor withdrawal in the first interview. Meanwhile, only 62 percent of those who chose the extreme hawkish alternative (military victory) had favored escalation in the first interview.

All this indicated that Americans have been rather ambivalent or confused on the issue of the Vietnam war. Since about half of these

1968 respondents failed to give the same Vietnam opinion twice in a row, we may conclude that at least 50 percent did not have steadfast opinions at the time. Indeed, since Converse's analysis suggests that many who respond "consistently" do so by a process of "guessing" the same response both times,[7] the portion of the adult public with firm convictions about the proper course of the war in 1968 may have been well under a majority.[8]

Obviously, the lack of depth to many of the "opinions" that get counted in surveys creates the danger that poll results can sometimes be misleading. One possible problem is that the truly attentive public—who follow politics closely and have developed genuine opinions on the issue at hand—might occasionally have viewpoints quite different from the responses of the less attentive. To our knowledge, however, no study has reported patterns of systematic differences between opinions expressed by the most and least politically informed and involved, beyond what would be expected on the basis of the different status characteristics of the two groups. For instance, although the most attentive are relatively "conservative" on social welfare questions but more "liberal" than the general population on other issues, the probable reason is that people with high education and prestigious occupations tend to take such stands.[9] (The impact of status on opinions is discussed in Chapter Five.)

Polls that ask people to reveal the intensity as well as the direction of their opinions reveal occasional instances in which the preferences of the strongly opinionated differ somewhat from those who say their opinions are not so strong. Two examples, from the Survey Research Center's 1960 study, are shown in Table 2-4. According to this table, people who offered "strong" views were most in favor of a government guarantee of employment, while on the question of foreign aid, favorable attitudes were more frequently expressed by the "not so strongly" opinionated. On rare occasions, most likely when a political personality is involved, a weakly opinionated majority will be found opposed by an intense minority. Such an instance is shown in Table 2-5, which presents the results of a 1953 poll, in which the public was asked to indicate its attitude toward the controversial Senator Joseph McCarthy on a 10-point scale from plus 5 (very favorable) to minus 5 (very unfavorable). Although a slight majority of opinion holders was favorable to McCarthy, among the minority with very intense opinions of the Senator, McCarthy was opposed by a ratio of over two to one. Results such as this, although unusual, suggest that we must continually be alert for instances in which the distribution of opinion changes shape once we take into account the intensity dimension.

TABLE 2-4 Opinion Distributions On Two Issues in 1960, By Strength Of Opinion

| | Agree Strongly | Agree, but Not Very Strongly | Not Sure, It Depends | Disagree, but Not Very Strongly | Disagree Strongly | Percent Who "Agree" | |
						Among "Strong" Opinion Holders	Among "Not so Strong" Opinion Holders
"The United States should give economic help to the poorer countries of the world even if these countries can't pay for it"	34%	25%	17%	7%	17%	67%	78%
"The government in Washington ought to see to it that everybody who wants to work can find a job"	54%	12%	9%	8%	18%	75%	59%

Source. Survey Research Center 1960 election data. "No opinion" and "Don't know" responses are excluded.

TABLE 2-5 **Intensity of Support and Opposition to Senator Joseph Mc-Carthy, 1953**

Value	Percentage at Each Value	Majority and Minority Totals	Average Intensity Score for Majority and Minority
5 (most pro-McCarthy)	6		
4	4	Majority pro-McCarthy = 35%	2.7 Majority
3	9		
3	6		
1	10		
−1	7		
−2	4		
−3	3	Minority anti-McCarthy = 30%	3.4 Minority
−4	2		
−5 (most anti-McCarthy)	14		
No Opinion	35	35	
Total	100	100	

Source. Robert E. Lane and David O. Sears, Public Opinion (Englewood Cliffs, N.J. Prentice Hall, 1964), p. 113.

"Doorstep Opinions" and Survey Results

One very real difficulty with interpreting opinion data from surveys is that since many people are responding to questions to which they have not given much previous thought, their replies can vary with even subtle differences in the way the question is worded. Of course, this is not a real problem with questions about voting preference since there are only a limited number of ways to ask people how they will vote and because most people do have crystallized preferences. But on policy questions, on which many people do not have crystallized opinions, the wording of the question can often determine the apparent majority position on the issue.

As an example, let us consider what the polls tell us about attitudes toward federal aid to education, an issue on which the bulk of the public has not had very strong convictions over the years. In a number of surveys taken from the late 1930s into the 1960s, the percentage of affirmative responses was generally about two-thirds to questions such as, simply, "Do you think the federal government should give money to states to help local schools."[10] But other questions on the issue that have been only slightly loaded have produced much different opinion breakdowns. For example, back in 1938, when 68 percent responded affirmatively to the simple question indicated above, the approval rate rose to 81 percent among a similar sample who were asked a question that emphasized aid on the basis of need: "Do you think the federal government should give money to help local schools in the poor communities?" On the other hand, when the question makes it clear that state and local responsibility is the alternative to spending federal tax money, majorities have been found *opposed* to federal aid. Thus, only 35 percent gave the pro-aid response to the Gallup Poll in 1947 when it asked: "Would you be willing to pay more taxes to the federal government to raise education levels in the poorer states of this country—or should the poorer states take this responsibility themselves?" Similarly, in 1964 when the Survey Research Center asked respondents to decide whether "the government in Washington should help towns and cities provide education for grade and high school children" or whether "this should be handled by the states and local communities," anti-aid responses outnumbered pro-aid responses by a ratio of three to two. In sharp contrast, an equally responsible poll taken the same year (1964) found the public to favor federal aid by a margin of over two to one when presented with the question:[11] "A broad general program of Federal aid to education is under consideration, which would include Federal grants to help pay teachers' salaries. Would you be for or against such a program?"

Variations in the question format could not have influenced the distribution of opinion so greatly unless a sizeable portion of the public was so unconcerned or ambivalent on the issue that it could be swayed in different directions by slightly different versions of what was basically one question. Such people were reacting to the positive and negative symbols and images presented in the questions rather than on the basis of deeply felt conviction. Thus, if the question evokes the images of needy children, or if the question allows the issue to be viewed as a referendum on the value of education, many people will respond favorably to the principle of federal aid to education. But they may react negatively if the question evokes the image of tax money being spent or if the issue is presented as one of federal intervention versus the virtues of states rights and local responsibility.

The problem of different response distributions to slightly different questions is not limited only to the issues of lesser public concern, such as federal aid to education. Even on an issue as important as the war in Vietnam, the direction of public sentiment may be quite different as measured by questions evoking different symbolic images. For example, fewer people appear to be hawkish when asked whether "we did the right thing" getting into the war than when they are asked whether involvement was "a mistake."[12] The authors of an insightful book on *Vietnam and the Silent Majority* offer the following caution about interpreting polls about public attitudes toward the war.[13]

The fact that people do not hold very well-formed and thought out opinions on public issues—even issues as important and well debated as the war in Indochina—explains many of the inconsistencies and seeming rapid changes in public opinion. The specific words that go into a question asked by a pollster may be positive or negative symbols to an individual. If a question is asked in which negative symbols are associated with withdrawal from the war, people sound quite "hawkish" in their responses. Thus people reject "defeat", "Communist take-overs," and "the loss of American credibility." On the other hand, if negative symbols are associated with a pro-war position, the American public will sound "dovish." They reject "killings," "continuing the war," and "domestic costs." Turning the matter upside down, we see the same thing. If positive symbols are associated with the war, the American public sounds "hawkish." They support "American prestige," "defense of democracy," and "support for our soldiers in Vietnam." On the other hand, if positive symbols are associated with "dovish" positions, the people sound "dovish." They come out in support of "peace", "worrying about our own problems before we worry about the problems of other people," and "saving American lives."

Variation in question wording even yields evidence of public ambivalence on the crucial issue of pollution control. To a rather visible extent, the public has become conscious of the fact that some sort of environmental crisis exists. For example, between 1965 and 1970, the proportion of the public who would describe the local air-pollution problem as "serious" rose from 28 percent to 69 percent.[14] By 1971, "pollution control" became the area of Federal spending that, except after aid to education, the public was least willing to see cut. Still, the public is not entirely convinced that new government programs to combat pollution are urgent. For example, in 1969 only 52 percent told Harris that "programs for improvement of the national environment now receive too little attention and support from the government." When people are reminded that their tax bill might expand to pay for pollution control, they become wary. For example, in 1971 only 59 percent said they were "willing to pay $15 a year more in taxes to finance a federal program to control air pollution." Another survey (in 1969) found only 22 percent "willing" to spend $200 more yearly to "solve our national problems of air and water pollution." Indeed, ordinary people may believe it unfair that they should be the ones to pay for the cleanup of industry-created pollution. If there ever is some taxpayer's revolt against the cost of fighting pollution, patriotic symbols may work as an antidote. For example, a plurality did respond favorably to the following question:

"As you may know, America faces serious pollution problems that will be very expensive to solve. One recent estimate said it might cost more than $1,000 for each family in this country, in order to clean up existing pollution. Do you think that the American people can afford whatever it takes to clean up pollution, or can't they?"

Yes   48%
No   41%
Don't know   11%

Of course students of public opinion have long been aware of ways in which "question sensitivity" may contaminate survey results. It is known, for example, that "agree-disagree" types of items can produce different responses than questions presenting both sides of the issue. When people are asked to agree or disagree with a statement concerning a matter on which they do not have definite opinions, they tend to agree more often than disagree. Thus the percentage who agree with a statement will be greater than the percentage who disagree with a statement supporting the opposite point of view. For instance, compare the responses to two rather opposite statements about academic freedom that were presented to respondents in a 1968 California poll. When asked whether they agreed or disagreed with the statement, "professors in state supported institutions should have freedom to speak and teach the truth as they see it," Californians appeared to support academic freedom by a ratio of 52 to 39. But when opinions were sought on the statement, "professors who advocate controversial ideas or speak out against official policy have no place in a state supported college or university," the same ratio of 52 to 39 was found, but this time the majority was on the side favoring restrictions on academic freedom.[15] Taken out of context, the opinion distribution on either one of these statements would offer misleading evidence of where the majority stood on the right of professors to speak freely in the classroom. Taken together, these two opinion distributions suggest another case where a large portion of the public was without crystallized attitudes.

Another problem of question sensitivity is that if the question includes the hint of how the political parties are polarized on the issue, respondents will gravitate more than usual to their party's position. For example, in 1960 the Survey Research Center twice asked the same respondents whether they agreed or disagreed with the statement, "The government in Washington should see to it that everybody who is willing to work has a job." In one instance, but not the other, the query was prefaced by the obvious partisan cue: "Over the years most Democrats have said that the government in Washington ought to see to it that everyone who wants to work can find a job. Many Republicans do not agree that the government should do this." Table 2-6 shows that Democrats were much more likely to agree with the statement—and Republicans to disagree—when they were told that these were their parties' positions. Evidently opinions on the issue of full employment were so shallow that many people "shifted" when they "learned" which side of the issue a good Democrat and a good Republican would take.

TABLE 2-6 **The Impact of a Partisan Cue on "Guaranteed Job" Opinion**

"The government should see to it that everyone who is willing to work can get a job."	No Party Cue		Told Democrats Are for and Republicans against	
	Democrats	Republicans	Democrats	Republicans
Percent Agree	78	61	81	42
Percent Disagree	22	39	19	58
	100	100	100	100
N	(498)	(304)	(495)	(305)

Source. Survey Research Center 1960 election data (unweighted sample). Nonopinion holders and undecided are excluded from analysis.

In similar fashion, people without firm convictions on an issue are likely to support the side that they are led to believe is the "official" or existing policy. This may explain the considerable disparity in levels of support for capital punishment between California, Minnesota, and the nation as a whole, as shown in Table 2-7. Nationwide, the public was about evenly split in 1965 on whether death should be the penalty for murder. But in the California poll, in which people were told (correctly) that the state allowed the death penalty, capital punishment was supported by a 2 to 1 ratio. In the Minnesota poll, in which the sample was told (correctly) that the state had abolished the death penalty, the public came out 2 to 1 *against* capital punishment. The two states are not sufficiently different in political attitudes to expect such a large difference in opinion if the identical question had been asked in both states. Nor is it likely that most of the Californians or Minnesotans were aware of their states' policy toward capital punishment before the question was asked. Therefore it is probable that the pollsters' questions provided the cue that influence respondents to support what they were told was the existing practice in their state.

TABLE 2-7 **Question Variation and Opinion on Capital Punishment**

	For Capital Punishment	Against	No Opinion
Nationwide: 1965			
Are you in favor of the death penalty for persons convicted of murder?	45%	43%	12%
California: 1963			
As you know, this state has capital punishment—that is, execution—as a form of punishment for criminals. How do you personally feel about capital punishment—would you be in favor of doing away with the death sentence, or do you feel the death sentence should be kept as punishment for serious crimes, as it is now?	56	28	16
Minnesota: 1963			
Minnesota does not have the death sentence for any crime. Do you think Minnesota should or should not permit the death sentence for convicted murderers?	31	62	7

Source. Hazel Erskine, "The Polls: Capital Punishment," *Public Opinion Quarterly, 34* (Summer, 1970), pp. 291–296.

DISTRIBUTIONS OF OPINION ON MAJOR ISSUES

The preceding discussion may create the erroneous impression that opinion polls are rather useless instruments for gauging public opinion. Our intent was simply to make the reader aware of some of the pitfalls that are involved in the interpretation of polls. Certainly, when they are interpreted with proper caution, polls are an extremely valuable source of information for the study of public opinion.

Sometimes little caution is necessary. For example, when 94 percent say that they "would like to see college administrators take a stronger stand on student unrest" at the same time when polls indicate that "student unrest" is most often stated as the "most important problem facing this country today," the conclusion that many Americans are concerned about the more extreme behavior of student activists is fairly well grounded. But normally, when the polls show that X percent appear to favor a certain policy at a given time, as based on a particular question, we need some anchor by which to measure the significance of the finding. We have already seen that by comparing responses to similar questions with only slightly different wordings, we can determine whether opinion on the issue is rather soft and malleable or rather hard and firm. Also, by comparing the responses to one question to those on slightly different but related issues, we can see what distinctions the public makes to the kinds of policies it is willing to support. Certainly the best anchor is to compare findings over the course of time. If the public displays a different level of support for some policy today than it did a few years ago when asked the same question, then we can say that we have located an important *change* in public opinion.

Unfortunately, the data that would allow the accurate assessment of trends in political opinion are not as available as one might expect. The reason is that although various polling organizations have been collecting vast amounts of opinion data over the years, it is not very often that they ask the same question in different years. Pollsters naturally ask questions on issues that are of current interest, and since the issues that are salient change, so do the questions. For example, questions dealing with civil liberties were asked most often in the "McCarthy era" of the early 1950s when many people thought our basic liberties were threatened. Questions dealing with race relations were not often asked in the 1930s and 1940s when the aspirations of the black minority were given little thought. Today, the public is not often polled on economic issues as frequently as had been the case in past decades when differences over the proper extent of government activity in the social welfare sphere comprised the dominant political cleavage of American politics.[16] Even when the polls monitor opinions on the same issue continually over a long time interval, they often vary their questions somewhat so that the "trends" that develop may be functions of different question wordings.

In the following section we will present a brief overview of what the polls do tell us about the distributions of public opinion—both today and in the past—on the broader long-standing political issues. Where possible, trend data will be employed. We have divided the issues into four broad issue domains: economic or "social welfare" issues, foreign policy, civil rights, and "social issues." Opinions in each of these four domains will be examined separately.

Social Welfare

From New Deal days to the present, the American public has generally been receptive to government programs to accomplish social objectives. In fact, it is often said that on social welfare legislation, mass opinion is usually well ahead of congressional action. For example, the earliest polls revealed an overwhelming majority in favor of "old age pensions" prior to the adoption of Social Security in 1936.[17] Continually, majority approval has been found prior to each increase in the federal minimum wage.[18] Also, polls show that most people were at least mildly favorable to federal aid to education and Medicare long before these programs were finally enacted into law in 1965.

Even the most controversial of existing social welfare programs receive overwhelming support from the public. For example, Table 2-8 shows that in the mid–1960s very few wanted reductions in the federal antipoverty, housing, and urban renewal programs enacted under the Johnson administration. The distributions in this table clearly demonstrate that there is little public sentiment for the extreme "conservative" position that the vast set of government social welfare programs should be dismantled. However, most people do not insist on a vigorous *increase* in the federal government's role either.

When given a choice between an increase in government activity, a decrease, or the continuation of the status quo, more people choose the middle category than either extreme. Such a pattern can be seen in Table 2-9 from the results of two polls—one from 1952 and one from 1964. Thus, the most accurate statement about public attitudes toward federal social welfare legislation may be that the public tends to accept the existing role of the federal government and is somewhat favorably disposed toward the least controversial new proposals.

To the extent it is possible to evaluate trends by comparing the results of similarly worded questions that have been asked the public in different years, it appears that the level of mass support for social welfare legislation has been remarkably stable over recent decades. The clearest evidence is from poll questions on government subsidization of medical care. The stability of support for government help in paying medical expenses is illustrated in Figure 2-2. It shows that between 1956 and 1968, the portion of opinion holders who agreed that the government should "help people get doctors and hospital care at low cost" stayed fairly constant, within the range of 62 to 75 percent.[19] Polls also indicate that over the years a consistent majority has believed that the government has a responsibility to insure full employment. In several polls from 1939 to 1960, opinion holders were 2 to 1 in favor of the notion that the government should insure "that everyone who wants to work has (or "can find") a job.[20] In 1964, 75 percent agreed that "the Federal Government has a responsibility to try to reduce unemployment," while only 18 percent dissented.[21]

TABLE 2-8 **Opinions on Selected Federal Social Welfare Programs in the Mid-1960s (in Percent)**

	Kept at Least at Present Level	Reduced	Ended Altogether	No Opinion
(1964) Under the federal housing program, the Federal Government is making grants to help build low-rent public housing. Do you think government spending for this purpose should be....	63	12	10	15
(1964) Under the urban renewal program, the Federal Government is making grants to help build run-down sections of our cities. Do you think government spending for this purpose should be....	67	10	11	12
(1967) Under the Community Action program, the Federal Government makes grants to city governments and private organizations so that they can carry out local projects with the idea of combatting poverty. Do you think spending by the Federal Government for this purpose should be....	54	25	10	11
(1967) Under the Head Start program, the Federal Government finances schooling for very young children from poor families even before they reach the usual school age with the idea of improving their educational opportunities. Do you think spending by the Federal Government for this purpose should be....	67	10	16	7
(1967) As part of the antipoverty program, the Federal Government is providing funds for retraining poorly educated people so they can get jobs. Do you think spending by the Federal Government for this purpose should be....	75	13	8	4

Source. Lloyd A. Free and Hadley Cantril, *The Political Beliefs of Americans,* (New York: Simon and Schuster, 1968), pp. 11–14.

TABLE 2-9   **Opinion of the Power of the Federal Government**

(1952) "Some people think the national government should do more in trying to deal with such problems as unemployment, education, housing, and so on. Others think that the government is already doing
too much. On the whole, would you say that what the government
has done has been. . . ."

too much	18%
about right	48%
not enough	16%
no opinion, other	18%

(1964) "Which one of the statements listed on this card comes closest to
your own views about government power today?

1. The Federal Government today has too much power.   26%
2. The Federal Government is now using just about the
right amount of power for meeting today's needs.   36%
3. The Federal Government should use its powers even
more vigorously to promote the well being of all
segments of the people."   31%
4. Don't know   7%

Sources. Survey Research Center; Lloyd A. Free and Hadley Cantril, *The Political Beliefs of Americans* (New York: Simon and Schuster, 1968), p. 19.

However, this consensus in favor of government programs designed to give jobs to the unemployed does not extend to majorities
in support of a government responsibility to insure everybody a
good standard of living or a guaranteed income. For example, when
the Survey Research Center asked its 1964 and 1968 samples whether
"the government in Washington should see to it that every person

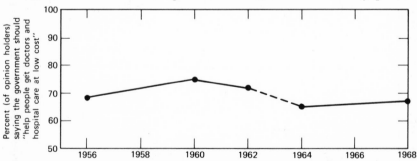

Figure 2-2.   Opinion of government subsidization of medical expenses.
(*Source.* Survey Research Center. The broken line indicates a
slight change in question wording.)

44   *Opinion Polls and Public Opinion: An Introductory View*

has a job and a good standard of living" or whether "the government should just let each person get ahead on his own," only about two-fifths of the opinion holders favored government assistance. The unwillingness of the public to support a guaranteed income is clearly revealed from the results of a 1969 Gallup Poll:[22]

"As you may know, there is talk about giving every family an income of at least $3200 a year, which would be the amount for a family of four. If the family earns less than this, the government would make up the difference. Would you favor or oppose such a plan?"

Favor 32%   Oppose 62%   No Opinion 6%

In contrast, a followup question yielded the following results:

"Another proposal is to guarantee enough work so that each family that has an employable wage earner would be guaranteed enough WORK each week to give him a wage of about $60 a week or $3200 a year. Would you favor or oppose such a plan?"

Favor 79%   Oppose 16%   No Opinion 5%

Results such as these show that there are limits to the public's willingness to support innovative social welfare proposals. As innovative suggestions turn toward such matters as guaranteeing each family a minimum income, mass opinion is clearly lagging behind the thinking of reformers and government leaders. One reason for this resistance is the widespread mass belief that people who receive financial assistance ought to work for their money, even if the work they do is of little use. Also, when government programs are perceived as benefiting only the lowest income groups—slum dwellers, welfare recipients, and potential "rioters"—few people see themselves as beneficiaries of these policies. As a result, the bulk of the public now sometimes appears on the "conservative" side of current social welfare controversies. For example, when in 1970 Gallup asked whether Congress should "try to improve the lot of the poor people and try to get at the cause of social problems," or "give more support to the police and get tougher with lawbreakers," less than 4 in 10 chose the former alternative.[23] But such conservative manifestations do not necessarily mean that the public is reacting to specific proposals any differently than it did (or would have done) in the past. Instead, the change has been in the nature of the proposals rather than in public thinking. As the public welfare proposals that are the topic of public debate appear more and more "radical" from the mass perspective, the nonmoving public now sometimes appears to be more conservative than liberal on social welfare issues.

Civil Rights

With the possible exception of the Vietnamese war, no issue is more responsible for the current polarization of American politics than the struggle for racial equality. We have already seen that mass attitudes on racial questions are probably more highly crystallized than political attitudes on other kinds of issues. Yet if we attempt to locate majority sentiment on civil rights issues, very different opinion distributions can often be obtained with slight variations in the questions and issues put to respondents. For example, in 1968 the Survey Research Center asked people to choose which statement they agreed with most: "White people have a right to keep Negroes out of their neighborhoods if they want to," or: "Negroes have a right to live wherever they can afford to, just like white people." Since 78 percent of those venturing an opinion picked the second statement, there seemingly was a strong consensus in support of equal rights on the volatile issue of open housing. Yet, a year earlier (in 1967), when Gallup asked whether Congress should enact a national "open housing" law, only 35 percent of those who said they knew what the term "open housing" means favored it.[24]

On the issue of school integration too, estimates of the public mood depend on the particular question that is put to survey respondents. Some of this variation is shown in Table 2-10. If white parents are asked whether they would object if their children are sent to a school where a few Negroes attend, the vast majority say that they would go along. If the issue is whether "the government in Washington should see to it that white and Negro children are allowed to go to the same school," the public is split about evenly. If the question is whether the federal government is pushing integration too fast, too slowly, or at about the right speed, those who say it is pushing "too fast" vastly outnumber those who say it is going "too slow." On school busing to achieve racial balance, there is overwhelming public opposition.

Whatever else can be concluded from the sampling of civil rights attitudes, polls clearly show that white America has at least rejected the prevalent "white supremist" ideology that pervaded mass attitudes as recently as a few decades ago. Poll data from the 1930s and 1940s suggests that, in those past decades, perhaps a majority of white Americans believed Negroes to be intellectually inferior and undeserving of equal status with whites. For example, in 1939 only 13 percent agreed that "Negroes should be allowed to live wherever they want to live, and there should be no laws and social pressures to keep them from it."[25] In 1944, only 42 percent of a national sample thought "Negroes should have as good a chance as white people to get any kind of job." As evidence of change, by

TABLE 2-10 **Opinion Distributions on Racial Integration of Schools (in Percent)**

	Pro-Integration	Anti-Integration	No Opinion, Other
(1969) Would you, yourself have any objection to sending your children to a school where a few of the children are Negroes? (asked of white parents only)	89	11	—
(1968) Should the government in Washington "see to it that white and Negro children go to the same schools . . . or stay out of this area as it is none of its business?"	38	44	18
(1969) Do you think the racial integration of schools in the United States is going too fast or not fast enough?	22	44	34[a]
(1970) In general, do you favor or oppose the busing of Negro and white children from one school district to another?	14	81	5

Sources. Gallup Opinion Index, September, 1969, p. 5 (question 1); Survey Research Center (question 2); Gallup Poll News Release, August 17, 1969 (question 3); *Gallup Opinion Index,* March, 1970 (question 4).
[a] Includes "about right" response (volunteered).

1963 82 percent of adult whites were willing to agree with this statement.[26] A similar change can be seen in white estimates of Negro intelligence. While as late as 1944 only 44 percent believed that "Negroes are as intelligent as white people," the percentage had risen to 77 percent by 1956.[27]

The steady rise in support for racial integration is shown in Figure 2-3, which displays the rates of agreement with the prointegration alternatives in three civil rights questions that were asked white cross-sections periodically between 1942 and 1970. On the basis of the three questions, public support for integration of schools, housing, and public transportation facilities all increased by over 30 percentage points over this period.[28] Other poll questions that have been continually asked since 1963 generally show that the rise in prointegration sentiment has continued. For example, from 1963 to

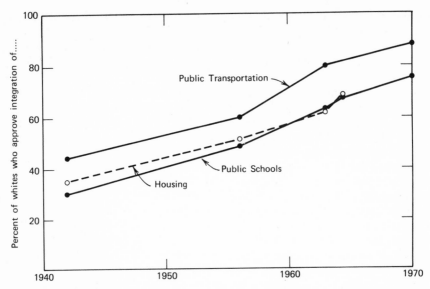

Figure 2-3. Trends in approval of school, housing, and transportation integration. (*Source.* Adapted from Paul B. Sheatsley, "White Attitudes toward the Negro," *Daedalus* (Winter, 1966), pp. 219, 222, 235; Andrew M. Greeley and Paul B. Sheatsley, "Attitudes toward Racial Integration," *Scientific American,* 225 (December, 1971), pp. 13-19.)

1970 the percentage of white parents who said they would have objections to sending their children to "schools where half of the children are Negro" dropped from 33 percent to 24 percent in the North, and—more dramatically—from 78 to 43 percent in the South.[29] Similar declines can be found since 1963 in the percentages who would object to voting for a "qualified Negro" presidential candidate, who oppose the right of Negroes to live in homes they can afford, and who say they favor "strict segregation of the races."[30]

Despite the clear decline in the frequency of explicitly "racist" sentiment expressed in surveys of the white public, this trend has not kept pace with the rise in black aspirations. One reason for this statement is that support for *federal action* in the civil rights sphere has remained at a lukewarm level over the years. For example, in the period following the 1954 Supreme Court ruling that school segregation was unconstitutional, public support for the decision in the Gallup Poll rose only from 54 percent in 1954 to 62 percent in 1961.[31] From 1956 to 1970, the public has remained about evenly divided on whether the federal government should see to it that "white and Negro children go to the same schools."[32] Also, throughout the 1960s the proportion of the public who thought the federal government was moving "too fast" on integration remained at a fairly constant level.[33]

Polls show that one factor hindering a reduction in civil rights conflict is the persistently unfavorable attitude of most whites toward the civil rights movement. Even in the early 1960s, when Negro activism emerged in the form of nonviolent demonstrations against institutional segregation in the South, most whites reacted negatively to "demonstrations," "freedom rides," and "sit-ins."[34] As early as 1963, a year before the periodic outbreak of urban Negro riots began, a majority of whites thought the civil rights movement was "more violent than peaceful." Polls taken in 1963 and thereafter have continually shown that the vast majority feel that civil rights leaders are pushing "too fast," and that the civil rights movement has "hurt more than helped" the Negro cause. This tendency can be seen in the poll results reported in Table 2-11.

There is, of course, some pattern to findings we have examined. By and large, most Americans give at least "lip service" to the principles of racial integration and equality. Yet far fewer believe that the federal government should do anything to implement these goals.

TABLE 2-11   **Opinion on the Civil Rights Movement**

Issue	1964	1968	1970
Some say that the civil rights people have been trying to push too fast. Others feel they haven't pushed fast enough. How about you: Do you think that civil rights leaders are trying to push too fast, are going too slowly, or are they moving about the right speed? (Percent too fast.)	71	65	55
During the past year or so, would you say that most of the actions Negroes have taken to get the things they want have been violent, or have most of these actions been peaceful? (Percent violent.)	64	74	69
Do you think the actions Negroes have taken have, on the whole, helped or, on the whole, have hurt their cause? (Percent hurt.)	64	69	65

Source. Survey Research Center. Nonopinion holders are excluded from the percentages.

Fewer still favor *accelerations* of federal civil rights activity. And the entire civil rights movement is viewed with distrust by most Americans.

Foreign Policy

Because issues of foreign policy are quite removed from everyday experience, "foreign policy" attitudes are generally held less firmly than opinions on domestic policy. We have already examined the extent to which mass opinions are uncrystallized regarding the war in Vietnam. Taken out of context, responses to any one foreign policy question seldom provide an accurate portrayal of American opinion. For instance, one might believe most Americans favor a more belligerent foreign policy than our national leaders from the fact that in 1964 the statement "the United States should take a firmer stand against the Soviet Union than it has in recent years" was approved by a ratio of 5 to 2. Yet in the same survey an even greater ratio of support was found for the milder, somewhat contrary view that the United States "should continue to negotiate with Russia with a view toward reducing armaments on both sides."[35] The "foreign aid" issue offers another instance of ambivalent opinion, since most Americans have only the haziest notion about this subject. Table 2-12 shows how in the mid-1960s the opinion distribution on foreign aid varied with the question asked. Although most Americans say they support economic aid for needy countries and have a favorable image of "foreign aid" in general, polls continually reveal the public to be quite receptive to cuts in the foreign aid budget and unfavorably disposed to aiding nations that refuse to follow the U.S. lead in foreign policy.

Given variable results such as these, our understanding of foreign policy attitudes can best be served by following observable trends in opinion. On foreign policy questions, public opinion has undergone several visible shifts since the first days of opinion polls. Most dramatic is the change—precipitated by World War II—in majority sentiment from isolationism to an internationalist outlook regarding the United States' role in world affairs. A glimpse at the results of opinion polls from the late 1930s reveals the extent of isolationist sentiment in that decade and before. In 1937, 70 percent of opinion holders said the American entry in World War I had been a mistake.[36] The same year 94 percent of opinion holders said the United States should "do everything possible to keep out of foreign wars" rather than "do everything possible to prevent war, even if it means threatening to fight countries which fight wars."[37] Although only an infinitesimal number of American citizens supported the German or Japanese side when war broke out in 1939, only about 60 percent of

TABLE 2-12   **Opinion Distributions on Foreign Aid (in Percent)**

	Pro-Aid	Anti-Aid	No Opinion, Other
(1964) Should "we give aid to other countries if they need help?"[b]	52	19	29
(1966) In general, how do you feel about foreign aid—are you for it or against it?	53	35	12
(1964) And now, what about economic aid to foreign countries? Do you think government spending for this purpose should be kept at least at the present level, or reduced or ended altogether?	32	59[a]	9
(1966) Suppose another country—which is receiving aid from the United States —fails to support the United States in a major foreign policy decision, such as Vietnam. Do you think the United States should continue giving aid to that country, reduce aid, or cut off aid completely?	16	75[a]	9

Sources. Survey Research Center (question 1); *Gallup Opinion Index,* March, 1966 (questions 2 and 4); Lloyd A. Free and Hadley Cantril, *The Political Beliefs of Americans* (New York: Simon and Schuster, 1968), p. 72 (question 3).

[a] Combination of responses favoring a reduction and those favoring an end to aid.

[b] For the complete wording of the first question, see the Appendix.

those venturing opinions were willing to go as far as to help Britain and France "except at the risk of getting into war ourselves." Between 1939 and late 1941, the percentage who said they would vote in favor of entering the war against Germany only rose from 13 percent to 32 percent. Although by October 1941, 70 percent of voters with opinions considered it more important that Germany be defeated than that America stay out of the war, the number saying it was "more important to help Britain win" than "keep out of war ourselves" had been only 36 percent 17 months before. Support for war with Japan prior to our entry was even lower; even a month before Pearl Harbor, only 19 percent felt "the United States should take steps to keep Japan from becoming too powerful, even if this means risking a war with Japan."

Once the Japanese attacked Pearl Harbor and we consequently entered World War II, Americans were unified behind the war effort —more so than during any other war in our history. Internationalist sentiment expressed in opinion polls naturally increased also, and did not recede once the war was over. For example, between 1942 and 1954 the percentage agreeing that "we take an active part in world affairs" seldom strayed from the average of 71 percent.[38] Also, although a majority in the 1930s thought it would be a mistake for the United States to join the League of Nations, the postwar percentage favoring U.S. withdrawal from the United Nations has never risen above 1 in 8. The low point of isolationist feeling among the mass public probably occurred in the mid-1960s, just before full American involvement in the Vietnam conflict. In 1964, only 18 percent agreed with the "isolationist" statement that "the United States should mind its own business internationally and let other countries get along as best they can on their own."[39]

If the extent of support for the war in Vietnam is a valid indicator of the level of internationalism, then isolationist sentiment is increasing once again. Between 1966 and 1971, the percentage who told Gallup that they thought our involvement in Vietnam was a mistake rose steadily from under one-third to a decisive majority. On foreign policy questions that do not deal directly with the war in Southeast Asia, support for the "isolationist" opinion has also been increasing. Whereas in 1964 74 percent of opinion holders told the Survey Research Center that the United States "should give aid to other countries if they need help," only 59 percent did so in 1968. Similarly, the proportion who said "It would be better for the United States to keep independent in world affairs" rather than "work closely with other nations" more than doubled—from 10 percent to 22 percent between 1963 and 1969.[40]

Of course, today the relevant foreign policy question may not be the *extent* of American involvement in world affairs so much as the *manner* in which the powerful United States conducts its foreign policy, particularly in relation to the Communist world. Through the years, mass attitudes toward the Soviet Union have generally followed the lead of foreign policy. During World War II, when the United States and Russia were allies, favorable attitudes toward the U.S.S.R. grew until at war's end 55 percent said "Russia can be counted on to cooperate with us once the war is over." Such trust diminished rapidly thereafter; by October 1946 the percentage who thought Russia could "be trusted to cooperate with us during the next few years" dropped to 28 percent. By the late 1940s, most people thought it more important "to stop Soviet expansion in Europe and Asia than avoid major war." During the Korean War in

the early 1950s, a majority of Americans polled said they expected
a war with Russia during their lifetime.[41]

Since the mid-1950s, Americans have taken a more relaxed stand
in respect to the Soviet threat. Only decreasing minorities in the
1960s foresaw war with Russia in the near future. The melting of
Cold War attitudes can be seen in the growing frequency with which
Americans said they felt "favorable" toward the Soviet Union—
from 7 percent in 1957 to 18 percent in 1967 and 40 percent in 1972.[42]
Americans even began to reject the notion that Communist nations
always act in concert. For example, by 1967 most who ventured
opinions thought that "if trouble ever broke out between the United
States and China . . . Russia would be more likely to be on our side
than on China's side." By the same date, China had replaced the
Soviet Union as the major threat to world peace in the eyes of over
75 percent of the opinion-holding public. Even so, support for admission of Red China to the United Nations has been rising steadily. As
Figure 2-4 shows, support in Gallup Polls for Chinese admission rose

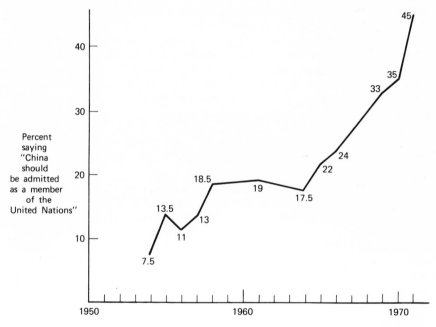

Figure 2-4. Increasing support for admitting China to the UN. (*Sources:*
Hazel Erskine, "The Polls: Red China and the UN," *Public
Opinion Quarterly, 35* (Spring, 1971), p. 125; *Gallup Opinion
Index,* June, 1971, p. 16.

Distributions of Opinion on Major Issues **53**

steadily between 1954 and 1971.[43] This trend is perhaps the clearest indication from the polls of the long-term change in American attitudes toward the Communist world.

The "Social Issues"

In recent years, a new set of issues has entered the American political arena. We refer to the various components of what has been termed the "Social Issue" in American politics.[44] In its broadest context, the term "social issue" might apply to all conflicts between the forces of change and the forces of resistance to deviations from the "traditional moral values." Here we shall focus on the political aspects of the social issues—"law and order," "permissiveness," "dissent," "campus unrest," and the like.

The increasing public concern about these issues has been reflected in the kinds of questions the commercial polls have been asking in recent years. Some examples of the Gallup Poll's recent "social issue" questions and the responses are shown in Table 2-13. Overwhelmingly in some instances, the public clusters on the "conservative" side of these issues. A similar pattern is found in the results of a series of survey questions on protest and dissent that were asked the public in 1968 and 1970. As Table 2-14 shows, majorities of opinion holders gave unqualified disapproval to peaceful sit-ins, violating laws one feels to be unjust, and (in 1968) even lawful protest. The bulk of the remaining minority chose the option that their approval or disapproval of the kind of activity in question would "depend on the circumstances." This hostility to even the milder forms of political protest is consistent with earlier findings regarding the public's tolerance level for dissent. For example, in the early 1950s, majorities rejected the right of Communists, Socialists, or opponents of churches and religion to speak in their communities.[45]

Since most of the issues reflected in Tables 2-13 and 2-14 are relatively new, it is difficult to establish trends. Probably if these questions had been asked of a national sample 20 years ago, the public would have responded even more conservatively than it does now. However, from the scattering of relevant questions that have been repeatedly asked in polls, a more recent trend toward an apparent increase of conservatism is evident at least on "law and order" related issues. For example, between 1965 and 1969 the proportion who said that the courts in their area were "not harsh enough" rose from 48 percent to 75 percent.[46] Capital punishment is one "law and order" issue on which the public has been polled continuously over a long period of time. As Figure 2-5 shows, opposition to the death penalty rose steadily from the late 1930s into the 1960s but has noticeably declined, at least temporarily, since then. The prestige

TABLE 2-13 Opinion Distributions on "Social Issues" (in Percent)

		"Liberal"	"Conservative"
(1965)	Do you think there is any police brutality in this area?	Yes, 9	No, 79
(1968)	Should divorce in this country be easier or more difficult to obtain than it is now?	Easier, 18	More Difficult, 60
(1969)	Do you favor or oppose having federal loans taken away from students who break laws while participating in college demonstrations?	Oppose, 11	Favor, 84
(1969)	Here are some questions about obscene literature sent through the mails . . . Would you like to see stricter state and local laws on such literature or not?	No, 8	Yes, 85
(1969)	What about the magazines and newspapers sold on newsstands. Would you like to see stricter state laws on such literature or not?	No, 17	Yes, 75
(1969)	Would you favor or oppose a law that would permit a woman to go to a doctor to end a pregnancy any time during the first three months?	Favor, 40	Oppose, 50
(1970)	Do you agree or disagree with college students going on strike as a way to protest the way things are run in this country?	Agree, 15	Disagree, 82
(1972)	Do you think the penalty for use or possession of marijuana should be less strict . . .?	Yes, 30	No, 64

Source. Issues of *Gallup Opinion Index* for the years cited.

Distributions of Opinion on Major Issues **55**

TABLE 2-14 Opinion Distributions on the Right to Protest (in Percent)

Issue		Approve	Depends on Circumstances	Disapprove
How about taking part in protest meetings or marches that are permitted by the local authorities?	(1968)	19	27	54
	(1970)	13	38	49
How about refusing to obey a law that one thinks is unjust, if the person feels so strongly about it that he is willing to go to jail rather than obey the law?	(1968)	15	24	61
	(1970)	11	36	53
Suppose all the methods have failed and the person decides to try to stop the government from going about its usual activities with sit-ins, mass meetings, demonstrations, and things like that?	(1968)	8	18	74
	(1970)	7	28	64

Source. Survey Research Center. Nonopinion holders are excluded from the percentages.

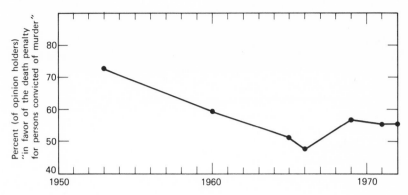

Figure 2-5. Changing attitudes toward capital punishment. (*Sources.* Recomputed from Gallup polls reported in Hazel Erskine, "The Polls: Capital Punishment," *Public Opinion Quarterly, 34* (Summer, 1970), pp. 291–296; *Gallup Opinion Index,* March, 1972.

of the Supreme Court has also been affected by the "social issue" preoccupation. Between 1963 and 1969, the portion of the public who rated the Court as "excellent" or "good" dropped from 43 percent to 33 percent.[47]

STABILITY OF OPINION DISTRIBUTION OVER TIME

From the periodic fluctuations in presidential election results, it sometimes appears that the American public undergoes periodic swings of political mood—either from "liberal" to "conservative" or vice versa. An increase in the vote for the Democratic party is often interpreted as a sign that the voters are becoming more liberal, while a Republican trend in the vote is sometimes taken as a signal of increasing conservatism on the part of the electorate. In Chapter One, we saw that the frequencies of Democratic and Republican *party identification* within the electorate remain stable even when party fortunes in presidential contests undergo sharp changes. Similarly, we have found that trends in public opinion on policy issues are not nearly as volatile as short-term swings in the election fortunes of the two major parties would suggest. Our review of the results of opinion surveys has disclosed a few instances in which the distribution of opinion on an issue has changed somewhat over the course of time. But these shifts—such as the declines in white racist sentiment and in "cold war" attitudes—can best be seen over a span of many years. In the short run, opinion distributions on long standing issues are generally quite stable.

TABLE 2-15 **Opinion on Nine Issues in 1964 and 1968**

Belief	Percent Support among Opinion Holders	
	1964	1968
The government in Washington should "help people get doctors and hospital care at low cost"	64	66
The government "should see to it that every person has a job and a good standard of living"	42	41
The government in Washington "should help towns and cities provide education for grade and high school children"	40	37
The government in Washington "should see to it that Negroes get fair treatment in jobs"	49	47
The government in Washington "should see to it that white and Negro children go to the same schools"	52	47
The government should "support the right of Negroes to go to any hotel or restaurant they can afford"	55	61
The United States "should give aid to other countries if they need help"	74	59
"Our government should sit down and talk to the leaders of the Communist countries and try to settle our differences"	88	91
Our farmers and businessmen "should be allowed to do business with Communist countries"	39	44
Mean . . .	56	55

Source. Survey Research Center. For the full forms of the questions, see the Appendix.

As a demonstration of this stability, Table 2-15 compares the distributions of policy preferences in 1964 and 1968 on nine long-standing issues of American politics. Respondents in two surveys were asked the identical set of questions on nine issues. Despite the Republican trend in presidential voting from 1964 to 1968, there was no tendency over this period of an increase in "conservative" responses to the nine questions shown in Table 2-15. On only five of the nine issues did the percentage of opinions that were "liberal" decrease. And, except for the decline in support for foreign aid, all the "shifts" were within the range expected on the basis of sampling error. A similar stability can be found in the opinion distributions to the series of questions asked by the Survey Research Center over the 1956 to 1960 period.

Seemingly the best way to locate trends of liberalism or conservatism on the part of the public would be simply to record changes in the degree to which people call themselves "liberals" or "conservatives." As shown in the next chapter, self-rankings as "liberals" or "conservatives" are of questionable value for the reason that many people lack adequate understanding of these terms. Yet we are obliged to note an obvious recent trend in self-placement on the liberal–conservative spectrum. In polls taken between the late 1930s and the mid-1960s, the public remained about evenly divided between people who called themselves "liberals" and self-declared "conservatives."[48] But then a "conservative" shift began, so by 1970 "conservatives" were outnumbering "liberals" as much as 2 to 1. (More recently, the "liberal" label has begun to regain some of its lost ground—see Table 2-16). This post-1964 wobble in the "liberal-

TABLE 2-16   The Trend in Self-Identification as "Liberal" or "Conservative," 1964–1972

	Very Liberal	Fairly Liberal	Middle-of-the-Road	Fairly Conservative	Very Conservative	Don't Know
Fall 1964	6%	20%[a]	34%	24%[a]	6%	10%
October 1970	4	16	35	31	9	5
May 1971	7	19	29	28	11	6
April 1972	8	18	33	23	14	4

Sources. (1964) Lloyd Free and Hadley Cantril, The Political Beliefs of Americans (New York: Simon and Schuster, 1968), p. 222; (others) Gallup Opinion Index.
[a] Wording in 1964 was "moderately" liberal or conservative.

conservative" trend line is puzzling since, as we have seen, the public's stand on traditional political issues did not noticeably become more conservative over this period. Most likely, the sudden shift toward "conservatism" reflects the increasing public concern about the so-called "social issues," on which people are generally conservative. It used to be that the popular conception of the difference between liberals and conservatives involved the dimension of relative willingness to support federal programs on which the public gives relatively "liberal" responses. But, in recent years, the terms "liberal" and "conservative" have been most frequently applied to the dimension of "tolerance" or "permissiveness" versus a more "strict" attitude on social issues on which people are generally conservative. Thus, in one sense, the relative "liberalism" of the public can shift with changes in the issues that are considered to be most important, even though on particular issues there is no general shift of opinion.[49]

CONCLUSION

In this chapter we have examined what can be learned from simply examining the distributions of opinion on political issues that are reported in the tabulation of survey results. We have seen that poll results are often contaminated by the responses of the many people who have less than well-formed opinions. Especially, we find that slight differences in the question wording can sometimes produce dramatic differences in the distribution of opinion. Because of this difficulty, the best way to analyze opinion breakdowns on policy issues is to follow opinion on a question over time. Doing this discloses some instances of opinion change. But, especially in the short run, the distributions of policy positions remain stable over time. That is, even though individuals often have opinions so underdeveloped that they seem to change their minds on political issues from one interview to the next, there is usually little change in the net breakdown of pro and con opinions from one time period to the next.

The findings in this chapter far from exhaust the kinds of information that can be extracted from opinion polls. By merely looking at the simple raw distributions of opinion we have only scratched the surface. For example, survey analysis allows us to examine the relationships between opinions on different issues, to locate group differences in opinions, and to examine the important question of the relationship between issue opinions and voting behavior. These and other topics that demand the employment of survey research will be explored in the following chapters.

FOOTNOTES FOR CHAPTER 2

[1] Philip E. Converse, Aage R. Clausen, and Warren E. Miller, "Electoral Myth and Reality, The 1964 Election," *American Political Science Review*, 59 (June, 1965), pp. 332–335.

[2] Gallup Poll News Release, July 27, 1969.

[3] Philip E. Converse, "The Nature of Belief Systems in Mass Publics," in David Apter (ed.), *Ideology and Discontent* (New York: The Free Press of Glencoe, 1964), pp. 238–245; Philip E. Converse, "Attitudes and Non-Attitudes: Continuation of a Dialogue," in Edward R. Tufte (ed.), *The Quantitative Analysis of Social Problems* (Reading, Mass.: Addison Wesley, 1970), pp. 168–189.

[4] Converse, "The Nature of Belief Systems . . . ," p. 239.

[5] This estimate of partisan conversion rate is derived from the tables in Philip E. Converse, "A Major Political Realignment in the South?" in Alan P. Sindler, (ed.), *Changes in the Contemporary South* (Durham: Duke University Press, 1963), pp. 195–222.

[6] Converse, "Attitudes and Non-Attitudes . . . ," p. 176.

[7] The possibility that most Vietnam "converts" were actually guessing is supported by the fact that the time interval between the successive interviews did not appear to affect the turnover rate. We compared the turnover rate for those interviewed in October and November (short interval) with the rate for the portion of the sample interviewed in September and December (long interval) and found the turnover rate to be slightly higher among the group with the shortest time between interviews. If opinion turnover represented true conversion, then turnover should have become greater with the increase in the time lag between interviews.

[8] The generalizations about the extent of opinion turnover of course apply to the public as a whole, and not to the more politically articulate subpopulation. A long-term study of Bennington College students in the 1930s disclosed a remarkable consistency between the political attitudes they held during college and their attitudes 25 years later. See Theodore M. Newcomb, et al., *Persistence and Change: Bennington College and its Students after Twenty-five Years* (New York: John Wiley and Sons, 1967).

[9] For examples of differences in opinion responses between the relatively attentive and the relatively inattentive, see Donald J. Devine, *The Attentive Public* (Chicago: Rand McNally, 1970), Chapter 5.

[10] Except where noted, this and the following survey questions dealing with the subject of federal aid to education are from the Gallup polls reported in Frank J. Munger and William F. Fenno, Jr., *National Politics and Federal Aid to Education* (Syracuse: Syracuse University Press, 1962), pp. 91–96.

[11] Lloyd A. Free and Hadley Cantril, *The Political Beliefs of Americans* (New York: Simon and Schuster, 1968), p. 13.

[12] John E. Mueller, "Trends in Popular Support for the Wars in Korea and Vietnam," *American Political Science Review, 65* (June, 1971), p. 363.

[13] Milton J. Rosenberg, Sidney Verba, and Philip E. Converse, *Vietnam and the Silent Majority* (New York: Harper and Row, 1970), pp. 24–25.

[14] This result, and others reported in this paragraph, are found in Hazel Erskine, "The Polls: Pollution and Its Cost," *Public Opinion Quarterly, 36* (Spring, 1972), pp. 120–135.

[15] These questions are from the Field Research Corporation's "California Poll" of January 1968, as reported in *Gallup Opinion Index*, March, 1968, p. 11.

[16] A tabulation of some of the shifts in the types of questions that pollsters ask is found in Hazel Gaudet Erskine, "The Polls: Some Gauges of Conservatism," *Public Opinion Quarterly, 28* (Spring, 1964), pp. 154–155.

[17] For example, in one of the first national polls on the subject, in 1935 89% said that they were "in favor of old-age pensions for needy persons." Source: Hadley Cantril, *Public Opinion: 1935–1946* (Princeton: Princeton University Press, 1951), p. 541.

[18] Hazel Gaudet Erskine, "The Polls: Attitudes toward Organized Labor," *Public Opinion Quarterly, 26* (Summer, 1962), p. 293; *Gallup Poll Index*, September, 1965, p. 17.

[19] The wording of the Survey Research Center's "medical care" question changed slightly between 1962 and 1964. In the earlier surveys, respondents were asked whether they agreed or disagreed with the statement: "The government ought to help people get doctors and hospital care at low cost." In 1964 and 1968 they were asked whether the government in Washington should "help people get doctors and hospital care at low cost" or whether the government should "stay out of this." The shift from the earlier agree-disagree format may account for the slight dip in promedical care responses between 1962 and 1964. Subsidization of medical care has received majority support in virtually every poll asked since the 1930s. For examples, see Cantril, *op. cit.*, pp. 432, 444.

[20] When asked whether the government should see to it that everyone who wants to work has a job, national samples have distributed themselves as follows:

	Should	Should Not	No opinion, Other
1935 (Fortune)	77	20	3
1939 (Fortune)	61	32	7
1956 (SRC)	56	27	17
1958 (SRC)	57	26	17
1960 (SRC)	59	24	17

Sources. Cantril, pp. 893, 897; Survey Research Center. The exact form of these questions varies slightly; in 1935, people were asked: "Do you believe that the government should see to it that every man who wants to work has a job?" In 1939, the question was, "Do you think our government should or should not be responsible for seeing to it that everyone who wants to work has a job?" In the three latter polls, people who first stated that they had an opinion on the issue were asked whether they agreed with the statement that "the government in Washington ought to see to it that everybody who wants to work can find a job."

[21] Free and Cantril, p. 14.
[22] *Gallup Opinion Index,* January, 1969, pp. 20–21.
[23] *Gallup Opinion Index,* November, 1970, p. 12.
[24] *Gallup Opinion Index,* April, 1967, p. 15.
[25] Hazel Erskine, "The Polls: Negro Housing," *Public Opinion Quarterly, 31* (Fall, 1967).
[26] Hazel Erskine, "The Polls: Negro Employment," *Public Opinion Quarterly, 32* (Spring, 1968), p. 132.
[27] Hazel Gaudet Erskine, "The Polls: Race Relations," *Public Opinion Quarterly, 26* (Spring, 1962), p. 138.
[28] The exact forms of these questions were: "Do you think white and Negro students should go to the same schools, or to separate schools?" "If a Negro with the same income and education as you have moved into your block, would it make any difference to you?" "Generally speaking, do you think there should be separate sections for Negroes in streetcars and buses?" In some instances in Figure 2–3, the results of more than one survey taken the same years are averaged together.

[29] *Gallup Opinion Index,* May, 1970, p. 5.

[30] The proportion who said they would vote for their party's presidential nominee if he was a "well-qualified man" and "happened to be a Negro" rose from 47% in 1963 to 67% in 1969. (Source: *Gallup Opinion Index,* April 1969, p. 6.) According to Survey Research Center data, the percentage of opinion holders who agreed that "Negroes have a right to live wherever they can afford to, just like white people" rose from 69% in 1964 to 78% in 1970. Between 1964 and 1970, the percentages of opinion holders telling the Survey Research Center that they favored "strict segregation" (rather than "desegregation" or "something in between") declined from 23% to 16%. Over the same period, the percentage favoring "desegregation" rose slightly from 32% to 41%.

[31] Erskine, "The Polls: Race Relations," p. 140.

[32] Questions asked on this subject by the Survey Research Center between 1956 and 1968 have varied somewhat. In 1956, 1958, and 1960, the percentages of opinion holders who disagreed with the statement "the government in Washington should stay out of the question of whether white and colored children go to the same school" were, respectively, 47%, 48%, and 51%. In 1962, the percentage agreeing with the statement "the government in Washington should see to it that white and colored children are allowed to go to the same school" was 61%. In 1964, 1966, 1968, and 1970, respondents were asked whether the government should "see to it that white and Negro children go to the same schools" or whether the government should "stay out of this area as it is none of the government's business." The percentages of opinion holders giving the prointegration response were 52% in 1964, 58% in 1966, 47% in 1968, and 57% in 1970.

[33] See the tabulations reported in Hazel Erskine, "The Polls," *Public Opinion Quarterly, 32* (Fall, 1968), pp. 513–514, and (Winter, 1968–1969), p. 702. The question was: "Do you think the Kennedy [Johnson] administration is pushing racial integration too fast, or not fast enough?"

[34] A summary of poll results on public attitudes toward racial demonstrations is found in Hazel Erskine, "The Polls: Demonstrations and Race Riots," *Public Opinion Quarterly, 31* (Winter, 1967–1968), pp. 654–677.

[35] Free and Cantril, pp. 83–84.

[36] Ibid., p. 62.

[37] This and the remaining findings reported in this paragraph are from an unpublished paper by Alfred O. Hero, Jr., "Public Reactions to Federal Policy: Some Comparative Trends."

[38] William R. Caspary, "The 'Mood Theory': A Study of Public Opinion and Foreign Policy," *American Political Science Review, 64* (June, 1970), pp. 536–537.

[39] Free and Cantril, p. 64.

[40] *Gallup Opinion Index,* March, 1969, p. 21.

[41] Hero, *op. cit.*

[42] *Gallup Opinion Index,* July, 1972; Gallup Poll Release, May 8, 1967.

[43] For some of the years for which poll results are represented in Figure 2–4, the results displayed are the average of the results of more than one poll.

[44] See especially the popular treatment by Richard M. Scammon and Ben J. Wattenberg, *The Real Majority* (New York: Coward-McCann, 1970).

[45] Samuel Stouffer, *Communism, Conformity, and Civil Liberties* (Garden City: Doubleday, 1955).

[46] *Gallup Opinion Index,* March, 1969, p. 12.

[47] Gallup Poll Release, June 15, 1969.

[48] Results of polls from 1938 to 1962 that asked the public to pick between the "liberal" and "conservative" choice are summarized in Erskine, "The Polls: Some Gauges of Conservatism," pp. 155–158.

[49] We can see evidence of the changing meanings of the terms "liberal" and "conservative" from the dramatic changes in the self-ranking tendencies of different groups. Southerners were once more inclined to call themselves "liberals," while the reverse is true today. Similarly, reflecting the former impact of economic issues, self-declared liberals were most frequently found among the least educated. However this relationship is also reversed today. Also, although there once was little tendency for the young to be more "liberal" than their elders in self-identification, this gap has increased markedly since the early 1960s.

THREE

IDEOLOGY AND POLITICAL OPINIONS: THE SEARCH FOR CONSISTENCY IN PUBLIC OPINION

Although the term "ideology" is evasive in meaning, it is generally assumed that a person's "political ideology" is his set of beliefs about the proper order of society and how it can be achieved.[1] One can think of a strong ideology as a "prism" that filters a person's view of the political world: the central elements of a person's belief system restrict or constrain the individual's views on specific political issues. The role of ideology is most apparent when we examine the set of beliefs held by people with viewpoints so unusual that they are labeled political "extremists." For example, the devout members of the John Birch Society are forced by their belief in a pervasive internal Communist conspiracy toward the conclusion that the American involvement in Vietnam was actually a Communist plot.[2] On the other hand, strict adherents to Marxist ideology interpret the Vietnam adventure as a war of capitalist imperialism. To most Americans both views appear to go against the grain of reality.

Although few Americans have ideological outlooks of either the far left or the far right, it is often assumed that there exists a more modest division of the American people between "liberals" and "conservatives." This distinction has considerable meaning when one describes the opinions or behavior of very politically active people. For example, an individual's political opinions on even widely disparate subjects (such as a foreign policy issue and a domestic policy issue) are somewhat predictable from one another, if one is talking about delegates to national political conventions[3] or congressional candidates.[4] The same appears to be true for people such as syndicated political columnists. If one knows a columnist's orientation toward most political issues, one can often successfully predict what he would write about another.

This chapter takes the reader on a search for patterns of internal consistency among the political opinions held by members of the mass public. The previous chapter showed that the public does not display strong opinions on most political issues. Consistent with this pattern, most Americans are largely indifferent to the liberal versus conservative battles fought among members of the more activist strata. To be sure, a respectable portion of the public understands the common meaning of the terms liberal and conservative. Yet people do not normally behave as self-conscious liberals or conservatives, aligning their beliefs according to a general ideological commitment. Partisanship, as we shall see, plays a slightly greater role in shaping political opinions, since many people do achieve some consistency between their issue stances and those that predominate among the leaders of their favored political party.

IDEOLOGY AS LIBERALISM-CONSERVATISM: ARE AMERICANS IDEOLOGUES?

To what do the ideological terms liberal and conservative actually refer? At the philosophical level, political thinkers who have reputations as liberals and conservatives depart from each other in several, somewhat overlapping, ways. Conservatives view society as a control for man's intrinsically base impulses; liberals view man's condition as relative to the quality of his society. Conservatives consider men to be inherently unequal and due unequal rewards; liberals are equalitarian. Conservatives venerate tradition and— most of all—order and authority; liberals believe planned change brings the possibility of improvement.[5] Of course, people who are liberal or conservative in their practical politics need not be strict adherents to the "philosophy about man" that is associated with their particular ideological label. Nevertheless, we can see the implications of these philosophical distinctions at work in the common application of the ideological labels to particular political points of view. Conservatives are more afraid than liberals of "big government," except on matters of law and order; in foreign policy, conservatives are more aggressive than liberals in their Cold War posture and are more fearful of Communism. Conservatives are more likely to see harmful consequences of government attempts to help the disadvantaged, while liberals see the advantages.

These kinds of relative distinctions are familiar to people who follow politics closely. But does the language of ideology have any meaning for the general public? When asked in a survey, most people will categorize themselves as either liberal or conservative, since few will refuse such labels when given forced-choice questions. But since many people respond arbitrarily to survey questions, the significance of the apparent willingness of people to give themselves ideological labels may be cast in doubt. Indeed, when people are also given the "safe," "middle of the road" alternative, about one-third will choose it. Moreover, when people are asked whether they feel "warm," "cold," or "neutral" toward "liberals" and "conservatives," only about 20 percent clearly differentiate between the two ideological groups by responding "warm" toward one, but "cold" toward the other.[6]

Knowledge of the Ideological Terms

To learn whether the mass public has much understanding of the ideological terms, we can examine what people say the terms stand for, and whether in fact self-classification as liberal or conservative is a good predictor of the opinions a person will express on particular issues. Actually, many people do seem capable of assigning the correct meanings to the ideological terms. For example, a study by Louis Harris found that substantial percentages of the American public correctly perceived the conservative and liberal positions on various issues of the day.[7] Forty-four percent felt that to advocate the "abolition of welfare and making people who collect it go to work" was a conservative position while only 20 percent thought it was a liberal position. Forty-six percent versus 22 percent saw wanting to "stop being permissive with student protesters" to be the conservative rather than liberal position, and "getting tougher on the subject of crime and law and order" was seen by most to be a conservative position, 48 percent to 23 percent. Liberal positions may be more clearly seen. "Help(ing) blacks move faster toward equality" was thought to be liberal by 54 percent, with only 17 percent thinking it to be a conservative position; and 51 percent versus 19 percent thought "increasing federal programs to help the poor" to be liberal.

These percentages can be viewed in two ways. From one point of view, majorities or near-majorities can correctly identify the liberal and conservative sides of major political issues. But one must also recognize that some 20 percent were persistently incorrect in their labeling, and another 30 percent claimed not to know. Also, on some additional issues (for example, Vietnam, taxing corporations), Harris found no public consensus on how the ideological terms should be applied.

Although there is a considerable amount of "guessing," people do tend to apply the correct ideological labels to visible political figures and to issue stances. Public ratings of Johnson and Goldwater during the 1964 presidential campaign are shown in Table 3-1. Most people viewed President Johnson as liberal or moderate. Senator Goldwater, Johnson's Republican opponent who consistently espoused the conservative viewpoint, was generally seen as a conservative, or even radical when this option was offered. (Apparently to the general public, the term "radical" is easily applied to extremism of either the political right or the left.) Correct ratings of politicians

TABLE 3-1   **Public View of Presidential Candidates' Political Philosophies, 1964**

	O.R.C. Survey		Gallup Survey	
	Johnson	Goldwater	Johnson	Goldwater
Conservative	16%	38%	15%	50%
Moderate	35	7	29[a]	16[a]
Liberal	30	5	47	11
Radical	3	29	[b]	[b]
Don't know	16	21	9	23
	100%	100%	100%	100%

Sources. Opinion Research Center survey: Thomas W. Benham, "Polling for a Presidential Candidate: Some Observations on the 1964 Campaign," *Public Opinion Quarterly, 24* (Summer, 1965), p. 190; Gallup Survey: Lloyd A. Free and Hadley Cantril, *The Political Beliefs of Americans* (New York: Simon and Schuster, 1968), p. 45.
[a] "Middle of the Road"
[b] "Radical" category not offered in Gallup Survey

on the liberal-conservative scale is not an isolated phenomenon peculiar to the ideological nature of Goldwater's campaign. Back in 1939, over 90 percent of a Gallup sample could label President Roosevelt as "liberal" or "radical" and correctly tag former President Hoover with the appropriate "conservative" label.[8]

In another study, described by Converse,[9] people were asked (in 1960) which party they, or most people, considered to be most conservative. People who responded with an answer or a guess were then asked what "people have in mind when they say that the Republicans (Democrats) are more conservative than the Democrats (Republicans)?" From the responses, it was concluded that slightly greater than 50 percent of the public could be taken as the "maximum estimate of reasonable recognition" of the ideological labels and their proper association of the Republican party with the label of "most conservative."[10] This figure represents the percentage who said the Republicans were considered more conservative and who gave some sort of "correct" meaning for the term conservative. Thus, about half the public emerges again as an estimate of the extent of recognition of the ideological labels. But, rather than raising questions of "broad philosophy," most of the "correct" answers focused instead on narrow issues, such as unemployment compensation or highway building, with many focused on the somewhat narrow distinction that conservatives save money and liberals spend it. Typical respondents said the Republicans were most conservative because "they vote against the wild spending sprees the Democrats get on," and because "they pay as you go."[11] In Converse's study, respondents were classified as able to conceptualize the "conservative" label in terms of broad philosophical distinctions if they touched on such matters as postures toward change, toward the welfare state, toward the power of the federal government, or toward the relationship between the government and the individual. Only 17 percent of the sample associated the conservative label, by some correct philosophical definition of the term, with the Republican party. Perhaps the lesson of this analysis is that people find it easier to apply the ideological terms to policy positions that are emphasized in the political rhetoric of the moment than to long-standing or abstract philosophical orientations. In 1960, the year of the survey we have been discussing, it was easy to apply the ideological terms to the dimension of government spending versus balanced budgets—a topic that is no longer as much in the news. Today, such distinctions as conservatives are firm on "law and order," while liberals are more "soft" or "permissive" have entered into the public's conceptualization of the terms.

When survey respondents are asked to classify themselves on the liberal-conservative spectrum, are they reasonably correct in doing so? That is, can one predict that self-identified liberals will take liberal viewpoints on particular issues, and that the opposite stands will be taken by those who call themselves conservatives? The limited evidence on this subject does show an association of this kind. Data provided by Free and Cantril show that self-classified liberals tend to favor a strong role for the federal government, and to identify with the Democratic party. Details are shown in Table 3-2. Even more clearly, the minority of the public who feel warmly toward liberals but cold to conservatives takes more liberal stands on issues and votes more Democratic than does the opposite minority who feel warmly toward conservatives but cold toward liberals. Examples are shown in Table 3-3. Although the direction of these relationships is hardly surprising, their strength suggests that at least to an important minority of the public, the liberal-conservatism distinction has genuine meaning.

The historical trend regarding the way self-described liberals and conservatives divide on issues suggests that the meanings of the liberal and conservative concepts among the mass public have undergone considerable evolution. According to Hero's extensive analysis of historical poll data, it was during the New Deal Era of the 1930s when self-declaration as a liberal or conservative was the best predictor of one's social welfare opinions.[12] But it is only relatively recently that the liberal-conservative distinction has been connected

TABLE 3-2　**Opinion and Partisan Characteristics of Self-Rated "Liberals" and "Conservatives"**

	Opinion on Power of Federal Government				
Self Identification	Too Much	About Right	Should Use More	Don't Know	Total
Liberal	11%	41%	43%	5%	100%
Middle of Road	23	41	30	6	99%
Conservative	46	28	22	4	100%

	Party Identification				
Self-Identification	Republican	Inde-pendent	Democratic	Other, Don't Know	Total
Liberal	12%	20%	66%	2%	100%
Middle of Road	22	29	47	1	99%
Conservative	41	21	37	1	100%

Source. Lloyd A. Free and Hadley Cantril. *The Political Beliefs of Americans* (New York: Simon and Schuster, 1966), pp. 220, 235.

in the public mind with civil rights or foreign policy. Prior to the Supreme Court's outlawing of segregated schools in 1954, people with prointegration views called themselves liberals at an only slightly higher than average rate. But by the late 1960s, self-declared liberalism or conservatism had become almost as good a predictor of a person's civil rights views as of his social welfare opinions. As a stark indication of the change, the South had once been the region with the greatest percentage of self-declared liberals.[13] Correlations between self-declared liberalism or conservatism and foreign policy views have always been weak, since most people do not associate the terms with stands on international problems; but these correlations have been increasing since the 1930s when they were virtually non-existent.[14] Shifting meanings of ideological terms to the mass public suggest that changes in how the public as a whole rates itself on the ideological spectrum are responses to new meanings instead of actual mass opinion shifts on the issues of the day. For example, as discussed in Chapter Two, the sudden gravitation of the public toward the "conservative" label in the late 1960s appears to be more the result of the public's realization that the conservative label fits the popular pro "law and order" position rather than changes of opinion on particular issues.

TABLE 3-3 **"Ideological" Preference and Opinions on Selected Policy Issues, 1968**

Belief	Percent Support Among Opinion Holders	
	Liberal[a]	Conservative[a]
The government should "help people get doctors and hospital care at low cost"	81%	38%
The government "should see to it that white and Negro children go to the same schools"	71%	40%
The government "should allow farmers and businessmen to trade with Communist countries"	68%	39%
Those who do not disapprove all "protest meetings or marches that are permitted by the local authorities"	79%	52%

Source. Survey Research Center, 1968 election data. For the full text of the opinion questions, see the Appendix.

[a] People classified as liberal are respondents who feel warm toward liberals but cold to conservatives. People classified as conservatives report the reverse feelings toward the ideological labels. Of 1557 total respondents, 6 per cent are classified as liberals, 14 per cent as conservatives.

Use of Ideological Language

Although the ideological terms are within the vocabularies of a large share of the American public, few actually employ them to defend their choices of parties and candidates, such as by arguing that some candidate is "too liberal" or "too conservative." During the 1956 presidential campaign, the Survey Research Center's interviewers asked persons in its national sample to describe both what they disliked and liked about both political parties and their presidential candidates, Eisenhower and Stevenson. The profile of the public's responses to these questions is reported in *The American Voter,* a classic study of American voting behavior.[15] The researchers were interested not only in the individuals' images of the parties and candidates but also in the conceptual *sophistication* of the responses. Respondents who spontaneously and knowledgeably evaluated the parties and candidates in terms of their placement on the liberal-conservative spectrum were labeled "ideologues." Even with a generous definition of what the ideologue response would demand (to include what *The American Voter* calls near-ideologues), only 12 percent of the 1956 sample fit the ideologue category. A typical ideologue response was that of an Ohio woman who, when asked what she liked about the Democratic party, answered, "nothing, except it being a more liberal party, and I think the Republicans as being more conservative and interested in big business." A weaker ideologue response was given by a Texan: "I think the Democrats are more concerned with all the people . . . they put out more liberal legislation for all the people."[16]

An added 42 percent of the 1956 sample expressed their likes and dislikes about the candidates and parties in terms of the groups they represent. Farmers often expressed this "group-benefits" orientation to explain their partisan preferences. Typical was the response of an Ohio farm woman when asked what she liked about the Democrats: "I think they have always helped the farmers. To tell you the truth, I don't see how any farmer could vote for Mr. Eisenhower."[17] Most group-benefits responses were somewhat class related, evoking the notion that Republicans favor "big business" while the Democrats favor "the little man." Whereas most ideologues were Republican in preference, most group-benefits respondents were Democrats. Though not ideologues, the people who give the most sophisticated group-benefits responses may be said to operate from an "ideology by proxy." They do often express a set of opinions that are consistent with their group interest, but only when this group interest is an obvious guide to their responses. On issues for which their group identifications cannot be a valuable cueing device, they do not behave in an ideologically predictable way.

At a lower level of conceptualization, another 24 percent in 1956 referred to "the nature of the times" the different parties are associated with when in power. "Nature of the times" voters do not evaluate the parties and candidates in terms of their policies or their group benefits, but do make an effort to evaluate the results they might produce, on the basis of past performance indicators, such as which party brings economic prosperity or which party keeps most of its "promises." However, many nature of the times responses are simply rationalizations of party preference. An interesting example is that of a Kentucky woman. When asked what she liked about the Democrats, she responded: "I like the good wages my husband makes." When the interviewer pointed out that the Republicans were then in power, she replied, "I know, and it's sort of begun to tighten up since the Republicans got in."[18]

Finally, 23 percent were found to offer no issue content whatsoever when asked to describe their partisan and candidate likes and dislikes. Typical was the North Carolina man who answered as follows (with interviewer questions abbreviated):[19]

(Like about the Democrats?) "No, Ma'am, not that I know of."
            (Dislike?) "No, Ma,am, but I've always been
                        a Democrat, just like my daddy."

(Like about the Republicans?) "No."
(Dislike?) "No."
This distribution of how people conceptualize partisan politics may be interpreted to mean that the American public is not very ideological, and in one sense this would be correct. The authors of *The American Voter* account for the few ideologues in terms of the public's "cognitive limitations," such as the lack of intellectual ability to think in terms of ideological abstractions.[20] But our knowledge that the public knows the liberal-conservative terms and can apply them to issue positions suggests the alternative interpretation that the American public simply does not find the ideological terms particularly useful to describe their partisan likes and dislikes, even though they do often understand their meaning or current usage. Consistent with this argument, the use of ideological language increases when the ideological differences between political candidates become magnified. Researchers have discovered that ideological references increased dramatically during the 1964 presidential campaign contested by Johnson and Goldwater, a campaign that commentators saw as more clearly defined on ideological grounds than any others of recent times.[21] Table 3-4 shows that the

TABLE 3-4 **Levels of Political Conceptualization in 1956 and 1964**

Conceptual Level	1956	1964
Ideologue[a]	12%	27%
Group interest	42	27
Nature of times	24	20
No issue content	23	26
Total	101%	100%
N	1684	1564

Sources. For 1956, Angus Campbell, et al., *The American Voter* (New York: Wiley, 1960), p. 249; and, for 1964, recomputed from John C. Pierce, "Party Identification and the Changing Role of Ideology in American Politics," *Midwest Journal of Political Science, 14* (February, 1970), p. 35.
[a] Including "near ideologues."

percentage of people classified as ideologues jumped dramatically between 1956 and 1964—from 12 percent to 27 percent. From the distributions, it appears that the new ideologues were added from the ranks of the kinds of people who previously gave group-benefits responses. Since the percentages in the lower two conceptual strata did not decline, the ideologue increase does not represent a general uplifting of political sophistication from the 1956 pattern. Rather, the extensive use of the "liberal" and "conservative" terminology by the candidates and mass media during the 1964 campaign was picked up by the public to defend their choices of parties and candidates. Thus, the authors of one study of the 1964 election comment, "the number of people volunteering the language of ideology is subject to considerable fluctuation."[22]

IDEOLOGY AS LIBERAL OR CONSERVATIVE CONSISTENCY

Do people have fundamental orientations toward politics (such as liberalism or conservatism) that link their judgments of several issues? One might suspect that many people are actually quite liberal or conservative in the opinions they express, even when they do not spontaneously choose these terms to describe their political orientation. But actually, relatively few people are consistently liberal or consistently conservative over a wide range of issues. Figure

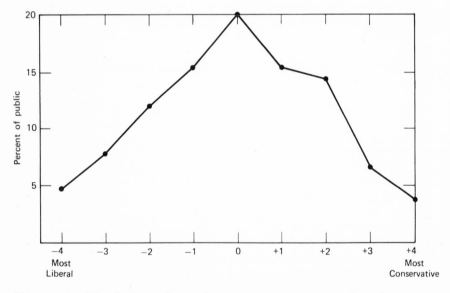

Figure 3-1. Distribution of cumulative opinion scores on four disparate policy issues—Medicare, school integration, foreign aid, and peaceful protest. (*Source.* Survey Research Center 1968 election data.) See the Appendix for opinion questions. Scores are the sum of conservative responses minus the liberal responses.

3-1 shows one distribution of the American public's liberalism-conservatism "scores," as measured by their cumulative responses to four opinion questions dealing with medical care, school integration, peaceful protest activity, and foreign aid. A person offering a liberal viewpoint on all four issues would have a score of −4, while a person who expresses conservative outlooks on all four issues would have a +4 score. Few people are at either extreme (five percent extreme liberals, four percent extreme conservatives). Most are near the midpoint of the scale, indicating that their liberal and conservative viewpoints balance each other out.

Since over a series of issues most people give some liberal and some conservative positions, there is the temptation to label the bulk of the public as political moderates. But these voters in the center cannot be grouped together as sharers of a common moderate ideology because they differ greatly in the pattern of their responses to individual issues. For example, one voter with "balanced" liberal and conservative views may be liberal on social welfare issues and civil rights, but conservative on foreign policy and law and order, while another with balanced views possesses exactly the opposite opinions. Still a third person may have an overall score that is neither very conservative nor very liberal for the reason that he expresses few opinions at all.

The Dimensions of Liberalism-Conservatism

When describing the ideological distribution of the mass public, it makes more sense to consider several separate dimensions of liberalism-conservatism rather than just one. One plausible ordering is along separate dimensions for each of the four issue areas we discussed in Chapter Two: social welfare policy, civil rights, foreign policy, and law and order versus civil liberties. Figure 3-2 shows the public's opinion distribution on separate liberalism-conservatism scales constructed for each of these four policy domains, with scores on each scale based on the responses to four opinion questions relevant to the particular issue area. On foreign policy the opinion scores cluster in the middle of the spectrum, indicating that few people have consistently liberal or conservative viewpoints on foreign affairs. But on the other three dimensions, opinions cluster more toward extreme scores, indicating some division between relative liberals and relative conservatives.

Interestingly, domestic political leaders and groups are viewed by the public along something close to these same three dimensions of domestic policy. Jerrold Rusk and Herbert Weisberg "factor analyzed" the public's ratings of political objects in 1970 and found the objects arranged in the three dimensional space shown in Figure 3-3

Ideology as Liberal or Conservative Consistency **75**

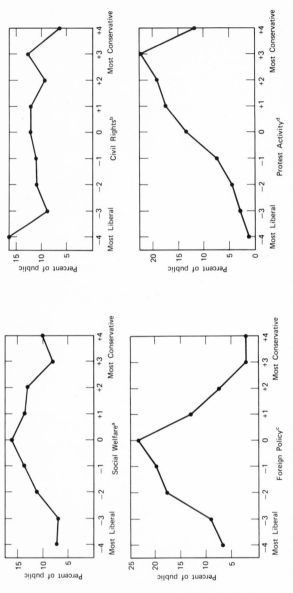

Figure 3-2. Distribution of opinion on four separate dimensions of liberalism-conservatism. Scores are the sum of conservative responses minus the sum of liberal responses. (a) Issues are Medicare, guaranteed standard of living, federal aid to education, and government power; (b) Issues are school integration, public accommodations, job discrimination, and self-rating on a segregation-desegregation scale; (c) Issues are trading with Communist nations, talking with their leaders, admitting Red China to the UN, and foreign aid; (d) Issues are lawful protest, civil disobedience, sit-ins, and the Chicago riot. See Appendix for details of the issue questions. Where three opinion options are offered (all protest activity items and the segregation-desegregation item), the "in-between" opinions are counted in neither the liberal nor conservative direction.

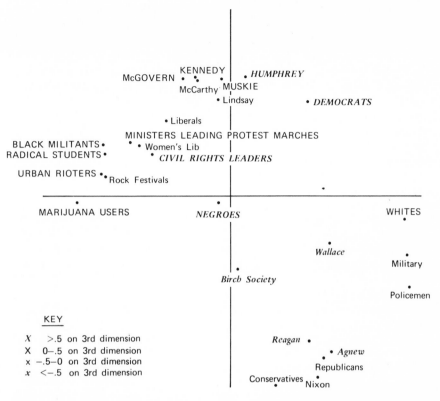

KENNEDY
McGOVERN • •. •   • *HUMPHREY*
        McCarthy MUSKIE
            • Lindsay   • *DEMOCRATS*

        • Liberals

        MINISTERS LEADING PROTEST MARCHES
BLACK MILITANTS •   • • Women's Lib
RADICAL STUDENTS •   • *CIVIL RIGHTS LEADERS*

URBAN RIOTERS •• Rock Festivals

                                    •

        •   •
MARIJUANA USERS   *NEGROES*   WHITES
                                                •

                                    •
                                Wallace   •
                                            Military

                    •
                Birch Society   •
                                            Policemen

    KEY

X   >.5 on 3rd dimension   *Reagan* •
X   0–.5 on 3rd dimension   •• *Agnew*
x   −.5–0 on 3rd dimension   Republicans
x   <−.5 on 3rd dimension   Conservatives •
                                    •   Nixon

Figure 3-3. 1970 candidate group space. (*Source.* Jerrold G. Rusk and Herbert F. Weisberg, "Perceptions of Presidential Candidates: Implications for Electoral Change," *Midwest Journal of Political Science, 16* (August 1972), p. 397.)

(one dimension goes in and out of the two dimensional page).[23] The closer together any two objects are in this space, the more highly correlated are their ratings by the public. Thus the graph is the best representation of how the typical citizen associates or dissociates these objects with one another in his mind. The up-down dimension appears to represent social welfare and partisanship, with liberal Democrats at the top. The left-right dimension obviously represents law and order (on the right) versus permissiveness, while the in-out dimension represents race and civil rights. Seemingly, the public applies these three standards in judging political leaders and organizations.

Ideology as Liberal or Conservative Consistency **77**

Correlations Between Opinions

To what extent can one predict an individual's opinions on one political issue from his opinion on others? Only when issues are part of the same general policy domain do peoples' opinions tend to cluster into visible patterns of liberal or conservative consistency. For example, some consistency between a person's opinion on government subsidization of medical costs and his opinion on government efforts to provide everyone a job and a good standard of living is created by his *general* view (if he has one) of the proper involvement by government in social welfare activities. Table 3-5(a) shows that most people are either liberal or conservative on both of these issues. Since more people accept Medicare than accept government guarantee of a good standard of living, there naturally must be some people who think Medicare is all right, but think guaranteeing a good standard of living is going too far. But very few are inconsistent in the opposite pattern, and these instances are expected if only for the reason that many opinions that people express in surveys are of the "doorstep" variety. Even more strongly than the social welfare example, people's attitudes toward racial integration force a pattern of consistency between their views toward school integration and toward integration of public accommodations (see Table 3-5(b)). A much weaker pattern of consistency is shown between foreign aid opinions and opinions toward trading with Communist nations (Table 3-5(c)). The slight consistency that is found is due to the responses of people who do have a general view of how far the United States should go in peaceably becoming involved with other nations. Many opinions on these two issues are of the doorstep variety, however, or made consistent by other rationales, such as that the United States should combat communism by giving aid to friendly nations and by not trading with Communist ones.

The lack of perfect or even near-perfect correlations in the top row of Table 3-5 suggests that we cannot carry the consistency argument very far. For example, the people who are most willing to support social welfare spending also tend to be the people who agree with the statement that "the government ought to cut taxes, even if it means putting off things that need to be done."[24] Since how much a government taxes and how much it spends are obviously related, one ought to try to figure out the source of this inconsistency, rather than simply reject public opinion as irrational. Perhaps the people who feel most in need of social welfare activities are also those who feel the tax bite most.

Among the most politically alert strata of society, there is strong consistency of viewpoints even when one crosses from one issue domain to another. For example, Table 3-6 shows that one could

TABLE 3-5 **Correlations Between Opinions on Selected Issues, 1968**

(a)

		Medicare	
		Pro	Con
Guaranteed Good Standard of Living	Pro	38%	5%
	Con	27%	29%
		phi = .40	

(b)

		School Integration	
		Pro	Con
Public Accommodations Law	Pro	41%	20%
	Con	6%	33%
		phi = .51	

(c)

		Foreign Aid	
		Pro	Con
Trade With Communist Nations	Pro	32%	15%
	Con	28%	26%
		phi = .17	

(d)

		Medicare	
		Pro	Con
School Integration	Pro	38%	11%
	Con	28%	24%
		phi = .26	

(e)

		Medicare	
		Pro	Con
Foreign Aid	Pro	42%	19%
	Con	26%	14%
		phi = .04	

(f)

		School Integration	
		Pro	Con
Foreign Aid	Pro	34%	25%
	Con	13%	27%
		phi = .24	

Source. Survey Research Center, 1968 election data.

Ideology as Liberal or Conservative Consistency **79**

TABLE 3-6 Medicare-Foreign Aid Consistency

		U.S. Senators (Roll-Call Votes)			SRC Public Sample (Opinions)	
		Foreign Aid Bill, 1964			Foreign Aid, 1964	
		Pro	Con		Pro	Con
1965 Medicare Bill	Pro	56%	13%	Medicare, 1964 Pro	50%	25%
	Con	10%	21%	Con	16%	9%
		phi = .47			phi = .03	

Sources. Senatorial data—*Congressional Quarterly;* and public opinion—Survey Research Center.

have had fairly good success in predicting a U.S. senator's vote on passage of the Medicare bill from how he voted on passage of the 1965 foreign aid bill, or vice versa. Nothing approaching this general consistency is found for the general public, however, as Table 3-6 shows medicare attitudes of the general public in 1964 to have been almost totally unrelated to opinions expressed on foreign aid. Similarly, civil rights opinions and foreign policy opinions are only weakly correlated, as are social welfare opinions and civil rights opinions (see the bottom row of Table 3-5). Clearly, the few people whose opinions on remotely connected issues are guided toward ideological consistency by applications of general liberal or conservative orientations are too scarce to make their presence obvious in a pattern of results of a general public sample. For most people, the simultaneous holding of liberal and conservative viewpoints on issues that are not obviously connected does not create any disturbing inconsistency, even though they may recognize that their opinions are not all liberal or conservative.

The full pattern of relationships between opinions on 10 issues are summarized in Table 3-7. The more positive the correlation coefficient shown, the more consistent the opinions on the two issues. The maximum possible correlation (which is not approached) would be 1.00, indicating that all the liberals on one issue are liberals on the other, and all the conservatives on one issue give conservative responses on the other. The opposite extreme is a correlation of -1.00, which would occur if liberalism on one issue were perfectly correlated with *conservatism* on the other. In between, the .00 benchmark indicates the perfect absence of a statistical relationship—when liberals and conservatives on one issue respond in identical patterns on

Table 3-7 **Correlations Between Opinions, 1968**[a]

Issue	Medi-care	Standard of Living	School Inte-gration	Public Accom-moda-tions	Foreign Aid	Trade with Commu-nists	Vietnam Involve-ment	Vietnam Policy	Lawful Protest	Civil Disobe-dience
Medicare										
Standard of Living	.40									
School Integration	.26	.22								
Public Accom-modations	.13	.26	.51							
Foreign Aid	.04	.13	.24	.24						
Trade with Communists	.01	.04	.15·	.19	.17					
Vietnam Involvement	.08	.03	−.07	−.10	−.23	−.04				
Vietnam Policy	.13	.16	.18	.12	.09	.18	.23			
Lawful Protest	.09	.17	.18	.22	.20	.16	−.00	.11		
Civil Disobedience	.09	.17	.12	.08	.14	.13	.05	.07	.26	

Source. Survey Research Center, 1968 election data. For the full text of the opinion questions, see the Appendix.
[a] Correlation coefficients are phi's.

the second. The correlation coefficients (phi's) shown for the patterns in Table 3-5 may also be a useful reference point for interpreting the correlations in Table 3-7.[25]

Is Ideological Constraint Increasing?

We have seen that ideological constraint or consistency is often quite weak, especially when we compare people's viewpoints on issues that are linked by little more than the fact that each has alternatives that are often labeled liberal and conservative. For example, support of Medicare does not logically demand support for trading with Communist nations, even though someone with a general liberal philosophy would be expected to support both. The low correlation between opinions on these two issues suggests that few people approach these two questions from the standpoint of their position on a general liberal-conservative spectrum applied to both issues. Yet earlier we noted an increase in the frequency with which people employ references of liberalism and conservatism to describe party differences, at least over the period from 1956 through 1964. Could this trend be an indicator of an increase in ideological constraint as well, so that correlations between opinions are increasing to become more consistent with conventional ideological expectations? If we follow the trend over time of how opinions on different issues are correlated with each other, correlations do seem to be increasing, with the greatest jump around the turn of the 1964 "ideological" election. Figure 3-4 depicts this trend for the interrelation of opinion

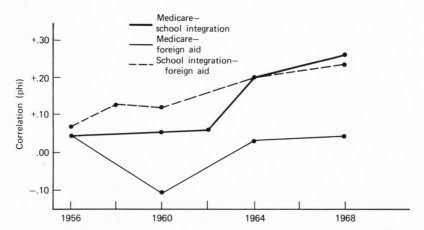

Figure 3-4. Correlations between opinions. (*Source.* Survey Research Center election data.)

82 *Ideology and Political Opinions: Search for Consistency*

on three issues that have been monitored by the Survey Research Center over several election years—Medicare, foreign economic aid, and school integration. It should be emphasized that the trend toward increasing correlations between opinions indicates that previous patterns of correlations were once even weaker than the ones we have been describing.

Even the most feeble of positive correlations between opinions on foreign policy and opinions on domestic policy have begun to emerge only in surveys conducted in the 1960s and 1970s. To cite one historical example, in the late 1940s, people who favored and people who opposed a higher minimum wage had virtually equal distributions of opinions toward the Marshall Plan to aid European economic recovery from World War II.[26] Throughout the brief historical period of opinion surveys, civil rights opinions have been more correlated with views toward international cooperation than social welfare opinions have been. In the 1940s, for example, people who favored abolition of racial segregation on all interstate transportation were a few percentage points more likely to favor the Marshall Plan than were civil rights opponents.[27] Judging from the accumulation of evidence, to the mass public the question of how cooperative the United States should be with other nations has been more closely tied (although weakly) to the question of federal help to aid the Negro than to social welfare policy. Also, to a lesser extent, civil rights views are generally more related to foreign policy views than to those on domestic social welfare policy.

Opinion on Vietnam as an Example

Referring back to Table 3-7, a particularly striking pattern is the general absence of correlations between Vietnam opinions and opinions on other issues. The two Vietnam items are not even very highly correlated with each other, indicating that many people (in 1968) viewed U.S. involvement in the war as a mistake (Vietnam involvement), but favored its escalation (Vietnam policy), or, alternatively, opposed escalation but applauded U.S. involvement. This pattern suggests that the public does not fall into predictable or consistent dove-hawk patterns on the war. Opinions on Vietnam were not related in a strong positive direction to opinions on other issues either, including even other foreign policy issues. One of the two Vietnam items (involvement) is actually *negatively* correlated with opinion on foreign aid. This means that people who viewed the war as a mistake (presumably the liberal opinion) tend to be the ones who oppose economic aid being sent to other countries, a pattern explained by the isolationist-internationalist foreign policy dimension rather than conventional liberalism-conservatism.

The intrusion of the Vietnam issue provides an example of what not to expect in the way of ideological consistency on the part of the American public. Although elites such as the highly visible members of the U.S. Senate have reacted to the war in a way consistent with their general ideology (the liberals were the first to oppose the war), no clear tendency of this sort is found in public surveys. Consequently, one cannot argue that liberal political orientations have led some people to oppose the war while conservative orientations have compelled others to support it. Both doves and hawks have been found within the ranks of the people who show up as liberal and those who appear conservative on nonwar related issues. Even attitudes toward war *protesters* are unrelated to attitudes toward war policy.[28]

One reason why it is so difficult to predict how people would respond to the war from their other attitudes is that opposition to the war is a liberal yet isolationist position, whereas other isolationist foreign policy views are generally regarded as conservative. Many people evidently have reacted to Vietnam according to their isolationist versus internationalist perspective, which makes *trading* with Communist nations and *fighting wars* of anticommunism compatible with internationalist viewpoints and their opposite pair of attitudes the logical extension of the old isolationist perspective that the U.S. should avoid foreign entanglements of any kind. The simple isolationist-internationalist dimension regarding foreign policy appears to be more salient for older voters than the liberal-conservative dimension of international cooperation versus aggression. Table 3-8 illustrates this. In 1968, older voters were more likely to oppose

TABLE 3-8 **Relationship Between Opinions on Trading with Communist Nations and Opinion on Vietnam Involvement, by Age, 1968 (in Percent)**

Opinion on U.S. Involvement in Vietnam	Born before 1915		Born 1915-1928		Born after 1928	
	Pro-trade	Anti-trade	Pro-trade	Anti-trade	Pro-trade	Anti-trade
Oppose	68	74	56	54	56	48
Favor	32	26	44	46	44	52
	100	100	100	100	100	100
$N =$	(149)	(152)	(150)	(175)	(128)	(166)
phi =	−.06		+.02		+.08	

Source. Survey Research Center 1968 election data.

Vietnam involvement if they opposed trade with Communist nations. Younger people, however, followed the opposite pattern consistent with notions of liberalism-conservatism: those who favored the war also tended to be those who opposed trading with Communist nations. Both tendencies are rather weak, however.[29]

Non-Liberal-Conservative Orderings

The complication of the isolationist-internationalist dimension when one tries to predict Vietnam attitudes suggests that, in other instances as well, portions of the public may operate in some sort of loose ideological fashion that is at variance with conventional notions of liberalism-conservatism. Robert Axelrod has discovered that an interesting, though weak, tendency of this sort applies to the patterns of attitudes held by very uninformed people.[30] Within the less politically involved strata (for example, nonvoters, less educated), Axelrod found that a weak "populism" scale best describes their attitudes, with support for social welfare, resistance to taxes, opposition to civil liberties, and foreign policy isolationism correlated with each other. The least informed tend either to support or to oppose the cluster of populist positions more so than they tend to be liberal or conservative in the conventional sense. Other research shows these populist positions, and segregationist sentiments as well, are most typical among people who are also politically alienated.[31] At the same time, Axelrod found that opinions become increasingly correlated in the way one would ordinarily predict if one isolates the relatively *informed* segment of the public. Thus, although the most politically alert people approach some attitudinal consistency that can be predicted from their liberal versus conservative orientations, their contribution to the overall pattern gets canceled out to some extent by that of the less alert segment of the public who may be responding to an entirely different set of ideological constraints.

One further qualification on the general lack of opinion consistency can be made: in a study of opinion patterns in two Oregon communities, Luttbeg found considerable structure to *local*-issue opinion patterns, although with opinions again ordered along several separate dimensions rather than the simple liberal-conservative pattern.[32] The major dimension of local-issue opinion involved issues related to a good "community environment" for children (for example, public kindergartens, special education programs, water fluoridation), with people falling into consistent patterns of either supporting or opposing these programs. Other dimensions involved the general issues of taxation, community growth, improving the city core, and increased recreational facilities. A somewhat different set of issue dimensions (once again, not liberalism-conservatism) was found for community leaders. Little constraint is found among people's attitudes toward state-level issues, however.[33]

Summary

While the American public displays some familiarity with the terminology of liberalism and conservatism, most people cannot be said to order their political viewpoints by means of a general ideological anchor. Many people can describe their position on a liberal-conservative continuum accurately, in the sense that they can sum up the tendency of their viewpoints on various issues to describe their net position. Yet the fact that there is little consistency among people's viewpoints—especially when the opinions cut across issue areas—demonstrates that few people use their ideological position as a cueing device to arrange their responses to the political world. The kind of attitudinal constraint that motivates people toward consistently liberal or moderate viewpoints on issues that are not related in obvious fashion is reserved for a small politically active segment of the American public. Yet to the extent there is any historical trend, it is toward an increase in the ideological consistency of people's viewpoints.

Of course, the failure of the average citizen to arrange his opinions in predictable liberal or conservative clusters does not necessarily mean that his opinions are *logically* inconsistent with one another. Instead of viewing the mass public as somehow incapable of consistency when thinking about politics, it may be more accurate to view each individual as bringing to bear his own unique ideology toward the political world.

PARTISANSHIP AND THE ORGANIZATION OF OPINIONS

So far, our discussion of opinion consistency has ignored the role of partisanship in creating opinion change. In the previous chapter, we saw that compared with people's opinions on policy issues, the party identification a person holds is quite stable over time. As will be elaborated in Chapter Five, the source of one's party identification is often the political values that were transmitted in the family during childhood. At the other end of the causal chain, party identification is the best predictor of how people vote. Following the sequence through, we find that people vote for the party with which their parents had identified.

Since party identification appears to be the most central element in most people's political belief systems (except, perhaps, for consensual opinions on which almost all Americans agree), one might suspect that people use their party identification as a cue to order the remainder of their political beliefs. An alert Republican, for example, would eventually learn that a good Republican is supposed to subscribe to conservative opinions on certain issues and would begin to respond accordingly. At the same time, one might suspect that the few people who change their party identification often do so out of awareness of the fact that their views on issues are out of alignment with their partisan heritage. These causal processes could not occur, however, unless people were aware of Democratic and Republican partisan differences on the issues of the day.

Perceptions of Party Differences on Issues

Although prominent political figures may argue that there is "not a dime's worth of difference" between the two major American political parties, it is commonly assumed that political leaders within the Republican party often subscribe to conservative viewpoints and most Democratic leaders, except perhaps in the South, subscribe to liberal ideas. As we will discuss in Chapter Nine, there is much truth to these assumptions. Here we may ask the question: To what extent does the public perceive these partisan differences on issues?

In its periodic election surveys, the Survey Research Center asks its respondents which party is more likely to do more in certain policy areas. Results from the 1968 poll are shown in Table 3-9. On the selected issues, only near-majorities on domestic policy and fewer on foreign policy saw the Democratic party as the one most willing to enact the policy in question (the liberal alternative). On the other hand, very few guessed "incorrectly" on each issue—that the Republicans would do more. Thus, among people who do see partisan differences, the direction of the perception is almost always that the Democrats would follow what are regarded as liberal policies and the Republicans the opposite.

Interestingly, although many argue that the relevance of partisanship has been decreasing, the public's perception of partisan differences on issues has been decidedly *increasing*. Figure 3-5 shows this trend for three issues monitored by the SRC over several points in time. Particularly striking is the fact that prior to 1964, no public consensus existed regarding which party was most in favor of school integration and of foreign aid (or other civil rights and foreign policy issues as well). Before 1964, the public only saw the parties as having opposite policies on social welfare issues—a tendency that goes back to the New Deal era of the 1930s when the parties did begin to develop opposite philosophies toward the role of the federal government in the economy. The then less-salient civil rights and foreign policy issues had also been a frequent source of sharp par-

TABLE 3-9 Public Perceptions of Party Differences on Issues, 1968

"Which party do you think is more likely to. . . ."	Entire Sample			Of Those Seeing a Party Difference	
	Democrat	Republican	No Difference, Don't Know, No Interest	Democrat	Republican
. . . Help people get doctors and hospital care at low cost	46%	7%	47% = 100%	87%	13% = 100%
. . . See to it that every person has a job and a good standard of living	42	10	48 = 100	81	19 = 100
. . . See to it that white and Negro children go to the same schools	42	7	51 = 100	86	14 = 100
Favor the . . . right of Negroes to go to any hotel or restaurant	40	6	54 = 100	87	13 = 100
Give aid to other countries	31	6	63 = 100	84	16 = 100
Allow farmers and businessmen to trade with Communist countries	19	9	72 = 100	67	33 = 100

Source. Survey Research Center 1968 election data.

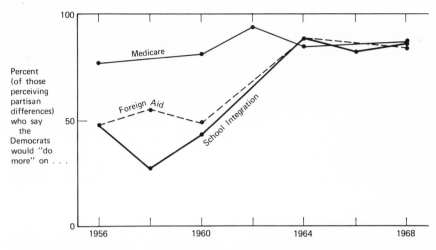

Figure 3-5. Changing perceptions of partisan differences on selected issues, 1956-1968. (*Source. SRC* election data.)

tisan division in Congress, but the people apparently failed to notice. The spur to the increased public awareness of party differences, as to so many other changes, appears to have been the ideological Goldwater election of 1964.[34]

Party Identification and Policy Preferences

On most political issues the views of Democratic and Republican identifiers will diverge in predictable ways, although the amount of difference is often slight and varies from issue to issue. Some examples from 1968 data are shown in Table 3-10. Although the views of "weak Democrats," "Independents," and "weak Republicans" are often indistinguishable from one another, the differences between "strong Democrats" and "strong Republicans" are often rather sharp. Quite clearly, strong Democrats and strong Republicans are most divided on social welfare issues, which is understandable given the fact that the public has only recently begun to perceive that the parties are different on other kinds of issues as well.

The trend in how Republicans and Democrats are divided on issues follows the trend in perceptions of partisan differences. As shown in Figure 3-6, it used to be that rank-and-file Republicans were more "liberal" on issues like school integration and foreign aid than their Democratic counterparts. This trend has now been reversed, although only barely in the case of foreign aid. Meanwhile,

Partisanship and the Organization of Opinions **89**

TABLE 3-10 **Relationship Between Party Identification and Policy Opinions on Selected Issues, 1968**

Percent Liberal of Opinion Holders	Strong Democrat	Weak Democrat	Independent	Weak Republican	Strong Republican	Correlation (Gamma)[a]
Medicare	83	76	61	43	47	.433
Standard of Living	59	45	31	30	31	.325
School Integration	62	48	40	42	35	.237
Public Accommodations	69	60	61	56	56	.112
Lawful Protest	52	43	49	45	40	.064
Civil Disobedience	42	38	41	34	34	.071
Foreign Aid	63	58	59	61	56	.039
Trade with Communists	52	43	42	51	37	.086
Vietnam Involvement	60	65	61	64	71	−.054
Vietnam Policy	69	63	57	64	62	.073
Mean	61	53	50	49	47	

Source. Survey Research Center, 1968 election data. For full texts of policy questions, see the Appendix.
[a] Gammas are based on results with full seven-point party identification scale.

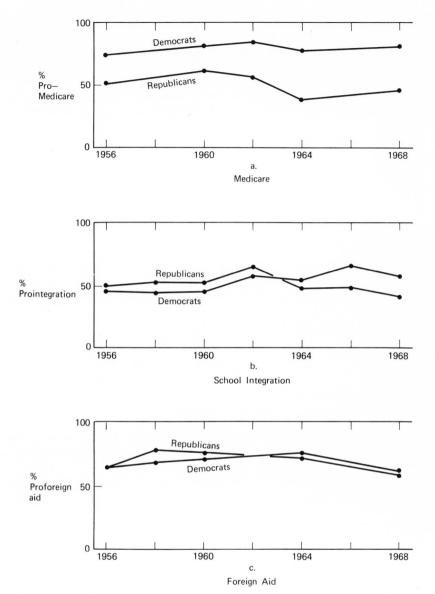

Figure 3-6. Changing partisan differences in opinion, 1956-1968. (*Source.* SRC election data.)

Democratic and Republican identifiers have been consistently divided on social welfare issues such as Medicare.

Is the source of the consistency between political opinions and party identification the result of people learning their political opinions from their party identification or the reverse pattern of political opinions shaping party identification? For instance, is a liberal Republican more likely to change to a conservative Republican or a liberal Democrat? Undoubtedly, both causal processes are at work, but their relative contributions to consistency between party identification and political opinions can only be roughly estimated. Because one's party identification is often a strongly held attitude, while stands on issues are typically casual at best, most writers on the subject assume that partisanship normally shapes policy opinions rather than the reverse, even though the rare partisan convert often is reacting to issues when he makes his change.[35] William Flanigan captures this conclusion:[36]

"It is relatively unusual in American politics for an issue to become so important that it disrupts party loyalties for large numbers of people. But in rare cases where individuals feel important issues are at stake, it is most unlikely that partisan loyalty... will overcome strongly felt interests."

Let us consider the usual case first. When President Nixon instituted a thaw in the U.S. relationship with mainland China, which culminated in his 1972 visit to China, it represented something of an upset of partisan stereotypes, since previously it had been liberal Democrats in Congress who had most visibly urged such a change of policy and Republican congressmen and leaders (Nixon included) who were most insistent on a hard-line policy. Before Nixon's presidency, Gallup polls usually showed the identical partisan pattern in the casual attitudes expressed by public samples—for example, Democrats were somewhat more in favor of admitting China to the United Nations than Republicans were. But Nixon's policy change apparently had a greater effect on the China attitudes of Republicans than Democrats, so that by 1972, Republicans had become more in favor of admitting China to the U.N. than Democrats were.[37] Naturally, it was easier for "anti-China" Republicans to change their attitudes toward China than to change their partisan identification.

A slightly different kind of example is provided by changes in the relationship between partisanship and Vietnam opinion. When Lyndon Johnson was President, more Republicans than Democrats viewed the war as a mistake. But when a Republican administration took over, it became easier for Democratic identifiers to oppose war policy and more difficult for Republicans not to justify it. And for this reason, the partisan transition of the Presidency following the

1968 election saw Democratic identifiers beginning to emerge in the Gallup polls as the partisan group most consistently viewing the war as a mistake.[38]

These limited foreign policy examples suggest that the typical explanation for correlations between party identification and issue stances is that party identification causes the issue response rather than the reverse. Yet not every instance when the issue stances of Democrats and Republicans diverge can be accounted for in this way. Although people are normally stable in their partisan preferences, an unusual amount of shifting may occur when the political parties make major changes in their policy orientations. When this happens, the electorate is said to undergo "partisan realignment."[39] To a certain extent, realignment goes on all the time, as each change in a party's policy emphasis is likely to produce a response on the part of the segment of the electorate that has the most vital stake in the issue. For example, World War I and World War II, both fought under Democratic administrations, cost the Democrats the allegiance of some of their German-American adherents.[40] As our previous discussion indicates, the emergence of civil rights as a partisan issue in the 1960s and 1970s has caused some partisan realignment, although not yet as extensively as at crucial times in America's past.

Two crucial realignment periods were around the time of the 1896 presidential election and later, from the late 1920s into the 1930s. The 1896 realignment is evident from the fact that geographic voting patterns that had been stable for decades suddenly became disrupted, first as a short-term response to the 1893 Depression, and then compounded by the unusual issue-polarization of the 1896 presidential election. In its 1896 convention, the Democratic party accepted much of the platform of the Populists, a rising third party of economic protest, and nominated William Jennings Bryan who campaigned for the inflationary program of "free silver." This new issue division attracted adherents to the Democratic cause but panicked a greater number into leaving. Consequently, the Republicans became the dominant party until the 1930s.[41]

The more recent major realignment came in two stages. First, the decision of a badly divided Democratic party to oppose Prohibition caused it to gain urban support but lose rural support in the 1928 election. More importantly, President Roosevelt's "New Deal" policies, which expanded the role of the federal government in the economy to cope with the hardships of the Great Depression, caused voters to realign further in the 1930s.[42] Trace evidence of the issue base of this realignment can be found even in recent surveys, as older voters who claimed to have left the Republican party in the 1930s are decidedly liberal in their social welfare orientation, while those who shifted their party identification in the opposite direction are quite conservative in their social welfare views.[43]

A major cause of contemporary partisan shifting appears to be the public's increasing awareness of partisan differences on the highly salient dimension of civil rights. For example, the data of Table 3-11 show that people who in 1964 reported a recent shift away from the Democratic party were decidedly more conservative on the civil rights issue of school integration than their counterparts making the reverse shift away from the Republicans. By comparison, the difference between the Medicare opinions of the two groups of shifters was rather mild, suggesting that social welfare opinions did not spur much switching.

TABLE 3-11 **Policy Opinions and Partisan Shifts, 1960-1964**

	Reported Change in Party Identification, 1960-64	
Opinion, 1964	Away from Democrats	Away from Republicans
Percent pro-school integration	38% (47)	62% (55)
Percent pro-Medicare	44% (45)	57% (51)

Source. Survey Research Center 1964 election data.

To date, the contemporary currents of partisan realignment appear mild in comparison with major realignments of the past. Although the number of people who call themselves political independents has been increasing, with the biggest jump from 23 percent in 1964 to 29 percent in 1966 (according to SRC data), no basic change has yet occurred in the ratio of Republican to Democratic identifiers or in the frequency with which people report a recent change in their party identification. Moreover, the issues that divide Republican and Democratic identifiers the most are still the issues on the social welfare dimension, as a result of the partisan realignment of the 1930s.

At the same time, the increasing public perception of significant partisan differences on nonsocial welfare issues is the major source of the partisan shifting that has been occurring. Given this increased awareness, a lack of clear-cut partisan differences on issues does not appear to be a sound explanation for the increase in the number of independents. Instead, many of the new group of independents (who, as we shall see in Chapter Six, come mainly from the core of young voters) may be rejecting their inherited party affiliation *because* the partisan issue differences are coming into clearer focus. Also, the increased awareness of party differences appears to be one cause of the electorate's trend toward increasing liberal-conservative polarization on issues. As perceived party differences expand beyond the social welfare realm to include differences within other policy domains as well, the public may be becoming more ideologically polarized by simply following the lead of the major parties.

FOOTNOTES FOR CHAPTER 3

[1] For one inventory of definitions of "ideology," see Robert Lane, *Political Ideology* (New York: The Free Press of Glencoe, 1962), pp. 13–16.

[2] For an interesting account of how the John Birch Society dealt with this ideological trap, see Stephen Earl Bennett, "Modes of Resolution of a 'Belief Dilemma' in the Ideology of the John Birch Society," *Journal of Politics, 33* (August, 1971), pp. 735–772.

[3] For a demonstration that the most liberal convention delegates are the most internationalist in their foreign policy views, see Herbert McClosky, "Personality and Attitude Correlates of Foreign Policy Orientation," in James N. Rosenau (ed.), *Domestic Sources of Foreign Policy* (New York: The Free Press, 1967), pp. 82–86.

[4] Philip E. Converse, "The Nature of Belief Systems in Mass Publics," in David E. Apter (ed.), *Ideology and Discontent* (New York: The Free Press, 1966), pp. 227–231.

[5] For one inventory of the philosophical distinctions between liberalism and conservatism, see Herbert McClosky, "Conservatism and Personality," *American Political Science Review, 52* (March, 1958), pp. 27–45.

[6] This finding is based on an evaluation of SRC data. Most people respond either "warm" or "neutral" toward both liberals and conservatives.

[7] Louis Harris, "Political Labels Depend on Who Applies Them," *St. Petersburg Times* (January 18, 1971), p. A10.

[8] Hadley Cantril, *Public Opinion 1935–1946* (Princeton: Princeton University Press, 1951), pp. 577–578.

[9] Converse, pp. 219–227.

[10] Ibid., p. 222.

[11] Ibid., p. 223.

[12] Alfred O. Hero, Jr., "Liberalism-Conservatism Revisited: Foreign vs. Domestic Federal Policies, 1937–1967," *Public Opinion Quarterly, 33* (Fall, 1969), p. 400.

[13] Ibid.

[14] Ibid., pp. 400–401.

[15] Angus Campbell, Philip E. Converse, Warren E. Miller, and Donald E. Stokes, *The American Voter* (New York: John Wiley and Sons, 1960), pp. 216–249.

[16] Ibid., p. 232.

[17] Ibid., p. 236.

[18] Ibid., p. 244.

[19] Ibid., p. 246.

[20] Ibid., p. 253.

[21] John O. Field and Ronald E. Anderson, "Ideology in the Public's Conceptual-

ization of the 1964 Election," *Public Opinion Quarterly, 33* (Fall, 1969), pp. 380–398; John C. Pierce, "Party Identification and the Changing Role of Ideology in American Politics," *Midwest Journal of Political Science, 14* (February, 1970), pp. 25–42.

[22] Field and Anderson, p. 388.

[23] Jerrold G. Rusk and Herbert F. Weisberg, "Perceptions of Presidential Candidates: Implications for Electoral Change," *Midwest Journal of Political Science, 16* (August 1972), pp. 388–410.

[24] Campbell, et al., pp. 194–197.

[25] Similar tables of correlations between opinions are found in various sources: for 1958 data, see Converse, *op. cit.*, p. 228; for 1956 data, see Robert Axelrod, "The Structure of Public Opinion on Policy Issues," *Public Opinion Quarterly, 31* (Spring, 1967), pp. 51–60. Another set of correlations based on opinions in 1968 is found in Robert G. Lehnen, "Assessing Reliability in Sample Surveys," *Public Opinion Quarterly, 35* (Winter, 1971–72), pp. 578–592. The reader should be cautioned that each study employs a somewhat different measure of correlation, so that the magnitudes of correlations from one study to another are not comparable.

[26] Hero, "Liberalism-Conservatism," p. 102.

[27] Ibid., p. 405.

[28] Philip E. Converse, et al., "Continuation and Change in American Politics: Parties and Issues in the 1968 Election," *American Political Science Review, 63* (December, 1969), p. 1087.

[29] The most thorough examination of the dimensions of foreign policy opinion is William R. Caspary, "Dimensions of Attitudes on International Conflict: Internationalism and Military Offensive Action," *Peace Research Society Papers, 12* (1970), pp. 1–10.

[30] Robert Axelrod, *op. cit.*

[31] Marian E. Olson, "Alienation and Political Opinions," *Public Opinion Quarterly, 29* (Summer, 1965), pp. 200–212.

[32] Norman R. Luttbeg, "The Structure of Beliefs Among Leaders and the Public," *Public Opinion Quarterly, 32* (Fall, 1968), pp. 388–409.

[33] Norman R. Luttbeg, "The Structure of Public Beliefs on State Government Policies: A Comparison with Local and National Findings," *Public Opinion Quarterly, 38* (Spring, 1971), pp. 114–116.

[34] Our discussion of the changing perceptions of party differences closely parallels the interpretations of Gerald M. Pomper. See his "Toward a More Responsible Two-Party System? What, Again?" *Journal of Politics, 33* (November, 1971), pp. 916–940; and "From Confusion to Clarity: Issues and American Voters, 1956–1968," *American Political Science Review, 66* (June, 1972), pp. 415–428.

[35] Angus Campbell, et al., pp. 212–215.

[36] William H. Flanigan, *Political Behavior of the American Electorate*, 2nd ed. (Boston: Allyn and Bacon, 1972), p. 98.

[37] Between 1966 and 1971, the percentage of Democratic opinion holders who told Gallup they favored UN admission for China rose from one-third to nearly half. Meanwhile Republican support rose from 1 in 4 to a clear plurality in favor of admission.

[38] The following table illustrates the partisan shifting on the war. Question: "Do you think the United States made a mistake sending troops to fight in Vietnam? Figures are percentages responding "yes".

	March 1966	Feb. 1968	July 1971
Democrats	24	41	64
Republicans	27	53	58

(Source. Gallup Opinion Index)

[39] On the concept of partisan realignment, see Campbell, et al., pp. 531–538.

[40] Samuel Lubell, *The Future of American Politics,* 2nd ed. (Garden City: Doubleday and Co., 1956), pp. 143–159.

[41] On the 1896 realignment, see Walter Dean Burnham, *Critical Elections and the Mainsprings of American Politics* (New York: W. W. Norton and Co., 1970), pp. 119–120.

[42] On the New Deal realignment see Everett Carll Ladd, *American Political Parties: Social Change and Political Responses* (New York: W. W. Norton and Co., 1970), pp. 207–228.

[43] For example, people in SRC's 1964 sample who reported that they shifted from Republican to Democratic in the 1930s favored Medicare by an overwhelming margin of 17 to 2. Respondents who reported making a reverse Democrat to Republican shift in the 1930s opposed Medicare 2 to 8.

FOUR

PUBLIC OPINION AND DEMOCRATIC STABILITY

This chapter continues our concern with the patterns of opinion and the degree of public acceptance of certain opinions and beliefs. Here, we turn to opinions deemed important to a society's stability and its government's use of powers granted to it for achieving social needs. The avoidance of conflict also looms important from this perspective, since a political system devoting too much of its efforts to resolving conflict can do little to achieve the collective needs of its society, thereby further adding to the potential for conflict.

In a democracy, public opinion is important because it can influence the decisions that political leaders make. Certain opinions have particular significance because the very functioning of democracy may depend on their widespread acceptance by the citizens. In this chapter we examine the attitudes that are considered to be necessary to maintain a democracy and the degree to which Americans appear to hold them. Ideas about what is vital to a system's stability can be divided into four types:

First, there should be public consensus in favor of the rules of democracy. An analogy here is the rules of the road for driving an automobile. If everyone did not accept the rule that one is to drive on the right, chaos would ensue. Two of the most important rules of democracy are the principles of majority rule and the protection of minority rights. We examine the extent to which Americans accept these rules.

Second, democracy's stability may rest on sufficient agreement on long-term social goals and values to allow peaceful resolutions of conflicting demands placed on government. Too great of a division may overtax even the best procedures for resolving conflict. We approach this problem by examining the extent of an American consensus on basic values to be achieved.

Third, if people are to accept government decisions, they must believe that their political actions can be effective and that they can trust the government to respond to their interests. Presumably, when government unresponsiveness leads to a withdrawal of public trust, the stability of the political system is threatened. In this chapter we look at some indicators of the extent of public trust in political leaders.

Fourth, in coping with personal anxieties and needs, many find comfort in blaming others as a class, such as a Catholic seeing Protestants as responsible for his unemployment. When such personalities are common and focus on a single minority, democracy insistence on minority rights and even its stability may be threatened.

Before examining these issues from the perspective of public opinion, some words are in order concerning the relationship between the opinions people hold and their actual behavior. People may engage in the same action on the basis of different attitudes and opinions, and the same attitudes and opinions may motivate people to different actions depending on the presence or absence of other opinions motivating them at the same time. Consider Figure 4-1. At the far right we place those actions by the public that have political significance, in this case the act of picketing the President of the United States in protest to his Vietnam War policy. The vertical line to the left of this signifies the division between action and thinking about it. All concepts to the left of the line are ideational, that is, within the minds of the individuals. Such concepts are not observable. We know of them only by way of asking people their opinions, attitudes, and beliefs; and we bother to ask because we expect that these expressions will help us better predict their actions than if we had to rely solely on the way they dressed, combed their hair, or otherwise differed physically. Often, such as when a self-proclaimed liberal opposes a particular liberal program, an individual's action will seem to contradict his expressed opinions. Sometimes this happens because we lack knowledge of other attitudes the person holds.

Each column of attitudes and opinions in the figure represents different degrees of abstraction and generality, with those closest to the behavior being more specific and limited in scope.[1] Generally we would expect that the more specific the attitude solicited, the more likely it is to prove predictive of actual behavior. For example, the most specific attitude listed in the Figure is attitude toward picketing the President at a specific time and place in protest to the war in Vietnam. This is substantially more specific than attitude toward war in that it includes the suggestion of action toward a specific individual and is limited to a single war. It is also more specific than attitude toward the war in Vietnam, again because it specifies action against the President. Each of these more specific attitudes moving to the right side of the figure starting with attitude toward war should better predict behavior. For example, if we tried to predict which individuals would picket solely on the basis of their attitude toward war in general, such as a man who has no strong objection to war in general but who strongly feels this particular war is a mistake, we would often be wrong. If we know his opinion

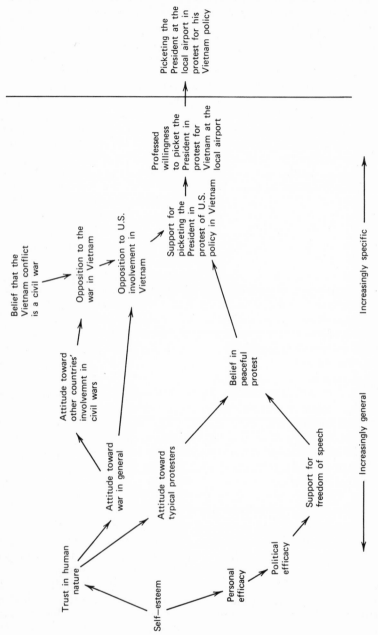

Figure 4-1. A hypothetical connection of actions, attitudes and beliefs.

Actions

Picketing the President at the local airport in protest for his Vietnam policy

Professed willingness to picket the President in protest for Vietnam at the local airport

Support for picketing the President in protest of U.S. policy in Vietnam

Belief that the Vietnam conflict is a civil war

Opposition to the war in Vietnam

Opposition to U.S. involvement in Vietnam

Attitude toward other countries' involvemnt in civil wars

Attitude toward war in general

Attitude toward typical protesters

Belief in peaceful protest

Support for freedom of speech

Trust in human nature

Self-esteem

Personal efficacy

Political efficacy

⟶ Increasingly general   Increasingly specific ⟶

on the war in Vietnam, we would less often be in error; but he may also not believe in protest, so we could still err.

In short, our greatest expectation of correctly predicting behavior would be to know a man's attitude on going out to the municipal airport to picket the arriving President to demand that he remove all U.S. troops. Knowing this attitude would give us maximum prediction, but persons agreeing to it may do so out of many motivations. Some may do so out of desire to force confrontation with the police, caring little about the cause; mothers may do so hoping to protect their draft age sons; and others out of opposition to war in general. To understand behavior we need to move away from the specific; to predict we need to move toward the specific. In the chapter we will generally be moving from more specific to more general attitudes and opinions.

PUBLIC ACCEPTANCE OF DEMOCRATIC "RULES OF THE GAME"

The beliefs that acts of government should reflect the wishes of the majority and not the minority, and that the minority must be assured fair treatment and the right to strive to become the majority, are commonly agreed to be essential to democracy. It would seem reasonable, then, that the public should believe in these ideas. Thus we would expect that nearly all Americans would agree to the following statements:

Democracy is the best form of government;
Public officials should be chosen by majority vote;
Every citizen should have an equal chance to influence government policy;
The minority should be free to criticize majority decisions;
People in the minority should be free to try to win majority support for their opinions.

James Prothro and Charles Grigg report their samples (from two cities) do indeed give consensual support of 95 to 98 percent for the above statements.[2] But these are very abstract and unspecific attitudes distant from possible public actions or reactions in specific instances, such as how they would react to avowed Communists teaching a course on revolution in a public university. This will be our first example that people may come to hold opinions for many reasons. In this case, many members of the public do not form their specific opinion on the basis of consistency with their more general support for majority rule and, especially, minority rights.

TABLE 4-1   **Percentage of "Democratic" Responses to Specific Applications of the Basic Principles of Democracy**

Majority Rule	
In a city referendum, only people who are well-informed about the problem being voted on should be allowed to vote.	49%
In a city referendum deciding on tax-supported undertakings, only taxpayers should be allowed to vote.	21
If a Negro were legally elected mayor of this city, the white people should not allow him to take office.	81
If a Communist were legally elected mayor of this city, the people should not allow him to take office.	46
A professional organization like the AMA has a right to try to increase the influence of doctors by getting them to vote as a bloc in elections	45
Minority Rights	
If a person wanted to make a speech in this city against churches and religion, he should be allowed to speak.	63
If a person wanted to make a speech in this city favoring government ownership of all the railroads and big industries, he should be allowed to speak.	79
If an admitted Communist wanted to make a speech in this city favoring communism, he should be allowed to speak.	44
A Negro should not be allowed to run for mayor of this city.	76
A Communist should not be allowed to run for mayor of the city.	42

Source. James W. Prothro and Charles M. Grigg, "Fundamental Principles of Democracy: Bases of Agreement and Disagreement," *Journal of Politics, 22* (Spring, 1960), p. 281. Data are from Ann Arbor, Michigan and Tallahassee, Florida.

Compared with the consensual support given to the general opinions noted above, we see in Table 4-1 that many hold "undemocratic" opinions on more specific instances in that they would condone violating "democratic" standards of majority rule and minority rights. On six of the ten questions, less than a majority give "democratic" responses. For example, most would allow only taxpayers to vote on city referenda. Apparently their opinion that taxpayers have the most to gain or lose in such elections is more important in their reaction to this specific issue than their support for unbridled majority rule.

The failure of Americans to apply the principles of free speech and tolerance of minorities to such minorities as Communists and atheists has also been demonstrated by many other researchers.[3] In a 1954 nationwide sample, Samuel Stouffer noted that 66 percent would remove a book by a known Communist from the public library, 60 percent would not allow someone to speak against churches and religion in their community, and 68 percent would not allow an admitted Communist to speak publicly.[4] If a man swears under oath that he is not a Communist despite a congressional committee's inquiry into his involvement, most people (70 percent) would allow him to speak publicly. Perhaps this suggests the limits of the public's willingness to deny unpopular minorities the right to free speech.[5] Of course, from another perspective this man is guilty of nothing, but 21 percent would deny him his rights.

To the degree that these expressions of public opinion could be marshalled behind a public policy to remove the rights of certain elements of our society, the public can hardly be conceived as the backbone of democracy. But many questions remain unanswered, such as a full enumeration of those to whom the public would deny rights. Limited research suggests that only extremist groups and those engaging in extreme actions would be denied their rights.[6] But these are statements of what people claim they would do, not their actions. Would the conscience of the public allow it to act out these sentiments in support of a political leader who would deny rights to some persons? While the following is only one incident, Prothro and Grigg note that shortly after 42 percent of Tallahasseans supported denying an elected Negro mayor his office, a black did run with no protest. But it was 1971 before a black did win and take a city council seat. The public's response to these questions, as in those we previously studied, may not reflect strongly held opinions that would shape their actions if aroused, but the basic findings are sobering!

Support for democratic principles proves more extensive among the young and better educated. In Stouffer's survey, 47 percent of those between 21 and 29 were "more tolerant" contrasting with only 18 percent of those 60 and older, and 66 percent of college graduates were "more tolerant" versus only 16 percent of those with only a grade school education.[7] Although education appears to cause political tolerance, possibly the most educated people give the most prodemocratic responses in surveys because they are more aware of the "proper" responses expected of them and not because they would oppose antidemocratic actions more vigorously.

These antidemocratic attitudes can of course be encouraged by political leaders. Fortunately, political activists and men in official positions seem to be above average adherents to the democratic "rules of the game." Comparing delegates to the 1956 presidential conventions with a national sample, Herbert McClosky noted that while the delegates were only 10 percentage points more democratic on general rules questions, they were 18 percentage points more democratic on specific applications of the rules.[8] The delegates gave the more democratic responses to every question. Similarly, 66 percent of the community leaders in Stouffer's study proved "more tolerant" (on a combined measure across issues) versus only 31 percent for the public sample. And none of the 14 community leadership groups studies proved as intolerant as the public.[9] Disturbingly, however, Stouffer found five percent of the community leaders to be "less tolerant"; and 26 percent of McClosky's delegates typically proved undemocratic on specific applications of free speech and procedural rights. More specifically, seven percent of the delegates agreed that "the majority has the right to abolish minorities if it wants" while 13 percent agreed that, "almost any unfairness or brutality may have to be justified when some great purpose is being carried out."[10] How many undemocratic leaders can a democracy endure? As yet, such a question has no answer. Two of the most blatantly undemocratic events in recent American history, the gathering of American citizens of Japanese ancestry into internment camps early in World War II and the yielding to Joseph McCarthy's unsubstantiated charges of Communist infiltration, were actions taken by elected officials without pressure from an insisting public.

One prevalent characteristic of political activists in democratic societies is their relatively greater education. Thus it may well be that political leaders are relatively more tolerant because of their education and not, as McClosky hypothesizes, because they "are unavoidably exposed to the liberal democratic values which form the main current of our political heritage."[11] From Stouffer's data, Robert Jackman investigated whether political leaders are in fact more tolerant than others who share their education, sex, and other distinguishing characteristics.[12] Table 4-2 shows that leaders are no more tolerant. Since leaders in our society are no more resolutely democratic than their equally educated counterparts among the public, apparently no great affinity for democratic rules arises as a result of day-to-day experience in the working of democracy among political activists.[13]

While support for the "democratic rules" would intrinsically seem important to the quality of democracy and the high levels of undemocratic opinion within both the public and leaders disturbing, our alarm may be unfounded. Because these limited studies fail to demonstrate that the undemocratic opinions have the implied threat to the preservation of democracy, they may even prove irrelevant to its quality. Does it matter to the health of a country that its average

TABLE 4-2   Mean Tolerance Scores Within Educational Categories for the Mass and Elite Samples with Region, Sex, and (for the Mass Sample Only) City Size Controlled

Education	Mass	Elite
College Graduate	87	85
Some College	79	77
High School Graduate	71	74
Grades 9-11	66	70
Grades 0-8	59	63

Source. Robert W. Jackman, "Political Elites, Mass Publics, and Support For Democratic Principles," Journal of Politics (August, 1972), p. 765.

citizens' beliefs show them not to be strong adherents of democracy? Researchers have yet to answer this question.

POLITICAL EFFICACY AND POLITICAL ALIENATION

According to many theorists, democracy works best when the citizens believe that their political actions will be effective, and that government decisions will be in their interests. For example, William Gamson says that "the loss of trust is the loss of system power, the loss of a generalized capacity for authorities to commit resources to attain collective goals."[14] In other words, democracies cannot function unless government actions are believed to be benevolent.

The person who feels he will be effective in his dealings with government is said to be "politically efficacious." Another concept, "political alienation," would seem identified by a lack of such political confidence. Originally developed to explain why some people fail to vote,[15] a set of questionnaire items measures people's placement on a scale of political efficacy-alienation. Typical items on this efficacy scale include:

People like me don't have any say about what the government does.
Voting is the only way that people like me can have a say about how the government runs things.
Sometimes politics and government seems so complicated that a person like me can't really understand what's going on.
I don't think public officials care much what people like me think.[16]

Agreement with each of these statements indicates political alienation; disagreement indicates political efficacy. Although very few variables are correlated with political efficacy scores, education is one strong exception. For example, while 77 percent of citizens with no formal education agree that public officials do not care what they think, only 10 percent of those who have completed college agree.[17]

The portion of the electorate evidencing efficacy has not been stable over time, as indicated in Figure 4-2. Despite a steady increase in the percentage of the electorate with college education, which

Figure 4-2. Trends in Responses to Political Efficacy Items, 1952-1970, (*Sources*. Philip E. Converse, "Changes in the American Electorate," in Angus Campbell and Philip E. Converse (eds.), *The Human Meaning of Social Change* (New York: Russell Sage Foundation, 1972), p. 328; Survey Research Center, 1970 election data.

would be expected to increase the number who feel politically efficacious, the zenith for such confidence in government was reached in
1960 and has since fallen to levels lower than in 1952. Only belief
that acts other than voting can or must be used to affect government
officials has resisted this trend. Even this item may be reflecting a
loss of confidence in the meaningfulness of just voting. This decline
in efficacy has unclear implications since political interest and participation have increased during this period, as would be expected,
given the improving education of the American electorate.[18] Possibly
the American public's growing lack of efficacy makes it ripe for
recruitment to movements expressing its discontent, or possibly the
termination of our involvement in Vietnam and an improvement in
the economy at home will see a return to a more efficacious electorate. Also, while it is entirely plausible that such feeling adversely
affects a political system, no evidence can be cited.

POLITICAL CULTURE

In their book *The Civic Culture*, Gabriel Almond and Sidney Verba
see political efficacy as only one of the elements that form the ideal
political culture of a stable democracy.[19] They view the ideal citizen as believing in the success of his political actions (efficacy),
believing that he is obligated to participate (citizen duty), but rather
inactive politically in actual practice (apathy). While conceding that
"unless there is some control of government elites by nonelites, it is
hard to consider a political system democratic," Almond and Verba
also argue that elites must have the power to "initiate and carry out
policies, adjust to new situations, meet internal and external challenges," and generally make authoritative decisions.[20] Thus, low
participation gives government room to operate, while the strong
confidence of the people that their participation would be successful
assures their acting to get a responsible leadership.

Almond and Verba see the best manifestations of the desired
political culture in the United States and Great Britain. They argue
that the citizens of these countries have a strong sense of civic duty
to participate and great confidence that participation would be effective. Yet they view the American and British public as relatively
politically apathetic in practice.[21] They base their conclusions
on the findings of their ambitious survey of opinion in the United
States, Great Britain, West Germany, Italy, and Mexico. The major
findings are presented in Table 4-3.

The first five differences among the countries shown in the Table
support their conclusion. Americans and Britons are more likely to
admit their responsibility to be actively involved in their community
and to feel they can do something about both local and national

TABLE 4-3   **Evidence of Civic Cultures in Five Democracies**

	United States	United Kingdom	Germany	Italy	Mexico
Percent believing the ordinary man should be active in his community	51	39	22	10	26
Percent who say they can do something about an unjust national regulation	75	62	38	28	38
Percent who say they can do something about an unjust local regulation	77	78	62	51	52
Percent who follow accounts of political and governmental affairs regularly	27	23	34	11	15
Percent who say they have attempted to influence local government	28	15	14	9	6
Percent reporting they regularly or occasionally discuss politics	76	70	60	32	38
Percent saying they would likely have success if they tried to change harmful local regulation	52	36	32	22	37
Percent saying they would likely have success if they tried to change harmful national regulation	41	25	13	11	29

Source. Gabriel A. Almond and Sidney Verba, *The Civic Culture.* Pages respective to items above: p. 169, p. 185, p. 185, p. 89, p. 116. The last two items are taken from the Inter-University Consortium For Political Research Codebook, *The Five Nation Study* (Ann Arbor: ICPR, 1968), pp. 29 and 83.

unjust or harmful regulations. And, like their fellow citizens in the other countries, they show little actual participation, at least as judged by admitting to attempts to influence local government and failing to follow regularly accounts of political and governmental affairs. However, the key questions showing high percentages of Americans and Britons feeling they could do something about unjust or harmful regulations are really questions that ask respondents what they could do to *try* to change policy and not questions concerning their likelihood of success. But the final two questions in the Table, which deal specifically with likely success were they to make the effort, blur the distinctiveness of Americans and Britons versus the others. Americans continue to be the most optimistic, but generally the citizens of all five countries prove pessimistic about the likely success of their actions.

If we identify the actual percentage in each country showing the three attributes of the ideal citizen identified in *The Civic Culture*, that is, (1) believing he should be active, (2) optimistic that he would be successful were he active, and (3) actually showing little political activity, their conclusion that the United States and Britain come closest to satisfying the model political culture receives slight support. The percentage of the population in each cðuntry showing all three properties is:

United States	22%
United Kingdom	17
Germany	9
Italy	3
Mexico	10.[22]

These minorities would hardly seem to be an adequate base on which to build stable democracies, if the stability of democracy does indeed rest on such beliefs. The sole unique opinion of citizens of the United States and the United Kingdom would appear to be their sense of civic duty.

THE SEARCH FOR AN AMERICAN CONSENSUS

We turn next to the degree that Americans concur on basic values. General agreement on values would limit the number of political issues that arise and reduce the number of areas of controversy with which government must deal. These consensual values might differ from country to country, but the attributes of a stable democracy might be consensus on values compared with division in unstable democracies.

An entire literature exists that searches for such consensus on values and orientation within different nationalities. What we are seeking here is evidence of a national character in the consensus within the public on attitudes and values that condition public responses to issues. As V. O. Key notes, we all have caricatures or stereotypes of authority-loving Germans, excitable Frenchmen, and optimistic and humanitarian Americans.[23]

From his study of public opinion, Key saw unique elements of consensus within the American character: Americanism, suspicion of authority, fairness in the game of government, individualism, willingness to accept the majority's decision, and political pragmatism rather than ideological thinking.[24] By Americanism, Key means smug and often intolerant satisfaction with things American. Almond and Verba asked their five national samples, "Speaking generally, what are the things about this country that you are most proud of?" As we see in Table 4-4, Americans give more responses than other nationals and focus more on governmental institutions.

This strong nationalism of Americans appears again in Table 4-5. Each person interviewed was asked if he could identify with a person of his own social class abroad and then if he could identify

TABLE 4-4 **Aspects of Nation in Which Respondents Report Pride, by Nation (in percent)**

Percent Who Say They Are Proud of	United States	United Kingdom	Germany	Italy	Mexico
Governmental, political institutions	85	46	7	3	30
Social legislation	13	18	6	1	2
Position in international affairs	5	11	5	2	3
Economic system	23	10	33	3	24
Characteristics of people	7	18	36	11	15
Spiritual virtues and religion	3	1	3	6	8
Contributions to the arts	1	6	11	16	9
Contributions to science	3	7	12	3	1
Physical attributes of country	5	10	17	25	22
Nothing or don't know	4	10	15	27	16
Other	9	11	3	21	14
Total percent of responses[a]	158	148	148	118	144
Total percent of respondents	100	100	100	100	100
Total number of cases	970	963	955	995	1,007

Source. Gabriel Almond and Sidney Verba, The Civic Culture (Princeton: Princeton University Press, 1963), p. 102.

[a] Percentages exceed one hundred because of multiple responses.

TABLE 4-5   Relative Influence of National and Class Identity, 1948

	Identify with Country Not of Own Class	Identify with Class Not of Own Country	Difference
United States	77% (Yes)	42% (Yes)	35
Germany	64	30	34
Norway	64	41	23
Mexico	56	40	16
France	63	48	15
Australia	78	67	11
Britain	67	58	9
Italy	50	41	9
Netherlands	56	61	−5

Source. William Buchanan and Hadley Cantril, How Nations See Each Other (Urbana: University of Illinois Press, 1952), p. 18. Cited in: Donald J. Devine, The Political Culture of the United States (Boston: Little, Brown and Company, 1972), p. 95.

with someone of his nationality but of a different class. The second column of the Table shows low class consciousness among Americans but not lower than in Germany, Norway, Mexico, or Italy. Americans, however, see themselves as quite capable of putting nationality before class. Only the Australians prove more capable. The index of the difference in these two responses suggests that American political leaders could more heavily rely on nationalism to unify the country than could officials in other countries, especially the Netherlands.[25]

Key's second estimate, that Americans suspect authority, seems unsupported in The Civic Culture data since only nine percent of the American sample thought they would not receive fair treatment by a government office or the police and courts as compared with much higher percentages for Italians and Mexicans.[26] But by fairness in the game of government, Key meant that Americans do not believe anyone should have a disproportionate say in what government does. For example, he finds that only 22 percent of a national sample said that neither labor nor business should be restricted by government from having much say in how the government is run. Thirty-four percent favored restricting both.[27]

Individualism is the American disposition to rely on one's own efforts. In coping with unjust or harmful government regulation, large percentages of both Americans and Britons (57 and 44 percent, respectively) claimed they would directly contact officials or the press.[28] In a study of public attitudes in education, in which people were asked what they would do if they were unhappy with how their child was taught in school, only five percent were at a loss as to what to do. More importantly, 77 percent would go directly and individually to the teacher or principal; and when the interviewer persisted in asking what they would do if each succeeding effort failed, 31 percent ultimately said they would solve the problem at home if their other individual efforts failed.[29] Key insists that the low salience of government reflects the individualism of Americans in that they prefer self-improvement to governmental support.[30] But we must also note that Americans are not unique in paying little attention to the government.

Our earlier discussion of Americans' support for the democratic rules of the game might suggest that Key errs in claiming that Americans accept or tolerate majority rule. As we note here, they believe in majority rule in the general sense while abandoning it in specific applications. But the tolerance, Key sees among Americans, is in their actions and not in their opinions. Finally, he sees Americans as politically pragmatic in that their responses, "to public issues are not fixed in advance by a rigid pattern of belief that produced predictable and firmly held positions on most public issues."[31] Our discussion in the previous chapter supports the absence of ideology among Americans, but this might not be unique to America. In short, there would seem to be much substance to the beliefs that Key sees among Americans, but this agreement would seem far short of being consensual and hardly characteristic of Americans only.

Values can be distinguished from more specific opinions. According to Milton Rokeach, values are:

"... modes of conduct and end-states of existence. To say that person has a 'value' is to say that he has an enduring belief that a specific mode of conduct or end-state of existence is personally and socially preferable to alternative modes of conduct or end-states of existence. Once a value is internalized it becomes, consciously or unconsciously, a standard or criterion for guiding action, for developing and maintaining attitudes toward relevant objects and situations, for justifying one's own and others' actions and attitudes, for morally judging self and others, and for comparing self with others."[32]

Clearly values, like attitudes, help people order and react to what happens to them, but values are more fundamental, more enduring, and fewer in number. An American consensus on the less numerous and more general values seems more likely than, for example, on attitudes toward the war in Vietnam and social protest. Rokeach assesses the two types of values he sees present among people: modes of conduct, and end-states of existence. The latter, called terminal values, refers to the unattainable but desired lives or world we hope for, for example, a world at peace, a comfortable life, or salvation. Modes of conduct, or instrumental values, are the values associated with the means to be used in striving for our goals.[33]

Rokeach's instrument for assessing values asks people to rank a list of values in order of personal importance. Table 4-6 presents the percentage of a sample ranking each of the values among their top five in personal importance. For example, 59 percent personally rank a world at peace as one of their five most important terminal values. While these data come from a Florida sample, the ordering of the two value sets by this sample very closely follows that of a national sample only partially reported by Rokeach.[34] Hadley Cantril's earlier study, with 13 samples from throughout the world, strongly indicates that Floridians' ranking of these terminal values may not be unique but rather seem to be shared worldwide.[35]

We find little evidence of agreement on which terminal values should be emphasized. Although it is possible that every respondent could rank a world at peace or any other value as the most important value of the 18, or at least place it within the top five in importance, this does not happen. Six out of 10 people, however, put world peace and family security among the top five. Twelve of the 18 values are placed among the top five personal values by at least one person in four, suggesting great diversity in American values. Thus a value consensus is clearly absent.

Among the instrumental values, honesty comes closest to being consensual, since only three out of every 10 adults do not place it among their top five. Strikingly, three of the public's top five values stress social control and one—"ambitious"—is central to proper behavior in our economic system. In a culture based on rationality and responsiveness to changing circumstances, the deemphasis of "logical" (17th), "imaginative" (18th), and "intellectual" (14th) might prove dysfunctional.

From one perspective, one might argue that the public is consensual in that beauty, an exciting life, social recognition, pleasure, and imaginativeness are not most valued, but the strongest impression from the table is great value diversity. A society may enjoy stability and freedom from social strife if it is consensual in its underlying values. But a diversity in motivating values, short of a single divisive schism, may cushion the task of government.[36] While the above analysis only suggests the absence of consensus, further research finds no evidence of different groups ranking the values in opposite ways.[37] Thus while there would seem to be no consensus, there is also no polarization.

TABLE 4-6   The Personal Values of Adults in the State of Florida, 1969

Terminal Value N=629	[a]
World at peace	59%
Family security	59
Freedom	49
Self-respect	43
Salvation	38
Wisdom	38
Happiness	33
Sense of accomplishment	32
Equality	28
Comfortable life	26
National security	26
Inner harmony	24
True friendship	14
Mature love	13
World of beauty	7
Exciting life	5
Social recognition	4
Pleasure	3
Instrumental Value N=613	
Honest	69
Responsible	48
Ambitious	46
Broadminded	35
Self-controlled	30
Courageous	30
Forgiving	30
Capable	29
Clean	28
Independent	26
Helpful	25
Loving	23
Polite	18
Intellectual	17
Cheerful	16
Obedient	13
Logical	11
Imaginative	8

[a] Percentage of persons placing this value among the top five of 18 values ranked as important to them as "guiding principles" in their lives.

PERSONALITY AND PUBLIC OPINION

Students of personality criticize approaches such as survey research on the grounds that they lack comprehensiveness and theoretical guidance. Still, the study of personality has yielded little predictive information as to what opinions we might expect of certain types of personalities.[38] While we must fully grant the importance of thoroughly understanding the motives of people for holding the opinions they do, we also need an evaluation of the strength and consistency of the noted relationship. The basic attribute of personality, as characteristically defined by psychologists, is the similarity of an individual's responses across a broad range of situations or stimuli caused by his personality.[39] All or most of the concepts previously discussed belong to such a broadly defined concept of personality. As we will be using the concept here, however, it is restricted to the innermost needs and conflicts of a person, especially those bordering on the abnormal.[40]

The basic elements here are the enduring, abstract perspectives that people adopt for the ordering of the world around them, to be socially attractive, and to meet the complexity of their personal needs. Students of personality see personal needs, such as believing one is individually important, as basic to understanding behavior. Thus, while personality psychologists strive to work across the full range of abstractness and specificity in our Figure 4-1, striving to uncover the nexus or pattern of relationships that connect more general and underlying concepts with specific attitudes and behaviors, their goal is an understanding of how different personalities perceive and react to events and people around them.

While trait psychologists have tried to associate personalities with specific attitudes and behavior, most researchers interested in personality dismiss such efforts as simplistic and naive, and pursue instead very thorough research across the full spectrum of attitudes on the specificity and abstraction dimension. As might be expected, such extensive and time-consuming assessments for each individual result in few individuals being evaluated. The most frequently cited studies of personality and political behavior examine no more than 24 individuals. Such groups can in no way be considered a sample of any meaningful segment of the population. If the dynamics of personality and behavior noted in those limited groups were universal or identical to those of other people, as is often claimed, these works would be definitive. But their primary contribution is insight into what makes some people other than ourselves tick and a comfortable feeling that we know them in contrast to the impersonality of the

tabular presentations of 1000 responses from survey research.
M. Brewster Smith, Jerome Bruner, and Robert White's study of 10 better-educated Boston men's opinions of Russia offers insight into how a person's personal frustrations affect his opinions. While the personalities of these men show dependence, guilt, inferiority, and demandingness reflecting their personal adjustment, the authors' conclusion is:

"Our data support no illusory hope that favorableness to Russia can be traced to any single trait or complex of traits. They do strongly support the assumption, firmly rooted in personality research, that there is congruence among the various instances of a person's thinking, feeling, and deciding about features of his world."[41]

Some men need to externalize their strivings and needs and careful study of individuals will unveil the sources of their consistency in responding to and evaluating events and things around them. In addition to the importance of personalities, these authors stress the gains in understanding the individual's opinions if one knows how a person perceives the situation and the world around him. Personality is important but so are perceptions.[42]

Robert Lane's study of 15 primarily Catholic, working-class men in Connecticut, considers the "loosely structured, unreflective statements of the common men," as Lane labels their ideology. He also finds much that is understandable in their opinions once one fully understands their perspective on the world.[43] But more important, his extensive evaluation of their personalities unearths no attributes or attitudes that determine their evaluation of society and government. He evaluates a multitude of different pathologies or deviant personality attributes, which others suggest might be important in explaining antisocial and antidemocratic behaviors, and identifies the three highest scores on each pathology. He finds different men guilty of different pathologies, and concludes that society is safer given this diversity and the resulting diversity of ideologies satisfying to these pathologies.[44] These two monographs and Lane's latest work, a study of how 24 college students' political thoughts satisfy their personal needs,[45] may well serve as the beginning of a thorough exploration of the consistency between characteristics of one's personality and political attitudes and opinions. But because they focus so intensively on a few individuals, many regularities in their thoughts and behavior may be overlooked or even ignored. We now turn to a personality characteristic that originated in such an intensive clinical examination but that has since been applied to large samples—authoritarianism.

The Authoritarian Personality

The Authoritarian Personality, published in 1950, represented the fruition of five years of complex and varied inquiry into the sources of anti-Semitism.[46] The authors found that personality needs were gratified by a person's disposition toward authority. Persons having the authoritarian personality are submissive to those having authority over them and are demanding of submission when in a position of authority.[47] Theodore Adorno notes a vivid depiction of such a personality in German folklore—the bicyclist's personality: above they bow, below they kick.[48] Jews, being a minority, are expected to be submissive, and thus persons with the authoritarian personality tend to be anti-Semitic. The obvious referent of this study is Nazi Germany.

Although the book's revelation that many people are submissive is hardly startling, it did offer a new measurement called the F (fascism) scale that could be administered to large numbers of individuals. Typical items on the F-scale include: "No sane, normal, decent person could ever think of hurting a close friend or relative" and "Most people don't realize how much our lives are controlled by plots hatched in secret by politicians."[49] Unfortunately, this particular instrument and its development are not as perfected as was first assumed. The major fault rests on the then unforeseen tendency of many to agree to a statement regardless of what it says. This "response set" is more common among the less educated; as a result of their agreeing to the authoritarian statements, the authoritarian personality type seemed prevalent and concentrated among the working class.[50] To test for response set, in 1956 the Survey Research Center included five original authoritarian items that required positive responses and five questions requiring authoritarians to disagree. People who were authoritarian on one scale were not authoritarian on the second. Furthermore, focusing only on those who were consistent across both scales, they found so few significant relationships with issues that they dismiss the concept's relevance other than to the better educated segment of the society from which it was developed.[51] Thus the one personality concept that promised more general results fails to do so. As Fred Greenstein concludes, "the difficulties of the literature (on the authoritarian personality) have resulted from promiscuous, atheoretical use of a handy but imperfect instrument."[52]

Research on authoritarianism and other possible antidemocratic personality traits has continued. Believing that the F-scale focuses only on the extreme right of ideology and that it is better to distinguish sharply between the structure of a person's beliefs and the content of these beliefs, Rokeach has developed and partially tested a Dogmatism Scale that discriminates among people's belief structures.[53] The dogmatic person identified by Rokeach, whether his beliefs are of the left or right, proves intolerant of those disagreeing with him and has beliefs that are closed to change. Finally, David McClelland and his associates have developed three scales that assess a person's need for power, association with others, and achievement.[54] Either because the concepts dealing with personality were focused on behaviors other than opinion holding, as is the case with McClelland, or failed to be tested in large samples and broad ranges of public opinions, as is the case with Rokeach, these efforts have yielded little definitive information as to how personality links with political opinions.

Greenstein vividly depicts our conclusion in this exploration of research on personality and public opinions, "the small population of students of personality and politics has as yet not contributed enough that is well established on the impact of personality on politics."[55] The insight from their work might well serve as hypotheses for further work, but the promise is unfulfilled.

SUMMARY

The United States and other developed democracies have proved to be remarkably stable political systems in an otherwise politically unstable world. The multitude of characteristics of these societies seen as encouraging this distinctiveness, however, find little confirmation. We cannot be sure, for example, that the American public would resist an antidemocratic movement perpetrated by political activists. Furthermore, we have no information as to the level of public acceptance of general and specific democratic rules of the game in nondemocratic or developing democratic societies that would permit our judging America's uniqueness. The numerous attitudes and patterns of attitudes variously conceived as buttressing a democracy seem only weakly related to relevant political behavior. They also seem not sufficiently common to make a majority of any society prodemocratic, and they hardly seem unique to so-called "developed" democracies.

Although there may be an American consensus, we have yet to witness a convincing demonstration of it. Even if it were present, the remaining differences of opinion within our society could easily generate demands that government would not be able to fulfill, and no one has demonstrated that more consensual societies place fewer demands on their government. Finally, the search for a "democratic" personality seems even less rewarding. While many researchers have indicated with rich detail how the frustrations of some individuals affect their opinions and behaviors in the political sphere, we know little about the distribution of solutions to personal problems in our society or whether we are blessed with more benign personalities than less stable democracies. The available findings strongly suggest that an educated populace is more supportive of democracy than a less-educated populace. The educated are more tolerant of minority positions, more efficacious, seemingly less frustrated in their daily lives, and more willing to grapple with the complexities of problems instead of forcing them into simple solutions. The recent decline in efficacious attitudes, despite steadily increasing education, suggests that it is not sufficient to improve the education of a society to assure it high efficacy.

Research on the importance of public opinion to the stability of democracy has only just begun to yield information. Certainly none of the facile conceptualizations of the uniqueness of developed democracies has been adequately documented, but the answer to the sources of democratic stability clearly merits continued inquiry.

FOOTNOTES FOR CHAPTER 4

[1] This presentation is broadly derived from the "funnel of causality" notion presented by the authors of The American Voter. Angus Campbell, Philip E. Converse, Warren E. Miller, and Donald E. Stokes, The American Voter (New York: Wiley, 1960), pp. 24–37.

[2] James W. Prothro and Charles M. Grigg, "Fundamental Principles of Democracy: Bases of Agreement and Disagreement," Journal of Politics, 22 (Spring, 1960), p. 281.

[3] Samuel A. Stouffer, Communism, Conformity, and Civil Liberties (New York: Wiley, 1955); and Herbert McClosky, "Consensus and Ideology in American Politics," American Political Science Review, 58 (June, 1964), pp. 361–382.

[4] Stouffer, pp. 33–41.

[5] Stouffer, p. 36.

[6] David H. Everson, "The Substantive Context of the Rules of the Game." Public Affairs Bulletin, Southern Illinois University, Carbondale, Ill. (May-June, 1970).

[7] Stouffer, p. 93.

[8] Recomputed from data in Tables in 2 and 3 of McClosky, pp. 366–367.

[9] Stouffer, p. 51.

[10] McCloskey, p. 365.

[11] Herbert McClosky, "Consensus and Ideology in American Politics," American Political Science Review, 58 (June, 1964), p. 375.

[12] Robert W. Jackman, "Political Elites, Mass Publics, and Support for Democratic Principles," Journal of Politics (August, 1972), pp. 753–773.

[13] This failure of respect for democracy to grow with political participation challenges the faith in participation expressed by Jack Walker, who urges greater mass political participation to offset the bias of elites in existing democratic societies and to reduce the antidemocratic attitudes of the masses by giving them more experience with the process of making decisions in a democracy. Jack L. Walker, "A Critique of the Elitist Theory of Democracy," American Political Science Review, 60 (June, 1966), pp. 285–295.

[14] William A. Gamson, *Power and Discontent* (Homewood, Ill.: Dorsey, 1968), p. 43.

[15] Campbell, et al., p. 104.

[16] John P. Robinson, Jerrold G. Rusk, and Kendra B. Head, *Measures of Political Attitudes* (Ann Arbor, Mich.: Institute for Social Research, 1968), p. 635.

[17] Philip E. Converse, "Change in the American Electorate," in Angus Campbell and Philip E. Converse, (eds.) *The Human Meaning of Social Change* (New York: Russell Sage Foundation, 1972), p. 326.

[18] Converse, p. 332.

[19] Gabriel A. Almond and Sidney Verba, *The Civic Culture* (Princeton, N.J.: Princeton University Press, 1963), p. 496.

[20] Ibid., p. 476.

[21] Ibid., p. 479.

[22] Recomputed from data supplied from the Inter-University Consortium for Political Research.

[23] V. O. Key, *Public Opinion and American Democracy* (New York: Knopf, 1961), p. 42.

[24] Ibid., pp. 43–49.

[25] Donald J. Devine, *The Political Culture of the United States* (Boston: Little Brown, 1972) p. 95.

[26] Almond and Verba, p. 108.

[27] Key, p. 46.

[28] Almond and Verba, p. 203.

[29] Norman R. Luttbeg, Florida Educational Needs: Public Satisfactions and Dissatisfactions with Their Schools, an unpublished manuscript, p. 41.

[30] Key, p. 47.

[31] Ibid., p. 49.

[32] Milton Rokeach, *Beliefs, Attitudes and Values* (San Francisco: Jossey-Bass, Inc., 1968), p. 160.

[33] Milton Rokeach, "The Measurement of Values and Value Systems," in Gilbert Abcarian and John W. Soule (eds.), *Social Psychology and Political Behavior* (Columbus, Ohio: Charles E. Merrill, 1971), p. 21.

[34] Using a measure, Spearman's r, which would be 1.00 were both samples to order the values in the identical manner and −1.00 were they oppositely ordered, Floridians very much reflect national terminal values, .97, and only slightly less so instrumental values, .88. The national orderings are recomputed from Tables 3 and 4 in Rokeach, "The Measurement of Values and Value Systems," *op. cit.*, pp. 31 and 32.

[35] Cantril generalized from his data to conclude that 549 million people hope for an improved or decent standard of living and 372 million fear war. Hadley Cantril, *The Pattern of Human Concerns* (New Brunswick, N.J.: Rutgers University Press, 1965), pp. 276–278.

[36] Key, p. 40.

[37] David H. Vomacka, *Attitudinal Constraint in Public Value Types*, unpublished doctoral dissertation, Department of Government, Florida State University, 1970.

[38] M. Brewster Smith, Jerome S. Bruner, and Robert W. White, *Opinions and Personality* (New York: Wiley, 1964), p. 9.

[39] Fred I. Greenstein, *Personality and Politics* (Chicago: Markham Publishing Co., 1969), p. 3.

120   *Public Opinion and Democratic Stability*

[40] Ibid., p. 4.

[41] Smith, Bruner, and White, p. 259.

[42] Ibid., p. 287.

[43] Robert E. Lane, *Political Ideology: Why the American Common Man Believes What He Does* (New York: The Free Press of Glencoe, 1962), p. 16.

[44] Ibid., p. 465.

[45] Robert E. Lane, *Political Thinking and Consciousness* (Chicago: Markham Publishing Co., 1969).

[46] Theodore W. Adorno, Else Frenkel-Brunswik, Daniel J. Levinson, and R. Nevitt Sanford, *The Authoritarian Personality* (New York: Harper, 1950).

[47] Although other traits are frequently cited as elements of the authoritarian personality, Greenstein notes these two properties, authoritarian aggression and authoritarian submission, are the most central traits. See Greenstein, p. 103.

[48] Cited by Greenstein from Theodore W. Adorno, "Freudian Theory and the Pattern of Fascist Propaganda," In Geza Roheim, (ed.) *Psychoanalysis and the Social Sciences* (New York: International Universities Press, 1951), p. 291n.

[49] Greenstein, p. 114.

[50] H. H. Hyman and Paul B. Sheatsley, "The Authoritarian Personality: A Methodological Critique," in Richard Christie and Marie Jahoda, (eds.) *Studies in the Scope and Method of "The Authoritarian Personality"* (Glencoe, Ill.: The Free Press, 1954), pp. 69–123; and Richard Christie, Joan Lavel, and Bernard Seidenberg, "Is the F Scale Reversible?" *Journal of Abnormal and Social Psychology*, 56, 1958, pp. 143–159.

[51] Campbell et al., p. 515.

[52] Greenstein, p. 114.

[53] Milton Rokeach, *The Open and Closed Mind* (New York: Basic Books, Inc., 1960), p. 14.

[54] David C. McClelland, *The Achieving Society* (New York: Van Nostrand Co., 1961).

[55] Greenstein, p. 152.

FIVE

THE LEARNING OF POLITICAL OPINIONS: THE AGENTS OF POLITICAL SOCIALIZATION

According to most views of the matter, the democratic ideal is approached when the government does what the people want. But what happens to the person who consistently finds his positions unsupported by the majority? Suppose we approach this question from the standpoint of the "liberal" who prefers busing children to achieve racial balance in schools, legalization of marijuana, and a repudiation of "immoral" wars like the one fought in Vietnam. If such an individual sees himself in a perpetual minority position, he can blame the public's misplaced values for this state of affairs—most people are "racist," "authoritarian," or "indifferent to human slaughter." More optimistically, he may argue that the people have the proper values but are simply misinformed—they "overestimate the extent of court-ordered busing," they "haven't heard yet that 'pot' is less harmful than alcohol," or they are "unaware of the deaths and devastation our bombs have caused in Vietnam." Similar complaints might be raised by a person at the opposite end of the political spectrum—for example, the "conservative" who sees himself out of step because people do not generally agree with him that it is time to get tougher with the Communist powers, dismantle the federal bureaucracy, and somehow reverse all the forces of social change.

In either case, our minority observer can rationalize his dilemma of supporting democracy when not getting his own way by arguing that an otherwise virtuous public has simply been misled. Complaints about improper influences on the public's values usually focus on the agents of childhood learning. From one side, the education system, or perhaps the American family, is too "permissive." The other side claims that, on the contrary, it is too "authoritarian." Charges of factual misguidance of the public usually center on the mass media ("they present too much—or too little—controversy"), the power of the President as a stingy monopolizer of information, and the sneaky propaganda efforts of assorted "demagogues" and the "special interests."

Although we have deliberately raised the possibilities in what some would say is a hysterical fashion, it is true that an individual's political beliefs are a function of his family upbringing, his education, what he learns or does not learn from the mass media, what the President says, isolated propaganda campaigns, and a variety of other forces that intrude on his life. This chapter focuses on how these forces shape how people think about politics and government—what political scientists call the process of "political socialization." Unfortunately, our review of what social scientists have learned about the influence of the various agents of political socialization cannot directly answer the larger questions raised above—for example, whether our hypothetical liberal or conservative is correct about the influences on public opinion. Instead, the questions social scientists try to answer are the "smaller" ones that can be researched on a factual and hopefully scientific basis. But the accumulation of answers to these questions can give a firmer factual base to anchor one's inferences about what is right or wrong with the state of public opinion today.

THE PRE-ADULT YEARS: THE INFLUENCE OF FAMILY AND SCHOOL

When a person first ventures into the voting booth or makes his first evaluation of a politician's speech, he is not without relevant opinions and biases that temper his impressions and reactions. Although he may be largely powerless in the political arena until he is 18, others around him will seek to shape his values and orientations, many of which will have relevance to his political actions. Before taking his first politically relevant action, he will already possess what Richard Dawson and Kenneth Prewitt call his "political self." This includes, "... his entire complex of orientations regarding his political world, including his views toward his own political role," such as what others expect of him when he takes political actions.[1]

Students of childhood political socialization approach their subject from a variety of perspectives. Dawson and Prewitt present perhaps the most inclusive conceptualization of the field as they argue "adult political behavior is the logical extension of values, knowledge, and identifications formed during childhood and youth."[2] Freud's basic premise that variations in human behavior originate in early childhood experiences undoubtedly underlies this perception of the field.[3] Others see the planting of ideas and values in youth as part of a social process in a continuing society that is essential to the society's stability and survival.[4] Societies, they argue, must see to the training of each new generation of citizens. Of course, if this training results in a total commitment to societally acceptable beliefs, the forces for change and improvement in society would be greatly handicapped. Indeed, one insistent view is that the public schools provide an authoritarian and overly conservative environment that (perhaps unintentionally) trains its inmates improperly for an activist role in a democracy.[5] While the question of the system's dependence on properly socialized citizens and the nature of societally acceptable values and attitudes was the focus in Chapter Four, our initial task here is the description of the development of the child's political learning.

The Development of Children's Political Orientations

A child betrays some initial political awareness at an early age. From a study by Robert Hess and Judith Torney, Table 5-1 traces the early

TABLE 5-1   Children's Party Preferences by Grade in School

Grade Level	N	Republican	Democrat	Some-times Democrat, Some-times Republican	Don't Know Which	Don't Know What Demo-crat and Republican Mean
2	1639	22.4%	13.4%	9.4%	21.1%	33.7%
3	1668	24.8	17.2	10.2	19.8	28.1
4	1738	30.1	19.0	15.0	16.9	19.0
5	1794	30.0	25.2	21.5	14.5	8.8
6	1744	28.2	28.8	26.0	12.6	4.5
7	1715	24.5	31.9	28.6	12.5	2.6
8	1685	20.5	32.5	31.6	13.8	1.6
Teachers	383	19.8	23.8	55.4	1.0	[a]

Source. Robert D. Hess and Judith V. Torney, The Development of Political Attitudes in Children (Chicago: Aldine, 1967), p. 90.
Note.—Item: If you could vote what would you be? Choose one.
[a] No DK alternative.

growth of familiarity with the two major political parties and an early willingness to identify with one or the other. Already by the second grade, 36 percent of the children profess a party orientation. By the fifth grade, 55 percent do so. All but 9 percent of the fifth graders have some understanding of the Democratic and Republican labels, although this familiarity normally means little more than rooting for a presidential candidate.[6] For example, under Republican and Democratic presidents, fewer than 20 percent of third graders have been unable to identify the President's party.[7] Also, after Kennedy's election those children labeling themselves Democrats expressed the greatest happiness with his victory.[8]

While the overall process of politics remains a mystery to them, grade school children do notice the President and view him as a benevolent leader, particularly when he is of their parents' political party. Quite apparently, the early meaning of government for children centers on people rather than ideas, and the government *is* the President. By the eighth grade, however, more abstract institutions of government, such as Congress and the right to vote, begin to define the meaning of government.[9] (See Figure 5-1.) But even for eighth graders, the President remains the government agent "who helps you and your family most."[10]

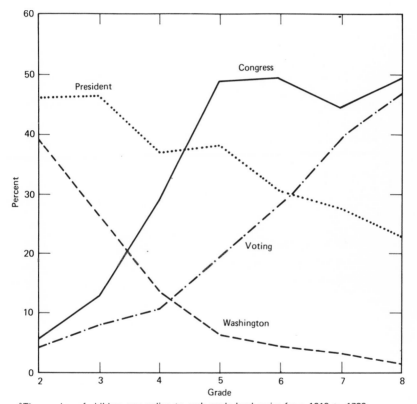

^aThe number of children responding to each grade level varies from 1619 to 1789.

Figure 5-1. Development of a cognitive image of government: the four dominant symbolic associations. (*Source.* David Easton and Jack Dennis, *Children and the Political System: Origins of Political Legitimacy* (New York: McGraw-Hill, 1968), p. 115.)

Throughout the grade school years, the evolution of children's attitudes toward government is one of growing respect for the tasks undertaken by the President and the government, but declining expectations that officials are trustworthy and virtuous men who would be concerned with one's personal problems. Figure 5-2 depicts the erosion of the expectation of presidential benevolence and Figure

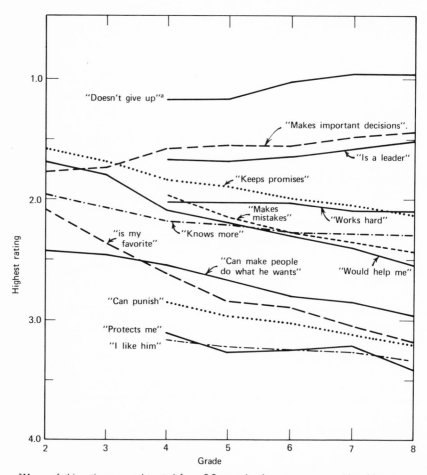

aMeans of this rating were subtracted from 6.0 to make them more comparable with the rest.

Figure 5-2. Mean ratings of the President on thirteen attributes by grade. (*Source.* David Easton and Jack Dennis, *Children and the Political System: Origins of Political Legitimacy* (New York: McGraw-Hill, 1968), p. 178.

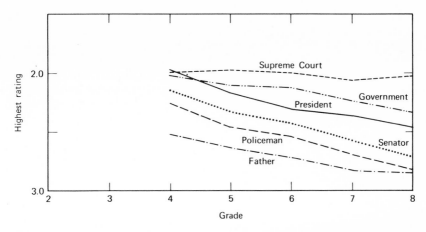

Figure 5-3. Mean rating by grade on "makes few mistakes" for father, senator, policeman, government, Supreme Court, and President. (*Source.* David Easton and Jack Dennis, *Children and the Political System: Origins of Political Legitimacy* (New York: McGraw-Hill, 1968), p. 263.)

5-3 shows the parallel trend in the development of attitudes toward other governmental agencies. This atrophy coincides with a growing acceptance of the citizen's active responsibility to be involved in government. Table 5-2 shows that through the grade school years emphasis on *passive* citizenship (helping others and obeying laws) is displaced by greater support for voting and especially taking an interest in the way the country is run. The child also becomes confident that he will be able to cope successfully with unvirtuous officials by engaging in the act of voting.[11]

During this period, the child also learns the "civics book" norm of not always voting for the same political party but, instead, for the "best man." Forty-nine percent of Hess and Torney's fourth graders say a good citizen would join a political party and vote for its candidates rather than vote for the best man. But only 26 percent of the eighth graders agree. Thirteen percent of their teachers take this position, indicating the strong consensus in civics education against party voting.[12]

The positive view of government that children first acquire becomes less positive, but remains quite favorable, as the child grows older. David Easton and Jack Dennis find 72 percent of fourth graders willing to say that the President rarely or almost never makes mistakes, a figure that only drops to 51 percent of eighth graders. Throughout the early grades, most children will say that

TABLE 5-2 **Changes by Grade in Perception of Qualities of the Good Citizen**[a]

Someone Who:

Grade Level	N	Works Hard	Every-body Likes Him	Votes and Gets Others to Vote	Helps Others	Interested in Way Country is Run	Always Obeys Laws	Goes to Church	Don't Know "Citizen"
4	1719	13.5%	7.0%	26.4%	47.8%	28.2%	44.3%	23.6%	2.0%
5	1780	11.3	8.5	29.8	42.1	41.8	32.0	20.6	.6
6	1736	10.7	9.0	35.8	35.4	50.5	37.4	16.0	.6
7	1710	11.1	8.3	35.9	34.2	57.7	32.7	14.6	.2
8	1674	10.0	8.1	44.6	26.3	65.0	29.0	11.8	.7
Teachers	392	7.9	3.6	51.5	31.6	72.4	22.4	3.8	2.3

Source. Robert D. Hess and Judith V. Torney, *The Development of Political Attitudes in Children* (Chicago: Aldine, 1967), p. 37.

Notes.—Item: If the President came to your town to give prizes to the two grownups who were the best citizens, which grownups would he choose? Put an X beside [the pictures of] the two he would choose as the best citizens.
[a] Percentages do not always sum to 200 per cent for any given grade because some children chose only one alternative or chose "I don't know."

the President would almost always or always help them if they needed him, and that he works harder than most people.[13] For the child, government is what David Sears calls the "benevolent monolith"—not too different from his father or other persons with authority in his life.[14] These sentiments often take the course of disapproval of societal disagreement since across all the elementary grades better than 80 percent agree that "the government usually knows what is best for the people",[15] and their definition of democracy seldom includes the right to criticize the government (this definition peaks at only 54 percent of eighth graders).[16] As we note in Chapter Four, many theorists see such open acceptance of government and intolerance for dissent as dangerous to political stability. Perhaps people who continue to hold such attitudes into adulthood are incompletely socialized, with a stoppage to their political attitude development occurring in the elementary school years.

The major spurt in a child's political learning usually comes during his early adolescence. An important aspect of this growth is the ability to grasp the abstraction of community interest apart from self-interest. Joseph Adelson and Robert O'Neil find that ideas such as community and society are beyond the grasp of fifth graders—but not ninth graders.[17] When asked about the purpose of vaccinations, income tax, and public education the younger children see only individual or personal implications. For example, 70 percent of the fifth graders see the purpose of vaccination to be the personal avoidance of illness and only 23 percent mention the community interest of avoiding epidemics. Ninth graders, however, exclusively see the community purpose. The biggest change comes between grades seven and nine.

Similar growth patterns are found in other aspects of political development. For example, Herbert Hyman finds ninth graders to approach the adult level of opinionation on policy issues.[18] Hess and Torney find that the eighth grade represented a plateau level at which point students' orientations toward government and politics closely approximated their teachers' and changes little thereafter.[19] Similarly, Richard Merelman notes little change in students' sense of political efficacy after the ninth grade.[20] All of this suggests that the 13-year-old is almost as much a political man as he will become. Armed with the party identification he typically borrows from his parents, a sense of civic duty, and a positive orientation remaining from his early impressions of political actors, he changes little thereafter.

Much of what we know about the political orientations of high school students comes from M. Kent Jennings and Richard Niemi's study of a national sample of high school seniors and their parents, conducted in 1965.[21] If one subscribes to the view that the model citizen should be politically active yet trusting, tolerant, and supportive of major ongoing social changes, these high school seniors matched—or by some measures exceeded—the average adult level of "development" in political socialization. When asked to describe the traits of good citizenship, the seniors opted for an active, participant orientation or, to a lesser extent, the prescription of passive political loyalty instead of the nonpolitical roles that were more often suggested by their parents (for example, helping others, going to church, and working hard). Compared to their parents, the students (in 1965) also displayed a lesser amount of "political cynicism" in their questionnaire responses. The students also were 10 to 14 percentage points more approving of the "official" policies of opposition to school prayer and support for racial integration of the schools. By similar margins, the students were slightly more tolerant or libertarian than their parents—for example, more in favor of allowing a Communist to hold public office and allowing an antireligious speaker to have his say.

Yet high school students were somewhat less politically aware than their parents—by such measures as their awareness of party differences, the degree to which they followed public affairs, and the extent to which they monitored the news media. This finding is not surprising, since studies have shown that both political awareness and participation increase throughout adulthood, perhaps peaking in middle age.[22] Young adults who do not attend college score particularly low in tests of political awareness and participation, including the act of voting.[23] Thus, upon the verge of high school graduation, the soon-to-be adult has come a long way in his development as a potential political participant but still has a bit farther to go.

The Agents of Childhood Socialization

Having traced the development of an individual's political attitudes through the preadult years, let us try to sort out the agents most responsible for this development. The family seems the most predominant source of preadult opinions, but not an exclusive one. Schools certainly make an effort to indoctrinate children, and it seems unlikely that the effort is totally unsuccessful. Other possible agents or early political socialization include the mass media and childhood friends, but these have received less attention from scholars.

The Family

Party identification is one political attitude that is learned primarily within the family, since schools generally do not teach their pupils

TABLE 5-3   **Parent and Child Agreement in Party Identification**

	Child		
Parents	Democrat	Independent	Republican
Democrat	33%	13%	4%
Independent	7	13	4
Republican	3	10	14

$N = 1852$

Source. M. Kent Jennings and Richard G. Niemi, "The Transmission of Political Values from Parent to Child," *American Political Science Review*, 62 (March, 1968), p. 173.

to be Democrats or Republicans. Jennings and Niemi find (see Table 5-3) that most high school seniors share the identification of their parents. Only seven percent hold a party identification opposite from their parents. Notably, 92 percent correctly identify the presidential choice of their parents, and 71 percent can correctly identify their parents' party identification, with the mistaken students usually identifying with the party they *perceive* to be their parents'.

Naturally, a person becomes more likely to reject his parents' party identification after he leaves the parental home and enters adulthood. Indeed, the older the adult, the less able one is to predict his party identification from the reported party leanings of his parents when he had been growing up.[24] But even in national adult samples, about two-thirds of those who can recall their family's party leanings during their childhood continue to identify with the parental political party while only about 10 percent "defect" to the opposition. The remainder end up as "independents."[25]

The transmission of party identification from one generation to the next is an important source of the stability of the American two-party system. If people were to orient themselves politically without the anchorage of a parental influence, the basic division of the nation's partisan loyalties would be subject to considerable flux, as in France. In France, most adults are not even able to state what their parents' partisan leanings had been when they were growing up, which suggests that politics is not a frequent topic of discussion in the French home. As a result, the French have less stable party identifications than citizens of other democracies. This has the further consequence of reinforcing the tendency of French parties to rise or fall in popularity with great suddenness.[26] In the United States, the vast majority of adults can identify their parents' party leanings, and there is no reason to suspect that this awareness will not continue. But, as we will see in the next chapter, the infrequent

The Pre-Adult Years: The Influence of Family and School   **131**

partisan realignments of American voters in the United States are periods when an unusually high number of young adults reject their parental partisan heritage.

Transmission of political values from one generation to the next is far less complete once we leave the realms of party identification and voter choice. As Table 5-4 shows, there are only weak correla-

TABLE 5-4 **Correspondence between Parents' and Children's Opinion on Politically Relevant Opinions**

Presidential choice in 1964	.59
Party identification	.47
Federal Government's role in integrating the schools	.34
Whether schools should be allowed to use prayers	.29
Legally elected Communist should be allowed to take office	.13
Speakers against churches and religions should be allowed	.05
Warmth toward	
Catholics	.28
Southerners	.22
Labor Unions	.22
Negroes	.20
Jews	.18
Whites	.19
Protestants	.13
Big business	.08
Cynicism	.12
Cosmopolitanism-localism	.17

Source. M. Kent Jennings and Richard G. Niemi, "Transmission of Political Values from Parent to Child," *American Political Science Review,* 62 (March, 1968), pp. 172, 175, 176, 178, and 179.

tions between the attitudes of parents and their high school children regarding policy issues, groups, political activity, and political cynicism. For comparison, Jennings and Niemi note that this pattern of unsuccessful transmission of opinion between parents and children does not apply in the choice of religious domination, since 74 percent of their seniors share the church affiliation of their parents.[27] Considering the literature on the parents' imparting of political values and opinions on their offspring, Sears concludes that "in general, it would appear that only a few political and social attitudes are expressed in sufficiently vivid form in the average American family to be adopted by the children."[28]

School

While it is plausible that the child learns most of his political orientations from observing his parents or talking to them about politics, the schools also have great access to the minds of children. The school's greatest political role is in the child's gradual learning about government and the citizen role expected of him. Figure 5-4 presents the answers of the teachers in Hess and Torney's socialization study. Even in the second grade, 65 percent of the teach-

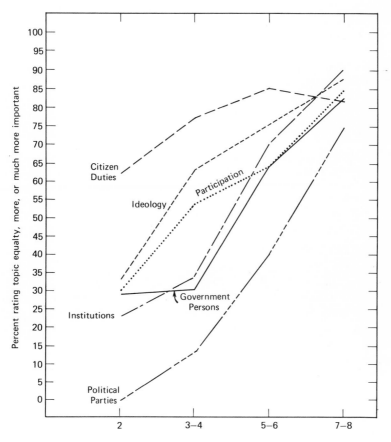

Figure 5-4. Comparison of teachers of different grade levels in view that political topics are at least as important as other subjects taught in their classrooms. (*Source.* Robert D. Hess and Judith V. Torney, *The Development of Political Attitudes in Children* (Chicago: Aldine, 1967), 109.)

ers claim to give as much attention to citizen duties as they do to reading and arithmetic. Much additional political material receives at least equal attention from many of the teachers, particularly in the later grades. Hess and Torney find that children's beliefs about government and citizenship from the second grade to the eighth grade evolve toward those of the teachers.[29] This pattern, they argue, indicates that "the school stands out as the central salient, and dominant force in the political socialization of young children."[30] But children are also affected by other agents of socialization as well— each intent on making them secure and adultlike. The teachers' opinions, to some substantial degree, represent those of all adults. Thus the convergence of student and teacher opinion may not represent the unique impact of teachers or the schools but of all socializers. The children themselves show little consciousness of any major political impact from the schools since no more than two percent ever mention the teacher as a source of advice on candidate choice. Fifty-eight percent in the fourth grade would rely on their parents for such advice. Although only 27 percent of the eighth graders give the same response, this decline in parental guidance reflects greater self-reliance than dependence on the teacher.[31]

If teachers do play a major socializing role, the most relevant teachers to examine may be social science teachers in the later grades. Social science teachers do appear to be somewhat politically different from the general population. After studying the political attitudes of the social studies teachers to whom their sample of seniors were exposed, M. Kent Jennings, Les Ehman, and Richard Niemi conclude that social science:[32]

"Teachers and parents strongly resemble each other only in the domains of party identification and intensity. Teachers are undoubtedly more politically trusting (not cynical) than parents, in some respects more efficacious, have more cosmopolitan political interests, stress the active, political side of citizenship behavior more, take somewhat more liberal stands on political issues, are more knowledgeable about the party system, and employ the printed media to a greater extent."

But the same authors find that teachers have an appreciable effect on student political thinking only when their views also coincide with those of the students' parents. Moreover, efforts to measure the impact of taking high school "civics"—the one course which specifically centers on political matters—disclose little or no evidence of change in political attitudes or awareness, except among students from culturally deprived backgrounds.[33] Perhaps, only drastic and innovative changes in school format and curriculum can give public schools more than a minimum political impact on their clients.

The Mass Media

Little is known about the impact of the mass media on childhood political socialization. For some reason, the frequently expressed concern about the impact of television violence on children results in little parallel concern about television's impact on childrens' political attitudes. We do not know, for example, whether the often comic portrayal of "cops" and other government agents in television cartoons decreases a child's expectation that the policeman or even the President can cope with real-life problems. In summarizing the limited studies of the impact of mass media on preadult political opinions, Merelman asserts that the media can affect levels of interest and involvement in politics but has no important effect on political opinions.[34] This is an area where the conventional wisdom strongly suggests the importance of an agent, but no reliable evidence exists.

Childhood Peer Groups

The political influence of a child's friends or "peer group" also remains rather unassessed. We do know that as children advance toward adulthood, they report more frequently that they talk politics with friends of the same age, suggesting that some peer group influence may be operating.[35] But, despite James Coleman's influential study of peer groups among adolescents[36] and the great wealth of research on a group's ability to enforce conformity on its members, no study has documented peer group influence in early political socialization. The low salience of politics and the great consistency in political opinion experienced by a child may make the effects on him of his peer group indistinguishable from the effects of his parents, schools, community, and media. The peer groups, too, may be inculcating the "establishment" point of view in the politics area. Indeed, Kenneth Langton finds evidence of peer influence only among lower-class Jamaican children who are involved in mixed social class peer groups. In time such children adopt the middle class political values of their peers.[37] Although disentangling the unique effects of a child's peers on his political opinions is most difficult, it seems unlikely that they will have much effect—not because they lack the capacity to affect their members but because they deviate little from the opinions being stressed by other agents of political socialization.

Yet the frequent suggestion that a new "youth culture" is brewing among American young people, including those of high school age, implies that peer groups are becoming important political socializers during adolescence. To explore the question of whether high school youths hold different values than their parents, we administered Rokeach's value scale (previously described in Chapter Four) to a sample of Florida high schoolers in order to compare their responses to those of an adult sample in the same state. One might expect youth to differ from previous generations by rejecting the Protestant work ethic, characterized by such values as family security and a comfortable life (although true adherents to the work ethic forego present enjoyment of a comfortable life for future enjoyment of an even more comfortable life). The essence of the new youth culture, by contrast, would seem to be respect for and love of others with maximum freedom to be oneself. Values and goals that pit one man against another are to be rejected.

Of course, vast differences in the hypothesized direction did not emerge from the responses. Indeed, the average ranking of the values were quite similar for students and adults (correlated at .86 on the terminal values and .71 on the instrumentals). But the values that are viewed most differently by parents and youth do follow the suggested pattern. Table 5-5 shows the values on which the adults and

TABLE 5-5 **Difference of 10 Percent or Greater in Stressing Different Values Between Adults and High School Students**

Students Give Greater Stress		Students Give Less Stress	
Value	Percentage Difference	Value	Percentage Difference
Freedom	22	Family security	26
Loving	16	Self-respect	17
Equality	14	Sense of accomplishment	15
World at peace	10	Capable	13
True friendship	10	Responsible	10
Exciting life	10	Ambitious	10

students differ most. Although one must interpret the data cautiously, the attributes of the new youth culture can be read into these differences. Interpersonal warmth is represented by the students' greater preference of "loving" and "true friendship," and the freedom from societal encumbrances is manifested in the higher student ratings for "freedom," "equality," and "world at peace." Although the youth culture notion of being true to oneself is not manifested by strong student support for "responsibility" or "self-respect" (possibly because these values are seen as internalized tools for social control), the values the youth reject more than their parents do tend to be those of the work ethic. Thus some change is apparent between high school youth and the previous generation, but not as great as some might expect. Of course, we cannot even be certain that these intergeneration differences would not have shown up if the test were administered in an earlier era—or that peer influence is responsible. Most studies of the political implications of a possible youth culture focus on college students—the group we turn to next.

THE POLITICAL IMPACT OF HIGHER EDUCATION

Today, almost 1 of every 2 high school graduates goes on to college. At the turn of the century most young people did not even graduate from high school, let alone contemplate attaining a college degree. Thus the proportion of the adult population with college experience has been rising steadily. For example, over the short time span from 1948 to 1968 the proportion with at least some college rose from 15 percent to 28 percent; the proportion with actual college degrees rose from 7 percent to 13 percent.[38] The trend will undoubtedly accelerate, as a lagged result of the post-World War II education boom, so that "the electorate of 1970 should look positively uninstructed by comparison with that of the year 2000."[39]

What are the political implications of the growth of the college-educated public? Although college students today are decidedly more liberal than the general population, this has not always been the case. As recently as 1960, Republican presidential candidates generally ran better in campus straw polls than in the actual elections. Despite such indicators, the college experience was generally regarded as a liberalizing one even before the upsurge in campus political activism beginning in the late 1960s. Even though college students may have been no more politically liberal than the general population, they presumably were to the political left of their upper-income parents. Evidence in support of this view is that in studies going back into the 1920s, college *seniors* were consistently found to be less conservative than entering freshmen.[40] Recent evidence that students move farther to the left as they increase their exposure to the liberal and college environment is shown in Table 5-6. Similarly, both today and in the past, college students frequently see themselves more to the political left of their parents than to the right.[41]

Of course, the political impact of the college experience will vary with the particular campus environment, or that segment of it to which the student is most exposed. For example, selection of a major in one of the social sciences exposes students to greater awareness of social problems and to the more politically liberal segment of the

TABLE 5-6   Ideological Self-Placement of College Students, by Year in
School, Late 1971 (in Percent)

	Far Left, Left	Middle-of-Road	Right, Far Right	Can't Say
Freshmen	28	56	14	2
Sophomores	31	52	15	2
Juniors	41	43	14	2
Seniors	40	46	9	5
Graduate students	63	24	11	2
All students	35	49	13	3

Source. *Gallup Opinion Index*, February 1972, p. 7.

faculty. But it is not clear whether or not one's college major generally influences one's attitudes—the reverse causal sequence is more evident.[42] Studies of older college graduates who left their campus environment prior to the recent upsurge of campus political activity possess the kinds of political attitudes typical of the institutions they attended—those who attended the relatively liberal "prestige" schools are more liberal today than the bulk of the college graduates who obtained degrees from ordinary institutions. For example, in 1964, prestige school graduates opposed Goldwater's conservative presidential candidacy at a higher rate than the general public, despite their generally Republican identification.[43] Graduates from elite schools are also unusually prone to oppose the Vietnam war, support civil rights, and prefer the "liberal" ideological label.[44] The remaining majority of college graduates who did not attend prestige schools maintain the political views typical of their higher socioeconomic group—generally conservative, but still (perhaps indicating the modest impact of their education) relatively liberal on matters of civil liberties and race relations and internationalist in foreign policy.

Although college students are more politically liberal today than their campus predecessors in generations past, the skimpiness of relevant survey data makes it difficult to draw the precise trend line. By 1961, a presumably representative sample of the campus population described itself as being on the political left rather than the right (60 percent versus 33 percent).[45] More recent Harris and Gallup surveys of college students from the late 1960s into the 1970s show a consistent ideological preference for the left over the right, typically like the distribution shown in Table 5-6. In the late 1960s, college students had become increasingly opposed to the Vietnam war,

TABLE 5-7   Shifting Self-Ratings as Vietnam "Doves" or "Hawks", 1967-1969 College Students and the Adult Public (in Percent)

	College Students		Adults	
	Dove	Hawk	Dove	Hawk
1967	35	49	35	52
1969	69	20	55	31

Source. Gallup Opinion Index.
1967 surveys were in spring (students) and December (general population); both 1969 surveys were in November.

although at a rate that only slightly exceeded that of the general population (see Table 5-7). Nixon's invasion of Cambodia in 1970 caused a further spurt of campus opposition not found in the general population. After the event, only 22 percent were willing to rate Nixon's presidential performance as "good" or "excellent." Fifty-nine percent gave him a rating of "poor". One year before, a campus majority had approved of Nixon's performance.[46] In 1970, most adults still did. The biggest change has been in the proportion of students who tell survey researchers that they have participated in demonstrations. According to Harris the demonstration rate increased from 29 percent in 1965 to 60 percent in 1970.[47] Except perhaps in the peculiarly silent 1950s, a small minority of students had always been active in what were considered "radical" causes at the time.[48] The frequency of such behavior by college students had increased dramatically in the late 1960s and the 1970s, keyed, of course, by revulsion again the Vietnam war.

Of course, the extent of student radicalism and liberalism should not be overdrawn. The overwhelming majority of college students see themselves to the political left of their parents and, of course, most are. But students appear to overestimate the extent to which the counterculture has taken hold. At least this would appear to be the inference from the interesting finding that students overestimate the extent of marijuana use among themselves. Sixty-five percent of one student sample guessed that a majority of students had tried marijuana, yet less than a third of the same sample told the interviewers (or were willing to do so) that they themselves had tried it.[49] Perhaps perceptions of student political radicalism are similarly distorted. When asked their political opinions, college students betray the same ambivalence characteristic of the general population—the distribution of their responses will vary greatly with the question

The Political Impact of Higher Education   **139**

wording. After the Kent State killings, Harris's sample of college students divided equally in assigning blame for campus violence between the authorities and the demonstrators.[50] But twice as many students told *Playboy* interviewers that the Kent State deaths were "attributable to the Nixon Administration's hostile attitude toward dissent" than said the students were at fault.[51] In a different vein, one study found a majority of college students in agreement, that "basically, this is a racist nation," but another study found only 16 percent denying that equal rights for minority groups could be achieved within our present form of government.[52]

Although the majority of students will not always give the "radical" answer to any question a pollster asks them, there does exist something of a gulf between the political opinions of college students and even noncollege youth. For example, using a scale based on responses to numerous political questions, a Yankelovich study for CBS found that 71 percent of noncollege youth but only 48 percent of college youth could be classified as "moderates" or "conservatives."[53] (The remaining categories were "reformers," "radical dissenters" and a few "revolutionaries.")

The impact of the college experience cannot account for all of this difference, as the least conservative adolescents are the ones who most frequently enter college.[54] Similarly, whether a particular college student will express leftist viewpoints or engage in protest behavior depends largely on the predispositions that the student brings with him. For example, although student demonstrations have been most frequent at the larger and more prestigious schools, it is the more liberal students who seek out these places. At least in the early stages of the student movement, student radicals were drawn most heavily from upper-middle-class homes where the parents were highly educated themselves and supportive of liberal political values.[55] Kenneth Keniston offers the interesting conclusion that where the father is supportive of the student's leftist leanings, the probability that the student will actively engage in radical behavior is enhanced, but when this parental support is missing, the radical student's alienation is more likely to produce withdrawal from society rather than political activism.[56] Evidently, radical students are more likely to have been raised in homes with "permissive" child-rearing practices, but there is reason to doubt a direct causal connection.[57]

Generalizations about the characteristics of student activists are beginning to lose some of their force as the radical student movement expands its base to include students who previously would not have belonged. But Seymour Martin Lipset suggests that the expansion of the student movement may actually be slow in comparison with the growth of earlier social movements.[58]

"Most radical movements, when new and small, tend to find their first recruits and supporters among the relatively more well-to-do and better educated, even though their program may be oriented to the manifest interests of the less privileged, and undereducated. The latter lack the psychic security and ability to work toward long-term goals which the former possess to a greater degree. When such movements grow, however, they usually secure the backing of the population groups who are quite different from the earlier members. It may, therefore, be argued that what is unusual about the growth of the American student movement is not that it has spread into diverse and less privileged student strata, but that it has done it so slowly—that the original associations between relatively privileged backgrounds and leftist commitment persist for so long."

At present, we cannot say for sure whether the relatively leftist political climate on college campuses will increase, or even that it will not be replaced by a genuine mood of political quiescence and conservatism. Whatever the case, a relevant question is whether or not current college students will lose their left-of-center views once they depart the college campus. The long-run implications of this question are obvious. If students become more conservative as they grow older, the liberalizing impact of higher education will be limited to the college generation of the moment. But if liberal students will retain their views in later life, then each graduating class will add to the cumulative totals of educated "liberals" within the general population. Relevant to this inquiry is the persistent finding that differences in attitudes among education levels decline with age.[59] Typical is the pattern shown in Table 5-8. One might interpret this table to mean that college-educated people gradually drift toward the conservatism of the rest of the population as the effects of their education wear off. But there is a case for a much different explanation that does not depend on a drift toward conservatism in the latter stage of the life cycle. The greater conservatism of older well-educated people may have resulted from the greater conservatism of their campus environment when they obtained their education. In other words, each successive college generation may be more liberal than those before it. There is indirect support for this view from the sketchy findings from the few panel studies that have followed college graduates in later life: over time, college graduates do not express more conservative views and may actually tend to drift in a liberal direction.[60] Although far from a sufficient amount of evidence, it appears that an increase in the "liberalizing" effect of higher education, plus the increase in the number of young people who go to college may portend an acceleration of the rate at which public opinion moves leftward.

TABLE 5-8   Views on Student Protest, by Education and Age (Percent Sympathetic to Student Protests)

Education	Age						Total[a]
	Under 25	25-34	35-44	45-54	55-64	65 and Over	
High school graduate or less	29	23	23	22	26	19	23
Some college or more	68	51	49	38	23	29	46
Total[b]	40	32	31	26	25	20	

Source. John L. Spaeth, "Public Reactions to College Student Protests," *Sociology of Education*, 42 (Spring, 1969), p. 204.
[a] Includes no answer on age.
[b] Includes no answer on education.

THE IMPACT OF THE MASS MEDIA

For some people who are disturbed by the course of certain political trends, the mass media and the people who run them are a convenient set of scapegoats. Certain perceived faults in how the public is thinking would disappear if the media would stop "biasing" the news, and public preoccupation with annoying governmental and societal problems would change in the desired direction if the news media would only give them different emphasis. These kinds of charges have come from both the political right and left. For example, an occasional book is published charging that the television networks are biased in a liberal direction or that they favor Democratic candidates, or alternatively, the reverse—that the network bias is in the conservative or Republican direction.[61] Newspapers are often criticized because of the obvious Republican leanings of their editorial pages; but in 1964, the Republican presidential candidate complained that he was not given a fair shake by the American press. Similarly, the content of what the media cover is often under fire from both ideological directions. While at one time the television networks were smarting from FCC chairman Newton Minnow's charge that TV was a "vast wasteland" with timid and limited news coverage of controversial topics, they have more recently been reeling from Vice-President Agnew's charge that the network news programs give too much coverage and respect to the views of those who find fault instead of what is good about America.

In an obvious but also limited sense, these kinds of charges are true. If the news media were to give more coverage to the topics we (or you) want and treat them in the way we (or you) desire, then the public would be influenced to think more like us. But this comment only serves to recognize the potential power of the news media to mold opinions. People in the communications trade feel the weight of the responsibility to report the news "objectively," while social scientists and mass communications researchers have the difficult chore of measuring bias and estimating its effect on public opinion.

Do Newspapers "Bias" Public Opinion?

The newspaper business in America has changed considerably over the years. In the 19th century, a town big enough to have a daily newspaper usually had more than one[62]—including at least one highly partisan Republican paper and one with an equally partisan Democratic leaning. This situation allowed the newspaper consumer to choose from among a diverse but hardly objective array of information sources. Over time, however, the number of publishing newspapers has dwindled, so that today no more than three percent of American cities with publishing newspapers have more than one newspaper under separate ownerships.[63] With this consolidation and with increased reliance upon wire services for newspaper copy, the bias to newspaper coverage—particularly of national and world events—has declined. Thus the choice of the newspaper consumer has decreased, while the "objectivity" of the product has increased. Beyond its local news coverage, the content of the typical newspaper reader's home town paper is much like that of the newspaper in the next town down the road. Of course there do exist unique and important exceptions—certain "prestige" newspapers with reputations for unusually good coverage of national and world events. National political and business leaders pay close attention to the prestige papers (most notably *The New York Times* and *The Washington Post*). People in the lower echelons of newspaper journalism also pay close attention to the prestige papers as a source of cues. One might wonder (although there has apparently been no research on this) whether people who reside in cities where a local newspaper has an unusually good reputation for thorough coverage (for example, St. Louis, Louisville, Milwaukee) are any more "enlightened" regarding political events than their less-fortunate brethren in other places.

There has been much speculation about the impact of the conservative and pro-Republican newspaper editorials on public opinion. An indicator of the ideological and partisan bias of newspapers is that in most presidential elections of modern times, American newspapers have endorsed the Republican candidate over his Democratic opponent by margins of greater than 3 to 1. Yet this distortion has limits, since the number of normally Republican papers that rejected Goldwater's extremely conservative candidacy in 1964 was sufficient to create a fairly even balance of Republican and Democratic endorsements that year.[64] The normal Republican tendency of the editorial page should not be surprising, since the publishers who determine editorial policy are wealthy businessmen who tend to reflect the ideology of their local business community in their own thinking. Also, major advertisers can influence editorial content threatening to withdraw their ads and the money they bring in if editorial policy does not suit them. A side benefit of the growth of local newspaper monopolies has been the decline of this form of pressure, however, since advertisers are reluctant to withdraw their ads from the only newspaper in town.

Does a newspaper's editorial stance influence the political opinions of its readers? Since editorials are not the most frequently read sections of newspapers, one might doubt the extent of direct influence. Newspapers usually magnify the extent of their editorial "bias" by presenting the reader with the writings of syndicated columnists who share the publisher's editorial stance. For example, Table 5-9

TABLE 5-9   **The 1959 Columnist Balance of Normally Republican Newspapers and Presidential Endorsements, 1964**[a]

	Columnist Ideological Balance			
Endorsement	Very Conservative	Conservative	Moderately Conservative	Moderately Liberal
Johnson	0%	27%	71%	100%
Goldwater	100	73	29	0
	100%	100%	100%	100%
N =	(6)	(22)	(21)	(8)

[a] Observations represent the summed characteristics of cities' newspapers. Where endorsements are neutral or divided, the city is omitted. For details, see footnotes 65 and 72.

shows that the political tendency of a normally Republican newspaper's columnists in 1959 was a good predictor of its presidential endorsements in 1964. Only those Republican papers with the least conservative columnists endorsed Johnson over Goldwater in 1964.[65]

There is some evidence, however, that newspapers are beginning to present more ideologically balanced arrays of columnists.[66] Although not all studies of the subject show the same thing, a newspaper's partisan leanings sometimes spill over (in moderate amounts) from the editorial page into the news columns.[67] This rule also appears to apply to coverage of issues. For example, a study of how Kentucky newspapers treated Medicare in 1962 (when it barely failed congressional passage) showed that the amount and bias of the news coverage of Medicare was strongly related to the newspaper's editorial stand on the issue.[68] At the same time, editors' attempts to guide news coverage into alignment with editorial policy appear to be decreasing. For example, from the late 1930s to the early 1960s, there was a decline in the rate at which Washington correspondents reported that their home newspapers killed or modified their stories.[69]

To some extent, the effect of conservative editorial opinion and its accompanying news bias is counteracted by the liberal Democratic tendency among working newspaper journalists. For example, Washington reporters—certainly a key group influencing what gets printed in the news pages—are predominantly Democratic in their partisan viewpoint.[70] Limited evidence also suggests that the editorial "gatekeepers" who make the day-to-day decisions regarding what news gets in their paper share the same partisan tendency.[71]

The failure of many Republican newspapers to endorse Goldwater in 1964 provides an unusual opportunity to estimate the impact of newspaper presidential endorsements. The very number of such papers allows us to compare the voting responses of their communities with the responses where the local paper did stick to their partisan tradition and support Goldwater. Table 5-10 shows the results of such an analysis. Counties with Johnson-endorsing papers (but previously Republican) and counties with Goldwater-endorsing papers were matched by geographic proximity and similar voting in the 1960 presidential election. In 17 out of 18 cases (the details are not shown for lack of space), the 1960–1964 Democratic vote gain was greatest in the county where the paper endorsed Johnson, with an average difference of 6 percent of the two-party vote.[72] Apparently, a publisher's decision to support Johnson over Goldwater (traceable, as we saw, to the paper's columnist leanings in 1959) added, on the average, about six percentage points to Johnson's local vote total. Inferentially, it would seem that the *normal* Republican trend of the press is worth at least a couple of percentage points to the Republican party nationwide. Humphrey might have defeated Nixon in 1968, for example, with a more equitable division of newspaper endorsements between the two major party candidates.

TABLE 5-10   Relationship between the 1964 Presidential Endorsement of Normally Republican Newspapers and the 1960-1964 Vote Shift in the County of Publication: Based on a Matching of Counties According to their 1960 Vote and Geographic Proximity[a]

Mean	Percent Democratic, of Two-Party Presidential Vote			
	1960	1964	Change	Number of Cases
Johnson endorsement	43.2%	61.8%	+18.6%	(18)
Goldwater endorsement	44.3	56.7	+12.4	(18)
Difference	− 1.1	+ 5.1	+ 6.2	

[a] For details of the county selection, see footnote 72.

For lower offices, the impact of newspaper endorsements is unclear, although one might expect that a newspaper would be more not less influential below the presidential level. Regarding local elections and issues, the content of newspaper coverage is often deemed crucial, although face-to-face communications are sometimes thought to neutralize the media impact on the most controversial issues.[73] Especially when the election is nonpartisan or involves an extremely long ballot, the newspaper's decision regarding what to report and who to endorse can be very important. As one newsman reportedly once said, "you can't tell the players without a scorecard, and we sell the scorecards."[74] Although studies show that newspapers have good success at endorsing local candidates who win,[75] this can be partially attributable to newspapers' endorsements of candidates who look like winners rather than any influence of the paper on the electoral decision. But statistical analyses of long-ballot elections suggest that the kind of election where voter confusion is maximum, newspaper support is the major key to victory.[76]

Does TV News "Bias" Public Opinion?

The vigor of the familiar debate over whether television stimulates violent behavior is an indicator of both the importance of television as a socializing agent and the difficulty of assessing its effects. Although it is generally assumed that television reporters are more politically "liberal" than the general public,[77] TV coverage is attacked in equal amounts from people to the political right and the political left, and appears to be scrupulously nonpartisan in a way that newspapers are not. When television journalists do make their values known, the impact may be slight. For example, even though the television coverage of the violence outside the Democrats' 1968 convention was clearly sympathetic to the demonstrators, polls showed that the public overwhelmingly sided with the police who were beating up the demonstrators.[78]

The more thoughtful critics of television news coverage are concerned more with what television treats as news than with any discovered bias in how they treat it. Since the typical 30 minute network news show would take no more than one page of *The New York Times* if it were set into print,[79] the obvious need for abbreviated news presentation places television in the role of the most important of news gatekeepers—deciding which subjects are newsworthy and which ones are not. Table 5-11 presents a comparison of how Amer-

TABLE 5-11 **Changing Issue Priorities of the American Public, 1965-1970**

Problem (in Order of Change in Concern)	1965	1970	Change
Reducing pollution of air and water	17%	53%	+36%
Reducing the amount of crime	41	56	+15
Improving housing, clearing slums	21	27	+ 6
Beautifying America	3	5	+ 2
Helping people in poor areas	32	30	− 2
Reducing racial discrimination	29	25	− 4
Improving highway safety	18	13	− 5
Conquering "killer diseases"	37	29	− 8
Reducing unemployment	35	25	−10
Improving public education	45	31	−14

Source. Gallup Opinion Index, June 1970, p. 8.
Question: Which Three of These National Problems Would You Like to See the Government Devote Most of its Attention in the Next Year or Two?

icans ranked certain problems in importance in 1965 with how they rated them in 1970. The most obvious change is a sharp increase in concern about pollution. One might wonder whether this change would have happened if the networks had not begun to publicize the urgent pleas of environmentalists. Conversely, would not present concern about the environment be greater if even more news about the environmental crisis were presented by the networks? One study of network news coverage over a two-month period in 1969 found that only one percent of the news items dealt with the topics of population and birth control, world hunger, pollution, and conservation.[80] By contrast, over three times as much news about accidents was broadcast over this time period.

Because people in the communications industry must be trend conscious, they naturally accelerate the pace of the acceptance of new ideas and new terminology, even if the process is an unwitting one. For example, television (and the other media) were responsible for the quick substitution of the word "black" for "Negro"—a shift that occurred even though as recently as 1970, polls showed most blacks preferred the word "Negro" or even "colored." Leo Bogart explains how the media fostered the change.[81]

"To the militant minority, the word 'Negro' carried a bitter historical burden which had to be cast off in the search for a proud new identity. This minority was concentrated within the spirited elements of urban youth who were not only more assertive and visible than their elders in contacts with authority, but also more likely to supply the Negro newsmen whom big city newspapers, television networks, and magazine were belatedly eager to recruit. White media practitioners in many instances fell in line with the terminology preferred by their own young Negro reporters, either in ignorance of what the Negro majority preferred or out of indifference to the whole matter. And since the term 'black' was daily reiterated by white reporters in the newscasts and in the press, it was also adopted by Negro publications, and entered the consciousness and usage of those to whom the term applied."

Constant coverage of a topic improves public knowledge about it. For example, the public was much more informed about previous presidential assassinations immediately after the killing of President Kennedy than it was a few months later.[82]

Public Perceptions of Media Bias

On November 13, 1969, in a speech in Des Moines carried by all three television networks in prime time. Vice President Agnew charged that the networks had been misusing their "vast power" by their "querulous criticism" of the Nixon administration. "Perhaps it is time," he said (and to some appeared to threaten), "that the networks were made more responsive to the views of the nation."[83] Shortly thereafter, Agnew extended his criticism to the printed media as well. A poll conducted for ABC shortly after the Des Moines speech found 51 percent agreeing with Agnew that the networks had been biasing the news, and only 33 percent disagreeing.[84] Lou Harris found the public to vote 2 to 1 that Agnew "was right to criticize the way TV networks cover the news."[85]

Pluralities in the Gallup poll agreed that both television and newspapers "tend to favor one side" rather than "deal fairly with both sides."[86] Mail streaming into the networks and their affiliates was even more one-sided, although the volume of mail to NBC was less than they received after the cancellation of "Star Trek."[87]

Were these signals valid indicators of public dissatisfaction with the way its news media presented the news? Apparently the pro-Agnew response was a combination of strong enthusiasm from a vocal minority and superficial acquiescence on the part of poll respondents, who, everything else being equal, like to support, a Vice President. Two years after Agnew's initial broadside against the media, antimedia responses in polls returned to their previous low levels, as a 1971 Roper survey disclosed when it asked its national sample the question, "Do you think television *is* fair or is *not* fair about showing different points of view?"[88]

Fair	69%
Not fair, too much to the left	7
Not fair, too much to the right	2
Not fair, too much conventional middle of the road opinion	6
Not fair, other or no elaboration	6
Don't know or no answer	10
	100%

Depending on one's view of media objectivity, figures such as these can be interpreted either as reassurance or as an indication that the public is being fooled.

The Impact of Television on Politics

The introduction of television into American homes in the late 1940s has caused people's media consumption to shift away from newspapers and other printed material. For example, since 1944 newspapers have actually declined in per capita circulation.[89] Even if we examine the trend since 1959, when almost all American homes already had TV sets, television has overtaken newspapers as the predominant news source for most people (see Table 5-12). Table 5-12 also shows that television has been increasing its lead over newspapers as the most believable information source. Still, on a given day, more people read a newspaper than watch television news. Moreover, newspapers predominate as the most valued news source among the most educated. Although newspaper reading rises with each step up the education ladder, watching television news does

TABLE 5-12   **The Public's View of Television and Newspapers, 1959-1971**

Source of Most News[a]	1959	1963	1967	1971
Both television and newspapers	25%	24%	30%	22%
Television but not newspapers	25	31	33	38
Newspapers but not television	31	29	25	26
Other media only	17	13	10	13
Don't know, no answer	1	3	2	1
Most believable[b]				
Television	29%	36%	41%	49%
Newspapers	32	24	24	20
Other media	22	22	15	19
Don't know, no answer	17	18	20	12

Source. "An Extended View of Public Attitudes Toward Television and Other Mass Media, 1959–1971", a report by the Roper Organization to Television Information Office, adapted from tables on pp. 2, 3.

[a] "First, I'd like to ask you where you usually get most of your news about what is going on in the world today—from newspapers or radio or television or magazines or talking to people or where?"

[b] "If you got conflicting or different reports of the same news story from radio, television, the magazines and the newspapers, which of the four versions would you be most inclined to believe—the one on radio or television or magazines or newspapers?"

not. For example, the 20 percent (in 1969) who regularly watch network news shows are disproportionately drawn from both education extremes—the early dropouts and the college educated.[90] For the least educated, frequent television watching is a typical pattern, while the highly educated watch the news to supplement what they learn from other media.

One might suppose that television has politicized the kinds of people who previously were not very politically involved. For example, at the time, many attributed the slight rise in the voting rate in 1952—the first television election—to the role of TV. But a careful comparison of turnout rates in areas that received television in 1952 with the turnout rates in places without TV reception showed that this popular hunch was untrue.[91] William Glaser's ingenious analysis of survey data reinforces the conclusion that television has not stimulated voter turnout; people who rely on television for their campaign information do not vote more frequently than predicted from their preelection intentions, although people who follow the campaign in newspapers do.[92] Some have argued that since the people who pay the closest attention to new information—and are best equipped to understand it—tend to be the ones who originally are most knowledgable on the subject, television has increased knowledge most among those already informed, thus actually increasing the knowledge gap between the informed and the uninformed public. Some indirect evidence has been gathered in support of this proposition.[93]

Although television may have little influence on general political awareness, its impact is heightened during campaign periods. Television has had its clearest impact in changing the nature of political campaigning. As Angus Campbell notes, with television "the public finds it easier to form an image of its leaders than it did through the older media."[94] Since television has made candidate personality a more important electoral factor than it was in the past,[95] campaign strategists now devote considerable time to the development of their candidate's TV image. When television first became a convenient medium for campaigning, campaign strategists often simply televised their candidate's speeches. They quickly learned, however, to exploit the shorter, more superficial "spot announcement" that gains the attention of the noninvolved viewer and, when longer messages are called for, artful montages of film clips showing the dynamic candidate at work.[96]

The technological sophistication demanded to run a television-oriented campaign has spawned an entire new industry of campaign managers who specialize in hiring themselves out to political clients. Their work includes polling research and evaluation, advising (or telling) the candidate what changes they should make in their appearance or issue stands, calculation of the proper mix of media exposure, and the creation of the media advertisements.[97]

The effects of this change—to which some apply the ambiguous "new politics" label—are several: first, it has taken campaigning out of the hands of the party professionals and put it in the hands of television image makers. Second, television ads during campaigns do undoubtedly cause a greater number of voters to stray from their normal partisan loyalties when they vote. Third, greater emphasis than before is placed on the image potential of possible candidates when the party leaders make their selection.[98] Finally, and perhaps most important, the costs of campaigning have leaped dramatically—total campaign spending (for all offices) more than doubled over the short time span from 1952 to 1968.[99]

The greatest danger of the new politics would appear to be the potential for the artificial creation of political leaders who meet the needs of candidate imagery rather than the needs of the offices they must fill. There are obvious limits to the ability of the image makers to bamboozle the public, however, if for no other reason than that the odds on the victory of the candidate who spends the most money on television or the one who hires the most highly touted set of campaign specialists are not that great. A look at the record of 1970 outcomes of gubernatorial and senatorial contests should make this clear. In the 32 senatorial contests (excluding those won by independents) the candidate who spent the most money on radio and television advertising won in only 56 percent of the cases. The victory rate of the 34 gubernatorial high spenders was only slightly greater—59 percent.[100] The record of the nine best-known media advisors in 1970 is also unimpressive. Excluding the several elections where their clients competed against each other, their record in statewide contests was an undistinguished eight wins and 12 losses.[101] Of course, how these figures should be interpreted is not exactly clear. As one astute image maker, Joseph Napolitan explained his losses, "the favorites very seldom come to us."[102] But one might also suspect that the favorite normally would be the most able to obtain the big campaign war chest necessary for a media campaign.

Although the results cannot be regarded as conclusive, the most rigorous study to date of the relationship between media spending and the vote finds that in 1970 House and Senate elections, "the winner's share of total broadcast expenditures had a significant positive effect on his margin of victory."[103] Media campaigns seem most effective in primary elections where name recognition is most important. Napolitan reports the instance where his candidate in a senatorial primary race was behind 2 to 1 the day before his 30-minute "documentary" ad was simulcast on all local channels, but led 55 to 45 the day after.[104] Even though the effective packaging of an otherwise undistinguished candidate probably does win an occasional election, political campaigning is still an art rather than a science. For example, there is no scientific way to translate poll data into a formula that tells the politician exactly what to do and say in order to win his election. Some systematic evaluation of what campaign techniques are most effective under varying circumstances is possible, yet little has been done. In the meantime, campaign consultants think they know what wins elections from what they did in previous victories, with each outfit having a unique formula. The important point is that many politicians apparently believe that candidates can be sold like toothpaste. As Robert MacNeil states,[105]

"Broadcasters and advertising men have a vested interest in demonstrating the power of their methods. Politicians, who are creatures of fashion, have found their claims irresistible. The new politics have captured most of the men who feel impelled to guide the large destinies of the states and the nation. No one has yet proved that the methods are not effective, and the candidates are paying heavily for their faith."

Mediating Media Impact: The Role of Interpersonal Communications

In trying to assess the impact of the mass media on public opinion, one should not have the image of the media consumer absorbing the media messages in isolation from others. Talking about politics with others is one source of political communications that modifies the effect of media transmission. The effect of talking about politics can either magnify or diminish the effect of mass media messages, depending on the circumstances. For example, a media campaign may have an indirect effect on the voting decision of a voter who manages to ignore it because the person decides how to vote after obtaining advice from someone who was attentive. On the other hand, a person who receives a message directly via the mass media that is discrepant with his voting predisposition can eliminate the resultant dissonance via discussion with others. Research regarding the role of personal influence on political opinions has focused on the characteristics of opinion leaders—those who say they have advised and/or been asked for their opinion. The fact that political opinion leaders are more politically informed than the average (as are those they talk to) suggests that their conversations generally magnify the net impact of the media's political messages.[106] The possibilities are limited, however, since people tend to talk about politics with people of similar political persuasion. Yet, the more a person talks about politics, the more likely he is to talk to people with opposite beliefs. Of particular importance is the finding that opinion leaders are highly represented among the electorally crucial "split-ticket" voters (at least in midterm elections),[107] while advice takers tend to be the late deciders. Because of the two-step flow of political communications from generally informed opinion leaders to followers, the influence of the informed public on the flow of public opinion is greater than their numbers would indicate. Unexplainably, however, research on this important process has virtually stopped since its initial discovery in the early voting studies.

PRESIDENTIAL LEADERSHIP

Because of the prestige of his office, the President has, potentially, more power to lead public opinion than any other individual or institution. Simply by taking his case to the people, a popular President supposedly can command broad support for his legislative program. One such incident apparently was President Johnson's appeal for a new Civil Rights Law enacted in 1964 to give Americans of all races equal access to public accommodations such as hotels and restaurants. Between June 1963 (during Kennedy's administration) and January 1964, public support for the proposed law rose from a slim plurality (49 to 42) in favor to a commanding majority of 61 to 31—a shift far greater than normally occurs over a seven month period on a controversial, emotional issue.[108] If Johnson's plea was responsible for this opinion shift, it was reinforced by the special circumstances of a new president pleading for enactment of the program of a martyred president. Other than this example, one can find little evidence that public support for domestic policy proposals rises and falls with the momentary public enthusiasm of the President. Although the absence of sufficient poll data relevant to this question may be partially responsible for this conclusion, another reason is that in domestic policy, the President is viewed as a partisan figure, representing unique constituencies rather than the public at large. In one well-documented instance, a well-publicized presidential proposal was followed by decreasing public support and congressional rejection. This was Roosevelt's short-lived effort in 1938 to expand the size of the Supreme Court in order to dilute the power of its then conservative majority.[109]

Presidential leadership in shaping the political opinions of Americans is greatest on matters of foreign policy—an area of limited public knowledge and interest. Insufficiently informed to guide foreign policy decisions, the public puts its faith in presidential leadership, on the seemingly sensible grounds that the President is better equipped than the people to make rational foreign policy decisions. As Seymour Lipset once put it, "the opinion data indicate that national policymakers, particularly the President, have an almost free hand to pursue any policy they think correct and get public support for it," for the reason that the public agrees on "certain larger objectives . . . and find it necessary to trust the judgment of national leaders as to what is possible given these purposes."[110]

Evidence from polls offers strong support for this general rule. For example, a sample of Detroit residents made the following selection between two alternatives regarding public versus presidential leadership in foreign policy.[111]

"The President is an inspired leader; he has ideas of his
own how to help the country. He should be able to make
the people and Congress work along with him."   52%
"It is up to the people through their Congressman to find
solutions to the problems of the day. The President
should stick to carrying out what the people and Congress
have decided."   40%
Combination or don't know   9%
                                                                    ──────
                                                                      100%

Seventy-five percent of the same sample, polled in the mid-1960s, agreed that if he felt it necessary, the President should send troops somewhere abroad where "fighting is breaking out" even if he knows "that most Americans are opposed to sending our troops there." The public will also give conditional support for unpopular soft-line action if the President decides it is the course to be taken. In polls taken in the mid-1960s, the proportion favoring mainland China's admission to the U.N. would substantially increase if respondents were asked what they would think if "the president suggested" it, or that "it would improve U.S.-China relations."[112] The fact that public attitudes toward China softened considerably once the President decided the time had come for a thaw confirms the role of presidential leadership in shaping the public's opinion toward China. If President Nixon had followed the public opinion polls in strict fashion, he would never have tried to open relations with China, and his popularity would not have increased the way it did following his China trip. Of course the public's previous response of verbal belligerence toward China was also a result of official policy at the time.

Public acquiescence to presidential decisions can be seen from simple comparisons of opinion before and after presidential decisions. Vietnam episodes provide several examples. Immediately prior to President Nixon's decision to send troops to Cambodia, only seven percent favored sending troops while 59 percent rejected such a step. After the President's speech explaining the new committment to enter Cambodia, 50 percent told the Harris poll that the President was right to send troops and only 43 percent said "no."[113] Each time the President stepped *down* the military action, public support for the particular policy in question increased also. For example, support for a bombing halt increased from 40 percent to 64 percent once President Johnson announced such a policy in 1968.[114] To take an example related to the same problem but at a different point in time, in repeated surveys in *1953–1954,* national samples voted almost 2 to 1 for sending ground troops to Indochina, if it appeared the French would lose control to the Communists.[115] President Eisenhower's failure to follow this expression of public opinion by sending troops did not hurt his popularity in the slightest.

Foreign policy crises are followed by upsurges in the public's rate of approval of the President's performance. By this index, Truman gained 9 points when he decided to resist the Communist invasion in South Korea, Eisenhower gained 8 points following the 1956 Suez crisis, and Kennedy gained 13 points following the 1962 Cuban missile crisis. More recent examples show boosts in popularity for Johnson after the Dominican Republic crisis (1965) and for Nixon after the Cambodia invasion (1970). Even crisis events that seem to reflect badly on the President's decision-making prowess normally produce upsurges of presidential popularity. Eisenhower gained following the U-2 incident and summit collapse in 1960 as did Kennedy after the Bay of Pigs invasion of 1961.[116]

As the case of Vietnam suggests, there are obvious limits to the President's ability to mobilize popular support for his foreign policy actions. What are these limits? The public reactions to both the Korean and the Vietnam Wars suggest that, whatever the short-term public reaction to presidential actions, the public becomes increasingly unwilling to support land wars fought to ambiguous conclusions over the long run. At the beginning of both the Korean and Vietnam adventures, the public did give the President broad latitude to act within the broad guidelines of combating Communist aggression while avoiding a larger war. But as the wars went on, presidents got boxed in by what they saw, perhaps incorrectly, as the possibility of even greater public opposition if they stepped outside the apparent in limits of decisionmaking latitude—either by stepping up the war drastically or ending it in apparent defeat. Johnson and Truman both suffered marked declines in popularity as the wars in Korea and Vietnam went on under their administrations. (Nixon avoided as great a decline in approval only because his stated goal was the withdrawal of troops—but at a slower rate than the majority was willing to support.) In Truman's case, the greatest decline in his popularity occurred following his firing of the popular battlefield leader, General Douglas MacArthur. The vast majority of Americans sided with MacArthur over Truman, and consequently registered disapproval of Truman's administration for the remainder of his term.[117] Johnson's greatest descent in the popularity polls was a seven point drop after the Viet Cong's Tet offensive in the winter of 1968 provided the necessary feedback to the public to belie the official optimism. Both turning points illustrate sources of the limits of presidential ability to command support in the foreign policy sphere. Truman's case illustrated that a president who is already low in the popularity polls cannot gain support by decisions as unpopular as the firing of a popular general. Johnson's decline shows that a president cannot register support indefinitely for a war effort that the overwhelming evidence from news reports shows to be going badly. In each case, the loss of public confidence limited the President's options severely, so that new changes in policy could not have induced the normal public acceptance. For example, it is generally assumed that Truman could not have gotten away with ending the Korean War on the same terms that Eisenhower did shortly after taking over the presidency. Similarly, perhaps if he wanted to, Nixon could have ended the Vietnam war on almost any terms immediately upon his takeover of the presidency.

PRESSURE GROUP LEADERSHIP

Propaganda efforts by organized pressure groups can be considered as one possible source of occasional change in mass opinion. The pressure groups with a large mass membership base, such as labor unions, place the greatest emphasis on public relations as a technique for influencing legislative and administrative action.[118] The public relations efforts of labor unions are largely aimed at influencing the opinions and voting behavior of its members. The success of these efforts are only limited, but still visible. For example, Table 5-13 shows that in the 1950s, rank and file AFL-CIO members were

TABLE 5-13 Opinions of Respondents in White-Collar and Blue-Collar Households with and without Union Members on Taft-Hartley Issue

	White-Collar[a]		Blue-Collar	
Opinion	Union[b]	Nonunion	Union	Nonunion
Repeal or change prolabor	23%	12%	29%	10%
Leave as is or change promanagement	20	20	12	9
Change, NA how	22	25	18	9
No opinion	35	43	41	72
	100%	100%	100%	100%
N	60	413	333	292

Source. V. O. Key, Jr., *Public Opinion and American Democracy* (New York: Knopf, 1961), p. 509.
[a] That is, the head of the household of the respondent was white-collar: professional, business, or clerical.
[b] The respondent falls in the union column if he or some other member of the household belongs to a union.

more opposed to the Taft-Hartley Act than their nonunionized counterparts of the same occupational class. On the other hand, most union members either did not support their union's views on Taft-Hartley, or failed to offer an opinion on this issue that stimulated such strong concern from union leadership. Union leaders also stimulate some influence on the *voting* behavior of its members. The best study of union influence on its members' voting finds that union members are about 20 percent more likely to vote Democratic than their nonunion counterparts in similar life situations.[119]

Since most pressure groups do not have a large mass membership, their efforts to indoctrinate their members cannot affect the mass opinion distribution very much even if their indoctrination efforts are entirely successful. However, ordinary pressure groups often spend vast amounts of money to influence the opinion of the general public. Such efforts hold the greatest promise of immediate rewards to the group when the public affects policy *directly* via referendum. Since public opinion is largely inert on an issue at the time it is put to a referendum, the propaganda effort of interested pressure groups is of sometimes great importance in deciding the outcome. For example, fluoridation referenda often go down to defeat, even though most people favor fluoridated water at times when it is not a "hot" issue in their community. Largely responsible for fluoridation defeats are the fear-exploiting propaganda of the antifluoridation forces, which overcome the more "establishment-oriented" propaganda from the other side. Facing a referendum decision on fluoridation, the previously uninvolved voter may ask a friend for the pros and cons and be told that one side says fluordiation minimizes tooth decay, while the other side says it causes unanticipated medical hazards and, besides, may be the first step toward the poisoning of our water supply by the Communists. Not being able to sort out the credibility of the arguments, our voter will assign them equal weight and go for the one that promises the least risk.[120]

The frequent and important referenda on pollution control show the effectiveness of fear-invoking propaganda, only this time emanating from the business groups that are fearful of stricter controls. When the issue is control of pollution, the propaganda antidote that can sometimes reverse public opinion is the exploitation of fear about lost jobs and, perhaps, higher prices.[121]

Not all propaganda efforts are successful however, as sometimes the intended audience manages to avoid the message entirely. Or the effort may backfire by alerting the intended audience to the issue without winning it to the intended side of the issue. For example, one recent study suggests that propaganda efforts in favor of school bond issues actually has the unintended consequence of provoking a stronger antibond issue vote.[122]

Organized propaganda efforts are not limited to referenda alone, since a pressure group may try to influence mass opinion in the hope that a change will influence the outcome of a legislative issue in its desired direction. Nationally, the past activity of the American Medical Association to reverse public support for Medicare proposals is the most visible example. Provoked by President Truman's proposal for a national health care program, the AMA launched a campaign to label it "socialized medicine." The AMA propaganda machine went to work once again in attempt to overturn public support for

President Kennedy's Medicare program, suggesting that the benefits from a private plan would be better. Although it cannot be proven, AMA propaganda may have been responsible for the temporary erosion of public support for Medicare during 1962:[123]

	Prefers Medicare	Prefers Private Plan	No Opinion
March 1962	55%	34%	11%
May 1962	48	41	11
July 1962	44	40	16

Although Medicare narrowly failed congressional passage in 1962, it was voted into law three years later despite further opposition by the AMA.

Scholarly observers generally agree that except when the public is alerted by its responsibility to vote in a referendum, pressure group activity is of little consequence in the shaping of mass opinion. As V. O. Key observes:

"The broad conception of pressure groups as activators of general public opinion which in turn softens up government seldom conforms with the reality. . . . The scale of operation necessary to have substantial impact on public opinion is beyond the resources of most groups. They may reach selected groups of political activists through one channel or another with considerable effect, but by and large their lone efforts to mold mass opinion must be of small consequence."[124]

The impact of pressure groups on policy, which is often considerable, does not rest with the success of propaganda efforts except for the possibility of an indirect effect when policy makers mistakenly measure the success of pressure group propaganda by its volume.

FOOTNOTES FOR CHAPTER 5

[1] Richard E. Dawson and Kenneth Prewitt, *Political Socialization* (Boston: Little Brown, 1969), p. 17.

[2] Dawson and Prewitt, p. 205.

[3] Richard M. Merelman, "The Adolescence of Political Socialization," *Sociology of Education*, 45 (Spring, 1972), p. 135.

[4] David Easton and Jack Dennis, *Children and the Political System: Origins of Political Legitimacy* (New York: McGraw-Hill, 1968), p. 9.

[5] Harmon Zeigler and Wayne Peak, "The Political Functions of the Education System," *Sociology of Education*, 43 (1970), pp. 115–142.

[6] Robert D. Hess and Judith V. Torney, *The Development of Political Attitudes in Children* (Chicago: Aldine, 1967), p. 81.

[7] Hess and Torney, p. 278.

[8] Hess and Torney, p. 210.

[9] Easton and Dennis, p. 116. They also conclude that since definitions centering on the picture of the Capitol increase at the expense of the pictures of Presidents Washington and Kennedy, the children are seeing law making as the central aspect of government, instead of law enforcement. This conclusion is unwarranted. These two sets of pictures differ not only in terms of the branch of government pictured but also whether a personality or an institution is pictured. It is equally likely that the children are moving from personalities to institutions in their definitions of government. Unfortunately, the researchers failed to show a picture of the White House or of a recognizable personality in Congress which would have permitted discriminating among these alternative conclusions.

[10] Easton and Dennis, p. 146.

[11] While only 16 percent of third graders score as politically efficacious—that they can affect changes in government, 54 percent of the eighth graders do so. David Easton and Jack Dennis, "The Child's Acquisition of Regime Norms: Political Efficacy," American Political Science Review, 61 (March, 1967), pp. 25–38.

[12] Hess and Torney, p. 84.

[13] Easton and Dennis, pp. 179–181.

[14] David O. Sears, "Political Behavior," in Gardner Lindzey and Elliot Aronson (eds.) Vol. 5, Handbook of Social Psychology (Reading: Addison-Wesley, 1969), p. 415.

[15] Easton and Dennis, p. 130.

[16] Hess and Torney, p. 66.

[17] Joseph Adelson and Robert P. O'Neil, "Growth of Political Ideas in Adolescence: The Sense of Community," Journal of Personality and Social Psychology, 4 (July, 1966), pp. 295–306.

[18] Herbert Hyman, Political Socialization (Glencoe: The Free Press, 1959), p. 59. See also the additional studies reviewed in Hyman's Chapter 5.

[19] Hess and Torney, p. 220.

[20] Richard M. Merelman, Political Socialization and Educational Climates (New York: Holt, 1971), Ch. 4.

[21] M. Kent Jennings and Richard G. Niemi, "The Transmission of Political Values from Parent to Child," American Political Science Review, 62 (March, 1968), pp. 169–184; M. Kent Jennings and Richard G. Niemi, "Patterns of Political Learning," Harvard Education Review, 38 (1968).

[22] Norval D. Glenn, "The Distribution of Political Knowledge in the United States," in Dan D. Nimmo and Charles M. Bonjean (eds.), Political Attitudes and Public Opinion (New York: David McKay, 1972), pp. 273–283; Don D. Smith, " 'Dark Areas of Ignorance' Revisited: Current Knowledge About Asian Affairs," Social Science Quarterly, 51 (December, 1970); Norval D. Glenn and Michael Grimes, "Aging, Voting, and Political Interest," American Sociological Review, 33 (August, 1968), pp. 563–575.

[23] Philip E. Converse and Richard Niemi, "Non-Voting Among Adults in the United States," in William J. Crotty, Donald E. Freeman, and Douglas S. Gatlin (eds.), Political Parties and Political Behavior, 2nd ed. (Boston: Allyn and Bacon, 1971), pp. 443–466; Louis M. Seagull, "The Youth Vote and Change in American Politics," The Annals (Spring, 1971), pp. 88–96.

[24] Bernard Berelson, et al., Voting (Chicago: University of Chicago Press, 1954), p. 89.

[25] It should be regarded that the transmission of party identification from one

generation to the next is far from complete. Only about 60 percent of national samples report that their parents had both been Republicans or both Democrats. The others can't recall, or report a parental conflict, that one or both were Independents, had been apolitical or were not citizens during the respondent's childhood. Adding these cases to those who clearly defect from their parental identification leaves only about one-half of the public for whom intergeneration transmittal may be inferred.

[26] Philip E. Converse, and Georges Dupeux, "Politicalization of the Electorate in France and the United States," Public Opinion Quarterly, 26 (Spring, 1962); Philip E. Converse, "Of Time and Partisan Stability," Comparative Political Studies, 2 (July, 1969), pp. 139–171.

[27] Jennings and Niemi, "The Transmission . . . ," p. 179.

[28] Sears, p. 381.

[29] Hess and Torney, pp. 200–202.

[30] Hess and Torney, p. 219.

[31] Hess and Torney, p. 86.

[32] M. Kent Jennings, Les H. Ehman, and Richard G. Niemi, "Social Studies Teachers and Their Pupils," unpublished paper.

[33] Kenneth P. Langton and M. Kent Jennings, "Political Socialization and the High School Civics Curriculum in the United States," American Political Science Review, 62 (September, 1968), pp. 852–877; Edgar Litt, "Civic Education, Community Norms, and Political Indoctrination," American Sociological Review, 28 (February, 1963), pp. 69–75.

[34] Merelman, "The Adolescence . . . ," p. 151.

[35] Hyman, p. 101; Hess and Torney, p. 71.

[36] James S. Coleman, The Adolescent Society (New York: The Free Press of Glencoe, 1961).

[37] Kenneth Langton, Political Socialization (New York: Oxford, 1969), p. 130.

[38] Extrapolated from Figure 4 in Philip E. Converse, "Change in the American Electorate," in Angus Campbell and Philip E. Converse (eds.), The Human Meaning of Social Change (New York: Russell Sage Foundation, 1972), p. 324.

[39] Ibid., p. 323.

[40] See the summary of the extensive literature on this point in Kenneth Feldman and Theodore M. Newcomb, The Impact of College on Students (San Francisco: Jossey-Bass, 1969), Vol. 2, pp. 16–24 and 49–56.

[41] Russell Middleton and Snell Putney, "Student Rebellion Against Parental Political Beliefs," Social Forces, 41 (May, 1963)́, pp. 377–383; Seymour Martin Lipset, Rebellion in the University (Boston: Little Brown, 1971), p. 84.

[42] Lipset, p. 82.

[43] Philip E. Converse, "Social Cleavages in the 1964 Election," in Crotty, Freeman, and Gatlin, op. cit., pp. 438–442.

[44] Ibid.; Milton Rosenberg, Sidney Verba, and Philip E. Converse, Vietnam and the Silent Majority (New York: Harper and Row, 1970), pp. 54–65.

[45] Middleton and Putney, p. 381.

[46] This shift of the campus mood is documented in Lipset, op. cit., pp. 44–45.

[47] Ibid., p. 45.

[48] For an informative account of student radicalism going back to the 1920s, see Ibid., pp. 159–196.

[49] Gilbert Marketing Group, February 1970 Omnibus Youth Survey, Tables 20A and 27A—cited in Ibid., p. 72.

[50] Ibid., p. 59.

[51] "Playboy Student Survey," Playboy, 17 (September, 1970), p. 184.

[52] Lipset, pp. 56–57.

[53] Ibid., p. 48.

[54] Langton, p. 18; Campbell, p. 65.

[55] Richard Flacks, "Who Protests: The Social Bases of the Student Movement," in Julian Foster and Durwood Long (eds.), Protest: Student Activism in America (New York: Morrow, 1970), pp. 147–152.

[56] Kenneth Keniston, "Notes on Young Radicals," Change, 1 (November-December, 1969), pp. 31–32.

[57] Lipset, pp. 102–104.

[58] Ibid., p. 87.

[59] Campbell, pp. 54–67; Norval D. Glenn, "The Trend in Differences in Attitude and Behavior by Education Level," Sociology of Education, 39 (Summer, 1966), pp. 255–275; Samuel Stouffer, Communism, Conformity, and Civil Liberties (New York: Doubleday, 1955); John L. Spaeth, "Public Reactions to College Student Protests," Sociology of Education, 42 (Spring, 1969), pp. 199–206.

[60] Erland Nelson, "Persistence of Attitudes of College Students Fourteen Years Later," Psychological Monographs, 68 (1954); Andrew M. Greeley and Joe L. Spaeth, "Political Change Among College Alumni," Sociology of Education, 43 (1970), pp. 106–113.

[61] Two recent examples are (from the left), Robert Cirino, Don't Blame the People (Los Angeles: Diversity Press, 1971), and (from the right) Edith Efron, The News Twisters (Los Angeles: Nash Publishers, 1971).

[62] Ben H. Bagdikian, The Information Machine (New York: Harper and Row, 1971), p. 137.

[63] Raymond B. Nixon and Jean Ward, "Trends in Newspaper Ownership," Journalism Quarterly, 38 (Winter, 1961), pp. 3–12.

[64] Newspaper endorsement data for particular presidential elections can be obtained from the polls of newspaper opinion reported during each presidential campaign by the trade journal Editor and Publisher.

[65] The observations of Table 5-9 are cities where newspapers are published rather than the newspapers themselves. For details of the sample, see footnote 72. Columnists were scored according to a rating scale devised by Ben H. Bagdikian, "How Newspapers Use Columnists," Columbia Journalism Review, 2 (Fall, 1964), pp. 20–24. When a county contained more than one newspaper, their average columnist score was obtained. Columnist data was secured from Press Intelligence Directory (Washington: Press Intelligence, Inc., 1961). Not all newspapers in the potential county pool could be scored.

[66] Ben H. Bagdikian, "How Editors Pick Columnists," Columbia Journalism Review, 5 (1966), p. 41.

[67] According to one review of studies of "biased" news coverage, the reported bias was in the direction of the newspaper's partisan leanings in 78 out of 81 cases. See Ben H. Bagdikian, "The Politics of American Newspapers," Columbia Journalism Review, 10 (March/April 1972), pp. 9–10.

[68] Lewis Donohew, "Newspaper Gatekeepers and Forces in the News Channel," Public Opinion Quarterly, 31 (Spring, 1967), pp. 61–68.

[69] William L. Rivers, The Opinion Makers (Boston: Beacon Press, 1965), pp. 174–178.

[70] Ibid., p. 78.

162   The Learning of Political Opinions

71 Bagdikian, *The Information Machine*, p. 108.

72 The matched counties were drawn from a pool of northern counties where newspapers published in the major city accounted for at least two-thirds of the county's newspaper circulation and reached at least two-thirds of the county households. Newspaper endorsement data was obtained from *Editor and Publishers* polls, supplemented by results of a postcard questionnaire sent to editor's who did not respond. Where the 1960 endorsement of a Goldwater-endorsing paper is unknown, it is assumed to be Republican. The matched counties were within the same state, and within at least eight percentage points of each other in their 1960 presidential two-party vote. No counties were matched if the largest city in one was more than three times as populous as the largest city in the other. Table 5-10 is part of a larger investigation of the influence of newspaper endorsements, in preparation.

73 James S. Coleman, *Community Conflict* (Glencoe: The Free Press, 1957), p. 24.

74 Edward C. Banfield and James Q. Wilson, *City Politics* (New York: Vintage Books, 1963), p. 159.

75 James E. Gregg, "Newspaper Editorial Endorsements and California Elections, 1948–1962," *Journalism Quarterly, 62* (1965), pp. 534–536; Reo M. Christenson, "The Power of the Press: The Case of the *Toledo Blade*," *Midwest Journal of Political Science, 3* (1959), pp. 230–239.

76 John E. Mueller, "Choosing Among 133 Candidates," *Public Opinion Quarterly, 34* (Fall, 1970), pp. 395–402; Michael Hooper, "Party and Newspaper Endorsement as Predictors of Voter Choice," *Journalism Quarterly, 43* (Summer, 1969), pp. 302–305.

77 Rivers, *op. cit.*

78 John P. Robinson, "Public Reaction to Political Protest," *Public Opinion Quarterly, 34* (Spring, 1970), pp. 1–9.

79 Robert MacNeil, *The People Machine* (New York: Harper and Row, 1968), p. 40.

80 Cirino, p. 40.

81 Leo Bogart, *Silent Politics* (New York: Wiley, 1972), p. 69.

82 Serena Wade and William Schramm, "The Mass Media as a Source of Knowledge," *Public Opinion Quarterly, 33* (Summer, 1969), p. 208.

83 Marvin Barrett (ed.), *Survey of Broadcast Journalism 1969–1970* (New York: Grossett and Dunlap, 1970), pp. 31–32.

84 Ibid., p. 33.

85 Hazel Gaudet Erskine, "The Polls: Opinion of the News Media," *Public Opinion Quarterly 34* (Winter, 1970–1971), p. 638.

86 Ibid., pp. 636, 637.

87 Barrett, *op. cit.*, p.32.

88 "An Extended View of Public Attitudes Toward Television and Other Mass Media, 1959–1971," A Report by The Roper Organization to Television Information Office, pp. 13–14.

89 Bagdikian, *The Information Machine*, p. 54.

90 John P. Robinson, "The Audience for National T. V. News Programs," *Public Opinion Quarterly, 35* (Fall, 1971), pp. 403–405.

91 Herbert A. Simon and Frederick Stern, "The Effect of Television on Voting Behavior in the 1952 Presidential Election," *American Political Science Review, 49* (June, 1955), pp. 10–13.

92 William A. Glaser, "Television and Voting Turnout," *Public Opinion Quarterly, 29* (Spring, 1965), pp. 71–86.

[93] P. J. Tichener, G. A. Donohue, and C. N. Olien, "Mass Media Flow and the Differential Growth of Knowledge," *Public Opinion Quarterly, 34* (Summer, 1970), pp. 159–170.

[94] Angus Campbell, "Has Television Reshaped Politics?" *Columbia Journalism Review 1* (Fall, 1962), p. 12.

[95] Over time, the rate at which people have voted against their partisan leanings has increased, with the biggest difference between the 19th century and the present. Converse argues that the growth of the mass media (with the introduction of TV accentuating the process) has been responsible for raising the public awareness of campaign issues to the information level necessary to allow an occasional vote against one's party leanings. See Philip E. Converse, "Information Flow and the Stability of Partisan Attitudes," *Public Opinion Quarterly, 26* (Winter, 1962), pp. 598–599.

[96] Harold Mendelsohn and Irving Crespi, *Polls, Television, and the New Politics* (Scranton: Chandler, 1970), pp. 247–317.

[97] Dan Nimmo, *The Political Persuaders* (Englewood Cliffs: Prentice-Hall, 1970), pp. 34–162.

[98] Mendelsohn and Crespi, pp. 297–298.

[99] Herbert Alexander, "Financing Parties in Campaigns in 1968," in William J. Crotty, et al. (eds.), *Political Parties and Political Behavior,* 2nd ed. (Boston: Allyn and Bacon, 1971), p. 316.

[100] Expenditure data was obtained from Federal Communications Commission, *Survey of Political Broadcasting* (Washington: Federal Communications Commission, 1971).

[101] "Political Consultants—Mixed Results in 1970 "Elections," *1970 Congressional Quarterly Almanac* (Washington: Congressional Quarterly, 1971), p. 1098.

[102] "T.V. Image Makers Given a Split Vote," *St. Petersburg* (Fla.) *Times* (November 7, 1970), p. 6.

[103] Paul A. Dawson and William E. Zinser, "Broadcast Expenditures and Electoral Outcomes in the 1970 Congressional Election," *Public Opinion Quarterly, 35* (Fall, 1971), p. 400.

[104] Joseph Napolitan, *The Election Game* (Garden City: Doubleday, 1972), p. 223.

[105] MacNeil, p. 227.

[106] The role of opinion leaders in elections has received the most extensive treatment in the earliest voting studies. See Paul Lazarsfeld, Bernard Berelson, and Hazel Gaudet, *The People's Choice* (New York: Duell, Sloan and Smith, 1944), Chapter 12; Bernard Berelson, Paul Lazarsfeld, and William N. McPhee, *Voting* (Chicago: University of Chicago Press, 1954), Chapter 6. Opinion leadership is most thoroughly studied in nonpolitical realms.

[107] John W. Kingdon, "Opinion Leaders in the Electorate," *Public Opinion Quarterly, 34* (Summer, 1970), pp. 256–261.

[108] AIPO news release, February 2, 1964. The exact question was, "How would you feel about a law that would give all persons—Negro as well as white—the right to be served in public places such as hotels, restaurants, theatres, and similar establishments? Would you like to see Congress pass such a law, or not?"

[109] Frank V. Cantwell, "Public Opinion and the Legislative Process," *American Political Science Review, 55* (1946), pp. 924–935.

[110] Seymour Martin Lipset, "Doves, Hawks, and the Polls," *Encounter, 27* (October, 1966), p. 39.

[111] Roberta S. Sigel, "Image of the American Presidency: Part II of an Exploration

164 *The Learning of Political Opinions*

into Popular Views of Presidential Power," *Midwest Journal of Political Science,* 10 (February, 1966), pp. 123–137.

[112] Hazel Erskine, "The Polls: Red China and the U.N.," *Public Opinion Quarterly, 35* (Spring, 1971), pp. 126–128.

[113] Milton J. Rosenberg, Sidney Verba, and Philip E. Converse, *Vietnam and the Silent Majority* (New York: Harper and Row, 1970), pp. 26–27.

[114] Gallup Poll, as reported in Mark V. Nadel, "Public Opinion and Public Policy" in Robert Weissberg and Mark V. Nadel (eds.), *American Democracy: Theory and Reality* (New York: John Wiley and Sons, 1972), p. 539.

[115] NORC polls, as reported in Kenneth N. Walz, "Electoral Punishment in Foreign Policy Crisis," in James Rosenau (ed.), *Domestic Sources of Foreign Policy* (New York: The Free Press, 1967), p. 286.

[116] Ibid., pp. 272–273; Fred I. Greenstein, "Popular Images of the President," *American Journal of Psychiatry, 122* (November, 1965), pp. 523–529; *Gallup Opinion Index.*

[117] John E. Mueller, "Presidential Popularity From Truman to Johnson," *American Political Science Review, 64* (March, 1970), p. 29.

[118] Lester Milbrath, "Lobbying as a Communications Process," *Public Opinion Quarterly, 24* (Spring, 1960), p. 45.

[119] Angus Campbell, Philip E. Converse, Donald E. Stokes, and Warren E. Miller, *The American Voter* (New York: Wiley, 1960), p. 306.

[120] Robert Abelson, "Computers, Polls, and Public Opinion: Some Puzzles and Paradoxes," *Trans-Action, 5* (September, 1968) pp. 20–27.

[121] For an interesting example, see William H. Rodgers, Jr., "Ecology Denied: The Unmasking of a Majority," *The Washington Monthly, 2* (February, 1971), pp. 39–43.

[122] M. Kent Jennings and L. Harmon Zeigler, "Interest Representation in School Governance," Paper presented at meeting of American Political Sceince Association, September 1970, pp. 41–43.

[123] Data reported in Nadel, *op. cit.*

[124] V. O. Key, *Public Opinion and American Democracy* (New York: Alfred Knopf, 1961), p. 515.

SIX

GROUP DIFFERENCES IN POLITICAL OPINIONS

It is common to think of differences in political opinion and voting behavior in terms of group stereotypes. Everyone is aware of the increasing polarization between black and white in this country. In addition, other group characteristics are often thought to be predictors of attitudes and voting. For example, we often hear that the young are more liberal than the old, or that Catholics and Jews are more Democratic than Protestant voters. Geography is also often assumed to make a difference: that is, the "liberal" Northeast and the "conservative" South, the "liberal" big cities versus the "conservative" small towns and rural areas. Social class is often thought to make a difference too, with working class people more Democratic and more liberal on economic issues than their middle-class counterparts. But on noneconomic issues, this polarity often seems reversed, with working class "hard hats" the group most opposed to change.

In this chapter, we will explore the validity of generalizations that are frequently made about group differences in attitudes and voting. Most of these generalizations we will find to be correct—but only to some degree. Knowing a person's group characteristics increases our ability to predict his political responses; but the exceptions make political predictions on the basis of group characteristics far from perfect.

ECONOMIC STATUS AND POLITICAL OPINIONS

An obvious source of political polarization is alignment along lines of economic class, with the poor or "have nots" disagreeing politically with the more wealthy. In most European countries the major political battle lines are drawn in this fashion, with a working class "socialist" party (and sometimes a significant Communist party) in opposition to one or more "middle class" parties. As indicated by the fact that the United States has never had an appreciable socialist movement, America has escaped the more extreme forms of class conflict. Even so, divisions on the basis of economic status are often found when the political attitudes and behavior of the American public are examined.

Class Differences on Social Welfare Issues

Typically, poorer people are more favorably inclined than the well-to-do toward government social welfare programs that are designed to raise living standards. To take an initial example, back in 1949, Gallup obtained a strong relationship between living conditions and opinion when he asked a national sample whether they thought "that the government should do more to improve the conditions of the poor people, that the government is doing just about the right amount of things now, or that the government has already done more for the poor people that is good for them:"[1]

	Do More	Right Amount	Too Much	No Opinion	Total
Prosperous	28%	42%	23%	7%	100%
Upper middle	35	38	20	7	100
Lower middle	44	36	12	8	100
Poor	57	27	7	9	100

The tendency for poorer people to be the most sympathetic to social welfare legislation persists today. Thus, when in 1968 a national sample of white voters was asked whether they would "favor more government programs to help the poor in things like medical care, education, or housing," 54 percent of the respondents in the manual or "blue-collar" occupational category gave the affirmative response, whereas only 45 percent of the nonmanual or "white collar" people did so.[2]

Figure 6-1 shows how family income is related to opinions on the issues of medical care and a guaranteed job and good standard of living among white respondents in the SRC's 1968 survey. Each of the five income groups compared contain approximately the same number of opinion-holding respondents. The figure shows that support for the belief that "the government should see to it that people can get doctors and hospitals care at low cost" is negatively related to income, since support for this "liberal" belief decreases gradually from 74 percent of the opinion holders in the lowest income group to only slight majorities in the highest income groups. On the question of whether the government should "see to it that everybody who wants to work has a job and a good standard of living," the relationship between income level and opinion is somewhat ragged. Even so, the percentage favoring this government guarantee ranges considerably from 48 percent among the poorest fifth to about 30 percent among the most prosperous. On both issues, the major opinion break within the sample of white respondents is between people in

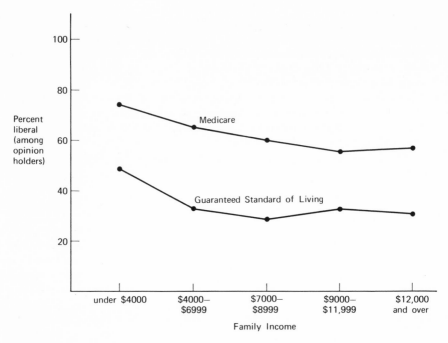

Figure 6-1. Family income and opinions on two social welfare issues, 1968 (nonwhites excluded). (*Source.* Survey Research Center, 1968 election data.)

the poorest income category and the remainder. We have not included nonwhites in our sample because we wish to show that wealth has an effect on social welfare attitudes that is independent of race. With nonwhites included, the opinion disparity between the least prosperous income category and the others would loom even larger, since prosocial welfare blacks and other racial minorities tend to cluster toward the bottom of the income scale.

Because income standards vary with the community, the occupation of the head of the respondent's household is generally preferred over income as a status indicator when a national sample is employed. Figure 6-2 compares the opinions on Medicare and a guaranteed job and good standard of living among whites in five occupational categories from unskilled manual workers at the lowest level to professionals (lawyers, teachers, and accountants, for example) at the top.[3] This figure shows that the major attitudinal difference among occupational groups is between unskilled workers and people in the remaining categories. Whereas 75 percent of the opinion holding respondents from households with an unskilled worker as its head agree that the government should help pay medical bills, the percentages in all of the remaining categories are much lower, varying only from 62 percent in the "skilled worker" category to 50 percent in "clerical and sales" households. This disparity between the unskilled and the remainder of the sample is even clearer on the guaranteed job question; although almost half of the unskilled (47 percent) support the notion of a guaranteed job and a good standard of living, only about 30 percent of the three middle categories do so. Interestingly, professionals—at the top of the occupational prestige ladder—appear to be the occupational group second most favorably inclined toward the government guarantee of a job and a good standard of living. With this one exception, the relationship between occupational status and social welfare opinion remains using income as the indicator and economic status: disproportionate support for social welfare measures within the lowest status category, but little variation among the remaining groups.

Programs of government assistance for medical care or a guaranteed job and good standard of living presumably give greatest bene-

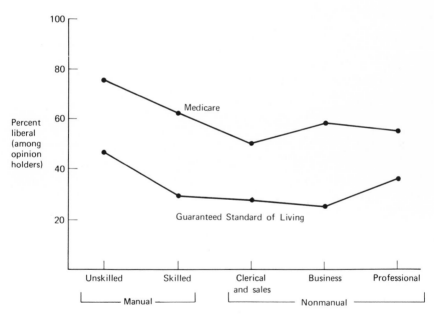

Figure 6-2. Occupational status and opinions on two social welfare issues, 1968 (nonwhites excluded). (*Source.* Survey Research Center, 1968 election data.)

fit to the poor. Therefore it is not surprising that support for these two programs generally decreases as one goes up the economic ladder. There are, however, more wealthy economic liberals and poor economic conservatives than one might expect if political attitudes were formed largely on the basis of economic self-interest. When the issue is a spending program that would presumably benefit all economic classes equally—such as the space program—it is the lower-income groups who usually are the *least* enthusiastic. For example, when in 1969, following the first successful landing of men on the moon, Gallup asked people whether they favored a proposal to "set aside money" for a project to "land a man on the planet Mars," the following distribution resulted:[4]

Income	Favor Mars Project	Oppose Mars Project	No Opinion
$7000 and over	46%	48%	6%
$5000-$6999	36	53	11
$3000-$4999	26	61	13
Under $3000	25	66	9

Similarly, it is usually people of relatively high economic status who are most in support of spending for foreign aid, national defense, or pollution control. It might be speculated that the greater opposition to these nonclass-related spending programs on the part of the lower economic groups may be indication that poor people feel strongly that priority should be placed on programs designed to raise the living standards of those who are economically less well-off.[5]

There is some indication that class differences in social welfare attitudes are not as great today as they have been in the past. Evidence of such a decline is shown in Figure 6-3. This figure displays the relationship between occupation and opinions toward a "guaranteed job" as measured by three surveys—in 1945, 1956, and 1968.[6] Since the line representing the relationship is much steeper for 1945 than for 1956 or 1968, the relative difference in economic liberalism between people of high and low status occupations appears to have declined during the post-World War II era. Apparently the change from the poverty of the Depression era to postwar prosperity was the cause of this shift. It should be noted, however, that the response to the increase in prosperity was not a noticeable net shift in social welfare attitudes on the part of the population as a whole. Instead, the change has been that the lower economic strata (among whites) has become less demanding of social welfare legislation while the more prosperous have become less resistant.[7]

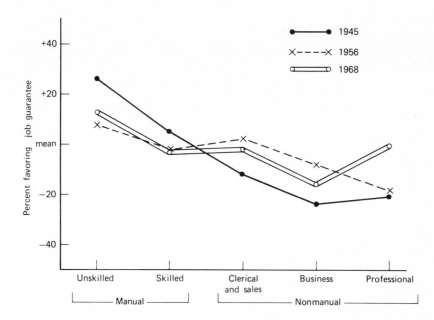

Figure 6-3. The changing relationship between occupation and opinion on a "guaranteed job," 1945-1968 (white male samples). (*Sources.* Richard Centers, *The Psychology of Social Classes* (Princeton: Princeton University Press, 1949), p. 62; Survey Research Center, 1956 and 1968 election data.)

Class Differences on Noneconomic Domestic Issues

On noneconomic issues liberalism tends to increase rather than decrease as one goes up the status ladder. Not atypical is the relationship between income and attitudes toward the legalization of marijuana reported by Gallup in April 1972:[8]

Income	Penalty for Marijuana Use SHOULD be Less Strict	Penalty for Marijuana Use Should NOT be Less Strict
$15,000 and over	42%	53%
$10,000-$14,000	30	65
$7000-$9999	32	65
$5000-$6999	24	68
$3000-$4999	29	65
Under $3000	16	72

Economic Status and Political Opinions **171**

When respondents in this survey are grouped by education level, the pattern is even sharper:

Education	Penalty for Marijuana Use SHOULD be Less Strict	Penalty for Marijuana Use Should NOT be Less Strict
College	47%	46%
High school	28	67
Grade school	17	76

Similar relationships between status indicators and opinion can be found on many other social issue questions. Table 6-1 shows how

TABLE 6-1 **Income, Education, and "Cultural Intolerance"**

	Percent "High" on Cultural Intolerance	Number of Cases
Education		
8th grade	52	(435)
High school	39	(836)
Some college	28	(204)
College graduate	12	(179)
Income		
Under $5000	47	(603)
$5000 to $9999	35	(649)
$10,000 to $14,999	29	(259)
$15,000 and over	27	(71)

Source. Seymour Martin Lipset and Earl Raab, *The Politics of Unreason* (New York: Harper and Row, 1970), p. 447, Table 78.
1964 national sample, nonwhites excluded.

income and education (among whites) are related to scores on a composite scale of "cultural intolerance" or "antimodernism" derived from survey data by Lipset and Raab. The table clearly shows that people with the least education and the lowest incomes tend to have the highest scores on "cultural intolerance."

Intolerance of minority viewpoints has continually been found to be most frequent among people in low-status categories—particularly among those with little education. This pattern has been found, for example, when people are asked whether Communists, Socialists, atheists, and other advocates of dissenting positions should be allowed to speak in their community.[9] Similarly, analysis of the SRC's of 1968 survey data reveals that people of higher status are the most likely to give at least qualified approval to lawful protest meetings or marches and "refusing to obey a law that one feels is unjust." These two tendencies are shown in Figure 6-4, using occupational categories as the status indicator.

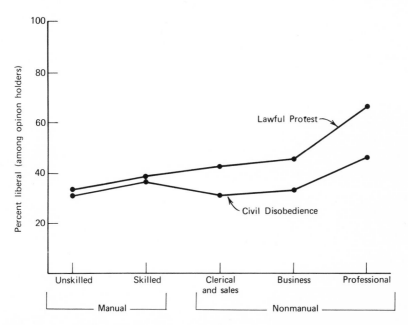

Figure 6-4. Occupational status and opinion on dissent, 1968 (nonwhites excluded). (*Source.* Survey Research Center, 1968 election data.)

Regarding white attitudes toward civil rights for Negroes, liberalism or prointegration sentiment increases somewhat with status. The relationship is far from strong, however. Typical is the relationship shown in Figure 6-5 between occupational status and opinions on federal involvement in school integration and the integration of public accommodations. The highly educated professional class stands out as the most liberal on these issues. The opinion distributions within the other categories are fairly constant. In fact, within this particular sample, the unskilled workers comprise what is apparently the second most liberal group.[10]

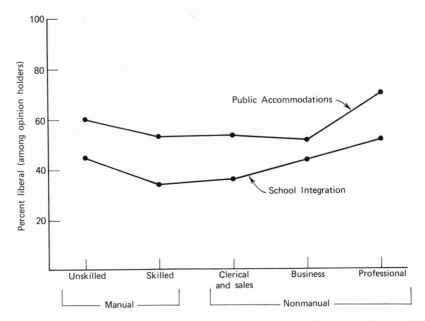

Figure 6-5. Occupational status and opinion on racial integration, 1968 (nonwhites excluded). (*Source.* Survey Research Center, 1968 election data.)

One clarification on the relationship between status and civil rights opinion is that the weak relationship between tolerance and status is more intense among white Southerners than among white Northerners. This is shown in Table 6-2, using family income as the status indicator. The table shows that in the North, "strict segregationist" sentiment varys little with family income. But among Southerners, the strict segregationist position becomes considerably more frequent with each step down the income ladder. Only within the highest income category does the percentage of Southerners who oppose the strict segregation approach the percentage in the North. A similar tendency is found when a vote for George Wallace in the 1968 presidential election is used as an indicator of anticivil-rights sentiment. Among Northern whites in the sample, voting for Wallace correlated positively with family income. But among Southerners a vote for Wallace became increasingly frequent with each step down the income ladder. These findings suggest that strong resistance to civil rights gains on the part of working class whites is for the most part a Southern phenomenon.

When tendencies have been found for intolerant or "illiberal"

TABLE 6-2 **Segregationist Sentiment and Wallace Voting by Family Income, North and South**

Family Income	Percent "Strict Segregationists"			Percent Voted for Wallace		
	North	South	Difference	North	South	Difference
Under $4000	19	47	28	6	42	36
$4000–$6999	9	31	22	6	27	21
$7000–$8999	12	30	18	6	35	29
$9000–$11,999	13	23	10	12	15	3
$12,000 and over	8	8	0	7	18	11

Source. Survey Research Center 1968 election data.
Nonwhites excluded.

attitudes on noneconomic issues to be most frequent among people in the lower economic strata, they have often been attributed to a syndrome of "working class authoritarianism." Many writers have suggested that the more rigid family upbringing in the working class promotes an authoritarian, intolerant, and perhaps even undemocratic tendency in the political beliefs.[11] There is evidence, however, that it is education rather than class upbringing that is the critical variable here.[12] If we examine the separate effects of income or occupation and education simultaneously, results such as those of Table 6-3 emerge. This table shows that within each of three income categories, liberal opinions on school integration and lawful protest increase with educational attainment. However, among people at the same educational level, the responses varied little in relationship to income. This pattern suggests that education has an independent effect on political attitudes—with noneconomic liberalism increasing with each increase in educational attainment. In turn, the impact of differing levels of education largely accounts for opinion differences between economic classes on such issues as civil rights and the right to dissent.[13]

Class Differences on Foreign Policy Issues

The major class difference in foreign policy attitudes is that people in the lower economic strata are continually more ready to take "isolationist" positions than the more "internationally minded" higher status groups. This tendency is shown in Figure 6-6, based once again on white voters in the SRC 1968 survey. The correlation between high status and approval of foreign aid is higher

TABLE 6-3   Joint Effects of Income and Education on Noneconomic
"Liberalism"

Percent Liberal (of Opinion Holders) on Lawful Protest

Family Income	Education		
	Non-High School Graduate	High School Graduate	Some College
Under $6000	27% (214)	33% (76)	55% (61)
$6000–$9999	29 (113)	41 (143)	48 (103)
$10,000 and over	39 (57)	44 (140)	71 (181)

Percent Liberal (of Opinion Holders) on School Integration

Family Income	Education		
	Non-High School Graduate	High School Graduate	Some College
Under $6000	35% (226)	43% (72)	49% (55)
$6000–$9999	33 (120)	42 (144)	43 (101)
$10,000 and over	36 (59)	42 (139)	49 (181)

Source. Survey Research Center, 1968 election data. For the full text of the opinion questions, see the Appendix. A "liberal" position on "lawful protest is defined as "approval" or "depends on circumstances" response toward "protest meetings or marches that are permitted by the local authorities."
Nonwhites excluded. Numbers in parentheses are the numbers of cases on which the percentages are based.

than that between status and any other opinion variable in the 1968 study. The issue of whether American farmers and businessmen should be allowed to trade with Communist nations, reveals a trace of upper-status internationalism. Since internationalism on such issues has often been equated with a liberal outlook, the isolationist tendency among the lower occupational groups has often been cited as another example of working-class authoritarianism. But complications arise with this interpretation, for if the working class people are authoritarian in their foreign policy attitudes, they ought to have a relatively aggressive and warlike attitude toward other nations. Actually, the accumulation of survey evidence indicates that economic status has virtually no impact on the aggressiveness of one's foreign policy stance. See, for instance, the lack of class differences on the Vietnam issues as shown in Figure 6-7.[14]

Comparing people with different educational attainment, the ever-

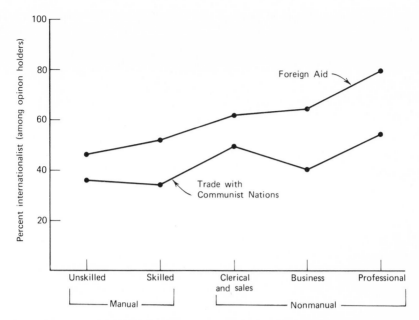

Figure 6-6. Occupational status and opinions on two foreign policy issues, 1968 (nonwhites excluded). (*Source.* Survey Research Center, 1968 election data.)

so-slight tendency, shown in Table 6-4 and replicated in other polls, is that nonhigh-school graduates tend to be more opposed to the war than people with a college background. This regularity is most clear in response to the question of whether the United States did the right thing in getting involved in Vietnam. For example, among white opinion holders in the 1968 SRC sample, the percentage saying that U.S. involvement was wrong ranged from 68 percent among nonhigh-school graduates to 58 percent among people with a college background. This may seem surprising since the most visible war opponents have been found on college campuses. Only if we refine the education index to isolate the small segment of voters with graduate degrees or four-year degrees from the more prestigious universities do we find disproportionate antiwar sentiment at the top of the education ladder.[15]

One cannot extract too much significance from class differences in foreign policy attitudes because the nonopinion rate on foreign policy questions increases dramatically as one goes down the status ladder.[16] Apparently people in the lower-status categories find little time to devote to questions of foreign policy. This makes the answers

Economic Status and Political Opinions **177**

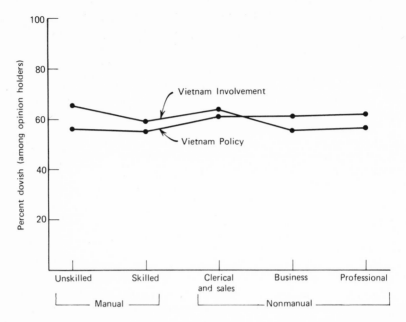

Figure 6-7. Occupational status and opinion on the war in Vietnam, 1968 (nonwhites excluded). (*Source.* Survey Research Center, 1968 election data.)

that they do offer on foreign policy questions somewhat suspect. We may particularly suspect that poor people and people with little education often grope for what they perceive to be the "official" policy when asked to give their foreign policy views.[17] Such a tendency may at least be the partial reason, for example, why, according to surveys, the less educated had been the most opposed to letting Red China in the United Nations. The better educated had the advantage of knowing that the idea of China's admission was gaining respectability. As the Vietnam example shows, the more educated also have a propensity to support the official foreign policy position. The more education one has, the more one is able to identify accurately the official or government position. Thus, when in the early 1960s the government position on a nuclear test ban flip-flopped, the poll responses of the more educated respondents changed accordingly, while those of the less educated remained stable.[18] Such a pattern may only occur if considerable sophistication is demanded in order to follow changes in the official line or in main currents of thought; the "dovish" trend on the war, for example, developed among people in all education categories.

TABLE 6-4   **Education and Vietnam Policy Preference, 1968**

	Non High School Graduates	High School Graduates	Some College
Withdraw	24%	17%	20%
Stay, but try to end fighting	38	43	39
Expand war	39	40	41
	100%	100%	100%
Number of cases	(441)	(426)	(368)

Source. Survey Research Center, 1968 election data.
Non-whites excluded.

Economic Status and "Liberalism-Conservatism"

We have seen that the direction of the relationship between status and political liberalism depends on the issue. On domestic issues, people of higher status tend to be the most conservative if the issue taps the social welfare dimension but are often the most liberal on civil rights and, especially, social issue questions. On many foreign policy questions, higher-status people are the most internationalist— a position that is generally associated with liberalism except when foreign policy belligerence is involved.

These tendencies are shown schematically in Table 6-5. Suppose

TABLE 6-5   **Typical Relationships Between Status and Opinions**

Type of Issue	Lower Status (Low Income, Education and Occupational Status)	Higher Status (High Income, Education and Occupational Status)
Social welfare (Medicare, guaranteed job)	more liberal	more conservative
Civil rights (racial integration)[a]	more conservative	more liberal
"Social issues" (dissent, civil liberties)	more conservative	more liberal
Foreign policy: general	more isolationist (conservative)	more internationalist (liberal)
Foreign policy: Vietnam, war and peace	————little difference———— [b]	

[a] Tendency shown is greater in South than North.
[b] If anything, upper status people are more "hawkish" or conservative.

Economic Status and Political Opinions   **179**

we try now to extract a relationship between status and a summary measure of liberalism, based on a composite of the opinions of each status group on a variety of issues. The relationship between occupational status and the average percentage of opinion holders who give the liberal response to the ten issue questions we have examined in the preceding graphs is as follows.

	Unskilled	Skilled	Clerical and Sales	Business	Professional
Average percent liberal	50%	45%	48%	47%	58%

The 10 issues include two social welfare issues, two civil rights issues, two issues on dissent and protest, two issues on general foreign policy, and two issues on Vietnam. There is no consistent relationship between occupational status and this measure of overall liberalism except for a tendency for professionals and their dependents to be more liberal than others.

Of course our method of constructing the summary index of the liberalism of each occupational group was entirely arbitrary. Let us instead examine the relationship between a person's status and his *self-ranking* as a liberal or a conservative. The relationship between status and self-rankings of the liberal–conservative dimension has undergone an interesting change in recent years. The change is most apparent using education as the status indicator, as in Table 6-6. In

TABLE 6-6 **Education and Self-Identification as a Liberal or a Conservative**

	Percent of Liberal and Conservative Identifiers Who Call Themselves Liberals[a]		
Education	1964	1972	Change
Grade school	51	30	−21
High school	46	41	− 5
College	45	51	+ 6

Sources. Lloyd A. Free and Hadley Cantril, The Political Beliefs of Americans (New York: Simon and Schuster, 1968), p. 223; Gallup Opinion Index, May 1972, p. 10.
[a] Percentages may be in error by about 1 percent, since they were recalculated from original tables in which middle-of-the-roaders and nonopinion holders were included in the percentage base.

1964, the higher a person's educational attainment, the more likely he was to call himself a conservative. But between 1964 and 1972, noncollege people became more inclined to call themselves conservative while the college educated became more liberal in their self-identification. As a result, by 1970 the college trained had suddenly become the most liberal of the three categories.

In Chapter Three, we had suggested that in popular usage the terms "liberal" and "conservative" had once referred mainly to differences in social welfare policy preference, whereas today the terms are more often applied to noneconomic issues. This interpretation would explain why the college educated were the most conservative group in 1964; the college trained, being relatively wealthy and therefore relatively conservative on economic issues, tended to call themselves conservative. Today the college trained are the most likely to call themselves liberals because they are more liberal than the average on most noneconomic issues. As mentioned earlier, the change in the popular meaning of the liberal-conservative terminology appears to indicate a change in the kinds of issues on which people give top priority. Since people are giving decreasing weight to economic issues, we are now more likely to find self-declared "liberals" among people of high economic status and education, whereas the reverse was true only a short while ago.

Class Differences in Party Preferences

Especially since the years of Franklin Roosevelt's presidency, the relationship between economic class and party preference has reflected class differences on economic issues, with preference for the Democratic party decreasing as one goes up the status ladder. In the 1930s, Roosevelt's efforts to expand the federal government's role in order to combat the economic effects of the Great Depression caused a "partisan realignment" of the American electorate. During this realignment of the New Deal era, the increased salience of economic issues pushed the relatively poor toward increasing loyalty to the Democratic party and the smaller group of relatively prosperous voters toward the Republicans. This basic partisan division of the American electorate, of course, remains today, largely because party identifications formed during the Depression era remain stable and are transmitted across generations.

Class differences in party identification and in presidential voting in 1968 are shown in Figure 6-8. To remove the impact of racial differences in party preference and voting, the sample excludes nonwhites. First, looking at the relationship between occupational status and party identification, we see that the percentage of party identifiers who call themselves Democrats rather than Republicans de-

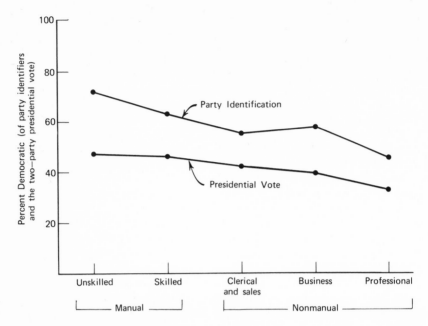

Figure 6-8. Party identification and presidential voting, 1968, by occupational status (nonwhites excluded). (*Source.* Survey Research Center, 1968 election data.)

creases as one goes up the status ladder, from 72 percent among unskilled workers to 45 percent among professionals for a difference of 27 percent. The five occupation categories, however, vary less in their support for Humphrey, the 1968 Democratic presidential candidate. The unskilled and the professionals differ by only 14 percent (47 percent versus 33 percent) in their frequency of Democratic voting.

Figure 6-9 traces the relationships between class and presidential voting going back to 1936. For simplicity, the voters are split into only two occupational categories—manual and nonmanual—for this comparison. The gap between the two classes in their frequency of Democratic voting is a useful indicator of "class voting."[19] No pattern stands out from this graph except for the fact that the voting gap between classes was highest in 1948. The reader may be surprised to notice that class voting in the Roosevelt elections shown here—1936 to 1944—was not unusually high. However, the Depression did have considerable impact on the era's young voters whose party identification had not yet crystallized. Consequently, during the 1930s and into the 1940s, young voters—who might be called the

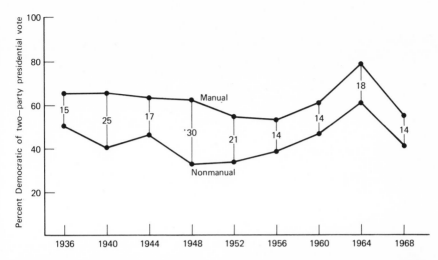

Figure 6-9. Occupational status and presidential voting, 1936-1968. (*Sources*. 1936-1960: Robert R. Alford, *Party and Society* (Chicago: Rand McNally, 1963), pp. 352-353, Table B-3. Alford has reported the results of more than one survey for each year. We have averaged the results together. 1964-1968: Survey Research Center, 1964 and 1968 election data.)

"Depression generation"—developed voting habits that were generally consistent with their class interests. It was the tendency of older voters to retain their pre-Depression party identification that prevented the overall degree of class voting during the Depression era from being unusually high.[20]

Despite the fluctuations in the degree of class voting over the years, class differences in party identification have remained stable. Examples from two widely separated years of the relationship between occupational status and party identification are shown in Figure 6-10. In 1939 and 1968, the relative Democratic tendencies (in party identification) among occupational groups was about the same. The only change over time has been an increase in Democratic identification across all five occupational categories. Some have suggested, however, that the New Deal partisan alignment along class lines is rapidly eroding and being replaced by a newer partisan alignment along noneconomic issues.[21] If so, evidence might be found in the partisan preferences of the newer generation of young voters. Some evidence of this can be found in Figure 6-11, which presents the relationship between ·class and party identification for different

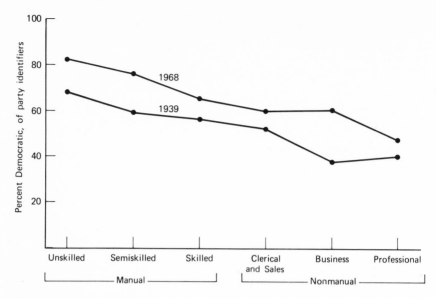

Figure 6-10. Continuity in the relationship between occupation and party identification, 1939-1968. (*Sources.* Hadley Cantril, *Public Opinion 1935-1946* (Princeton: Princeton University Press, 1951), p. 576; Survey Research Center, 1968 election data.)

age groups in both 1960 and, more recently, in 1968. This figure shows that the decline in class differences in party preference over the 1952–1968 period among the Depression generation—particularly those first eligible to vote in the 1932 and 1936 presidential elections. But most conspicuous is the low degree of class differences in 1968 among the youngest age group. In fact, the young party identifiers in the 1968 sample were more likely to call themselves Democrats if they were in nonmanual occupations than if they were in the manual or blue-collar category. This may be a sign of a possible new party alignment along nonclass lines.

If, in fact, economic classes of this country are becoming decreasingly polarized against one another in their voting behavior and party preference, this would not necessarily be a sign of increasing political stability. Great Britain, for example, is often cited as a model of stability; yet there are few other democratic nations where economic class is as important a determinant of electoral choice. British voters in the manual strata prefer the Labour party to the Conservatives by a ratio of about 3 to 1; whereas the reverse ratio

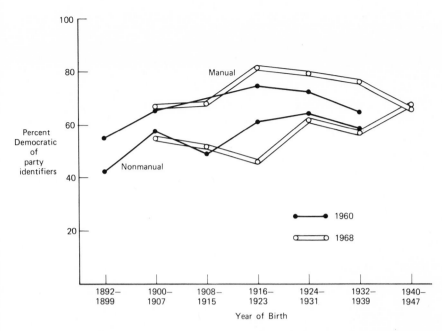

Figure 6-11. Occupational status and party identification, by age group, 1960 and 1968. (*Source.* Survey Research Center, 1960 and 1968 election data. Birthdates of 1960 respondents are approximated from age at time of interview.)

holds for nonmanuals.[22] France and Italy have less class voting but a more volatile brand of politics.[23] The major determinant of a nation's degree of class voting is the extent to which noneconomic issues play a role in shaping electoral decisions. In Great Britain, for example, no major noneconomic set of issues—either regional, racial, or religious—cuts across class lines. As a consequence, an Englishman's class interest substantially determines how he will vote. Even though France and Italy have sizeable Communist and Socialist parties, these countries have major divisions on noneconomic issues —particularly over the role of the Catholic Church. Thus, in these countries we find many lower status supporters of conservative parties (particularly among women) and many middle-class "leftists." The fact that class conflict has never dominated American partisan politics to the extent it has in Europe may have been one long-term source of the stability of the American political system. But a possible further decline in the political importance of the traditional class-related issues may augur something quite different from a

Economic Status and Political Opinions **185**

period of political tranquility, for the increasingly important racial, war-related, and social issues obviously could intensify political conflict in the years to come.

RACE AND POLITICAL OPINIONS

It is often said that Americans are becoming increasingly polarized on the basis of race. In this section we will examine one aspect of this racial division—differences between whites and blacks in their opinions on standard political issues and in voting behavior. In 1968, when the SRC's national sample was asked whether they favored "strict segregation" of the races, "desegregation," or "something in between" the difference between the responses of whites and blacks were as follows:

	Whites	Blacks
Desegregation	33%	78%
Something in between	50	18
Strict segregation	17	4
	100%	100%

Unlike what either a white racist or a black nationalist might prefer to believe, blacks are almost unanimous in rejecting racial segregation. Of course, no such consensus exists among whites. The polarization of the races might be seen even more clearly by comparing the responses of whites and blacks on the issue of whether civil rights leaders are trying to "push too fast," "too slowly," or "at about the right speed:"

	Whites	Blacks
Not fast enough	5%	63%
About right	24	29
Too fast	71	8
	100%	100%

Similarly, 66 percent of the black opinion holders in the 1968 sample said the civil rights movement was "peaceful," while a majority of whites (81 percent) said it was "violent." Also 83 percent of the blacks but only 23 percent of the whites said the civil rights movement "helped" the Negro cause. Clearly whites and blacks see the civil rights movement quite differently.

Even on issues that are tangential to civil rights, blacks are much more likely than whites to take the liberal position. Some examples from the SRC 1968 data are shown in Table 6-7. On the job guarantee and medical care questions, for example, black opinion holders are nearly unanimous in supporting government action.[24] More so than whites, blacks approve peaceful protest and civil disobedience. Even on foreign policy questions blacks are more liberal than whites. Blacks are the more favorably disposed toward foreign aid and trading with Communist nations, but more opposed to the war in Vietnam.

TABLE 6-7 **Race and Opinion on Selected Noncivil Rights Issues, 1968**

Belief	Percent Support Among Opinion Holders	
	Whites	Blacks
The government should see to it that every person has a job and a good standard of living	34	88
Our farmers and businessmen should be allowed to do business with Communist countries	43	65
Oppose "stronger" Vietnam stand that might mean invading North Vietnam	60	81
Do not disapprove all protest meetings or marches that are permitted by the local authorities	43	73

Source. Survey Research Center, 1968 election data. Black percentages are based on the "weighted" sample, including the "Negro supplement." For the full text of the opinion questions, see the Appendix.

In partisan preference, American blacks have undergone a long-term reversal in allegiance. Between the Civil War and Franklin Roosevelt's presidency, most Negroes who could vote opted for the Republican Party because it was the party of Lincoln. From the 1930s to the present, however, most black voters have supported the Democratic Party. Initially, this shift was a response to economic issues rather than any greater attempt on the part of the Democratic party to remove racial barriers. Only in recent years could the Democratic Party be identified as the party with clearly greater sympathy for the civil rights cause. But, as a consequence of the Democrats' increasing image as the more "pro-civil rights" party (beginning in the 1960s), the Democratic tendency in Negro voting at the presidential level has changed from only a tendency to near

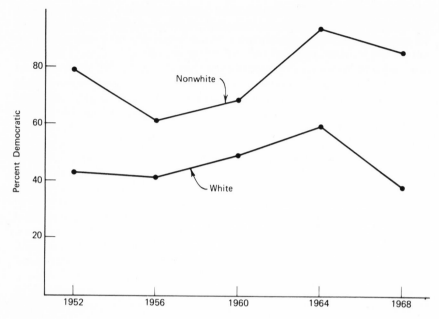

Figure 6-12. Race and presidential voting, 1952-1968. Percentages are of two-party vote, 1952-1964; of three-party vote, 1968. (*Source.* Gallup Poll.)

unanimity. This change is shown in Figure 6-12. Clearly the Democratic voting of blacks is a pivotal factor in presidential elections. In state and local elections, black voters will often vote for a Republican if he is the more liberal candidate on civil rights.[25] Thus the black voters' allegiance to the Democratic Party is contingent upon the Democrats giving at least somewhat more support than the Republicans do to the civil rights cause.

AGE AND POLITICAL OPINIONS

From the recent talk about the "generation gap," one might suspect that American public opinion is strongly polarized on the basis of age, with older people much more conservative than the young. Comparisons of young and old voters in samples of the adult electorate do reveal that opinions on most issues do vary somewhat with age, but not always by wide margins and sometimes not even in the predicted direction.

On most standard poll questions older people are found to be somewhat more conservative than young adults. Typical patterns are shown in Table 6-8 in which the political opinions of the under 30 generation are compared with those of people 50 years of age or older. The questions, taken from SRC and Gallup surveys, are ordered according to the percentage difference in the responses of the two contrasted generations. On 9 out of 10 issues, the younger generation is the most liberal, by margins of from 8 to 21 percentage points. Only on the medical care issue are members of the older generation understandably more likely to give a liberal (pro-Medicare) opinion.

The reader may expect the relationship between age and attitudes toward the war in Vietnam to be similar to the strongest relationships shown in Table 6-8. However, despite the fact that active opposition to the war has quite obviously been most prevalent among the young, it is older people, on the whole, who appear most dovish on the war issue. Although this statement may seem surprising, there can be little doubt of its accuracy. For example, virtually every Gallup poll taken on the issue shows agreement on the statement that getting into the war was a "mistake," to be more frequent among voters 50 years of age or older than among young voters in their twenties.[26] Much of the seeming antiwar sentiment of older people stems from their retention of the old isolationist belief that all foreign entanglements should be avoided instead of the humanitarian grounds offered by the more vocal opponents of the war. The isolationism of much of the older generation may explain, for example, why they can be the age group that is both most opposed to a war against communism in Vietnam and also the most opposed to the seating of Communist China in the United Nations. Certainly the antiwar sentiment of the older generation should not be taken to mean that people over 50 are the age group most sympathetic to antiwar protesters. Polls clearly show the opposite to be true.

With interesting exceptions on certain issues, young adults do hold more liberal opinions than their elders. Has this generation gap in opinions always been with us, or is it a new phenomenon? On most issues, the opinion differences between age groups are about the same as they had been in earlier surveys. But on youth-related issues, the gap between the opinions of the young and the old has been widening. For example, until the late 1960s, young adults—and even 18 to 20-year-olds—had been no more favorable to lowering the voting age than had the 50-and-older generation of the time. As recently as 1965, the 20 to 29 age group were only two percentage points more favorable than the 50-and-older people toward a lowered voting age. By 1971, the gap had widened to a 22 percentage point difference.[27]

Young and old voters are also becoming more polarized in their

TABLE 6-8 **Age and Opinion on Selected Political Issues**

		Percent of Opinion Holders Supporting Belief		
	Belief	21–29 Years Old	50 Years or Older	Difference
(1970)	Red China should be admitted to the United Nations	60	34	−26
(1968)	Do not disapprove all protest meetings or marches that are permitted by the local authorities	59	34	−25
(1972)	Penalties for the use of marijuana should be less strict	44	20	−24
(1968)	The government should support the right of Negroes to go to any hotel or restaurant they can afford	70	52	−18
(1968)	The United States should give aid to other countries if they need help	64	50	−14
(1968)	The government in Washington should see to it that white and Negro children go to the same schools	52	40	−12
(1969)	Do not believe their local courts deal not harshly enough with criminals	23	12	−11
(1968)	The government in Washington should help towns and cities provide education for grade and high school children	40	31	− 9
(1968)	The government should see to it that every person has a good job and a good standard of living	45	37	− 8
(1968)	The government in Washington should help people get doctors and medical care at low cost	61	69	+ 8

Sources. 1968 items from Survey Research Center 1968 election data; items from other years from *Gallup Opinion Index* for years cited.

Note: for Gallup data, percentages may be in error by about one percent, since they were recalculated from original tables in which nonopinion holders were included in the percentage base.

190 *Group Differences in Political Opinions*

TABLE 6-9   Age and Self-Identification as a Liberal or a Conservative

Age	Percent of Liberal and Conservative Identifiers Who Call Themselves Liberals[a]		
	1964	1972	Change
18–20	[b]	77	
21–29	50	58	+ 8
30–49	50	38	−12
50 and above	44	31	−13

Sources. Lloyd A. Free and Hadley Cantril, The Political Beliefs of Americans (New York: Simon and Schuster, 1968), p. 223; Gallup Opinion Index, May 1972.
[a] Percentages may be in error by about one percent, since they were recalculated from original tables in which "middle-of-the-roaders" and nonopinion holders were included in the percentage base.
[b] Not asked.

self-identification with liberal or conservative labels. As Table 6-9 shows, in 1964 young voters were only slightly more liberal than their elders in self-identification. By 1972, the gap had widened considerably. Also, the newly enfranchised 18 to 20 year olds display a much stronger gravitation to the liberal label than even the 21 to 29 year old group.

Why is it that older voters are generally more conservative than the young? One possibility—an "aging" explanation—is simply that people may become more and more conservative as they grow older. There is also another possible explanation that does not demand that people change their political attitudes as they age: the reason why older people are the most conservative may be that each generation entering the electorate is more liberal than those before them. To fully understand the relationship between age and conservatism, we need to monitor generations at several points in time to see if they become more conservative. For example, if people in a given generation—say those born between 1930 and 1935—give conservative responses to the same poll question year after year, then the "aging" explanation would be accepted. But if their answers remain constant over time, then an explanation in terms of generational differences would be proper. Unfortunately, adequate tests of the sort we have proposed have not been done, possibly because polls taken years apart generally ask different opinion questions that are not comparable.

One question that has continually been asked over the years is the party identification of the respondent. Consequently we may take

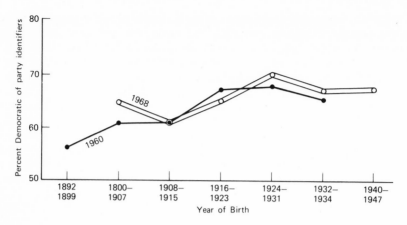

Figure 6-13. Age and party identification, 1960 and 1968. (*Source.* Survey Research Center, 1960 and 1968 election data.)

party identification as a rough measure of liberalism–conservatism and find out whether the party identification of various generations changes over time. If a trend toward increasing Republicanism on the part of each generation can be identified, we could infer that people become more conservative with age. Figure 6-13 shows the distribution of party identification for several eight-year generations at two points in time—in 1960 and in 1968. The figure shows than instead of changing, each generation's party identification is remarkably stable over the eight year period. Thus, if Republicanism equals conservatism, our crude test does not allow the inference that people become more conservative as they grow older.[28] The figure shows that the chief relationship between party identification and age is that people born in the 20th century tend to be more Democratic than those born in the previous century. The apparent reason for this pattern is that people born in the 19th century entered the electorate and developed their party identification before the impact of the Depression-based realignment of the 1930s that tipped the partisan balance somewhat in favor of the Democratic party.[29] Because the pre-Depression generation is a decreasingly small portion of the American electorate, the percentage of the electorate who call themselves Democrats has been increasing at a glacial pace over the years. This slight trend is stopping, however, since mortality has been reducing the pre-Depression generation to insignificant size. As the pre-Depression generation dies off, the relationship between age and party choice is also disappearing, since among voters born after the first part of this century there is virtually no relationship between age and party identification.[30]

192 *Group Differences in Political Opinions*

If the American electorate is now undergoing a new partisan realignment, it would probably be most evident among younger voters. We have already seen that the old class-based partisan alignment has eroded among the younger generation. Another clear trend in the party choice of young voters is the surprising degree to which they reject identification with either major political party. As Figure 6-14 shows, slightly over half of the SRC's 1968 sample in the 21 to 28 age bracket called themselves "Independents" rather than Democrats or Republicans. Although young voters had been the most Independent in other years, such as shown in the graph for 1960, the trend has never been as strong as in recent years. Indeed it is the rejection of the parties by young voters that explains the recent upsurge of Independent self-classification rather than a large-scale switching to Independent classification by older partisans.[31] The disinclination to identify with either party is, therefore, largely a characteristic of youthful voters alone. If one of the two major

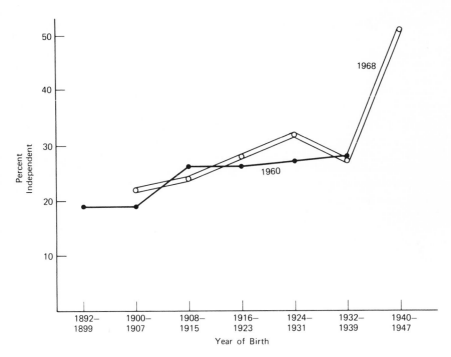

Figure 6-14.   Age and frequency of "Independent" self-classification, 1960 and 1968. (*Source.* Survey Research Center, 1960 and 1968 election data.)

parties eventually captures most of the support of young voters, it could establish itself as the dominant party of future decades.

RELIGION AND POLITICAL OPINIONS

In religion, Americans are divided into a Protestant majority, a Catholic minority of about 25 percent, and a still smaller but significant minority of about 3 percent who are Jewish. The partisan tendencies of the three major faiths are well known. Protestants are the most Republican group, Catholics tend to vote Democratic, and Jewish voters vote Democratic also, to an even greater extent than Catholics. Religious divisions were at their clearest in the 1960 presidential election when the Democrats broke tradition and nominated a Catholic, John F. Kennedy, for president. Among northern whites, the breakdown of the 1960 presidential vote by religion was as follows.[32]

	Protestant	Catholic	Jewish
Percent Democratic (Kennedy)	28%	83%	93%
Percent Republican (Nixon)	72	17	7
	100%	100%	100%

Almost three-fourths of the Protestant vote among northern whites were for Nixon, the Republican candidate, while over 80 percent of the Catholic and Jewish vote was Democratic. In more typical elections, without a Catholic candidate, the religious division is smaller, but still there. For example, the religious division in the presidential election of 1968—again among a northern white sample was the following.[33]

	Protestant	Catholic	Jewish
Percent Democratic (Humphrey)	26%	56%	89%
Percent Republican (Nixon)	66	39	7
Percent AIP (Wallace)	8	5	4
	100%	100%	100%

The temporal stability of the partisan differences between Protestants, Catholics, and Jews is shown in Figure 6-15. The figure shows, for each of five presidential years, the percentage of the party identifiers within each religious denomination (among northern whites only) who call themselves Democrats. Typically, the Democratic percentage (in terms of party identification) is about 90 percent among

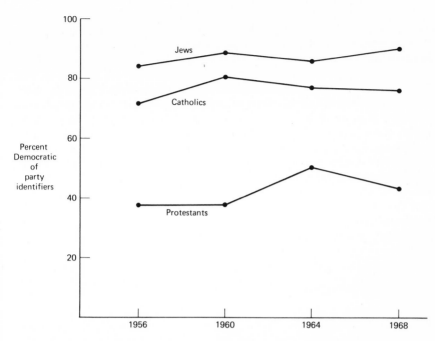

Figure 6-15. Religion and party identification (northern whites only), 1956-1968. (*Source.* Survey Research Center, election data.)

Jews, 70 percent among Catholics, but slightly less than half among Protestants. Since these differences are fairly constant from year to year, there is little reason to suspect that the fairly wide partisan divisions between religious denominations are eroding.

There are several possible explanations for the difference in the partisan tendencies of Catholics and Protestants. A small part of the explanation may involve differences in Protestant and Catholic theological emphasis: Protestant churches have placed somewhat greater stress on "individualism," which is indirectly linked with the conservative philosophy of the Republican party. More important, the Democratic party has from its time of origin made a greater effort than the Republicans and their forerunners to woo the immigrant voters, most of whom were Catholic. The payoff of this policy for the Democratic party has been the allegiance of most members of Catholic ethnic groups—especially the Irish, Italians, and Polish— many of whom are now several generations removed from immigrant status. The exceptions tend to prove the rule: in localities where the Republican party made a successful effort long ago to win over certain Catholic ethnic groups (such as the Italians in New

Haven), the Republican adherence persists today.[34] Still a simpler explanation for the Democratic voting of Catholics is that at one time American Catholics were much less affluent than their Protestant neighbors—a condition that would naturally cause them to gravitate to the Democratic party for economic reasons. But this explanation may be inadequate, for the reason that Catholics have now caught up to and even surpassed Protestants in average economic status. Also, in surveys going back to 1940, when most Catholics were poorer than Protestants, the more frequent Democratic voting by Catholics persisted even when economic status was held constant.[35] Certainly an economic explanation for the overwhelmingly Democrat tendencies of Jewish voters would certainly be ill-founded, since of the three major denominations Jews are clearly the wealthiest. Probably the Jewish allegiance to the Democratic party is partially a response to their status as an often persecuted minority; as with Negroes, and perhaps even Catholics, their minority status moves them toward the generally more liberal Democratic party. Additionally, the explanation for the liberal and Democratic tendencies of Jewish votes may involve the unique Jewish cultural heritage.[36]

Perhaps the best explanation for the Democratic allegiance of Catholics is simply that their minority status attracts them to the more "left-leaning" Democratic Party. As evidence, in countries where the Catholic Church is the major religion, its adherents are usually identified with the more conservative political parties. Some political observers have been predicting that the Catholic ethnic groups are ripe for massive conversions to Republicanism because of their supposed political conservatism. But the premise of a unique Catholic conservatism is false, since the partisan difference between Protestants and Catholics is also reflected in their political opinions.[37] Possibly the reason why Catholics are more liberal than Protestants on most political issues is that they have learned to identify with the liberal policy positions of their favored Democratic Party.

Table 6-10 shows a pattern of increasing political liberalism as one goes from Protestants to Catholics to Jews among northern whites in the SRC's 1968 sample. On all 10 issues shown, the Jewish respondents are the most liberal. Catholics follow, since they are more liberal than the Protestants in the sample on all but two of the 10 issues. These two exceptions ("trading with Communist nations" and "Vietnam involvement") are foreign policy questions on which differences between religions are slightest.

A further, but somewhat less fruitful, exploration of the relationship between religion and political opinion can be made by comparing the opinion tendencies of different Protestant denominations. Theological distinctions between Protestant denominations are often

TABLE 6-10   **Religion and Political Opinions (Northern Whites Only)**[a]

Issue	Percent Liberal Among Opinion Holders		
	Protestant	Catholic	Jewish
Medicare	57	66	84
Guaranteed standard of living	30	41	67
School integration	42	56	66
Public accommodations	60	69	86
Foreign aid	55	58	85
Trade with Communists	45	42	65
Vietnam involvement	61	58	71
Vietnam policy	60	65	83
Lawful protest	42	54	86
Civil disobedience	33	36	75
Mean Percent Liberal	*49*	*55*	*77*

Source. Survey Research Center, 1968 election data.

[a] For the full text of the opinion questions, see the Appendix. The liberal side of each issue is defined according to common usages and our usage in the text. On the three latter issues, the survey question allows three rather than two responses. On the Vietnam policy question, a liberal opinion is defined as opposition to the expansion of the war alternative. On lawful protest, and civil disobedience, both approval and responses of "depends on the circumstances" are counted as being relatively liberal.

thought to have political implications; the emphasis on personal salvation in the Baptist church and other "fundamentalist" groups seemingly should make members of the more fundamentalist denominations relatively conservative, while the more "worldly" involvement in social problems on the part of many leaders of nonfundamentalist groups (Presbyterians, Episcopalians, for example) ought to make their members relatively liberal. Very sharp differences of this sort have been found between the political attitudes of Protestant *clergymen* of fundamentalist and nonfundamentalist churches.[38] However, differences between the mass memberships of Protestant denominations are usually slight, and when they are found, they often reflect the strong economic and educational differences between denominations. For example, Table 6-11 shows that Baptists and other fundamentalists are actually more liberal than members of less fundamentalist Protestant groups on the economic issue of a guaranteed standard of living. This is because fundamentalists are relatively low on the economic ladder. The only other appreciable interdenominational difference found in Table 6-11 is that the few Episcopalians cited in the sample are noticeably more liberal than

TABLE 6-11   **Protestant Denomination and Political Opinions**

| | Percent Liberal Among Opinion Holders | | | | | |
| | Least Fundamentalist | | | | Most Fundamentalist | |
	Episcopal	Presbyterian	Methodist	Lutheran	Baptist	Fundamentalist Sects
Guaranteed standard of living	27	20	27	28	32	35
Social integration	36	38	42	33	28	38
Trade with Communists	58	39	41	42	36	40
Vietnam policy	69	56	60	64	54	60
Lawful protest	66	39	34	39	29	37

Source. Survey Research Center, 1968 election data. For the full text of the opinion questions, see the Appendix. Nonwhites are excluded. Denominations are arrayed in the order of decreasing frequency of belief (among SRC respondents) that "the Bible of God's word and all it says is true." The fundamentalist sects category includes the Pentecostal Church, and other denominations listed as neofundamentalist in the SRC's 1968 Codebook. Not all Protestant denominations are included in this table.

the Protestant norm on the issues of "trading with Communist nations" and "lawful protest." Since these two issues are ones on which high status individuals are clearly the most likely to take the liberal position, it is possible that the relative affluence and high education of Episcopalians explains their unusual liberalism, rather than the political liberalism of the Episcopalian clergy or the low support for fundamentalist religious doctrine among Episcopal churchgoers. When comparisons of members of different Protestant churches have included added controls for differences in economic status or education, opinion differences have not been strong enough to provide adequate evidence of a denominational effect. This is true for interdenominational differences in party preference and voting as well as for differences in political issues. Among Protestants, religious fundamentalism is normally related to support for the Democratic Party, for the reason that members of fundamentalist churches are drawn heavily from among the poor. A seeming exception occurred in 1968 when the "conservative" presidential candidacy of George Wallace received disproportionate support from Baptists and other religious fundamentalists.[39] Yet it is not clear that their religious affiliation was the *cause* of the fundamentalists' attraction to Wallace. Instead, it may have been a function of the low education, low status, and Southern origin of fundamentalist churchgoers.[40]

GEOGRAPHY AND POLITICAL OPINIONS

It is common to think of American political opinion as being somewhat polarized along lines of geographic region. The South stands out in particular for its political conservatism—especially on civil rights issues. Among the non-Southern regions, the East is often thought to stand out for its political liberalism. There have also been other regional stereotypes that once may have been valid but do not seem to be today. The South, for example, was once perhaps the most internationally minded region in foreign policy, largely because of the cotton growers' interest in unrestrained trade with other nations. The Midwest at one time had the reputation, seemingly deserved on the basis of poll results, of being the most isolationist (or least internationalist) region of the country.[41] Most regional differences in political opinion have been washing away, however, even to the extent that North–South differences on civil rights issues are less acute now than in the 1950s.

The basic similarity of opinion distributions in the four regions is shown in Table 6-12, from the SRC's 1968 survey data. For the most part, regional differences shown in this table are so slight that they could be attributable to sampling error. Since with this sample each

TABLE 6-12 **Regional Differences in Political Opinions**

	Percent Liberal Among Opinion Holders			
Issue	East	Midwest	South	West
Medicare	70	58	68	70
Guaranteed standard of living	44	34	41	45
School integration	54	45	38	55
Public accommodations	70	63	49	69
Foreign aid	61	58	59	58
Trade with Communists	46	46	39	51
Vietnam involvement	63	64	64	58
Vietnam policy	60	63	59	59
Lawful protest	64	48	37	51
Civil disobedience	56	65	61	64
Mean Percent Liberal	*59*	*54*	*52*	*58*

Source. Survey Research Center, 1968 election data. For the full text of the opinion questions, see the Appendix.

of the four regions shows up as the most liberal on at least one issue and as the most conservative on at least one other, clearly it does not make much sense to stereotype any one region as a center of unusual liberalism or conservatism.

Remindful of the basic regional similarities, we can cautiously assign liberalism scores to the four regional groups on the basis of averaging their responses to the 10 issues questions. When this is done, the South barely beats out the Midwest for the title of the least liberal region, largely because of the southern conservatism on the civil rights issues included. By another slim margin, Easterners defeat Westerners for the title of most liberal group in the sample. This relative ordering is typical of most regional breakdowns of opinion.

It has sometimes been hypothesized that regional differences in opinion reflect important differences in the political cultures of the various regions, with residents of different regions learning from their political environment to adapt to different sets of political beliefs.[42] But except for the resistance of white southerners to racial integration, no clear cultural differences emerge when we examine regional opinion differences on standard political questions. Even the small differences that appear between regional groups are for the most part simply a function of the different group compositions of the regions. For example, if the East is truly the most liberal region, it is because Easterners are more likely than residents of other regions to be a member of a liberal ethnic or religious minority group—either black, Catholic, or Jewish. If we limit our regional comparison to only the relatively conservative white Protestant majority, opinion differences between Easterners, Midwesterners, and Westerners wash away almost all together, as Table 6-13 shows.

TABLE 6-13 **Regional Differences in Political Opinions of White Protestants**

	Percent Liberal Among Opinion Holders			
Issue	East	Midwest	South	West
Medicare	56	52	60	68
Guaranteed standard of living	28	27	28	40
School integration	39	39	26	49
Public accommodations	61	57	35	61
Foreign aid	59	53	54	57
Trade with Communists	46	44	34	46
Vietnam Involvement	64	64	65	54
Vietnam policy	66	60	56	54
Lawful protest	40	40	29	46
Civil disobedience	39	30	35	34
Mean Percent Liberal	*50*	*48*	*42*	*51*

Source. Survey Research Center, 1968 election data. For the full text of the opinion questions, see the Appendix.

Comparison of only white Protestants, however, does accentuate the difference between the North and the South. Table 6-13 shows that white Protestants in the South are much more opposed to school integration and public accommodations laws than their Northern counterparts. The Southerners in the white Protestant sample are also clearly the most opposed to lawful protest and to trading with Communist nations. But on other issues, including Medicare, a guaranteed standard of living, and Vietnam, even white Protestants in the South give opinions that are much like those of their counterparts in the rest of the country.[43]

Regional differences are much more apparent on matters of partisan preference and voting than in opinions on national issues. Ever since the Civil War, the South has been the most Democratic region. Table 6-14 shows that this tendency still exists in party identification; whereas only slight majorities of party identifiers in the North call themselves Democrats, the ratio of Democrats to

TABLE 6-14 **Regional Differences in Political Partisanship**

	East	Midwest	South	West
Percent Democrat of party identifiers				
All respondents	57	59	82	60
White Protestants only	32	45	76	50
Percent Democrat 1968 presidential vote				
All respondents	47	41	38	36
White Protestants only	23	27	24	26

Source. Survey Research Center, 1968 election data.

Republicans in the South is 4 to 1. Examining the party identification of white Protestants alone, we still find Southerners to be the
most Democratic group in terms of party identification. Restricting
analysis to white Protestants also reveals partisan differences
among Northern regions. White Protestants in the "liberal" East are
considerably less likely than their Midwestern and Western counterparts to call themselves Democrats. This difference as late as 1968
reflects the historic tendency of the East to be the most Republican
region of the country.

In recent presidential voting, the regions have gone against their
historical trend. In 1968, the South, while not going overwhelmingly
Republican, did express its dissatisfaction with the national Democratic party by giving a large vote to George Wallace. The liberal
but historically Republican East, on the other hand, gave the most
support of any region to the presidential bid of Hubert Humphrey,
the Democratic presidential candidate. This Democratic tendency in
the presidential voting of Easterners is attributable to the disproportionate Negro, Jewish, and Catholic vote in the East. As the data
in Table 6-14 show, when only white Protestants are compared, it
was Easterners who were the least Democratic group in presidential
voting and party identification.

A somewhat better predictor of a person's political opinions than
the region he lives in, is whether he resides in a city, a suburb, or
the countryside. Most big cities are, relatively speaking, centers of
political liberalism and Democratic politics. Somewhat more conservative and Republican than the cities are the suburbs that surround
them. Residents of small towns and rural areas are also relatively

TABLE 6-15 **Urbanism and Political Opinions**

| | Percent Liberal Among Opinion Holders | | | | | |
| | Large Metropolitan Area | | Small Metropolitan Area | | | |
Issue	City	Suburb	City	Suburb	Small Town	Rural
Medicare	82	67	70	63	60	62
Guaranteed standard of living	60	38	42	40	37	34
School integration	64	40	58	47	45	39
Public accommodation	77	65	69	53	59	56
Foreign aid	70	73	61	56	55	52
Trade with Communists	57	38	46	40	47	44
Vietnam involvement	73	52	61	59	64	65
Vietnam policy	70	63	66	56	61	61
Lawful protest	66	46	55	48	39	38
Civil disobedience	46	39	44	44	36	33
Mean Percent Liberal	*67*	*52*	*57*	*51*	*50*	*48*
Percent Democratic (of party identifiers)	74	59	76	62	70	61
Percent Democratic, presidential vote	56	43	51	41	41	31

Source. Survey Research Center, 1968 election data.

conservative and, outside the South, relatively Republican in their politics. These tendencies among the general adult population are shown in Table 6-15.

As with region, most difference of opinion tendencies by area size can be explained in terms of the differences in the kinds of people who live in the different places. City residents show up as relatively liberal in surveys, for example, because people with relatively liberal group characteristics—Negroes, Catholics, and Jews —are more likely than others to live in the city. A major reason why suburbs are more conservative than their central cities is that blacks comprise a much smaller proportion of the suburban population. Small town and rural areas are conservative because normally they are predominantly Protestant and, outside the South, contain few blacks. Also, since the South is a relatively rural region, conservative Southerners are more likely than Northerners to be small town or rural residents.

Geography and Political Opinions **203**

In other words, if we hold constant the group characteristics of people by comparing only those with similar group characteristics, differences of opinion by area size tend to wash away. This is shown in Table 6-16, which compares Northern white Protestants in differ-

TABLE 6-16 **Political Opinions by Size of Place, Northern White Protestants Only**

| | Percent Liberal Among Opinion Holders | | | | | |
| | Large Metropolitan Area | | Small Metropolitan Area | | | |
Issue	City	Suburb	City	Suburb	Small Town	Rural
Medicare	72	59	70	61	53	53
Guaranteed standard of living	35	33	27	32	30	30
School integration	37	30	48	43	46	42
Public accommodations	61	65	53	51	61	62
Foreign aid	77	71	51	48	55	53
Trade with Communists	47	32	35	39	48	52
Vietnam involvement	58	48	73	58	61	65
Vietnam policy	59	54	63	60	61	60
Lawful protest	53	43	55	45	34	39
Civil disobedience	26	32	41	42	33	30
Mean Percent Liberal	*53*	*47*	*52*	*48*	*48*	*51*
Percent Democratic (of party identifiers)	31	41	43	42	51	41
Percent Democratic, 1968 presidential vote	23	26	34	20	36	21

Source. Survey Research Center, 1968 election data.

ent kinds of residence. The "mean liberalism" of the six size categories range only from 47 to 53 percent. Similarly, although the partisan tendencies in the six categories are varied, their relative ordering for northern white Protestants is nothing like the one based on entire population. For example, northern white Protestants in the sample most frequently call themselves Democrats when they live in a small town and most frequently call themselves Republicans when they live in large cities.[44]

In terms of population trends, big cities have been losing people while their suburbs have been gaining rapidly. In some popular discussions of voting trends, the suburban movement has been heralded as a sign of increasing voter conservatism and growing Republicanism.[45] As people move to the conservative suburbs, so the argument goes, they conform politically by adapting the more conservative opinions and Republican voting habits of their new neighbors. There are several flaws in this argument, however. We have seen, for instance, that people with similar group characteristics but in different places of residence, are pretty much alike politically. Second, even if suburbanites are slightly more conservative than their city counterparts with similar characteristics whom they left behind, the explanation could be that the most conservative city dwellers flee to the suburbs instead of becoming more conservative once they get there. Finally, even if it were true that people who move from city to suburb become more conservative as an adaption to suburban living, the reverse would also be true; the influx of allegedly liberal city folk would make the political norms of the suburbs more liberal.

Although the population movement to the suburbs may have little impact in terms of a national trend of opinion or partisanship, the flight to the suburbs is, of course, quite significant in regard to local politics. It has been forecast that if the present trend of white flight to the suburbs continues, most major cities will have black majorities in a few years, which may lead to a greater racial polarization of local politics than we have already. Also, since it is the more affluent who move to the suburbs, the financial base of the cities is becoming severely weakened at a time when their need to spend money for urban problems is becoming more acute. This growing urban crisis will in the coming decades become even more of a political focal point than it has in the past. As the cities demand more money from suburbanites who work but do not live in the city, from their often unsympathetic state legislatures, and from Congress, a heightened urban-rural conflict over spending priorities may be in development.

SEX AND POLITICAL OPINIONS

Differences in the political attitudes of men and women are so slight as to deserve only brief mention. Around the time female suffrage was implemented in the United States, with the ratification of the 19th Amendment in 1920, some observers voiced the apprehension that extension of the franchise to women would somehow transform the nature of American politics in a less desirable direction. Of course, no such fear was justified. For a while, women were less likely to exercise their right to vote than were men; yet this gap has decreased along with the disappearance of the cultural belief that political activity is incompatible with the feminine role. In political attitudes and voting, men and women are seldom different.

At one time, women were slightly more Republican than men in their partisan preference. But even this difference apparently has disappeared.[46] On political issues, differences between men and women are virtually nonexistent. Even on the issue of liberalized abortion laws—a key issue of the Women's Liberation movement, polls show that men and women have similar attitudes. Some exceptions to the rule are shown in Table 6-17. One apparent pattern shown is that women react to some political issues in what might be

TABLE 6-17 **Opinion Differences Between Men and Women on Selected Issues**

Opinion	Percent of Opinion Holders Supporting Belief		
	Men	Women	Difference
(1967) Favor a law that would require a person to obtain a police permit before he or she could buy a gun	66	83	−17
(1969) Oppose the death penalty for persons convicted of murder	36	51	−15
(1968)[a] Oppose stronger Vietnam stand that might mean invading North Vietnam	55	69	−14
(1968)[a] We should have stayed out of Vietnam	57	69	−12
(1968)[a] The government in Washington should see to it that every person has a job and a good standard of living	37	43	− 6
(1969) Oppose stricter laws dealing with obscene literature	13	6	+ 7
(1972) The penalties for the use of marijuana should be made less strict	36	28	+ 8
(1969) Divorce in this country should be easier to obtain	24	15	+ 9
(1971) Red China should be admitted to the United Nations	56	46	+10

Sources. [a] Survey Research Center, 1968 election data; others from *Gallup Opinion Index,* for years cited.
Note: for Gallup data, percentages may be in error by about one percent, since they were recalculated from original tables in which nonopinion holders were included in the percentage base.

called a more "tender-minded" fashion than men. For example, women are more opposed to the war in Vietnam and to capital punishment, but more favorable to a guaranteed job and gun control legislation. On some questions on what might be called social issues, women show what apparently is a more "puritanical" streak: they are more opposed to the legalization of marijuana and liberalized divorce laws, and more favorably inclined toward a crackdown on pornography. Even these differences can hardly be called significant, however.

CONCLUSION

Although the divisions we have discussed in this chapter do not exhaust all the possibilities for consideration, we have examined those that politicians and students of politics think are most important. Some of a person's group characteristics do make some difference in his opinions and voting behavior. For example, the more affluent one is, the more likely he is to resist government help for the less advantaged and to vote Republican. Blacks and whites are politically divided over even nonracial issues. Perhaps because of their minority status, Jews and Catholics support the Democratic party and its programs more than do Protestants. But some group characteristics do not appear to exert much influence on political opinions or voting behavior. Although Southern whites are certainly rather conservative on civil rights, and will vote accordingly, they are hardly different from their Northern brethren on other kinds of political issues. Whether a person lives in the cities, suburbs, or countryside does not seem to influence his political attitudes either. It is important to keep in mind that even when a group distinction does have some political importance, the identified social group will be far from uniform in its political opinions and voting behavior. Moreover, it is rare for any group to make a dramatic shift in its voting pattern that is different from the movement of the rest of the population.

Over time, certain group distinctions may rise or decrease in importance. For example, the distinction between farmers and non-farmers has receded in relevance with the decline in the farm population. Certain group distinctions that may increase in importance are divisions between young and old, the highly educated and the less educated, and perhaps even men and women. Although the women's liberation effort has yet to achieve manifestation in a male-female division in political polls, evidence of issue polarizations along lines of age and education are beginning to emerge. Although it has not happened yet, these additional sources of polarization on issues may also become more powerful as sources of voting alignments as well, replacing or joining the usual partisan distinctions between rich and poor, Northerner and Southerner, Protestant and non-Protestant, and white and black.

FOOTNOTES FOR CHAPTER 6

[1] "The Polls," Public Opinion Quarterly, 12 (1948), p. 781.

[2] These figures are recomputed from Table 63 in Seymour Martin Lipset and Earl Raab, The Politics of Unreason (New York: Harper and Row, 1970), pp. 402–403.

[3] Because farmers, as a group, cannot be meaningfully placed either high or low on the status hierarchy, they are excluded from our analysis of the relationship between occupational status and political attitudes. The dwindling number of farm owners and managers are more politically conservative than the national average. In terms of partisan politics farmers often shift their votes between Republicans and Democrats according to the economic conditions they face and the party in power at the time. On agrarian political behavior in the modern era, see Angus Campbell, et al, The American Voter (New York: John Wiley & Sons, 1960), Chapter 15.

[4] Gallup Opinion Index, August 1969, p. 20.

[5] There is evidence that on local referendums concerning proposals that if passed would raise property taxes to pay for various local projects, richer homeowners vote "yes" more frequently than do low-income property owners. See Edward Banfield and James Q. Wilson, "Public Regardingness as a Value Premise in Voting Behavior," American Political Science Review, 58 (December, 1964), pp. 876–887; Dennis S. Ippolito and Martin L. Levin, "Public Regardingness, Race, and Social Class: The Case of a Rapid Transit Referendum," Social Science Quarterly, 51 (December, 1970), pp. 628–633. Banfield and Wilson offer the provocative but controversial interpretation that upper-income groups are more "public regarding" than the "private regarding" poor taxpayers. By "public regarding," they mean that the affluent place the greater priority on the value of spending for "the public interest" or the "welfare of the community," as opposed to narrowly conceived "self-interest."

[6] The "job guarantee" questions employed in the three surveys are slightly different. In 1945, respondents were asked: "Which of these statements do you most agree with? (1) The most important job for the government is to make it certain that there are good opportunities for each person to get ahead on his own. (2) The most important job for the government is to guarantee every person a decent and steady job and standard of living." In 1956, people were asked whether they agreed or disagreed with the statement that "the government in Washington ought to see to it that everybody who wants to work can find a job." The 1968 question was whether "the government in Washington should see to it that every person has a job and a good standard of living" or whether "the government should just let each person get ahead on his own". Because the 1945 sample contained only white males, the analysis of the latter surveys is limited to white males also. The decline in the relationship between economic status and "job guarantee" opinion was first demonstrated by Philip E. Converse, "The Shifting Role of Class in Political Attitudes and Behavior," in Eleanor E.

Maccoby, et al. (eds.), *Readings in Social Psychology*, 3rd ed. (New York: Holt, Rinehart, and Winston, 1958), pp. 388–399.

[7] Detailed empirical assessment of the declining role of economic class in the shaping of social welfare attitudes is difficult, because of the frequent changes in the questions pollsters ask. The most complete evidence of the shifting importance of economic class is found in Philip E. Converse, "The Shifting Role of Class in Political Attitudes and Behavior," *op. cit.*

[8] *Gallup Opinion Index*, April 1972, p. 19.

[9] Samuel A. Stouffer, *Communism, Conformity, and Civil Liberties* (Garden City, N.Y.: Doubleday and Company, 1955); James W. Prothro and Charles Grigg, "Fundamental Principles of Democracy: Bases of Agreement and Disagreement," *Journal of Politics*, 22 (1960), pp. 276–294.

[10] For further evidence concerning the relationship between status and civil rights attitudes, see Paul B. Sheatsley, "White Attitudes Toward the Negro," *Daedalus* (Winter, 1966), pp. 217–238; Charles H. Stember, *Education and Attitude Change* (New York: Institution of Human Relations Press, 1961); Harlan Hahn, "Northern Referenda on Fair Housing," *Western Political Quarterly*, 21 (September, 1968), pp. 483–495; Howard D. Hamilton, "Voting Behavior in Open Housing Referenda," *Social Science Quarterly*, 51 (December, 1970), pp. 715–729; and Angus Campbell, *White Attitudes Toward Black People* (Ann Arbor: Institute for Social Research, 1971).

[11] Seymour Martin Lipset, *Political Man* (Garden City, N.Y.: Doubleday and Company, 1960), Chapter 4.

[12] Stember, *op. cit.*; Lewis Lipsitz, "Working Class Authoritarianism: A Re-Evaluation," *American Sociological Review*, 30 (1965), pp. 103–109.

[13] As we saw in the previous chapter, the gap between the political opinions of the more- and less-educated decrease with age.

[14] When whites and blacks are analyzed together in the same sample, the tendency is clearly for high status to be associated with foreign policy belligerence. See Richard Hamilton, "A Research Note on Mass Support for 'Tough' Military Initiatives," *American Sociological Review*, 33 (June, 1968), pp. 439–445; Martin Patchen, "Social Class and Dimensions of Foreign Policy Attitudes, *Social Science Quarterly*, 51 (December 1970), pp. 649–667. Also, a careful analysis of voting in local referendums on the Vietnam issue has shown that the lower status voting precincts were the ones with the greatest sentiment for withdrawal, see Harlan Hahn, "Correlates of Public Sentiments about War: Local Referenda on the Vietnam Issue," *American Political Science Review*, 64 (December, 1970), pp. 1186–1198.

[15] Milton J. Rosenberg, et al, *Vietnam and the Silent Majority* (New York: Harper and Row, 1970), pp. 54–65.

[16] V. O. Key, Jr., *Public Opinion and American Democracy* (New York: Alfred A. Knopf, 1961), p. 134; see also, the data reported in Richard Hamilton, *op. cit.*, and Patchen, *op. cit.*

[17] For a discussion on this problem in interpreting polls on foreign policy, see Milton J. Rosenberg, "Images in Relation to the Policy Process: American Public Opinion on Cold-War Issues," Chapter 8 in Herbert C. Kelman (ed.), *International Behavior: A Social-Psychological Analysis* (New York: Holt, Rinehart, and Winston, 1965), pp. 290–291, 317–318.

[18] Eugene J. Rosi, "Mass and Attentive Opinion on Nuclear Weapons Tests and Fallout," *Public Opinion Quarterly*, 29 (1965), pp. 280–297.

[19] This simple measure of "class voting" was first employed by Robert R. Alford in *Party and Society* (Chicago: Rand McNally, 1963).

[20] On the Depression's impact upon the relationship between class and voting among the "Depression generation," see Campbell, et al, *The American Voter,* pp. 356–361.

[21] Walter Dean Burnham, *Critical Elections and the Mainsprings of American Politics* (New York: W. W. Norton and Co., 1970).

[22] Computed from Tables 4.3 and 4.8 in David Butler and Donald Stokes, *Political Change in Great Britain* (New York: St. Martin's Press, 1969), pp. 70, 77.

[23] In 1956, 70 percent of France's industrial workers and 42 percent of its non-farm nonmanuals voted Socialist or Communist. The comparable figures for Italy in 1953 were 68 percent and 31 percent. (Recomputed from Lipset, *op. cit.,* tables on pp. 225–227.) On internation differences in class voting within other nations, see Alford, *op. cit.;* and Seymour M. Lipset and Stein Rokkan (eds.), *Party Systems, and Voter Alignments* (New York: The Free Press, 1967).

[24] Even blacks in higher status occupations are nearly unanimous in supporting social welfare programs. The black–white differences in social welfare opinion may be thought of as one form of class polarization—that is, the dominant white majority versus the black "underclass." Black–white differences are especially acute on the question of solving the problems of the urban ghetto.

[25] An example of high black voting for a Republican candidate occurred in the 1966 gubernatorial election in Maryland. The Democratic primary winner campaigned on the single issue of opposition to open housing legislation. As a consequence, the black wards of Baltimore voted overwhelmingly for the successful Republican candidate—Spiro T. Agnew. For an analysis of the election statistics of this contest, see Burnham, pp. 152–159.

[26] Hazel Erskine, "The Polls: Is War a Mistake?" *Public Opinion Quarterly, 34* (Spring, 1970), pp. 66–69.

[27] Hazel Erskine, "The Polls: The Politics of Age," *Public Opinion Quarterly, 35* (Fall, 1971), pp. 482, 486–487.

[28] The evidence that age cohorts do not become more Republican with time is quite convincing. See Neal E. Cutler, "Generation, Maturation, and Party Affiliation," *Public Opinion Quarterly, 33* (Winter, 1969– 1970), pp. 583–588; and Norval Glenn and Ted Hefner, "Further Evidence on Aging and Party Identification," *Public Opinion Quarterly, 36* (Spring, 1972), pp. 31–47.

[29] According to *The American Voter,* the sharpest cutting point in the relationship between age and party identification is between voters who came of political age before the Roosevelt era and those who entered the electorate during the earlier Thirties or later. See Campbell, et al, *op. cit.,* pp. 153–159.

[30] Thus, although age is apparently becoming a good predictor of people's isssue attitudes, it is declining as a predictor of presidential voting or party identification. See the Gallup data reported in Erskine, "The Polls: The Politics of Age," at pp. 491–494.

[31] See also Glenn and Hefner.

[32] Source: Survey Research Center, 1960 Election data. In this table and the following comparisons of Protestants, Catholics, and Jews, only Northern whites are compared in order to control for regional and racial differences. Almost all Southerners and Negroes are Protestants. In party preference, they are predominantly Democratic. Consequently, inclusion of Southerners and blacks would mask the importance of religion as a determinant of party preference.

210 *Group Differences in Political Opinions*

[33] Survey Research Center, 1968 election data.

[34] Raymond E. Wolfinger, "The Development and Persistence of Ethnic Voting," Lawrence H. Fuchs (ed.), *American Ethnic Politics* (New York: Harper and Row, 1968), pp. 163–193.

[35] Bernard R. Berelson, et al, *Voting* (Chicago: University of Chicago Press, 1954) pp. 64–66.

[36] Lawrence H. Fuchs, "American Jews and the Presidential Vote," in Fuchs, *op cit.*, pp. 144–162.

[37] For the most complete examination of what surveys show to be the political attitudes of Catholic ethnic groups, see Andrew M. Greeley, "Political Attitudes among American White Ethnics," *Public Opinion Quarterly, 36* (Summer, 1972), pp. 213–221.

[38] Harold E. Quinley, "The Protestant Clergy and the War in Vietnam," *Public Opinion Quarterly, 34* (Spring, 1970), pp. 43–52.

[39] Lipset and Raab, *op. cit.,* Chapter 10.

[40] However, one study of white Atlantans found evidence suggesting that even with education held constant, Baptists were more likely to vote for Wallace than were Protestant members of less fundamentalist denominations. See Anthony M. Orum, "Religion and the Rise of the Radical White: The Case of Southern Wallace Support in 1968," *Social Science Quarterly, 51* (December, 1970), pp. 674–688. Studies based on local samples of limited size suggest some support for a novel hypothesis regarding the relationship between fundamentalism and politics: the more frequently a fundamentalist attends church, the more politically conservative he is. But the more frequently a nonfundamentalist Protestant attends church, the more liberal is his politics. See Benton H. Johnson, "Ascetic Protestantism and Political Preference," *Public Opinion Quarterly, 26* (Spring, 1962), pp. 35–46; Benton H. Johnson, "Ascentic Protestantism and Political Preference in the Deep South," *American Journal of Sociology, 69* (January, 1964), pp. 359–366.

[41] To take but one instance of one-time regional differences in foreign policy "isolationism," when asked in 1945 whether the United States and Russia "should make a permanent military alliance," Southerners responded favorably by a ratio of greater than 2 to 1. At the other extreme, a slight majority of Midwesterners opposed such an alliance. See Hadley Cantril, *Public Opinion 1935–1946* (Princeton: Princeton University Press, 1951), p. 961. By the late 1950s, such disparities had largely disappeared. See Key, *Public Opinion and American Democracy,* pp. 106–107.

[42] Samuel C. Patterson, "The Political Cultures of the American States," in Norman R. Luttbeg (ed.), *Public Opinion and Public Policy* (Homewood, Ill.: Dorsey Press, 1968), pp. 275–292.

[43] The most politically relevant way of dividing states into regions may not be the customary division into East, Midwest, South, and West. For example, one study divided states on the basis of similarity of political characteristics with the result that three major regions emerged, labeled "Industrial," "Southern," and "Northwestern" states. See Norman R. Luttbeg, "Classifying the American States: An Empirical Attempt to Identify Internal Variations," *Midwest Journal of Political Science, 15* (1971). Even using this new classification scheme, there is little regional variation in mass political opinion, once we control for race and religion.

[44] Among the many studies of the political impact of suburban living are

Campbell, *op. cit.*, pp. 119–126; and Joseph Zikmund, "Suburban Voting in Presidential Elections: 1948–1964," *Midwest Journal of Political Science, 12* (May, 1968), pp. 239–258.
[45] Kevin P. Phillips, *The Emerging Republican Majority* (New Rochelle, N.Y.: Arlington House, 1969).
[46] According to Gallup data, the presidential voting of women was from three to six percentage points more Republican than that of men over the 1952–1960 period. But in the 1964 election, women were two percent *less* Republican than men. In 1968, women were four percentage points more likely to vote for Humphrey, the Democrat, and four percentage points less likely to vote for Wallace.

SEVEN

ELECTIONS AS INSTRUMENTS
OF POPULAR CONTROL

In a democracy, the public supposedly controls the behavior of its public officials by exercising its influence at the ballot box in a rational fashion. But the democratic institution of free elections is not in itself sufficient guarantee of public influence over governmental decisions. For example, it might be the case that none of the candidates the public can choose from offer the public what it wants. Or, through some combination of misguidance, ignorance, and indifference, the voters may behave "irrationally" when given a meaningful choice by failing to vote into office the candidates who would best represent their interests. Also, if officeholders *perceive* that the public is not watching, or that it does not care, they may feel free to make policy decisions without consideration of public opinion.

Looking at the matter in a positive rather than negative fashion, we can state the conditions that do allow elections to be an effective instrument for inducing policy decisions that are responsive to public opinion. First, the candidates should offer a meaningful choice of policy options for the voters to choose from and, once elected, the winner should try to carry out his campaign pledges and also respond to changes in public opinion and new policy demands. Second, the voters should be informed about the issues that separate the candidates and vote for those who best represent their own views. Clearly, the fulfillment of each of these two sets of conditions depends somewhat on the fulfillment of the other. For example, political leaders will pay greatest attention to public opinion when they believe that the public is alert enough to throw them out of office if they do not. Similarly, voters have the greatest opportunity to vote intelligently on the basis of policy issues when the politicians act from the assumption that they are going to do so.

In the present chapter we examine the behavior of the electorate when it carries out its assigned responsibility. Then in the following chapters we examine the responsiveness of political elites to public opinion.

POLITICAL CAMPAIGNS AND THE VOTER

Prior to each election, voters are bombarded by news and propaganda about the candidates who seek their favor. The amount of money that politicians spend on political campaigns is staggering. For example, approximately 300 million dollars (more than $4 per voter) was spent on behalf of the candidates for various offices in the 1968 election.[1] Judging by this attention that politicians give to the voters at election time, one might assume that the voter reacts to campaign stimuli in the fluid manner that, in his role as a consumer, he often reacts to advertising stimuli in the mass media. Just as the person about to purchase a product such as a detergent might vacillate in his choice of brands until the moment of purchase, so might the voter waver between the candidates until his entry into the voting booth forces him to make a final decision. But this image of the voting process exaggerates the number of voters available for seduction by political campaign appeals, since it ignores the typical voter's reliance on "brand loyalty" to one political party or the other.

As we have already discussed in Chapter Three, most American voters have a more or less permanent attachment to either the Republican or Democratic party. It is through the filter of party identification that most voters view the partisan aspects of the political world. The anchor of their party identification prevents most voters from wavering in their candidate choice during a campaign or in the party they vote from one election year to the next. For example, the Survey Research Center's panel study of the American electorate over the 1956–1960 period disclosed that of all the people who voted for President in both 1956 and 1960, 78 percent voted for the same party both times.[2] Similarly, during a presidential year most voters decide who they will support for president as early as convention time and stick to this choice over the course of the campaign. For example, panel studies of voter choices over the 1960 and 1964 presidential campaigns revealed that about 80 percent of the voters in each November election had voted consistently with their candidate preference in August.[3] When partisans do change their candidate choice during the campaign, the pattern is usually an initial attraction to the opposition's candidate followed by a return to the fold by election day. The percentage of the voters who stick with their party's choice is even higher in elections below the presidential level because the lesser amount of information that reaches the average voter is often too slight to give him any reason to go against his party. Only in nonpartisan elections and primary contests (in which party identification cannot be a criterion of choice) do voters vacillate in an erratic manner. In fact, voter preferences in primary contests are so fluid that pollsters have great difficulty predicting their outcomes even when they monitor opinion as late as a day or two prior to the election.[4]

Of course, if party identification were the sole determinant of how people vote, election results would simply reflect the balance of

Democratic and Republican identifiers. And since the ratio of Democratic to Republican identifiers is essentially stable over time, election results would be almost identical from one election to the next. This is the pattern in some multiparty democracies (for example, in Scandinavia and Holland) where party loyalties are hardened even more than in the United States due to the fact that parties concentrate their appeal on specific blocs of voters. But in America, as in other democracies where the parties make broad appeals to the electorate as a whole (for example, Britain, Canada), election results do often depart considerably from the voter division that would occur with a strict party line vote.

When an election is decided essentially on a party line basis, the result is called the "normal vote." Assuming a 50-50 split by Independents and only a minimum partisan defection rate that is equal on both sides, the normal vote in a national election would result in a victory for the Democrats who would obtain about 54 percent of the two-party vote.[5] This calculation reflects the Democratic edge in party identification (approximately three Democrats for every two Republicans) that more than counterbalances the effect of a higher turnout rate among Republicans than Democrats. The normal vote is approximated by the nationwide returns of midterm elections in which national issues are seldom important, while Republican and Democratic trends generated by various state and local contests cancel themselves out. The breakdown of the 1970 vote for the House of Representatives, by party, is shown in Table 7-1 and represents the typical midterm pattern. The low frequency of Democratic voting on the party of Republican identifiers is balanced by an equally low defection rate on the part of Democrats. The independent voters (whose turnout rate is particularly low in midterm elections) split their votes about evenly between the two parties.

When election results depart appreciably from the normal vote

TABLE 7-1 **Party Identification and the Congressional Vote, 1970**

Vote for House of Representatives	Party Identification			
	Democrat	Independent	Republican	Total
Democrat	83%	55%	12%	54%
Republican	17	45	88	46
	.100%	100%	100%	100%
N =	(304)	(168)	(209)	(681)

Source. Survey Research Center, 1970 election data.

expectation, the "short-term partisan forces" of the campaign favor one party more than the other. Unlike the national midterm pattern, strong short-term forces are often generated by the highly visible presidential campaigns, and push the election results away from the normal vote baseline. This tendency is shown in Figure 7-1, which

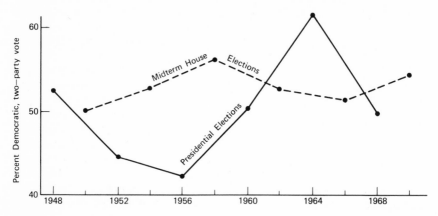

Figure 7-1. Voting trends in presidential and midterm House elections.

contrasts the variability of the vote for President with the stability of the normal vote pattern of midterm House election results. In three presidential elections shown (1948, 1960, and 1968), the results were close to normal. But the short-term forces greatly favored the Republicans in 1952 and 1956 when the popular General Eisenhower headed the Republican ticket and swung heavily in the Democrats' favor in 1964.[6] Actually, departures from normal voting in presidential races are due not only to public reaction to events over the short campaign period between the summer nominating conventions and the November election, but also to the public's accumulated four-year response to the incumbent administration and the public's images of the candidate once the major-party nominees are known. Generally the eventual victor's support peaks quite early in the campaign and declines somewhat thereafter, as the loser regains some support from the return to the fold of many of his party's usual followers once the campaign heats up. For example, the victories of Johnson in 1964 and Nixon in 1968 were both by smaller margins than predicted by preelection polls from a few months earlier. One notorious exception more or less proves the rule: in 1948, polls during the campaign indicated a Republican victory, but

a last minute surge toward Truman on the part of wayward Democrats who had been temporarily attracted to his opponent allowed
the final vote result to be a normal Democratic victory. Since normal
elections at the national level are won by the Democrats, the Republican party needs strong short-term forces in its favor in order to win
national elections. In fact, even when the Democrats win the presidency with less than 54 percent of the vote (the normal outcome),
as in 1960, it is actually the Republicans who have the edge in
short-term forces.

The departure of election results from the normal vote does not
signify that the usual role of party identification in shaping electoral
decisions has broken down. Instead, one finds that the party favored by the short-term forces is the beneficiary of most of the short-
term partisan defections and wins most of the Independent votes.
Figure 7-2 shows this pattern over the six presidential elections from
1948 through 1968. When the short-term forces favor the Republicans, Democrats "defect" beyond their normal rate, Republicans are
even more loyal to their party than usual, and Independents vote
overwhelmingly Republican. With pro-Democratic short-term forces,
the pattern is the reverse—with unusually frequent Republican
defections and a Democratic trend among Independents.

Short-Term Forces Below the Presidential Level

Relative to the excitement of presidential contests, campaigns for
office below the presidential level attract little voter interest. For

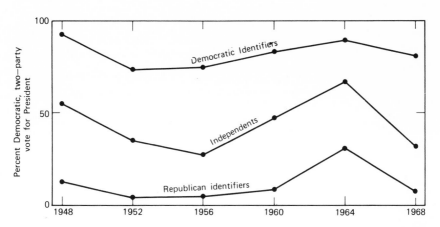

Figure 7-2. Party identification and the vote for president, 1948-1968.
(*Source.* SRC election data. The Wallace vote is not included
in the 1968 computations.)

Political Campaigns and the Voter **217**

this reason it is often assumed that campaigns waged for lower office have little impact on the election outcomes, with the results rarely deviating far from a simple reflection of normal voting strengths in the area, except for a possible adjustment in presidential years for the residual "coattail" impact of presidential contests. However, this extreme view that candidates and campaign issues are unimportant in nonpresidential elections exaggerates the importance of party identification. For example, it ignores the fact that, in some postelection polls, as many as half the respondents report that they split their ticket rather than vote for one party's candidates for all offices. Because of this ticket-splitting behavior, the same constituency often will vote the Democrats into one office and the Republicans into another—a practice that has been increasing over the years.[7]

Figure 7-3 offers one illustration of short-term forces operating in

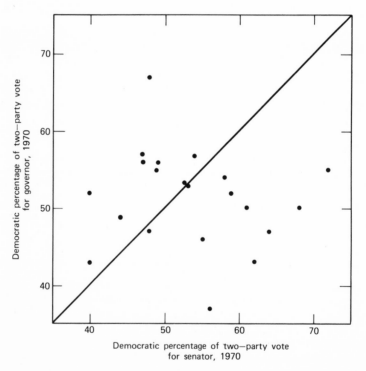

Figure 7-3. Relationship between vote for governor and vote for senator, by state, 1970. (Cases with third-party vote of greater than 10% are omitted.)

non-presidential campaigns. For states that elected both a governor and a U.S. senator in 1970, it shows the relationship between the statewide vote divisions for the two offices. If there had been no short-term forces generated by the separate campaigns for the different offices, all the observations shown in the graph would fall along the diagonal line—with the same vote division for each office. Instead, the states scatter on the graph without a pattern, so that one could not predict how a state was going to vote for governor from knowledge of the outcome of the race for senator, or vice versa.

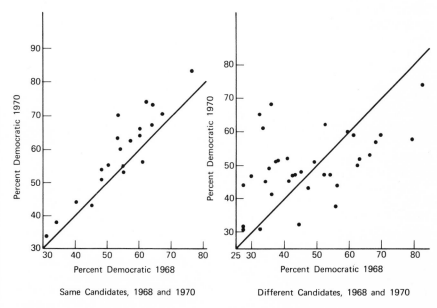

Figure 7-4. Partisan change in U.S. House elections as a function of candidate continuity.

Even the relatively invisible campaigns for the U.S. House of Representatives often have a sizable impact on the outcomes of these congressional contests. Figure 7-4 shows the distribution of the 1968–1970 shifts in the congressional vote for two types of districts —those in which each major party ran the same candidate in both 1968 and 1970, and those in which both parties ran different candidates in the two elections. Where the 1970 contests were rerun of the 1968 races with the same candidates, the vote shifts were uniform with slight shifts to the Democrats following the Republican 1968 election. But where each party fielded a new candidate, the vote shifts were quite varied, reflecting the change in the short-term forces produced by changes in the candidates running. Where the candidates changed, 30 percent of the districts also changed party hands, in some cases from Democratic to Republican against the national trend at the time.

Who Are The "Floating Voters"?

We have seen that the campaign stimuli that are presented to the voters have their own effect on elections independent of partisan loyalties, so that election results do often depart from the normal party vote. An important question is whether it is the most informed or the least informed voters who respond most to these campaign-generated short-term forces. If the "floating voters" who switch their vote in response to short-term campaign forces are more politically informed than the average, it would follow that election trends are essentially the response of the most politically alert segment of the public. But if the reverse were true—that floating voters are more politically ignorant than the average—then one might be compelled to support the more dismal conclusion that election trends are largely the result of campaign appeals that successfully reach the voters least capable of evaluating them.

Because of their "neutral" status, the Independents are more responsive to short-term forces than voters who develop identifications with one of the two parties. Since Independents lack the strong rooting interest in election outcomes that partisans often have, Independents vote less frequently than partisans do, and show up relatively low on tests for political involvement in campaigns. Although these indicators would seem to imply that Independents are also less politically *informed* than partisans, this is not true. Instead, the most accurate portrayal of voters selecting the Independent label appears to be that they are a heterogeneous lot, including voters too apolitical to articulate a partisan leaning, others temporarily disenchanted with the party to which they have previously given their loyalty, and also some "model" nonpartisan citizens ready to shift their political weight in response to the issues. Since the least informed Independents fail to attain the involvement "threshold" that would motivate them to vote in elections, the remaining Independents who do vote are actually slightly more informed than voting partisans. For example, Table 7-2 shows such a tendency present for the Survey Research Center's 1964 sample. On four crude measures of "political informedness," Independents show up as more informed than partisans.[8]

Although the least-informed voters are not overly represented among those who gravitate to the Independent label, they do display

TABLE 7-2 **Strength of Party Identification and Political "Informedness" of Voter (1964)**

	"Strong" Partisans	"Not so Strong" Partisans	Independent
Percent know mainland China to be Communist, not in UN	75	72	84
Percent interested in "government and politics"[a]	79	74	82
Percent high in mass media usage[b]	61	57	62
Percent who identify the Republicans as the most "conservative" party	65	63	66
Percent attended college	27	23	32
N =	(462-463)	(422-424)	(218-219)

Source. Survey Research Center, 1964 election data.
[a] Voters saying they follow government and politics either "all the time" or "some of the time" are scored as "interested." Other responses are "only now and then" or "hardly at all."
[b] "High" media usage means that the voter reports that he followed the campaign in at least three of the four mass media (newspaper, magazines, radio, TV).

the greatest susceptibility to changing their partisan leanings when new campaign information reaches them. It is the highly informed voter who is most resistant to the impact of campaign propaganda, because his accumulated storage of political information can bolster his initial views against the intruding information. For example, a Republican who is highly informed about politics is better equipped to discount Democratic propaganda than one who is more politically ignorant. But it does not always follow that the least attentive voters account for most of the voting trends of elections, because the least attentive voters sometimes receive no campaign information at all. Instead, the general rule appears to be that the least attentive voters are the ones most easily persuaded to vote against their initial partisan leanings—*but only when the campaign is visible enough to reach them.*[9] In a "low stimulus" election, in which the flow of campaign information is minimal, only the most attentive voters have sufficient knowledge to motivate a vote against their party. In contrast, even the least attentive voters usually receive some exposure to "high stimulus" presidential campaigns, thereby responding

Political Campaigns and the Voter **221**

more to the short-term forces of the campaign than the more attentive voters who follow the campaign closely.

U.S. House elections fit the category of low stimulus elections, since they are so invisible that only about half the voters claim to have read and heard anything about either of their local candidates before casting their ballot.[10] In such contests, only the most politically alert voters are able to respond to short-term forces generated by the campaign, but even they are usually able to act on only a bare minimum of information that reaches them. As Table 7-3 shows, the least informed voters in House elections are the least likely to vote against their party's candidate because they possess virtually no information about the candidates at all. Consequently, it appears that the electorate's response to short-term forces in low stimulus elections is largely the product of the minimal information obtained by the most attentive voters.

In high stimulus presidential contests, which attract high interest and high voter turnout, almost all voters receive some campaign exposure. For example, awareness of the candidates' names is nearly universal during a presidential campaign.[11] The general increase in the intake of political information during a presidential campaign temporarily loosens a greater number of voters from their partisan moorings—particularly among the least attentive voters. The tiny fraction of presidential voters who manage to avoid the campaign completely maintain stable candidate preferences throughout the campaign. But setting these few cases aside, partisan defections and preelection wavering in candidate choice are most frequent among voters with only slight exposure to the presidential campaign.[12] Similarly, voters who switch their presidential vote from one party to

TABLE 7-3 **Party Voting in U.S. House Elections, by Salience of Candidates in Contested Districts, 1958 (in Percent)**

	Voter Was Aware of		
Voted for Candidate	Both Candidates (N = 196)	One Candidate (N = 234)	Neither Candidate (N = 368)
Of own party	83	88	92
Of other party	17	12	8
Total	100	100	100

Source. Adapted from Table 4 in Donald E. Stokes and Warren E. Miller, "Party Government and the Salience of Congress," Public Opinion Quarterly, 26 (Winter, 1962), p. 541.

the other in successive presidential elections are on the whole less politically informed than voters who vote for the same party both times. The best demonstration of this rule is provided by the Survey Research Center's panel study of changing voter preferences over the 1956–1960 time period. Table 7-4 shows how the vote patterns of respondents who voted in both 1956 and 1960 varied with their degree of attention to the 1960 presidential campaign. Shifts in presidential voting from one party to the other were less frequent among the highly attentive voters (defined as those who monitored the campaign in three or more mass media—newspapers, radio, TV, magazines) than among the less attentive. Moreover, the shifts of the relatively inattentive were more uniformly in the predominant Republican to Democratic direction than were the less-frequent shifts of the more attentive voters. Consequently the net Democratic gain between 1956 and 1960 was greatest among voters who were low in attention (from 38 to 56 percent within the sample) than among voters who were high in campaign attention (only from 39 to 45 percent within the sample).[13]

From the kinds of findings we have just examined, it is often said that presidential election trends are largely determined by the behavior of the least informed voters. Converse states it this way: "not only is the electorate as a whole quite uninformed, but it is the least informed members within the electorate who seem to hold the critical 'balance of power' in the sense that alternatives in governing party depend disproportionately on shifts in their sentiment."[14] Indeed, one might even be tempted to conclude that the most effective kind of presidential campaign would be one aimed directly at the voter who is normally inattentive and uninformed about politics. But this interpretation ignores another consideration: the fact that the less malleable attentive voter is at least a more accessible target for campaign messages. Equally important is the fact that the contribution of relatively uninformed people to electoral trends is diluted by their low motivation to vote. As Table 7-5 shows (for 1956–1960), with nonvoters taken into account the net interelection vote shifts are not crucially different between information strata. Stated differently, although voters who respond to short-term forces of presidential campaigns tend to be somewhat less informed than the average *voter*, as a group they are about as informed as the average member of the eligible electorate.

THE ROLE OF ISSUES IN ELECTIONS

The previous section has shown that despite the constraint of fairly constant party loyalties, partisans cross party lines in sufficient numbers to produce considerable fluctuation in the parties' electoral

TABLE 7-4 **Presidential Vote Shifts, 1956-1960, by Mass Media Attention**[a]

		Low Mass Media Attention, 1960 [N = 259] 1956 Vote			High Mass Media Attention, 1960 [N = 467] 1956 Vote		
		Democrat	Republican	Total	Democrat	Republican	Total
1960 Vote	Democrat	33%	23%	56%	33%	12%	45%
	Republican	5%	39%	44%	6%	49%	55%
	Total	38%	62%	100%	39%	61%	100%

Source. Survey Research Center, 1956–1960 panel data.

[a] Mass media attention was classified as high if the respondent followed the 1960 campaign in at least three of the four mass media (newspapers, magazines, radio, TV), and low if the respondent followed the campaign in two or fewer.

TABLE 7-5   Net Vote Shifts, 1956-1960, by Media Attention Level[a]

Low Mass Media Attention, 1960				High Mass Media Attention, 1960			
	1956	1960	Change		1956	1960	Change
Democrat	24%	39%	+15%	Democrat	35%	44%	+9%
Republican	37	32	− 5	Republican	54	51	−3
Nonvote	39	29	−10	Nonvote	11	5	−6
Total	100%	100%		Total	100%	100%	

Source. Survey Research Center, 1956–1960 panel data.
[a] High media users are defined as those who followed the 1960 campaign in at least three mass media (newspapers, magazines, radio, TV). Low media users are the remainder.

fortunes. If elections cannot be successfully predicted simply on the basis of the underlying partisan division of the electorate, election issues (or candidates) must play a role in determining election outcomes. Although the term "issue" can refer to many different kinds of motivating factors, we focus here on policy issues—the proposals of the candidates as to how they will act on important policy questions.

Despite our current knowledge about voting behavior, scholars are not in full agreement on the actual role that policy issues play in elections. From what is known about the capabilities of the average voter, it is no surprise that many scholars reject the notion that it is meaningful to view election results as the response of the public to policy issues discussed during the campaign. For example, the authors of *The American Voter*, undoubtedly the single most influential book on voting behavior, offer the following, somewhat cynical, conclusion.

We have ... the portrait of an electorate almost wholly without detailed information about decision making in government. A substantial portion of the public is able to respond in a discrete manner to issues that *might* be the subject of legislative or administrative action. Yet it knows little about what government has done on these issues or what the parties propose to do. It is almost completely unable to judge the rationality of government actions; knowing little of particular policies and what has led to them, the mass electorate is not able to appraise either its goals or the appropriateness of the means chosen to serve these goals.[15]

There is a danger, however, in carrying the "voters are fools" argument too far, as the political sophistication of voters varies

The Role of Issues in Elections   **225**

widely. At the bottom of the scale is a sizeable fraction of the public who could be accurately labelled as political "know-nothings" because they are almost entirely devoid of political interest or knowledge. Found in all of society, these people seldom vote, however, and therefore exert little influence on elections. People who do vote make their electoral choices out of a variety of motivations. At a more or less superficial level, some are influenced by candidate "images" and personalities as they are portrayed in advertisements and in the news media. Others are at least able to judge past performances of government leaders—rewarding the incumbent party when its policies seem to work, and punishing it when they appear to fail. At the top of the scale are voters who choose candidates from a consideration of their offering of policy choices for the future. Since some voters are influenced by the candidates' policy offerings, this minority's views carry some weight in the determination of election outcomes, thus adding an element of rationality to the process. Though somewhat overstated, the argument pointing toward rationality in electoral decisions has been made by V. O. Key.

To be sure, many individual voters act in odd ways indeed; yet in the large the electorate behaves about as rationally and responsibly as we should expect, given the clarity of the alternatives presented to it and the character of the information available to it. In American presidential campaigns of recent decades the portrait of the American electorate that develops from the data is not one of an electorate straightjacketed by social determinants or moved by subconscious urges triggered by devilishly skillful propagandists. It is rather one of an electorate moved by concerns about central and relevant questions of public policy, of government performance, and of executive personality.[16]

The most balanced view of the role of policy issues in elections is that candidate policy stances are one of many determinants of election outcomes. If it were true that each voter selects the candidate who best represents his own policy views, then elections would be decided by the fact that a majority of voters preferred the policy views of the winning candidate to those of the loser. But because policy issues only influence some voters, and then in conjunction with other motivating forces, the candidate whose policy views are closest to those of the voters (or even to those of the most issue-oriented voters) cannot be sure of winning his election bid. For example, he might be threatened by a loss because he is less "well-known" than his opponent, because he lacks a favorable "image" in his television appearances, or, especially, if his party is the minority party in his area. For a candidate to win when his party is in the minority necessitates the successful encouragement of massive defections from the stronger opposition party, a task made difficult by the importance of party identification.

Are Voters Motivated by Policy Issues?

For voters to be influenced by policy issues when they cast their ballots, two conditions must be met. First, in order to cast a policy-oriented vote effectively, the voter must learn what the differences are between the policy views of the alternative candidates. In addition, the voter who possesses accurate recognition of the candidate stances must vote for the candidate whose views are closest to his own. Some understanding of the role policy issues play in motivating voter decisions can be obtained by examining how accurately survey respondents perceive the candidates' policy positions, and how often their reported votes go to the candidates who come closest to sharing their own stated policy views. Naturally, voters are most likely to be influenced by a policy issue when the divergence between the candidate stances is strong and the issue is of considerable importance to the electorate. Let us take a close look at evidence of policy voting from surveys conducted during recent presidential elections.

The Vietnam Issue in 1968

Did people vote for president in 1968 on the basis of their policy views on the Vietnam war?[17] First, let us examine the extent to which voters in 1968 were able to perceive differences between the Vietnam stances of their presidential candidates. To find the answer, the Survey Research Center asked its 1968 respondents to rate the Vietnam stances of each presidential candidate on a seven-point scale. The low end of the scale (a score of 1) represented the stand that "we should *withdraw completely* from Vietnam right now, no matter what the results." The high end (a score of 7) represented the opposite viewpoint that "we should do everything to win a *complete military victory,* no matter what the results." Thus, the higher the score a voter gave a candidate on this scale, the more "hawkish" he perceived the candidate's views to be.

The vast majority accurately perceived George Wallace's Vietnam position to be rather hawkish, resulting in an average score for him of 5.6 on the scale from 1 to 7. But there was less agreement on the stances of Nixon and Humphrey, since each received ratings for all parts of the scale (but mostly in the middle range). Their average ratings were only slightly divergent, as Nixon's average score was 4.6, while Humphrey's was only slightly more "dovish" at 4.2. The voters' average *self*-rating was nestled in between the average ratings for the two major-party candidates at 4.3.

The lack of voter agreement on where the major-party candidates stood on Vietnam does not necessarily mean that voters were not paying much attention to the Vietnam issue. Instead, it was quite difficult for even the most careful observer to detect what Humphrey and Nixon said they would do differently about Vietnam, since only a careful study of campaign statements would support the belief of the plurality of the public—that Humphrey's stand was slightly less hawkish than Nixon's.[18] In fact, given the vagueness of their stands, it is remarkable that there was as much voter agreement as there was on Nixon's and Humphrey's relative positions on Vietnam: 45 percent rated Humphrey more dovish than Nixon while 28 percent offered the reverse belief that Nixon was the relative dove in the race. The remaining 27 percent gave the two candidates identical ratings.

Because the major candidates' stances on Vietnam were far from crystal clear to the voters, the presidential decisions of 1968 voters were only slightly related to their policy views on Vietnam. As Table 7-6 shows, Vietnam hawks were the most likely to vote for

TABLE 7-6 **Vietnam Opinion and Presidential Voting, 1968**

	Scale Position						
	Immediate Withdrawal						Complete Military Victory
Voted For	1	2	3	4	5	6	7
Humphrey	53%	47%	49%	45%	39%	28%	32%
Nixon	38	49	51	48	55	50	46
Wallace	8	4	0	8	5	22	22
	99%	100%	100%	101%	99%	100%	100%
N =	(118)	(77)	(76)	(292)	(107)	(94)	(179)

Source. Survey Research Center, 1968 election data.

George Wallace, the most hawkish presidential candidate. But Humphrey, the most dovish candidate, received only a slightly greater percentage of the dove vote than from elsewhere on the Vietnam policy spectrum. Table 7-7 shows how the relationship between

TABLE 7-7   **Vietnam Opinion and the 1968 Presidential Vote, Controlling for the Effects of Party Identification**

	Percent Democratic of Two-Party Vote[a]		
	Vietnam Policy Preference		
Party Identification	Immediate Withdrawal (1, 2)	In Between (3, 4, 5)	Military Victory (6, 7)
Democratic	83% (86)	82% (201)	75% (94)
Independent	46 (46)	32 (113)	16 (56)
Republican	12 (50)	7 (133)	5 (63)

Source. Survey Center, 1968 election data.
[a] Wallace voters removed from the percentage computations for the table.

Vietnam opinion and the major-party vote looks with party identification held constant. Democratic identifiers who voted for Nixon tended to be more hawkish than those who stuck with Humphrey, while Republican identifiers who crossed over to vote for Humphrey tended to be the most dovish Republicans. Independents, presumably free of party ties, also voted more Republican if their Vietnam views were hawkish. But even dovish Independents gave more support to Nixon than to Humphrey, presumably for reasons other than the candidates' Vietnam stands.

One might wonder if Vietnam opinions would have been more highly related to voter decisions if the major party candidates had taken distinctly opposite viewpoints on the war. Suppose, for example, that instead of Nixon the Republican party had nominated Governor Reagan of California, a vocal hawk, while instead of Humphrey the Democrats had nominated Senator Eugene McCarthy, the outspoken dove who sought the nomination. We can estimate the extent to which voters would have divided along dove versus hawk lines in this hypothetical election by comparing the difference in the relative attraction to Reagan and McCarthy among doves and hawks.[19] The Survey Research Center's 1968 respondents were asked to rate their feelings toward both Reagan and McCarthy (along with other prominent politicians) as either "cold," "warm," or "neutral." Those who felt warm toward one of the two men but cool toward the other indicated a clear preference for Reagan or McCarthy if the choice were to be made between them. The relationship between these choices and the respondents' Vietnam opinions is as follows:

The Role of Issues in Elections   **229**

	Doves	In-Between	Hawks
McCarthy	82%	62%	32%
Reagan	18	38	68
	100%	100%	100%

McCarthy would have clearly won this "election," perhaps simply because he was better known than Reagan. But while McCarthy was favored by over four-fifths of the doves, Reagan was the choice of over two-thirds of the hawks.[20] Clearly people's Vietnam positions could have had considerable influence on their election choices in 1968 if the candidates had offered clearly divergent policy choices on the war.

The Urban Unrest Issue in 1968

Sharing the spotlight with Vietnam in the 1968 presidential contest was the issue of urban unrest and rioting.[21] After several years of episodic rioting in black ghettos, the presidential candidates were forced to give some indication of what they would do about it. More so than the other two candidates, Humphrey emphasized the approach of solving the problems of poverty as a means to dampening urban unrest. Wallace clearly favored the solution of massive use of force. Nixon's position was somewhere in between.

The Survey Research Center asked each 1968 respondent to rate the positions of the three presidential candidates and themselves on an "urban unrest" scale. The ratings were on a seven-point scale from 1 (correct the problems of poverty and unemployment that give rise to the disturbances) to 7 (use all available force to maintain law and order—no matter what the results).

Almost all voters agreed that Humphrey was to what might be called the left of center (average score of 2.7). The majority also saw Wallace as occupying the extreme "law and order" position (average score of 6.4). In between, the average placement of Nixon was very slightly to the right of center at 4.2. The average self-placement of the voters was at 3.4—or virtually midway between Humphrey and Nixon. Most voters (64 percent) correctly saw Nixon's position as more hardline than Humphrey's, while only 16 percent had the reverse—mistaken—impression. The remaining nineteen percent gave the two major-party candidates identical ratings on the urban unrest scale. Thus, in the 1968 campaign the bulk of the voting public was able to correctly perceive that Humphrey was the most liberal on the domestic problem of urban unrest, Wallace an extreme conservative, and Nixon somewhere in between.

TABLE 7-8 Urban Unrest Opinion and Presidential Voting, (1968)

Voted For	Scale Position						
	Solve Problems 1	2	3	4	5	6	Use Force 7
Humphrey	66%	52%	58%	35%	21%	22%	25%
Nixon	30	46	37	58	65	56	39
Wallace	3	3	4	7	14	22	36
	100%	101%	99%	100%	100%	100%	100%
N =	(175)	(114)	(107)	(284)	(104)	(74)	(102)

Source. Survey Research Center, 1968 election data.

Table 7-8 reveals a quite strong relationship between the voter's stand on urban unrest and his vote choice in 1968. For example, the majority of voters who placed emphasis on solving the causes of poverty voted for Humphrey, the candidate who best represented their views, while less than one quarter of the voters who opted for emphasis on use of "all available force" to quell rioting did so. Most of Wallace's support was from strong law and order people, while Nixon's was concentrated in the middle and right-hand side of the spectrum on the urban unrest issue. One reason why Humphrey ran best among urban unrest liberals is that Democratic identifiers are more liberal than Republicans on matters of social welfare—a dimension that is touched by the urban unrest issue. Consequently, the tendency would have occurred even if all partisans simply voted for their party's candidate. But the influence of the issue was also present in the pattern of party defections (see Table 7-9) as Democrats were most likely to vote for Nixon if they were strong law and order supporters, while the few Republicans who supported Humphrey were toward the liberal end of the political spectrum on the issue of urban unrest. Meanwhile, Independents were most likely to support Nixon over Humphrey if they favored a strong law and order stand.

Civil Rights as an Issue in 1964

Candidate differences on issues are the most clearly presented when the major party candidates take explicitly opposite stands on important legislative issues. One of these instances (which are surprisingly rare) occurred when President Johnson and Senator Goldwater took

TABLE 7-9 "Urban Unrest" Opinion, and the 1968 Presidential Vote, Controlling for the Effects of "Party Identification"

	Percent Democratic, of Two-Party Vote[a]		
	Urban Unrest Policy Preference		
Party Identification	Fight Poverty (1, 2)	In Between (3, 4, 5)	Use Force (6, 7)
Democrat	90% (161)	74% (176)	69% (51)
Independent	44 (57)	31 (137)	14 (29)
Republican	7 (61)	8 (143)	5 (43)

Source. Survey Research Center, 1968 election data.
[a] Wallace voters are removed from the percentage computations for this table.

opposite stands on the Civil Rights Act of 1964, which guaranteed all races equal access to public accommodations such as hotels and restaurants. President Johnson successfully pushed the bill through Congress where Goldwater, his eventual opponent, voted against it on the alleged grounds of its unconstitutionality. When asked for the candidates' stands on the Civil Rights law, an overwhelming 95 percent of the Survey Research Center's 1964 respondents who had heard of the act (over three quarters of the total sample) correctly stated that Johnson favored it, while 84 percent correctly stated that Goldwater opposed it.[22]

About three quarters of the voters in the Survey Research Center's 1964 sample expressed opinions on the Civil Rights law for that year, and said their mind was "made up" on the matter. The law's supporters and opponents disagreed considerably in their presidential voting. Johnson's share of the vote was only 47 percent among the law's opponents but an overwhelming 82 percent among its supporters.

Table 7-10 shows that many people broke with their party identification in order to achieve this consistency between their views on public accommodations and their candidate choice. For example, a majority of "weak Republicans" who favored the Public Accomodations Act voted Democratic for President while more than one third of the "weak Democrats" who opposed the act swam against the partisan tide to vote Republican for President. Only "strong" partisans remained reasonably loyal to their party when their views on the Public Accommodations law varied from those of their party's candidate.

TABLE 7-10   **Opinion on the 1964 Civil Rights Act and Presidential Voting, 1964**

	Percent Democratic, Presidential Vote	
	Pro Civil Rights Act, Mind "Made Up" (N = 477)	Con Civil Rights Act, Mind "Made Up" (N = 386)
Strong Democrats	99%	86%
Weak Democrats	94	64
Independents	79	42
Weak Republicans	58	27
Strong Republicans	27	4
All cases	82%	47%

Source. Survey Research Center, 1964 election data. For exact wording of the question on the Public Accommodations Law, see the Appendix.

Predicting Votes from Policy Stances

One's ability to predict how a voter will act on the basis of his policy views increases if the voters' views over a range of several issues are taken into account. For example, Table 7-11 shows that voters who gave consistently liberal responses to each item on a three-item issue scale (school integration, medicare, and foreign aid) voted overwhelmingly Democratic in 1964, while their consistently conservative counterparts voted overwhelmingly Republican. Although this example is taken from the uniquely "ideological" 1964 election, the same pattern can be replicated for relevant issues of most other presidential campaigns as well.[23] In similar fashion, the correlation between a voter's presidential preference and his policy views increases if the voter is allowed to choose the issues that concern him most.[24] Even the voter's self-identification as a liberal or conservative is a fairly good predictor of his vote for president and even (at least in California) for statewide offices.[25] In fact, on balance it appears that measures of voters' policy stances summed over several issues perform about as well as predictors of how people vote as do party identification and measures that tap voters' evaluations of the candidates' personalities.[26]

The Problem of Causality

Unfortunately, it is not clear how much of the consistency between the policy views people express and those of the candidates they vote for is a product of rational policy voting, since some portion of it is attributable to voters adapting issue stances to rationalize candidate choices made on other—possibly irrational—grounds. What is clear is that voters have a strong need to maintain cognitive con-

TABLE 7-11 **"Composite" Liberalism-Conservatism and Presidential Voting, 1964**

	Scale Scores[a]						
	Most Liberal						Most Conservative
Voted For	−3	−2	−1	0	+1	+2	+3
Johnson	90	89	75	68	50	35	20
Goldwater	10	11	25	32	50	65	80
	100%	100%	100%	100%	100%	100%	100%
N =	(177)	(156)	(260)	(177)	(204)	(81)	(35)

Source. Survey Research Center, 1968 election data.

[a] Scale scores are assigned according to the pattern of opinion on three issues: medical care, school integration, and foreign aid. Each respondent's score is the number of opinions, on the three issues, expressed in opposition to government activity in the particular sphere, minus the number of opinions expressed in favor of government activity in the particular sphere. No points were either subtracted or added for each response of "no interest," "don't know," or "depends." For the full texts of the three opinion questions, see the Appendix.

sistency between their issue stances, their perceptions of the issue stances of the candidates, and their choice of a candidate. Rational policy voting—the selection of a candidate on the basis of his policy stances—is only one source of this consistency.

Consider the possible modes of resolution for the voter whose beliefs are initially out of alignment—for example, he might have liberal views but be initially attracted to the candidate who he later learns is more conservative. How such a voter would resolve this dilemma depends on which of the three elements—his policy views, his perceptions of the candidates' policy views, and his candidate preference—is the weakest link. If the voter feels strongly about his views and is certain that his favored candidate opposes them, he could resolve the dilemma by changing his choice of candidate. This, of course, would be a pure case of policy voting. But if the candidate stands are sufficiently vague or only weakly publicized, the easiest way out would be to shift one's estimate of the candidate stances.[27] This process, known as *projection,* is perhaps the most frequent resolution of the dilemma. For example, many of the Nixon voters in 1968 who inconsistently held dovish views on the war in Vietnam incorrectly perceived Nixon's Vietnam policy stand to be more dovish than Humphrey's. Only when the candidate stances are unambiguously different and well-publicized, as those of Johnson and Goldwater in 1964 on the Public Accommodations Act, does a sizeable rate of false projection of candidate stances fail to occur.

A third resolution of the dilemma would be for the voter to change a relatively weak policy stance to make it consistent with that of his preferred candidate. We have already examined this process, known as *rationalization,* in the context of our discussion of the relationship between issue stands and party identification. Although some people switch their party identification to make it consistent with their issue stances (for example, the conservative Democrat who begins to call himself a Republican), probably the most frequent pattern is a switch of issue stances to align them with one's party identification. A similar pattern may work during a political campaign to change the policy stances of voters, including Independents, into alignment with those of the candidate to whom they are initially attracted for reasons that have nothing to do with their stances on the particular policy. Rationalization is most evident when a sudden or unexpected policy stance taken by a candidate causes the views of his supporters to be more in line with his position and those of his opponents to become more unfavorable. One rare instance when this process was clearly visible occurred during the 1956 presidential campaign when Adlai Stevenson, the Democratic candidate, unexpectedly announced that he was in favor of a cessation of nuclear testing, a stance that provoked strong opposition from President Eisenhower, his Republican opponent. Whereas normally there had been no difference between the views of Republican and Democratic voters on nucelar policy during the 1950s, the polarization of the candidates on this issue produced a temporary inflation of support for a nuclear test ban among Stevenson supporters and a temporary steep drop in support for a nuclear test ban among Eisenhower voters.[28] Since the complicated test ban issue was not one on which many voters had strongly crystallized opinions, people reacted to Stevenson's introduction of the issue by switching to their candidate's position rather than by shifting their candidate choice to correspond to their initial test ban views. Although injection of this issue into the campaign did not greatly influence the election outcome, it did serve the function of temporarily rearranging people's thinking on the subject.

The process of rationalization makes it difficult to disentangle fully the causal process which produces a correlation between voters' policy views and their candidate choice. Consider for example, the problem of interpreting the following results of a survey of Wisconsin voters conducted after a hotly contested gubernatorial election fought on the tax issue.[29] In this 1962 election, the Republican candidate for governor favored an increase in the sales tax to increase revenue, while his Democratic opponent favored an increase in the income tax instead. Two-thirds of the voters who favored the sales tax voted for the Republican candidate, who represented their views, while the same percentage of the income tax proponents voted for the Democratic candidate. At first glance, it would seem that many Wisconsin voters based their gubernatorial vote on some kind of evaluation of which candidate's tax policy would be better for their state. However, when the voters in the sample were asked the main reason for their candidate choice, only a tiny fraction gave tax policy as the reason. Apparently, then, the strong consistency between tax policy preference and candidate preference occurred mainly because many voters chose a stand on the complicated tax issue by adopting the views of their candidate instead of choosing between the candidates by evaluating the merits of their tax stands. (Also, Wisconsin Democrats and Republicans could have been somewhat divided on tax policy before the election campaign.) Here the candidates for governor gave Wisconsin voters a rare opportunity to choose a governor on the basis of clearly divergent tax proposals. Yet voters chose to use other criteria, essentially relying on their party identification.

The alert reader will notice that any example of consistency between voters' policy preferences and those of the candidates they vote for can in part be due to rationalization rather than policy voting. Consider our previous example of the sizeable correlation between opinions on the Public Accommodations Act and presidential voting in 1964. For some voters, the explanation for their voting for the candidate who represented their views may have been that their preference for Johnson on other grounds caused them to shift toward Johnson's favorable opinion of the law or, for others, that attraction to Goldwater provoked opposition to the law. Unfortunately, we have no way of directly testing whether this explanation or its rival—that voters shifted their candidate choice to correspond to their civil rights views—contains the greater validity. Undoubtedly both processes were at work, but in unknown proportions. Scholars who are consistently skeptical of the electorate's capabilities for policy voting may subscribe to one view, while others who prefer to see evidence of rational electoral decisions may subscribe to the other. To settle the matter of whether correlations between voter policy opinions and candidate choices are mainly due to voters picking a candidate first and then agreeing with his policy positions or to voters standing firm on their policy positions and then choosing a candidate who shares their views, we need to follow shifts in voters' policy stances and candidate choices over the course of a political campaign. But, unfortunately, this crucial evidence does not exist. Without such data we can only make educated guesses of the extent to which the process of rationalization accounts for the relationship between policy choice and candidate choice. On complicated and remote issues that do not attract much mass interest, it is a good guess that consistency is mostly a product of *post hoc* rationalizations of voting decisions. But on "gut" issues that attract public attention or visibly affect people's daily lives, a politician or observer would be foolish to predict that the number of voters who pick their candidate according to their policy views would be insignificant.

Issue Voting as Retrospective Judgment

Only a limited segment of the public is capable of policy voting in the manner we have described. People whose votes are shaped by the policy views of the candidates undoubtedly come largely from the ranks of "ideologues" and, to a lesser extent, from group-oriented voters, whose judgments about candidates and parties are formed by evaluations of the groups they represent (for example, rich, poor, black, white). Other voters evaluate the political world around them according to the "nature of the times." If times are perceived to be good, the incumbent party is rewarded; if times are bad, the incumbents are punished. As Richard Brody suggests, the typical citizen's "vote more nearly reflects his reaction to a party's past performance on an issue rather than his desire to give a mandate for a new policy direction."[30] For example, a very good predictor of whether a voter in 1968 would vote for Humphrey was his evaluation of "how President Johnson has done his job:"[31]

Rating of Johnson	Percent for Humphrey
Very good	80
Good	58
Fair	33
Poor	11
Very poor	4

The rule that voters react according to their satisfaction with the incumbent's handling of problems has the interesting implication that the voter will sometimes vote against the incumbent even if his only opponent takes policy stands that are even further removed from the voter's own apparent policy preferences. For example, this principle can be applied to voting behavior in the key New Hampshire presidential primary of 1968, in which Senator McCarthy, running on the issue of opposition to the Vietnam War, "upset" President Johnson. Although McCarthy received his strongest support (82 percent) from the state's few "doves," more of his protest votes came from the numerous hawks than from doves. In fact, hawks who also "disapproved" of Johnson's handling of Vietnam rejected Johnson at a greater rate (52 percent) than did the voters who were in between the dove and hawk ends of the Vietnam policy scale (38 percent).[32] What McCarthy's dove and hawk supporters had in common despite their different policy preferences was frustration with the status quo war policies of the Johnson administration—a frustration that was channelled into a victory for Richard Nixon that November. A surprising aspect of McCarthy's national constituency was that many of his supporters were also attracted to George Wallace.[33] Since McCarthy, the challenger from the political left, and Wallace, the challenger from the right, both opposed the established politics of the day, many "alienated" voters who were disturbed about the nation's political course could find comfort in dual support for both of the obvious advocates of change.

The voter whose issue voting is limited to retrospective judgments of the incumbent's performance should not necessarily be ridiculed, because given his limited political awareness of information, this behavior course may be the most rational one available. Many voters do not have the political involvement necessary to evaluate policy proposals for future action or to monitor the candidate's policy proposals. But they can take readings of the incumbents' performance to date, and throw the rascals out if the obvious signs indicate that it is time, in Campbell's words, to let "a new bunch of fellows run things" for a while.[34] Moreover, even informed voters may agree it is time for a change even though the incumbent's challenger fails to give a meaningful indication of what he would do differently if elected. For example, although Herbert Hoover was denied a second term in 1932 because he was unfortunate enough to serve during the onset of the Great Depression, the public did not know what it was getting when it decided to let Franklin Roosevelt run the country. Judging from Roosevelt's campaign rhetoric or from the difference between the prevailing Republican and Democratic ideologies of the time, one might have thought that Roosevelt would make even less use of the federal government to reverse the economic trend than Hoover was doing during his last days in office.[35] But buoyed by his mandate to try something different, Roosevelt's policies evolved into the New Deal program involving a far greater role of the federal government in American life than had been known before. Once Roosevelt's policies became crystallized, in 1936 the American public gave him an even larger mandate to continue the New Deal policies. Although Roosevelt's 1936 landslide victory can partially be interpreted as a simple "nature of the times" reward for valiant leadership, his policies also produced a massive realignment of voters according to their policy views, with social welfare liberals moving toward Roosevelt and the Democrats and conservatives moving away.

POLICY VOTING AND ELECTION SHIFTS

Since voters are sometimes influenced by policy issues, there is a potential for policy issues to play a decisive role in election outcomes. We have already noted that party fortunes in elections often fluctuate considerably from one election to the next. Could it be that these fluctuations are at least partially caused by the electorate's response to the alternative policies offered by the candidates? Alternatively, are fluctuations in party fortunes at election time caused by changing evaluations of the party's past performance record rather than their specific proposals for change?

Shifts in the Public "Mood"

The most obvious way in which issues could produce electoral change would occur if shifts in voter sentiment on policy issues produce changes in party fortunes. For example, political journalists often will interpret a Democratic victory as the result of a liberal mood on the part of the electorate and a Republican victory as a conservative reaction. But, as we saw in Chapter Two, cyclical swings in the public mood back and forth from liberal to conservative do not occur. Consequently, short-term public mood fluctuations between liberalism and conservatism cannot explain changes in partisan voting tides, because such mood fluctuations do not exist. To be sure, there can be rare but important exceptions, such as the public's change from predominantly hawkish to dovish views on Vietnam. But normally, when a question of public policy persists over a long period of time (for example, school integration, medicare, foreign aid), any changes in the distribution of mass opinion are glacial.

However, the public does often change its evaluations of the relative capabilities of the Democratic and Republican parties as solvers of key problems. Polling agencies have periodically asked public samples which party was most likely to bring about prosperity and which party was most likely to bring about peace. These judgments (see Figure 7-5), largely based on retrospective judgments of the

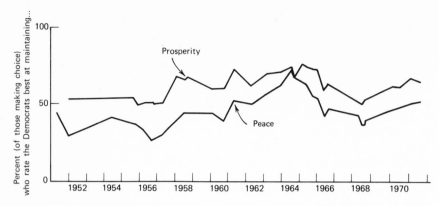

Figure 7-5. Ratings of parties on peace and prosperity. Questions: (prosperity) "which political party—the Republicans or the Democrats—do you think will keep the country prosperous?", (peace) "which political party do you think would be more likely to keep the United States out of World War III—the Republican party or the Democratic party?" (*Source. Gallup Opinion Index.*)

recent performance of the incumbent president's party, can operate as something of a barometer of election results. They follow predictable rules, such as that the incumbent party is most likely to be seen as the "prosperity" party when the economy is healthy, and most likely to be seen as the party of "peace" when the nation is not at war. For example, the Democratic party, which is normally seen as the prosperity party anyway, made strong short-term gains in its prosperity-producing image during the "Republican" recessions of 1958 and 1970. It is instructive that the Democrats made their best midterm showings since the 1930s in the elections of these two years, while the Republicans look back fondly of their 1946 "landslide" during the post-World War II period of relative economic deprivation and Democratic control of the Presidency. Elaborate statistical analysis of historical data going back to the prepoll area has shown that economic prosperity usually produces electoral gains for the party controlling the presidency.[36]

Following the course of public perceptions of which party is the party of peace is also instructive. Largely because the "Democrat-produced" Korean War lasted a frustrating three years, only to end in a bewildering stalemate, the public gave the Republicans the overwhelming edge as the peace party during the 1950s. However, the Democrats were able to reverse this trend slightly when they showed that they too could keep the nation out of war in the early

1960s. Then, of course, came the Vietnam war, which by 1968 had given the peace image back to the Republicans, who gradually began to lose it again once the war became theirs.

Which is the more important determinant of presidential election outcomes—the public's shifting evaluations of party capabilities on domestic policy, or on foreign policy? Although domestic policy views comprise the stronger factor in shaping *individual* voting decisions, in recent times it has been the public's foreign policy response that has caused the most electoral *change* at the presidential level. According to Donald Stokes' statistical analysis of the forces at work in presidential elections, the Republicans' foreign policy edge declined from a net advantage of about 3½ percent of the vote in 1952 to a slight net liability in 1964.[37] Over this period, the Democrats' net domestic policy advantage did not vary more than one percentage point from the average of one percent of the vote.[38]

Responses to foreign policy produce the greater short-term electoral change because the public can respond more readily to sudden international events than to the more gradual changes on the domestic scene. However, drastic changes in the nation's economy, though infrequent, do produce shifts in party fortunes that can be long lasting. The Great Depression beginning in 1929 did, of course, produce a long-term benefit to the Democratic party. Similarly, the more distant Depression of 1893 hurt the Democrats, in power at the time, so badly that they became the minority party for years thereafter.[39] Both of these post-Depression political changes were strong enough to be labelled "partisan realignments" of the American electorate.

Shifts in Candidate Issue Stances

Changes in the cast of candidates from one election to another bring about changes in the policy orientations of the candidates from which the voters must choose. If voters do reward and punish candidates on the basis of their policy stances, the fluctuation of candidate policy proposals can be a contributor to electoral change. It is part of the popular lore politics that in a two-man race the candidate who stakes out the middle ground of the political spectrum will win by virtue of his appeal to the moderate voters. Belief in this principle often causes opposing candidates to gravitate away from the liberal and conservative poles toward the more moderate range. Following a model developed by Anthony Downs,[40] this situation is depicted in Figure 7-6a. Assuming policy-oriented voters distribute themselves in a bell-shaped curve across the political spectrum, those to the left of center will vote for the candidate slightly to the left of center, while those to the right of center will vote for the candidate slightly

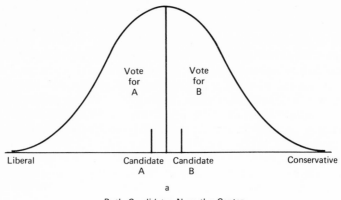

Vote
for
A

Vote
for
B

Liberal   Candidate Candidate   Conservative
                      A   B

a

Both Candidates Near the Center

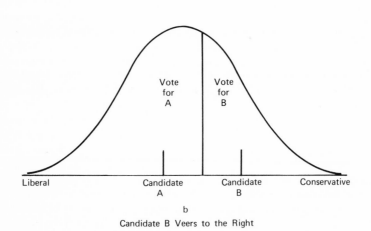

Vote
for
A

Vote
for
B

Liberal   Candidate   Candidate   Conservative
                          A   B

b

Candidate B Veers to the Right

Figure 7-6. Candidate ideology and voter response (hypothetical).

to the right. If the candidates are stationed symmetrically (equidis-
tant from the center), neither will have the policy edge. But if one
of the candidates veers toward one of the ideological extremes (as
does the conservative in Figure 7-6b), then the policy-oriented voters
in the middle of the spectrum will vote for the more compatible
candidate only slightly off center, giving him the victory.

Although only some unknown fraction of the public approaches the sensitivity to issues necessary for this model to work perfectly, the presence of some policy voting by the electorate allows the forces the model describes to have some bearing on election outcomes. If moderate candidates are the best vote getters, this would normally mean that the least conservative Republicans and the least liberal Democrats make the best candidates.

In U. S. House elections, conservative Republican congressmen are poorer vote getters than their Republican counterparts who represent the moderate-to-liberal wing of their party.[41] Table 7-12 shows this tendency at work in the 1970 midterm House elections. In 14 of 15 comparisons of relatively conservative and relatively liberal Republican congressmen from politically similar and neighboring districts, the more conservative congressman is the poorer vote getter, as measured by the difference in their vote leads over Nixon's 1968 performance in their district. Although the tendency is far less dramatic for Democrats, moderate Democrats in the House also appear to be somewhat better vote-getters than their more liberal brethren.

Although very few people possess more than the most superficial knowledge about their congressman, the tiny minority who are both knowledgeable and seemingly moderate in their preferences do shift their political weight in House elections, rewarding moderates and punishing those who by comparison are "extremists." A survey analysis of voting behavior in the 1964 House elections found that the electoral impact of the policy stands of Republican congressmen could be accounted for by the behavior of those Independents and Republicans who voted Democratic for President and were also highly informed about both their congressman and politics in general. Nine such voters who were picked up in the sieve of a national sample had a moderate-to-liberal Republican congressman seeking reelection, and all but one of the nine voted for him. Meanwhile of the six respondents meeting the outlined criteria who had the choice of voting for the reelection of a *conservative* Republican Congressman, all but one voted Democratic instead.[42]

If even a congressman's electoral margin is affected by his policy stance, certainly the outcomes of presidential contests must also be affected by the policy positions of the candidates. Unlike the case with party identification and issue orientation which are also good predictors of presidential voting, the public's relative attraction to the Republican and Democratic presidential candidate does change dramatically from one election to the next. On the basis of statistical analysis of voting data, Donald Stokes has calculated that these shifts in the public response to presidential candidates comprise the major determinant of presidential voting shifts.[43] For example, the public's net assessment of Eisenhower and Stevenson added about five percent of the vote to the Republican column in

TABLE 7-12   **The Difference in the Vote for Matched Conservative and Liberal Republican Congressmen in 1970**[a]

Congressman	State and District	ADA Score (Liberalism)	Republican Percent Two-Party Vote		Congress Minus President	Difference
			President 1968	Congress 1970		
Talcott	Calif. 12	24	50.2	65.2	15.0	
McClosky	Calif. 11	64	45.4	78.7	33.3	+18.3
Goldwater	Calif. 27	0	55.2	68.6	13.4	
Bell	Calif. 28	28	57.0	72.8	15.8	+ 2.4
Michel	Ill. 18	20	52.2	66.1	13.9	
Railsback	Ill. 19	48	50.9	68.2	17.3	+ 3.4
Morton	Md. 1	16	46.7	76.2	29.5	
Gude	Md. 5	80	44.4	63.4	19.0	−10.5
Keith	Mass. 12	40	43.0	50.4	7.4	
Heckler	Mass. 10	72	38.2	57.0	18.8	+11.4
McDonald	Mich. 19	24	44.3	59.2	14.9	
Riegle	Mich. 7	80	40.5	70.3	29.8	+14.9
Chamberlain	Mich. 6	12	52.1	60.3	8.2	
Esch	Mich. 2	52	48.1	62.5	14.4	+ 6.2
Nelsen	Minn. 2	16	51.9	63.3	11.4	
Quie	Minn. 1	40	47.3	69.3	22.0	+10.6
Langen	Minn. 7	12	47.0	45.9	−1.1	
Zwach	Minn. 6	44	44.2	52.3	8.1	+ 9.2
Foreman	N.M. 2	4	51.8	48.6	−3.2	
Lujan	N.M. 1	36	52.4	58.5	6.1	+ 9.3
Devine	Ohio 12	4	50.4	57.7	7.3	
Miller	Ohio 10	40	51.2	66.5	15.3	+ 8.0
Minshall	Ohio 23	12	58.3	60.1	1.8	
Mosher	Ohio 13	88	53.6	61.7	8.1	+ 6.3
Bow	Ohio 16	12	49.5	56.2	6.7	
Stanton	Ohio 11	52	45.1	68.2	23.1	+16.4
Corbett	Pa. 18	20	47.0	61.5	14.5	
Fulton	Pa. 27	56	44.1	61.2	17.1	+ 2.6
Johnson	Pa. 23	4	53.9	57.9	4.0	
McDade	Pa. 10	56	49.1	66.6	17.5	+13.5
Average	Conservative		50.2	59.8	9.6	
	Liberal		46.8	65.1	18.3	+ 8.7

[a] Republican congressmen are matched if they are (1) at least 25 points apart on the ADA liberalism index, (2) from neighboring districts within the same state (contiguous districts or districts within the same metropolitan area), and (3) their districts were no more than 5.0 percent of the vote apart in their vote for Nixon in 1968.

1952 and about eight percent in 1956. By contrast, the public's net evaluation of Johnson versus Goldwater in 1964 added about 10 percent of the votes to the Democratic column in 1964. In recent presidential elections, the major-party candidates who produced the most one-sided public reactions have been Eisenhower (very favorable) and Goldwater (very negative). A major reason for Goldwater's negative image was his extremely conservative policy orientation, as many voters viewed him as too conservative or even radical. The popular Eisenhower, on the other hand, represented the more moderate wing of the Republican party of his day. Although major reasons for his great appeal were his standing as a military hero and the warmth he projected, his appeal was undoubtedly enhanced by his avoidance of the divisive rhetoric of his party's right wing.

Shifts in the Importance of Issues

Still a third way in which election results can be influenced by policy issues is the possibility that the impact of policy issues on voting decisions varies from one election to the next. When issues stand out as a motivating factor behind voting decisions, the results might well be different than when issues are muted during a campaign. Although one cannot apply a general rule regarding the consequences of an issue-laden election (such as that either liberal or conservative candidates should usually be favored), it is evident that some elections are decided more on the basis of policy considerations than others. For example, in neither 1956 nor 1960 did policy issues appear to be responsible for many partisan defections. In 1956, the pervasive popular image of the incumbent President was the predominant force behind the massive Democratic defections. In 1960, most defections in each partisan direction were motivated by the unique "issue" of Kennedy's Catholicism. By comparison, policy issues played a much greater role in the 1964 and 1968 presidential contests. Largely responsible in 1964 was Goldwater's explicitly "ideological" campaign. In 1968, the Wallace entry was one cause, but the crisis-laden setting of the 1968 campaign was undoubtedly an additional factor.

Accompanying the trend toward increased policy voting is the recent increase in public perceptions of party differences on policy issues, note in Chapter Three. Civil rights issues in particular have become an increasingly strong source of Republican and Democratic division. As Figure 7-7 shows, in 1956 and 1960 the presidential vote divisions among supporters and opponents of federal activity to support school integration were nearly identical. But in 1964 and 1968 integration supporters began to outdistance opponents of integration activity in their rate of Democratic voting. The same increase in

Policy Voting and Election Shifts **245**

TABLE 7-13 **Social Welfare Issues and the Vote, 1936–1952**

1936: "Do you favor the compulsory old-age insurance plan, starting January first, which requires employers and employees to make equal monthly contributions?" (Social Security)

	Yes	No
Percent Roosevelt (Democrat)	69%	35%
Percent Landon (Republican)	31	65
	100%	100%
	($N = 2899$)	($N = 1263$)

1940: "During the next four years do you think there should be more or less regulation of business by the Federal government than at present?"

	More Regulation	About Same	Less Regulation
Percent Roosevelt (Democrat)	77%	79%	22%
Percent Willkie (Republican)	23	21	78
	100%	100%	100%
	($N = 1204$)	($N = 958$)	($N = 2346$)

issue voting can be seen, though on a lesser scale, if we examine foreign policy issues and social welfare issues. Figure 7-7 shows that foreign aid supporters have begun to vote more Democratic than foreign aid opponents, whereas in 1956 and 1960 the pattern had actually been the reverse. Although presidential voting decisions have been correlated with social welfare opinions since at least the 1930s, the gap between the Democratic voting rates of social welfare liberals and conservatives also has widened somewhat, as the figure illustrates for the medical care issue.

Is the strong issue voting found in 1964 and 1968 a new departure from previous elections? Actually a case can be made that the issue-free 1956 and 1960 campaigns, during a period of political tranquility, were the deviant cases. Foreign policy and civil rights issues did not exert much influence on presidential elections prior to 1956. But from the New Deal era through even 1952—the first Eisenhower election—social welfare liberals and conservatives were rather divided in their voting. Some examples from surveys over the 1936–52 period are shown in Table 7-13. The major difference be-

1948: "As things stand today, do you think the laws governing labor unions are too strict or not strict enough?"

	Too Strict	About Right	Not Strict Enough
Percent Truman (Democrat)	77%	58%	36%
Percent Dewey (Republican)	23	42	64
	100%	100%	100%
	(N = 460)	(N = 693)	(N = 637)

1952: "Some people think the national government should do more in trying to deal with such problems as unemployment, education, housing, and so on. Others think the government is already doing too much. On the whole, would you say that what the government has done has been about right, too much, or not enough?"

	Not Enough	About Right	Too Much
Percent Stevenson (Democrat)	56%	46%	11%
Percent Eisenhower (Republican)	44	54	89
	100%	100%	100%
	(N = 293)	(N = 650)	(N = 238)

Sources. 1936, 1940, 1948 percentages recomputed from tables in V. O. Key, Jr., *The Responsible Electorate* (Cambridge: Belknap Press, 1966), pp. 43, 45, 48. 1952 percentages recomputed from Table I in Angus Campbell, Gerald Gurin, and Warren E. Miller, "Political Issues and the Vote: November, 1952," *American Political Science Review,* 46 (1953), pp. 359–385.

tween the role that issues play today and 25 years ago is in the increased importance of nonsocial welfare issues in presidential campaigns.

THE POSSIBILITY OF ELECTORAL REALIGNMENT

The collective decisions the voter makes at election time contain elements of both stability and change. The fact that most voting decisions are based on long-standing partisan loyalty adds an element of stability, with election results fluctuating around the baseline figure of the "normal vote." Electoral change is evident from the departures of election results from the normal vote baseline.

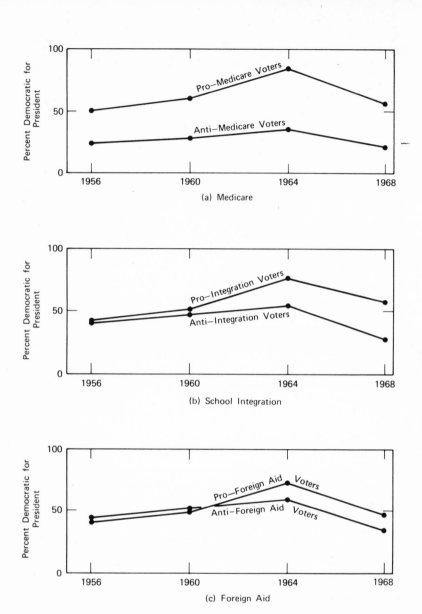

Figure 7-7. The relationship between three issues and the vote in four presidential elections. (*Source.* SRC election data.)

Although the exact amount cannot be measured with precision, the electorate's response to campaign issues plays some role—even if limited—in producing electoral change.

Electoral shifts are normally only temporary, because voters shifting toward the advantaged party or candidate do not change their party identification in the process. Consequently, they may surge in the opposite partisan direction in a subsequent election, or even do so when voting in another contest held on the same date. Yet it is conceivable that circumstances could be so polarizing as to cause permanent transfers of partisan loyalties, rather than temporary partisan defections. The most recent such realignment period, centered in the 1930s, produced a change from a considerable Republican advantage in national voting loyalties to a long-term Democratic edge in party identification that persists today. This change can be interpreted as at least a partial ratification by the American electorate of President Roosevelt's then unprecedented expansion of federal government services that were applied to cope with the equally unprecedented Great Depression. If another realignment is on the near horizon, it could restore the Republican party to the predominant position, or weaken it further. Or it could change the focus of the issues that separate the two parties without producing a *net* change in the distribution of partisan loyalties. If any of these possibilities become true, the public will have rearranged its partisan loyalties as a long-term electoral response to the decisive issues of the day.

FOOTNOTES TO CHAPTER 7

[1] Herbert E. Alexander, "Financing Parties in Campaigns in 1968," in William J. Crotty, et al. (eds.), *Political Parties and Political Behavior,* 2nd ed. (Boston: Allyn and Bacon, 1971), p. 316.

[2] Philip E. Converse, "Information Flow and the Stability of Partisan Attitudes," *Public Opinion Quarterly,* 26 (Winter, 1962), pp. 578–599.

[3] Thomas W. Benham, "Polling for a Presidential Candidate: Some Observations on the 1964 Campaign," *Public Opinion Quarterly,* 29 (Summer, 1965), pp. 177–178.

[4] Robert P. Abelson, "Computers, Polls, and Public Opinion—Some Puzzles and Paradoxes," *Trans-Action,* 5 (September, 1968), pp. 20–27.

[5] Philip E. Converse, "The Concept of the Normal Vote," in Angus Campbell, et al., *Elections and the Political Order* (New York: Wiley, 1966), pp. 7–39.

[6] On the concept of short-term partisan forces in elections, see Angus Campbell, "Issues and Voters: Past and Present," *Journal of Politics,* 26 (November, 1964), pp. 745–757.

[7] Walter Dean Burnham, *Critical Elections and the Mainsprings of American Politics* (New York: Norton, 1970), pp. 119–120.

[8] The question of the "informedness" of the Independent voter has been sub-

ject to some controversy. Apparently the earlier view that Independents are less informed than the average was solely inferred from the finding that Independents are less interested in campaigns, care less who wins them, and vote less often than the partisan. See, for example, Angus Campbell, et al. The American Voter (John Wiley and Sons, 1960), pp. 142–145. The finding that the Independents are actually not an especially uninformed group is a relatively recent discovery. See William H. Flanigan, Political Behavior of the American Electorate, 2nd ed. (Boston: Allyn and Bacon, 1972), pp. 47–48. Burnham has suggested that recent converts to the "Independent" category have added to the overall informedness of the Independent group (Burnham, op. cit., pp. 127–129). But Independents were not once any less informed, relative to partisans, than they are now, as the pattern shown in Table 7-2 can be replicated with data from earlier years as well as from 1964 and later.

[9] Converse, "Information Flow."

[10] Donald E. Stokes and Warren E. Miller, "Party Government and the Saliency of Congress," Public Opinion Quarterly, 26 (Winter, 1962), pp. 531–546.

[11] A Gallup poll during the 1948 presidential campaign found that 88 percent could recall the name of the Republican presidential candidate (Dewey) and 91 percent could name President Truman as the Democratic candidate. Presidential candidates are not always well-known prior to their nomination. For example, immediately prior to his Democratic nomination in 1952, only 34 percent could identify Adlai Stevenson. Recognition of vice-presidential candidates is, at least according to a 1948 poll, only around the 50 percent mark. For further details, see Hazel Gaudet Erskine, "The Polls: The Informed Public," Public Opinion Quarterly, 26 (Winter, 1962), pp. 669–677.

[12] Converse has shown that the most extremely uninformed voters (such as 1960 voters who deliberately avoided the televised debates between the candidates) are almost perfectly stable in their partisan preferences (Converse, "Information Flow"). However, a more recent analysis by William Dreyer suggests that people who vote in presidential elections without any information are too scarce to obscure the general tendency for the least informed to have the most stable partisan preferences. See William Dreyer, "Media Use and Electoral Choices: Some Political Consequences of Information Exposure," Public Opinion Quarterly, 35 (Winter, 1971–1972), pp. 544–553.

[13] Table 7-4 shows that in 1956 the informed and uninformed voted alike, while in 1960 the uninformed were more Democratic than were the informed. It is the 1960 pattern that is "normal," since voters in the lower socioeconomic strata tend to be relatively uninformed and also relatively Democratic in their voting habits.

[14] Converse, "Information Flow," p. 578.

[15] Angus Campbell, et al., The American Voter, op. cit., p. 543.

[16] V. O. Key, Jr., The Responsible Electorate (Cambridge: The Belknap Press of Harvard University Press, 1966), pp. 7–8.

[17] For analyses of the Vietnam issue in 1968 that are similar to ours, see Benjamin I. Page and Richard A. Brody, "Policy Voting and the Electoral Process: The Vietnam War Issue," American Political Science Review, 66 (September, 1972) pp. 979–995, and Richard W. Boyd, "Popular Control of Public Policy: A Normal Vote Analysis of the 1968 Presidential Election," American Political Science Review, 66 (June, 1972), pp. 429–449.

[18] For an analysis of the 1968 presidential candidates' campaign rhetoric on

Vietnam, see Page and Brody, pp. 984–985.

[19] The insights that can be gained from an analysis of a McCarthy-Reagan "election" was first suggested by Page and Brody, op. cit. They report that voters would also have reacted according to their Vietnam views in a hypothetical McCarthy-Wallace race.

[20] Our McCarthy versus Reagan analysis is limited to the responses of actual voters whose response was warm to one but cold to the other, a subsample of 211 respondents.

[21] An analysis of the urban unrest issue in 1968 similar to ours is found in Boyd, op. cit.

[22] Boyd, p. 444.

[23] For example, scores on a multi-issue "issue partisanship" scale were highly correlated with voting decisions in the 1952 presidential election. See Angus Campbell, Gerald Gurin, and Warren E. Miller, The Voter Decides (Evanston: Row, Peterson, and Co., 1954), pp. 112–143.

[24] David E. Repass, "Issue Salience and Party Choice," American Political Science Review, 65 (June, 1971), pp. 389–400.

[25] Modest correlations between self-rated liberalism-conservatism and voting decisions in both primary and general election contests are reported in Totten J. Anderson and Charles G. Bell, "The 1970 Election in California," Western Political Quarterly, 24 (June, 1971), pp. 252–273.

[26] Even in the relatively issue-free 1956 presidential election, issue orientation was a better vote predictor than candidate orientation, although a somewhat weaker predictor than party identification. See Angus Campbell and Donald E. Stokes, "Partisan Attitudes and the Presidential Vote," in Eugene Burdick and Arthur J. Brodbeck (eds.), American Voting Behavior (Glencoe: The Free Press, 1959), pp. 353–371. In 1964, issue orientation was almost as good a predictor as party identification (Repass, op. cit.).

[27] Drury R. Sherrod, "Selective Perception of Political Candidates," Public Opinion Quarterly, 35 (Winter, 1971–1972), pp. 554–562; Samuel Kirkpatrick, "Political Attitude Structure and Component Change," Public Opinion Quarterly, 34 (Fall, 1970), pp. 403–407.

[28] Eugene J. Rosi, "Mass and Attentive Opinion on Nuclear Weapons Test and Fallout, 1954–1963," Public Opinion Quarterly, 29 (Summer, 1965), pp. 280–297.

[29] This analysis of a Wisconsin election is drawn from Leon D. Epstein, "Election Decision and Policy Mandate; An Empirical Example," Public Opinion Quarterly, 28 (Winter, 1964); and Gerald M. Pomper, Elections in America (New York: Dodd, Mead, 1968).

[30] Richard A. Brody, "How Vietnam May Affect the Election," Trans-Action, 5 (October, 1968), p. 19.

[31] Boyd, p. 440.

[32] Robert E. Craig, "The Protest Coalition: Voting Behavior in the New Hampshire Democratic Presidential Primary, 1968," paper delivered at the 1971 annual meeting of the American Political Science Association, Chicago, Illinois.

[33] Philip E. Converse et al., "Continuity and Change in American Politics: Parties and Issues in the 1968 Election," American Political Science Review, 63 (December, 1969), pp. 1092–1095.

[34] Angus Campbell, "Issues and Voters," p. 755.

[35] Everett Carll Ladd, American Political Parties: Social Change and Political Response (New York: Norton, 1970), pp. 207–209.

[36] Gerald H. Kramer, "Short-term Fluctuations in U.S. Voting Behavior, 1896–1964." *American Political Science Review, 65* (March, 1971), pp. 131–143.

[37] Donald E. Stokes, "Some Dynamic Elements of Contests for the Presidency," *American Political Science Review, 60* (March, 1966), pp. 19–28.

[38] Stokes, *op. cit.*

[39] Burnham (*op. cit.*, pp. 38–39) traces the 1894–1932 Republican hegemony to the economic crash of 1893. From 1876 through 1892, interparty competition at the national level had been more evenly balanced than during any other period of American history.

[40] Anthony Downs, *An Economic Theory of Democracy* (New York: Harper and Row, 1957), chapter 8.

[41] Robert S. Erikson, "The Electoral Impact of Congressional Roll Call Voting," *American Political Science Review, 65* (December, 1971), pp. 1018–1032.

[42] Ibid., pp. 1029–1032.

[43] Stokes, *op. cit.*

EIGHT

THE PUBLIC AND ITS ELECTED REPRESENTATIVES

In the previous chapter, the public showed some ability to utilize elections as a policy expression to their representatives. While this public competence fell far short of the democratic "ideal," policy-responsive voters can alter the outcome of a close election. In this chapter and the next, we turn to the political leaders' ability to achieve consistency between public opinion and public policy by way of the five models of political linkage we discussed in Chapter One. The Rational-Activist Model requires many policy directed and participant voters, and a group of political leaders forced to be responsive by public elections. The Sharing Model considers the agreement between the opinions of both leaders and the public that may make policy consistent with public opinion, and the Role Playing Model focuses on the leader's personal concern to represent his constituency as he sees their preferences.

These three models receive the most extensive evaluation here as they posit characteristics of the representatives that condition their response to the public. The Pressure Group and Political Party Models, positing mediating institutions presumed to encourage political linkage, will be covered in the next chapter.

OPINION SHARING BETWEEN POLICY MAKERS AND THE PUBLIC

The simplest form of linkage between public opinion and the policy decisions of political leaders would be the simple sharing of common opinions by followers and leaders. Consider, for example, the result if we elected congressmen by lottery. Just as a randomly selected sample of survey respondents is representative of the general population within a certain margin of error, so would be an assembly of 435 randomly selected people acting as a House of Representatives. If such an assembly could act without being distracted by the demands of powerful interest groups or the rules of the actual Congress that impede change, then—for better or worse—its decision would reflect public opinion. In actuality the Congress is less representative than a random sample, if for no other reason than that its members are supposedly chosen for their superior capabilities rather than their typicality.

How then do our congressmen and our other political leaders differ from the general population? To answer this question we must find the traits that motivate some but not others to pursue a political career and the traits that produce success at achieving this goal. When people who are active in politics—whether as a local party official or an elected legislator—are interviewed, they often report that a spur to their political career was a very politically active family. The consensus based on several studies is that about 40 percent of the presently politically active grew up in politically active homes. Thus, assuming only about 10 percent of the public—at the most—are very active in politics themselves, almost half of our political leaders come from the 10 percent of the nation's families that are most politically active.[1]

Office holders are also differentiated from the general population by the forces that recruit them for office. Intense political interest alone cannot push a person into a political leadership role. In order to contest an election seriously, the would-be political leader must attract the base of support necessary to win. In some cases, the political leader is a "self-starter" who, because of his political interest and ambition, announces his candidacy and then is able to accumulate support. In other cases, the future leader is procured by the local business or party elite for the task of getting elected. Sometimes the community or party leaders can choose from among many active aspirants for the role. But often at the local level, previously nonpolitical people end up as office holders through the urging of friends or business associates. Kenneth Prewitt finds these "lateral entrants" to politics among members of the nonpartisan city councils he studies.[2] James Barber finds them among members of the highly partisan Connecticut legislature. Many are what he calls "reluctants"—serving not because of their raw ambition or political interest, but because of the insistence of others.[3]

Because the most wealthy and best educated are most likely to be politically interested and articulate and have the visibility to be tapped for a leadership role, it is not surprising that these are also the people who are represented among our political leaders. Put simply, there is an upper-status bias to the political leadership opportunity structure. For example, as Table 8-1 shows, the vast majority of American legislators have "professional" or "managerial" jobs in a society where only 19 percent of the work force are engaged in such occupations. Lawyers and businessmen are particularly overrepresented. Additionally, greater percentages of legislators are whites, males, Protestants and older people (nonyouth) than are found for the general population.[4]

In part, the overrepresentation of the affluent and educated in the councils of government stems from the middle-class leadership

TABLE 8-1   Occupations of American Legislators (in Percent)

	U.S. Senators (1947–1957)	U.S. House (1949–1951)	State Legislators (1951–1961)[a]	U.S. Labor Force (1960)
Professional, technical	64	64	37	11
Proprietor, manager, official	29	22	32	8
Farmer, farm manager	7	4	16	4
Craftsman, foreman, operative	—	—	5	14
Clerical, sales	—	4	8	22
Unskilled labor, servant, farm labor	—	2	[b]	34
Other, not known	—	2	3	7
Total	100	100	100	100

Source. (Legislators) Malcolm E. Jewell and Samuel C. Patterson, *The Legislative Process in the United States* (New York: Random House, 1966), p. 108, assembled from earlier studies; (population) U.S. Census.
[a] Average of nine states studied within the date range indicated.
[b] Less than one percent.

structure of the two major political parties. Even the Democratic Party—supposedly the more representative of the working man—draws its leadership from the middle class. By contrast, in many other democracies, the presence of a Socialist or Labor Party draws working-class people into greater political activity. In Norway, for example, political participation is not correlated with affluence as it is in the United States.[5] Although Socialist and Labor Parties do not draw their leaders exclusively from the working class that they represent, they do at least open a door for the political recruitment of blue-collar workers that is rather closed in this country.[6]

There is not anything inherently sinister about the status differentiation between political leaders and the general public, since the disproportionate concentration of political leadership skills in the hands of the better educated and prosperous may make it all but inevitable. For example, even the delegates to the "reformed" Democratic National Convention of 1972 were still far better educated and more affluent than the general population, although representative on the basis of race, sex, and age.[7] Even movements of economic protest draw their leaders from the most affluent strata

Opinion Sharing Between Policy Makers and the Public **255**

within the protest group. For example, Lipset finds this to be the pattern within agricultural protest movements: "The battle for higher prices and a better economic return for their labor has been conducted by the farmers who need it least."[8]

The status "bias" to the leadership structure does not necessarily mean that the political views of political leaders typify their class instead of the general public. For example, the 1972 delegates to the Democratic Convention obviously did not express the prevailing views of the economically comfortable. To be sure, there are potential sources of misrepresentation in the group background of political leaders. For example, one might suspect that state legislatures would be more eager to pass "no fault" insurance laws if they contained fewer lawyers. Or, the city council that is overstocked with local businessmen might well be suspected of reflecting the prevailing norms of the local business community rather than the views of the general population. A more general consideration is that whatever their individual ideologies, the generally affluent leaders might resist redistributive legislation that would work against their self-interest. For example, a study of the attitudes of national convention delegates (in 1956) found that one of the few issues on which delegates of *both* parties were clearly on the conservative side of the public was that of making the rich pay a greater share of the taxes.[9] Of course, one could argue that virtually all political viewpoints found in the general population are also shared by *some* of the prosperous and better educated—and these might be our leaders. Moreover, even among the more affluent, few are sufficiently politically motivated to run for public office, so it is unlikely that political representatives from such backgrounds even accurately represent the opinions of their economic group.[10] Thus, one can hope that there is sufficient diversity of viewpoint among the candidates for office from which the people make their selections at the polls. And if not, there is still the possibility that electoral pressure can divert the behavior of political leaders away from unrepresentative personal preferences.

We can also try a direct approach to the question of whether political leaders and the general public share the same opinions by comparing the political attitudes of the two sets of groups. As we saw in Chapter Four, the public gives less support for freedom of speech, including the right of all citizens to strive to implement their positions into public policy. In this instance, the more supportive political representatives better aid democracy in *not* sharing public opinion. But the lesser tolerance by the mass public does not negate the importance of representatives sharing their constituents' opinions on specific programs being considered by government. No amount of exceptional support for freedom of speech or democratic rules of the game by representatives would make their failure to create a public policy consistent with public opinion more palatable. Like V. O. Key, we see the importance of another standard for democracy, ". . . if a democracy is to exist, the belief must be widespread that public opinion, at least in the long-run, affects the course of public action.[11] He is referring here to the opinions on more specific programs and issues before government, and we presume that the belief that the public opinion counts rests on its really having an impact. Our inquiry turns now to the representatives' opinion on specific issues.

About the only published data from which we can assess the correspondence between the policy views of the public and its elected leaders is a CBS poll of Congress and the public in 1970. Comparisons on five issues are shown in Table 8-2. (A sixth issue—wage and price controls—is omitted.) Although a selection of other issues (such as national health insurance) might well reveal a different pattern, on the five issues shown, the senators (and representa-

TABLE 8-2 **Comparison of Public and Congressional Opinion on Key Policy Issues, 1970**

	Public	U.S. House Members	U.S. Senators
1. *Vietnam:* Percent say "speed up our withdrawal"	27	30	45
2. *Defense:* Percent say "place less emphasis" on military weapons programs	30	37	45
3. *Guaranteed Income:* Percent approve at least "$1600 for a family of four or more"	48	65	76
4. *Civil Rights:* Percent say government should go farther to improve blacks' conditions	53	58	76
5. *Supreme Court:* Percent deny it gives "too much consideration to rights of people suspected of crimes"	29	36	56

Source. "Candidates, Congress and Constituents," CBS News Poll, Series 70, No. 7, Report 5. All congressmen were surveyed.

Note: Except for question 5, the questions asked the public sample and the congressmen were not exactly identical, although close enough to each other to allow rough comparison.

tives to a lesser extent) held views that can be described as somewhat more liberal than the public's. One might say that in terms of accepting new ideas, congressmen were somewhat ahead of public opinion. Still, one should exercise caution in interpreting these results because the public sample and the congressmen were asked questions that had slightly different wordings. Given this caution, it is remarkable that the public's responses are generally only a few percentage points different from the House members'—though, of course, not the senators.'

Why are the opinions of congressmen and the general public in even rough correspondence? Possibly, the correspondence is evidence of the Sharing Model at work—congressional candidates are recruited from the same attitudinal milieu as the general population. But also, the similarity could, in part, be the result of elections weeding out the congressional candidates who do not share the public's views. In any case, we should not conclude from this table that policy is also congruent with public opinion. There are forces—such as the inertial drag of congressional rules and norms, the opposition of powerful pressure groups, and the failure of presidential leadership—that can prevent even a representative Congress from doing what the public seems to want.

We might also ask whether, in addition to the correspondence between congressional and public opinion in the aggregate, individual congressmen share the policy of their particular constituencies. As part of an ambitious study (of which more will be said later), Warren Miller and Donald Stokes collected the views of both congressmen and their constituencies following the 1958 election.[12] Although the questions asked congressmen and voters were not identical, they covered the same subjects. Consequently, we can ask whether the congressmen with the most liberal views represented the most liberal House districts. Comparisons were made in three policy domains: civil rights, foreign policy, and social welfare. As Figure 8-1 shows, in each domain the correlation between the congressman's personal attitude and the views of his constituency was positive: +.50 in civil rights, +.32 in foreign policy, and +.26 in domestic welfare. In other words, the most liberal districts do tend to elect the congressmen with the most liberal viewpoints. Although the relationships are far from perfect, there would be some correspondence between constituency preferences and the congressman's vote were he to vote solely on the basis of his personal preferences. Here again a major question is why. In part, it may be the result of simple sharing. For example, at least feeble public-congressional correlations would result if each district's congressman were determined by lottery. But, interestingly, the correlations between the views of nonincumbent congressional candidates (who usually lost)

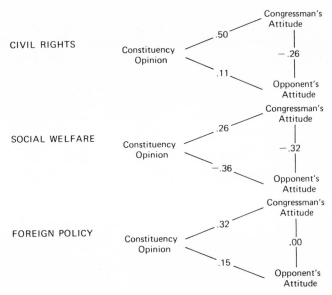

Figure 8-1. Relationship between congressmen's opinions, their opponents' opinions, and constituency opinion. Numbers are correlation coefficients. (*Source.* 1958 Survey Research Study of Representation. From personal correspondence with project director.)

and the districts that (usually) rejected them were much weaker than for the winners, and on social welfare were negative. Thus, the more liberal the district on social welfare, the more *conservative* the losing major-party candidate is likely to be. Although the full reason for this negative correlation defies simple explanation, the filtering process of elections was seemingly at work.[13]

LEADERSHIP RESPONSIVENESS TO PUBLIC OPINION

We have seen that there is some sharing of political preferences by people and their elected representatives. Thus, if the representatives' preferences guide their behavior in office, there exists some guarantee of at least a modest amount of linkage between public opinion and policy. Linkage would be more complete if representatives support the choice of the public over their own preference when there is a conflict between the two. For this Role Playing Model to work, two conditions must be met. First, the representative must have some incentive for choosing the public's preference over his own. This incentive may be the representative's belief that following public opinion is ordinarily the "right" thing to do or the belief that he will face electoral reprisals if he does not go along with public opinion. Second, the representative must know what public opinion is before he can follow it. Below, we will consider the evidence regarding how well these two conditions are met.

Seemingly crucial to the people having much real control over what their leaders do is a strong desire by public officials to take public opinion into account. But, as V. O. Key wrote in 1961:

"We have practically no systematic information about what goes on in the minds of public men as they ruminate about the weight to be given to public opinion in governmental decision."[14]

Despite more than a decade since Key's writing, his gloomy statement about the state of our knowledge about the public's direct influence on decision makers could, perhaps, be written today. There do exist bits of evidence, however, that tell us something about leaders' responsiveness to public opinion. Our task, then, is to link these pieces together.

How Legislators See Their "Roles"

For nearly every circumstance in which one human being interacts with another, such as being a father, asking a question in the classroom, interviewing for a job, or serving as a representative in a government, people hold beliefs as to what the proper behavior should be in those circumstances. These sets of beliefs prescribing behavior for each social position are normally labeled "roles." Roles vary greatly in their richness, with some encompassing very broad ranges of expected behavior while others give only minimal direction as to what is expected. Our concern here is with the role of the political representative and, more specifically, with that role as perceived by representatives.

Several researchers have explored the various aspects of how legislators see their role—their expected behavior, as they perceive it. Here we consider how legislators see their role vis-a-vis their constituencies. John Wahlke, Heinz Eulau, and their associates, who began the study of legislative roles, identified three types of possible representative roles. The "trustee" they define to be the legislator who "sees himself as a free agent in that as a premise of his decision-making behavior, he claims to follow what he considers to be right or just, his convictions and principles, the dictates of his conscience".[15] Moreover, the trustee is fully confident that his constituency expects him to behave in just that manner. At the opposite end of the pole from the trustee is the "delegate" who feels he should follow the wishes of his constituents even if they are contrary to his own. Finally, because the researchers found many representatives who claimed it was necessary to play trustee on some issues and delegate on others, they conceived of a conditional or mixed role, which they call the "politico". Elaborate questionnaires have been administered to state legislators and congressmen, in order to classify them according to representative roles.

If legislators do play the role assigned to them by their questionnaire responses, the public's only coercion on the trustee is its retrospective judgment at the polls regarding his decisions. The delegate and (to a lesser extent) the politico are additionally constrained by their apparently greater desire to work in behalf of constituency desires. Electoral coercion does appear to play a role here, as delegates face closer elections than trustees.[16] Presumably the causal connection is that safe seats allow the aloofness of a trustee and not that delegate behavior loses votes.

Table 8-3 shows the distribution of the three role types found within several state legislatures and the U.S. House of Representatives. Wisconsin's legislature stands out for its high proportion of delegates, perhaps because of the state's "progressive" political history. The U.S. House of Representatives also contains few trustees, and a high percentage of in-between politicos. A good guess is that if the role orientations of U.S. senators were measured, with the advantage of a lengthy six-year term, few would score as delegates.

There is little research focusing on whether or not the representative votes according to his role designation, and what little research there is finds little consistency.[17] Perhaps the difference in legislative roles better reflects the representative's personal needs than his behavior in the process of achieving correspondence between public opinion and policy.[18]

Many legislators seemingly do ponder the appropriate acts they should take, and there is disagreement among them. The most conducive role for political linkage—that of delegate—fails to be more than a minority in most legislatures. To be sure, many would find it too humiliating to admit to being merely the voice of others. Indeed most of us applaud the "courage" of the "statesmanlike" legislator who votes his independent judgment over the views of his constituency—particularly when we agree with that judgment. The legislator who we most often condemn is the one who votes neither his convictions nor the convictions of those he represents, but who is motivated by a different consideration—the payoff for supporting some special interest group.

TABLE 8-3 **Distribution of Representational Roles (in Percent)**

Representational Role Orientation	California N=49	New Jersey N=54	Ohio N=114	Tennessee N=78	Wisconsin N=89	Pennsylvania N=106	Michigan N=77	House of Representatives N=87
Trustee	55	61	56	81	21	33	35	28
Politico	25	22	29	13	4	27	31	46
Delegate	20	17	15	6	66	39	34	23
Not Classified	—	—	—	—	9	1	—	3

Sources. John C. Wahlke et al., *The Legislative System* (New York: John Wiley and Sons, Inc., 1962, p. 281; Frank J. Sorauf, *Party and Representation* (New York: Atherton Press, 1963) p. 124; Malcolm E. Jewell and Samuel C. Patterson, *The Legislative Process in the United States* (New York: Random House, 1966) p. 398; John W. Soule, "Future Political Ambitions and the Behavior of Incumbent State Legislators," *Midwest Journal of Political Science XIII*, No. 3 (August, 1969) p. 452; and Roger H. Davidson, *The Role of Congressman* (New York: Pegasus, 1969) p. 117.

The Fear of Electoral Reprisals

Instead of asking legislators how much they follow public opinion, we can ask them whether they perceive that their reelection chances depend on what they do in office. When asked by political scientists, most legislators will report that they fear electoral reprisals if they stray from satisfying public demands. Eighty-five percent of the congressmen interviewed by Miller and Stokes said their personal record and standing in Congress was either "quite important" or "very important" to their reelection.[19] By comparison, only 46 percent gave ratings of "quite" or "very important" for party loyalties or national issues. It is easy to see how the representative glorifies the politics of the public and comes to believe that he will be carefully judged by them in succeeding elections. The uncertainty of the representative as to why he won causes him to believe that reelection rests with his constituency's reaction to his performance in office.

A study of candidates for state and national office in Wisconsin reports that the *winners* saw the candidates and election issues to be more important than party labels, while losers were more inclined to see the importance of partisanship in determining the outcome.[20] The winner's greater optimism about both public interest and his ability to affect whether he won caused John Kingdon to conclude that the difference can be explained by what he labels a "congratulation-rationalization effect".

". . . winners develop complimentary beliefs about voters and losers develop rationalizations for their losses simply by virtue of the outcome of the election. Winners, the argument runs, believe that voters did a good job of choosing. Voters in their view are well informed about politics and vote according to the issues and candidates, rather than blindly following their party. Losers, on the other hand, rationalize defeat by saying that voters are ill informed and vote according to party label rather than the issues or men who are running for office."[21]

Apparently, legislators prefer to believe that they win elections because voters agree with their views rather than because they are successful at catering to public tastes. Many, in fact, resolve perceived disagreements with their constituencies by the psychologically satisfying perception that they are able to educate the voters to accept their views.[22] Regarding the extent of public monitoring of their performance, there is no consensus to the Congressmen's perceptions. Many are uncertain of how closely the voters are watching —and perhaps for this reason prefer not to take chances. Generally, they see reelection as largely a matter of maintaining the proper "image" back home. But they do not know how much their behavior in office shapes that image. Perhaps they have room for independence on smaller issues but not on the "big" ones.[23]

When acknowledging the public's power over them, elected officials do not always view it as wisely exercised. Key, for example, observes that "public men often act as if they thought the deciding margin in elections was cast by fools; moreover, by fools informed enough and alert enough to bring retribution to those who dare not demonstrate themselves to be equally foolish".[24]

Examining what congressmen do rather than what they say, there is some evidence that congressmen make the greatest adjustments in their behavior when they appear electorally threatened. Looking at the roll-call behavior of 1970 congressmen, we can see that deviation from their party's ideological standard in order to appeal to the moderate voter was most frequent on the part of the electorally insecure. Figure 8-2 shows that northern Republicans tended to vote rather conservatively, except those who represented districts that do not ordinarily vote Republican—where a majority of the 1968 presidential votes had been Democratic. Similarly, northern Democrats generally took liberal roll-call stands, except when their districts gave the threatening signal of a light Democratic vote for president.

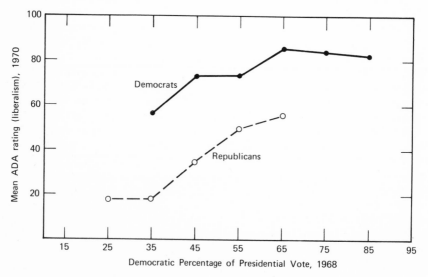

Figure 8-2. Roll-call liberalism of House members (1970) as function of their district's presidential vote, 1968 (Northerners only).

264 *The Public and It's Elected Representatives*

Political Ambition

The belief that his reelection chances hinge on how well he represents constituency opinion will not influence the officeholder much unless he cares about getting reelected. As Joseph Schlesinger has described the positive functions of political ambition, "no more irresponsible government is imaginable than one of high-minded men unconcerned for their political futures".[25] Politicians at the top of the political ladder usually try to continue in office as long as possible. For example, it is clear that presidents normally want to stay in office for their constitutional allotment of two full terms. Even Truman and Johnson, who both opted for retirement in the spring of their reelection years, did so only after the results of the first presidential primaries indicated that even renomination by their party would have been a difficult hurdle. Most governors also seek reelection when constitutionally able—for example, 86 percent out of 28 cases in 1970. Ambition for continuation is also rather high in the case of congressmen. For example, of the 35 senators up for reelection in 1970, only two did not seek reelection. The same year, only five of the 430 U.S. House members (there were five vacancies) voluntarily retired from public life. (Twenty-one others gave up their House careers to try for the higher offices of U.S. senator or governor.)[26]

Interestingly, the inclination of the congressman to hang onto his office for several terms is a relatively recent phenomenon. In the 19th century, House and Senate members quite frequently returned to private life after only a term or two.[27] This pattern still persists in the career pattern of lower-level office holders. Prewitt's study of Bay Area councilmen disclosed that almost one fifth did not (at the time of their interview) plan to seek reelection.[28] Although it is not known how prevalent this pattern is at the local level throughout the nation, the retirement rate of state legislators appears to be even higher.[29]

The rate at which members of a legislative body retire appears to have very delicate effects. Observers of Congress often moan that the institution is handicapped by the presence of too many old men who refuse to give up their seats. Students of state legislatures offer the opposite complaint: that frequent retirements (often to seek higher office as well as to go back home) produce a depletion of experienced personnel. Here our chief concern is that the retiring legislator may be relatively indifferent to public opinion.

One should not necessarily infer that the nonambitious officeholder's escape from electoral pressure typically frees him for pursuit of worthy goals that are too advanced for public opinion to accept. Many politicians are strongly motivated to advance their conception of the "public interest," and this pursuit of accomplishments feeds their ambition for further public service. This reasoning suggests the hypothesis that the political leader with the strongest policy motivations tends to feel the most pressure to satisfy public opinion—at least on matters that concern them least.

At the other extreme, we may, following Prewitt, identify a different type of policy maker whom Prewitt calls the "volunteer-citizen politician."[30] The volunteer's most frequent habitat is a low-paying post in a nonpartisan setting. Likely to have wandered into politics as a natural extension of his participation in civic organizations, he sees himself as performing a duty to serve a term or two. He does not see his role as satisfying constituency demands because, as Prewitt says, voters are not asked to "replace the inept church leader, the misguided little league organizer, or the irresponsible library board members".[31] Indeed, the public is not likely to monitor his performance closely; thus, the Rational Activist Model does not supply political linkage. Having entered politics from the local business establishment, the volunteer leader may not represent the views of the entire community. Thus, the Sharing Model also seems improbable. Only the Role Playing Model seems at all likely to be effective since, like most citizens of a democracy, he feels he should listen to what others say and give it his consideration. But little additional motivation seems likely and, in any case, the people he talks to will be members of his own circle. In short, models of political linkage seem ineffective in holding the volunteer accountable. But the number of such volunteers in political positions remains unassessed.

The Leader's Desire to Represent

We have tried to assess how much politicians fear electoral sanctions as a motivation for following public opinion. The existing evidence suggests politicians give greater credit to the public's monitoring capabilities than the evidence would warrant. Even more difficult to assess is the extent to which political leaders heed public opinion simply because they think it is what they ought to do. We cannot test the validity of this role-playing model directly, for it is impossible to enter politicians' minds and locate their value structures. However, some observers of politics have argued that the widespread belief that public opinion should be followed is a major source of what democratic linkage exists. V. O. Key, for example, argued that within the subculture of political leaders a value of fundamental importance is a "regard for public opinion, a belief that in some way or another, it should prevail".[32]

Miller and Stokes' study of congressional representation provides

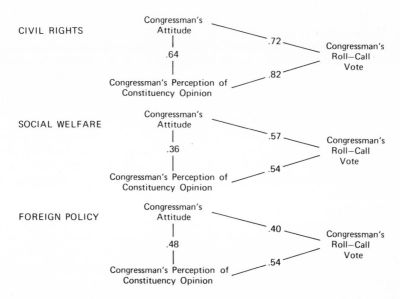

Figure 8-3. Relationship between congressmen's opinions, their perceptions of constituency opinions, and their roll-call votes. (*Source.* See Figure 8-1.)

some evidence of how frequently politicians follow their perception of constituency views. As part of this study, correlations were computed between the congressman's role-call behavior and both his own views and his perception of what his district wanted. Figure 8-3 shows that in the three policy areas examined, the representative's personal preference and his perception of constituency preference were about equally (and positively) correlated with his roll-call behavior. The positive correlation between the congressman's views and his perceptions of constituency views makes the matter difficult to disentangle further, beyond the tentative inference that congressmen typically give about equal weight to both considerations.

HOW ELECTED OFFICIALS LEARN PUBLIC OPINION

Even if the political decision maker wants to follow public opinion, he cannot do so effectively unless he knows what the people want. According to political lore, good politicians have acute political antennae that detect the prevailing political mood when they wander among the "grass roots". Of course, the policy maker is also sometimes able to "read" public opinion directly by examining the results of available opinion polls.

Unlike the President, the lower-level elected official (such as the state legislator) rarely has the resources to conduct his own poll. But one group of officeholders who do make frequent use of polls are members of the U.S. House of Representatives. Thanks to their franking (free mailing) privilege, House members can send questionnaires to each household in their district for only the printing costs. The number of House members who do take constituency polls has been steadily rising—from 11 percent in the early 1950s to 74 percent in 1969–1970.[33] Since these polls are administered by mailed questionnaires, they have a low-return rate (about 14 percent on the average)[34] that can permit the views of a small minority (typically the better educated and more wealthy) to be mistaken for "public opinion". But one might argue that since the minority who do take the trouble to respond to congressional polls presumably feel most intensely about the issues, any bias in the poll results would be weighted in favor of the more attentive segment of the public who will vote according to their beliefs.

How accurate are congressional polls, and how much weight do congressmen give them? One study of opinion on the fallout shelter · controversy in the early 1960s compared the results of congressional polls and professionally completed polls and found a high correspondence between them.[35] The study also found that congressmen often altered their votes on the shelter issue as a response to the declining public support for fallout shelters manifested in their own polls. But the increased use of polls notwithstanding, representatives remain reliant on other means of detecting constituency opinion as well. Tables 8-4 and 8-5 show that U.S. House members and Wis-

TABLE 8-4   **Extent of Reliance Upon Various Communication Channels by Congressmen From 116 Districts, 1958 (in Percent)**

Extent of Reliance	Personal Contact	Mail	Newspapers	Party Organization	Opinion Polls
		Source of Information			
A great deal	62	25	5	8	6
Quite a bit	19	30	27	10	7
Some	8	23	24	15	11
Not much	8	19	29	28	15
None	2	3	15	39	61

Source. Warren E. Miller, "Policy Preferences of Congressional Candidates and Constituents," paper presented at the 1961 Annual Meeting of the American Political Science Association.

TABLE 8-5   Use and Perceived Reliability of Various Sources of
Information among Wisconsin candidates (in Percent)

	Source				
Reliability	Polls	Party People	Volunteers	Past Statistics	Warmth of reception
Rely without qualification	13	21	19	45	57
Rely with qualification	5	16	19	38	8
Do not rely on source	8	48	29	5	31
No information from source	74	15	33	12	3
	100	100	100	100	99
N	61	61	58	60	61

Source. John W. Kingdon, *Candidates for Office: Beliefs and Strategies* (New York: Random House, 1966), p. 91.

consin candidates are more confident of other, more impressionistic ways of judging constituent opinion. Let us examine how precisely the politician can determine the most popular course to take from the techniques available to him.

Opinion Polls

Perusing the results of opinion polls gives the policy maker additional insight into what his constituency wants yet, like everybody else, the politician must read them with caution. Let us examine why the office holder who bases every decision on what the polls show to be the majority preference does not always take the most politically rewarding course. As we saw in Chapter Two, the distribution of opinion on an issue can vary with the exact question wording. Consequently, the side of the issue on which majority opinion lies may shift with the seemingly innocuous change in the question wording. Given such circumstances, following public opinion as registered by a single reading on the issue may make little political sense.

Actually, the policy option that would yield the political leader the most votes (and satisfy the most people) is not always the majority position anyway. For example, according to unsubstantiated political lore, the minority who are gun enthusiasts have man-

How Elected Officials Learn Public Opinion   **269**

aged to defeat several politicians who advocate strict gun control even though polls show a majority favor strict gun registration laws. Presumably, the average person who, when asked, will favor gun control does not translate these convictions into action at the ballot box, but the gun enthusiast will.

Paradoxically, the way to build a winning majority at the polls may sometimes be to create a coalition of intense minorities. Suppose, for example, opinion on three issues is divided 80 to 20, with the different minorities on each issue feeling several times more intensely about the matter than those on the other side do. Then if one candidate supports the majority side to all three issues, and the other appeals to the minority side, the candidate of the minorities could win 60 percent of the vote (20 times 3), assuming all vote on the basis of the issues. There would be nothing inherently undemocratic about the majority side losing out on each question, as a majority of voters would have more to gain more from their representation on the one question they feel strongly about than they would by representation on the two issues about which they care little. A related reason why finding an accurate profile of the entire population's opinion and acting on it may not be the best reelection strategy, is that money contributors and volunteer workers probably hold unrepresentative opinions and may respond unsympathetically to candidates articulating the representative public opinion.

Politicians may sometimes feel free to ignore the polls because they recognize that the public generally expects its political leaders to use their own judgment, acting as trustees rather than delegates. In one poll, a substantial part of the public (46 percent) favored the statement, "an elected legislator (congressman) should decide what he thinks best, and always vote accordingly, even if it is not what his district wants".[36] As we saw in Chapter Five, the public normally gives the President even greater latitude to use his own judgment. The public seems to react in displeasure at being asked to do what they think they elect officials to do, namely make decisions. For example, many defeats of fluoridation referenda seem based on public displeasure at their elected officials' failure to take a stand on the issue by passing the buck to the voters.[37]

Indeed, by following majority opinion, the politician may be discounting the potential effects of his own leadership. For example, President Nixon would not have reaped the political benefits of his trip to China if he had followed the lead of the opinion polls that showed that the public was hostile toward China. Here, the President was able to influence opinion by redefining the situation for the American public. Indeed, one might argue that a reasonably popular president can mobilize majority support for virtually any policy action he takes in the foreign policy spheres. Of course, the leadership potential of the politician depends on the prestige of his office, his own popularity and the nature of the issue. For example, a "lowly" congressman may not create much of a ripple in public thinking by advocating some new foreign policy course. Even a president cannot automatically count on the public following his lead in the domestic sphere.

Another reason why his own policy judgment may yield the office holder more electoral benefit in the long run than acting like a delegate is that, at election time, the voters will react more to the apparent success or failure of his performance in office than to their initial impressions of his decisions. If the politician knows he will eventually be rewarded or punished for the "nature of the times" he or his party seem to produce, polls of current public sentiment about what ought to be done are sometimes of little help. Obviously, a President would make economic policy on the basis of expert opinion rather than on what the polls say the public thinks would work best.

The Vietnam war provides one example of a discrepancy between the public's policy preference at the moment and the public's eventual reaction to the consequences of that policy. According to the polls, the public supported the war at the time the crucial steps of escalated involvement were taken. If the high officials in the Kennedy-Johnson administrations had foreknowledge of the extent of the public's eventual opposition to a prolonged war, perhaps they would have made different decisions. Here, politicians had to make crucial guesses about public reactions to their possible options—for which polls could not give answers.

These considerations undoubtedly comprise some of the reasons why office holders themselves place surprisingly little stock in polls. But other sources of their estimates of public opinion contain their own pitfalls. Crowd reactions, obviously, can be misleading indicators given the disproportionately politicized and partisan nature of political audiences. How accurate are other sources of opinion cues —election returns, constituency groupings, the mail, and the people back home to whom the representative talks?

Election Returns

After elections, it is a popular fad to decipher the results in terms of the new "mood" of the voters evident in who they elect. We saw earlier that changes in the voters' partisan preferences are not the result of ideological mood swings: Republican gains do not necessarily mean the public has swung farther to the right, for example. The winning politician who interprets his landslide victory to be a mandate for his favorite programs may find a sudden erosion of his popular support to be the result of his mistake. The urge to decipher meaning from particular issue-oriented election contests can also lead to errors, if the judgment is made without consideration of the general partisan trend. For example, in retrospect, an overinterpretation of election results by concerned political observers may have been the reason why official Washington overestimated the popular support for demogogic Senator Joe McCarthy in the early 1950s. Although, at first, other senators disassociated themselves from McCarthy's unsubstantiated claims that some indefinite number of known Communists were running loose in the State Department and elsewhere in government, the defeat of several of McCarthy's senatorial critics in the 1950 and 1952 elections silenced the remainder.[38] In retrospect, it is clear that most of the defeated McCarthy opponents would have lost anyway in the anti-Democratic tide.[39] Almost unnoticed, McCarthy himself trailed his party's ticket when he won reelection from Wisconsin voters in 1952. Actually, McCarthy never was supported by a clear majority of the public—with most of his supporters coming from predictable sources such as small-town Republicans. If otherwise alert politicians had paid closer attention to the polls than to isolated and misleading election returns, the "climate of opinion" that assumed McCarthy was invincible may never have been created. As it was, McCarthy's downfall—forced by his attack on the U.S. Army—was as sudden as the initial rise of what became known as "McCarthyism".

Group Characteristics

In their interviews with John Kingdon, the Wisconsin candidates claimed to cue off supporting groups, labor for Democrats, and business for Republicans, in judging the policy positions they need to make to insure support at election time.[40] More research is needed regarding the representative's reliance on guessing the social composition of his constituency and attributing opinions to it based on those characteristics. For example, if a politician's district contains an unusually high proportion of elderly voters, and he, therefore, concludes that they support extension of Social Security payments, is he correct? Such judgments with very diverse districts and for obscure programs can be quite difficult, but this type of assessment may be vital to the politician who seeks to know public opinion.

The Mail

Political officeholders place only slight stock in the mail they receive as a source of constituency opinion. Skepticism is highest when a barrage of letters clearly originates from a pressure group campaign.[41] But, setting such cases aside, is there any bias to the mail political leaders receive? Writing a letter to an elected official is not a regular activity for the average person. President Lincoln received about 44 letters each year for 10,000 literate adults, or from less than one-half of one percent of the population. Similarly, Wilson received about 47 per 10,000. Roosevelt received 160, meaning that about 2 literate persons in every 100 felt the need to write him.[42] The infrequency of this action causes us to suspect the representativeness of the letter-writing public. Key notes that the preponderance of letters to the White House are supportive or approving, which might cause the President to have a myopic view of public support for his program.[43]

Only about 15 percent of the public admit to ever having written a public official and about two-thirds of all letters written to officials originate from three percent of the public.[44] The politician who measures public opinion solely from the content of his mail or from Letters to the Editor would misjudge public opinion to be more conservative than it is. Figure 8-4 compares letter opinion (the opinions of those claiming to have written to public officials) with public opinion (the opinions of the total population measured in the sample survey) in 1964. If letter opinion was misperceived as being public opinion, we would conclude that in 1964, Goldwater held an appreciable lead midway in the campaign, that Republicans and Independents toasted his nomination above all other Republican candidates, and that Americans were upset with the growing strength of the Federal Government and held a decidedly conservative stance. Goldwater's optimism regarding the public reception of his conservative campaign might well have rested on misplaced confidence that volunteered opinion (rather than poll opinion) best reflected public opinion.

These findings have been replicated by a national survey that assesses public attitudes towards the war in Vietnam. Sidney Verba and Richard Brody find the relationships between various forms of participation and attitudes toward Vietnam shown in Table 8-6. If an official read the state of public attitudes from his mail, he would have found "a little more than one and a half times as many hawks as in the population as a whole."[45] The eight demonstrators in the sample, if proportionate to their number in the total population, would mean that approximately 750,000 people had taken part in a demonstration. Such numbers would, of course, attract considerable attention and might well cause the official to take this activity and its message as public opinion. Naturally, such a conclusion would yield an unrepresentatively dovish perception of public opinion. A third subgroup, the minority who tried to convince others, differed from the general public in still a different way—clustering more toward both the dove and hawk poles of the Vietnam spectrum.

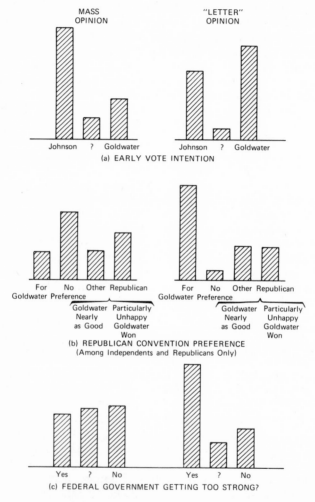

Figure 8-4. Public opinion as measured by people or political letters. (*Source.* Philip E. Converse, Aage R. Clausen, and Warren E. Miller, "Electoral Myth and Reality: The 1964 Election," *American Political Science Review, 59* (June, 1965), p. 334.)

MASS
OPINION

"LETTER"
OPINION

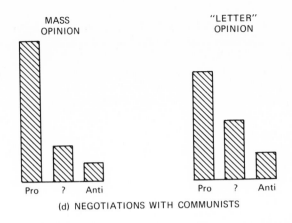

Pro   ?   Anti   Pro   ?   Anti
(d) NEGOTIATIONS WITH COMMUNISTS

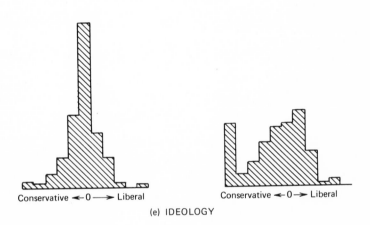

Conservative ◄–0—► Liberal   Conservative ◄–0–► Liberal
(e) IDEOLOGY

Attentive Constituents

Little is known about the constituents with whom officeholders do
maintain regular contact. As part of one study, Iowa legislators were
asked which constituents they would regard as politically knowledgeable and aware and whose advice they might seek on legislative issues or problems.[46] The attentive constituents thus identified
were then interviewed. From the perspective of achieving responsible representatives, the attentive constituents have many desirable
attributes: they are informed about the procedures of the legislature
and who controls it; interested in the political process to the point
of having extensive communication with state, local, and national

TABLE 8-6   **Position on the Hawk-Dove Scale of the Population as a Whole and of Various Activist Populations (in Percent)**

Vietnam Preferences	Whole Population	Those Who Have Discussed Vietnam	Those Who Have Tried to Change Opinions of Others	Those Who Have Written Letters	Those Who Have Demon- strated
Hawk	18	20	26	30	1 case
Mild hawk	31	31	28	33	None
Middle	26	26	19	10	1 case
Mild dove	13	12	10	10	None
Dove	12	11	17	17	6 cases
Total	100	100	100	100	100
Percent of population	100	68	13	2.5	.5

Source. Sidney Verba and Richard Brody, Participation, Policy Preferences, and the War in Vietnam," *Public Opinion Quarterly, 34* (Fall, 1970), p. 330.

officials (including playing an active part in their actual recruitment); and strongly supportive of the legislature. But in terms of their socioeconomic standing, these attentive constituents were an even more high-status group than the legislators themselves. For these influential men also to have contacts with the average citizen, the accurate exchange of opinions and attitudes would have to over-come a very substantial social gap. Consequently, it is quite unlikely that the constituents to whom officeholders talk are adequate con-duits for channeling the opinion of the public at large up to the political leadership.

How Accurately Do Officials See Public Opinion?

Given the multiple devices they employ to sense public opinion, how accurate are officeholders in their perceptions of public opinion? One approach to answering this question is to sample opinion and then see how closely the public's representatives can predict what it is. In their study of congressional representation, Miller and Stokes sampled opinions in 1962 congressional districts, and then asked the districts' representatives what they thought the opinion of their home constituency would be (see Figure 8-5). On civil rights

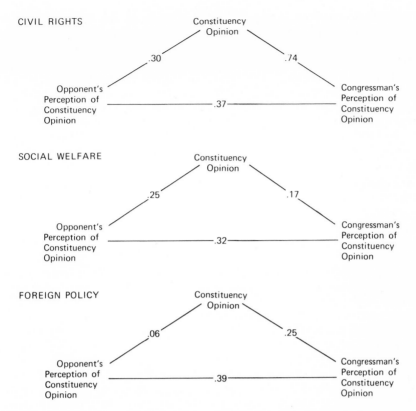

Figure 8-5. Relationship between constituency opinion and the perceptions of constituency opinion held by congressional candidates. (*Source*. See Figure 8-1.)

issues, the correlation between constituency opinion and the congressman's perception of it was a fairly robust +.74—a not surprising indication that representatives of procivil rights black constituencies and anticivil rights Deep South districts are aware of their constituencies' views. Correlations between constituency opinion and congressional perceptions of it are also positive on social welfare issues (+.17) and foreign policy issues (+.25).

But these correlations are relatively weak. In fact, on social welfare and foreign policy, the representative's own position is a better predictor of his estimate of constituency views than is actual constituency opinion (see Figure 8-6, p. 283). This suggests that their personal views biased their estimates of constituency preferences to appear more like their own. Moreover, as the correlations of Figure

8-5 also indicate, the congressmen were no better at predicting constituency opinion than were the challengers who were trying to defeat them.

Perhaps the most difficult test for the representatives' political antennae to pass is correct estimation of constituency opinion on issues that do not attract much public attention. Accordingly, Ronald Hedlund and H. Paul Friesema quizzed Iowa state legislators about their constituencies' majority preference on four statewide referendum questions that were about to be put before the voters.[47] On the four questions, the accuracy of the legislators' predictions varied from 64 to 92 percent. (Simply by random guessing, the legislators would have been correct half the time.) The predictions on home rule for cities (92 percent) and reapportionment (82 percent) were reasonably accurate. But the rates of successful prediction on annual legislative sessions (59 percent) and giving the governor the item veto (64 percent) were only slightly beyond the guess range. Hedlund and Friesema argue that the home rule and reapportionment referenda attracted greater public interest than annual legislative sessions and item vetoes. This suggests greater accuracy in representatives' predictions of public opinion in those areas where the public expresses the most interest.

Following up on the Iowa study, in 1972 the authors of this book asked Florida legislators to predict the percentage point breakdown in their district and the state on three "straw ballot" referendum issues. One of these straw ballot issues dealt with the volatile question of "forced" school busing to achieve racial balance. Here the legislators' estimates were not far off the mark; for example, the 56 responding House members erred by an average of only 7 percentage points in predicting their district's antibusing vote. But estimates were less valid on the less publicized remaining straw ballot issues. On the question of allowing prayers in schools, the average error in prediction was 11 percentage points; on the question of rejecting the dual (or segregated) school system, the average was 12 percentage points. Once again, the legislators' awareness of public opinion is weaker when the public focus on the issue is weak.

DO ELECTED OFFICIALS NEED TO FOLLOW PUBLIC OPINION?

We have seen that although politicians sometimes have difficulty reading public opinion, they apparently do at least try to consider public opinion when making decisions—partly from fear of electoral retribution if they do not. Actually, there are reasons for suspecting that public officials do not need to weigh public opinion very heavily in order to get reelected. Incumbent officeholders do not lose reelection bids at a rate that should stimulate electoral anxiety. Furthermore, most people do not monitor their leaders' policy decisions with sufficient attention to produce massive voter reactions.

Judging from the reelection rate of congressmen, incumbents are returned to office with astounding regularity. For example, in 1970 the reelection rate for members of Congress was 95 percent in the House and 80 percent in the Senate. Governors, however, are more vulnerable. For example, in 1970 only 61 percent of those who sought reelection were returned to office.[48] Governors appear electorally insecure because, like presidents, they get held accountable for the nature of the times during their administration.[49] Legislators face less electoral difficulty than executives because it is more difficult for voters to trace the consequences of legislators' actions or to hold them individually responsible for government outputs, such as the state of the economy.

To what extent do voters react to the content of their leaders' policy decisions and policy proposals for the future? In the previous chapter we saw that, in a presidential race, a sizeable share of the voters will be somewhat aware of major issues and be influenced by them. But in subpresidential contests, the public's information is usually far below the level to allow the expectation of much rational voting. The best data in this regard concerns public awareness of the U.S. House of Representatives and their particular congressman.

Congress is not a very salient institution to most people. When asked which party has more congressmen, more give the correct answer than the incorrect one. But with an adjustment for correct guessing, the best estimate is that typically less than half the congressional election voters cast their ballot with firm knowledge of which party is in control.[51] Once, following the 1966 election, a plurality in an SRC poll incorrectly responded that the Republicans controlled Congress—apparently confusing the big Republican gains that were reported in the news media with a Republican majority.[52] When people are asked how good a job Congress is doing, one might suspect that their response would depend on their party identification and the party in power—Democrats would like Congress best when the Democrats control it, for example. But it does not work out this way. A person more frequently rates Congress' performance as good when his party controls the White House but not Congress, than when his party controls Congress but not the White House.

When we turn to voters' knowledge of their individual congressmen and congressional candidates, no improvement is found. First of all, the local news media rarely give much coverage to the congressman's role-call stands or to the substantive issues of congressional campaigns.[53] Consequently, even if most people had the urge to follow the congressional politics of their district, they would have great difficulty in doing so. Only slightly more than half the public can even name their congressman.[54] Similarly, at election time only about half will claim to have read or heard anything about their representative in Washington or his opponent.[55] What information they do have about their representative turns out to be rather slim. When interviewers probe to find out *what* the voter has read or heard about the congressional candidate, the answer is typically a vague reference such as "he is a good man", or "he knows the problems". Specific references to the representative's legislative actions comprise only a fraction of the responses—"not more than a thirtieth" say Stokes and Miller, based on their 1958 survey.[56] Slim improvement is shown with application of a more generous test: only seven percent of the 1958 sample gave a reason for their candidate choice that "had any discernible issued content".[57]

On even heatedly debated congressional issues, few people know where their congressman stands. Table 8-7 condenses the results of an interesting survey that asked people how they and their congressman stood on the funding of the Supersonic Transport plan (SST) shortly after Congress rejected the SST. Most people polled were unable to state how their representative voted on the SST. Those who tried to answer the question were wrong almost as often as

TABLE 8-7 **Voters' Awareness Of Their Congressman's Position On The Supersonic Transport Plane, 1971 (in Percent)**

	Congressman Pro-SST		Congressman Anti-SST	
	Constituents' SST Opinion	Constituents' Perceptions of Congressman's SST Stand	Constituents' SST Opinion	Constituents' Perceptions of Congressman's SST Stand
Continue work	24	12	16	3.5
Stop spending	56	14	68.5	27.5
Not sure	19	74	15.5	69
	100	100	100	100

Source. Joseph Kraft, Inc., "A Review of Voter Attitudes in Ten Key Congressional Districts," August 1971, A Report to The American Businessmen's Committee for National Priorities.
Responses are district means. The 10 congressmen whose districts were sampled were: (pro-SST) Albert, Arends, Boggs, Bow, G. Ford, Hebert, Mahon, and Mills; (Anti-SST) J. Byrnes, O'Neil.

they were right—suggesting that even those who tried to answer were mostly guessing. Thus, the voters were almost totally unaware of how their congressman voted on an issue that had commanded a major share of newspaper headlines for a period of months. Evidently, congressmen were able to vote on the SST without stirring much public attention back home.[58]

From these survey findings, one might well wonder whether the congressman needs to pay any attention at all to his constituency's views when he weighs the alternatives of each legislative decision. As Warren Miller and Donald Stokes put it:

"Congressmen feel that their individual legislative actions may have considerable impact on the electorate, yet some simple facts about the Representative's salience to his constituents imply that this could hardly be true."[59]

Indeed, we may have a major political linkage between mass opinion and leader response that is generally overlooked— although the public is not watching, leaders sometimes do what they think the public wants because they *mistakenly* believe the public is paying attention! If this view is true, then leaders' responsiveness to public opinion would quickly evaporate once somebody points out to them that surveys show the public to be rather indifferent to what they do. But on the other hand, maybe the politicians do not exaggerate the importance of their record to their electoral fate as much as the polls seem to suggest. Let us explore the reasons why officeholders do have to tread carefully when they consider violating something called public opinion.

First, the easiest way for voters to become aware of their elected leader's record is when he does something that can be exploited by his opponent as a stand against public opinion. Therefore, although name recognition generally wins votes, lack of public knowledge of a political leader's policy stands may sometimes actually be a sign of his successful representation. Put another way, if congressmen became more casual in their consideration of constituency views— for example, if representatives of liberal districts started acting like conservatives and vice versa—the polls might show much more evidence of constituency awareness and, on election day, more would be defeated.

Also, one should note that there does exist a sprinkling of informed voters who shift their political weight according to the policy views of the candidates. Even if these alert voters comprise a tiny fraction of the total, their opinion leadership allows them to influence election outcomes to an extent beyond what their numbers would indicate. As information about the congressman diffuses downward from relatively informed opinion leaders to the mass public, it may be, as Miller and Stokes suggest, that many voters "get simple positive or negative cues about the Congressman which were provoked by his legislative actions but no longer have a recognizable policy content."[60] By responding to such cues, a significant number of voters may act as if they are relatively informed about their congressman's record. As a result, the collective electoral decisions in congressional contests may be more responsive to roll call records than our knowledge about individual voters would indicate.

In the previous chapter, we saw that the result of this process is visible in election returns. Congressmen lose votes when they take ideologically extreme public positions. Normally, a congressman's vote loss due to his policy stands is not sufficient to defeat him, since he is often protected by a modest incumbency advantage and a one-party district. But the few who do lose can often blame their own policy stands for their misfortune. The role of issues in determining defeat or victory is clearest for northern Republicans—those who lose tend to represent the more conservative wing of their party. For example, none of the eight northern Republican House members who were defeated for reelection in 1970 (excluding one who was pitted against a Democratic incumbent) were among the most liberal half of Republican northerners, as measured by the ADA index. Back in 1964, when better than one quarter of the northern Republican House members who sought reelection were rejected by the voters in the anti-Goldwater tide, most of the losers were archconservatives. For example, 41 percent of the 37 northern incumbent candidates who signed a preconvention statement promoting Goldwater's conservative presidential candidacy went down to defeat themselves in November 1964. In contrast, only 12 percent of the 33 northern Republican House members who publicly disassociated themselves from the Goldwater candidacy by accepting the support of the liberal "Committee to Support Modern Republicanism" lost their reelection bids.[61] The public's ideological selectivity when determining which Republic House members it will defeat has, therefore, had a moderating or liberalizing effect on the Republican House membership. If conservative and moderate Republicans lost reelection bids at equal rates, House Republicans would, as a group, be more conservative than they are.

CONCLUSIONS

In this chapter we have examined some of the possible factors that could compel the policy maker to make decisions that are congruent with public opinion. Complete understanding of the frequency or infrequency of linkage between public opinion and policy is beyond the present knowledge of political scientists. While the problems of

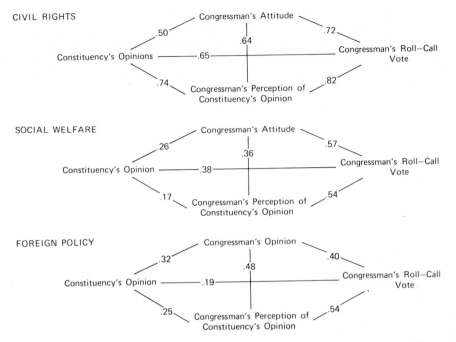

CIVIL RIGHTS

Congressman's Attitude

Constituency's Opinions —— .65 ——

.50 .64 .72

Congressman's Roll—Call Vote

.74 .82

Congressman's Perception of Constituency's Opinion

SOCIAL WELFARE

Congressman's Attitude

Constituency's Opinion —— .38 ——

.26 .36 .57

Congressman's Roll—Call Vote

.17 .54

Congressman's Perception of Constituency's Opinion

FOREIGN POLICY

Congressman's Opinion

Constituency's Opinion —— .19 ——

.32 .48 .40

Congressman's Roll—Call Vote

.25 .54

Congressman's Perception of Constituency's Opinion

Figure 8-6. The relationship between congressmen's opinions, perception of constituency's opinions, constituency's opinions, and the congressman's vote. (*Source*. 1958 Survey Research Center study of representation. From personal correspondence with project director.)

estimation will be explored further in Chapter Nine, here we can report the results of one study that did attempt to measure the overall linkage between policy decisions and constituency preferences. Once more, we are referring to Miller and Stokes' representation study. Figure 8-6 shows the correlations found between constituencies' preferences and the roll-call decisions for their congressmen, in addition to the correlations between the various links in the chains we have already examined. The relationship between constituency attitudes and the roll-call result is moderately high on civil rights (+.65), modest on social welfare (+.38), and almost nonexistent on foreign policy, (+.19). Given the public's disinterest in foreign policy details, particularly in the pre-Vietnam era when this study was conducted, the latter correlation is hardly surprising.

Since the number of voters whose views were sampled is very low in many of the districts examined, the correlations that Miller and Stokes report may be less reliable than we need to form firm conclusions about overall linkage. The strong point of Miller and Stokes' analysis is their statistical assessment of how the linkage that does exist gets achieved. Across all three domains examined, the congressmen prove as likely to vote their *perception* of constituency attitudes as they are to vote their own attitudes. Using the complicated analysis procedure known as "path analysis", Miller and Stokes report that in the area of civil rights, the congressman's roll call behavior is most adequately explained by his following perceptions of constituents' attitudes.[62] This would, of course, imply that linkage depends on the correctness of his perceptions. But they also report that in the area of social welfare, his behavior derives much more from his personal attitudes, suggesting that if congruence is achieved here, it is because congressmen and their constituents share the same views. As Miller and Stokes suggest, the Parties Model, discussed in the following chapter, may be relevant here.[63] Evidently the effective political linkage will vary with the type of issue. Without question, however, the civil rights area shows the highest overall quality of linkage between public opinion and policy, which in turn rests on linkage by way of the representative accurately perceiving his constituent's attitudes.

This chapter has dealt with the representative as an individual faced with the task of participating in the making of public policy as the spokesman for the constituency that elected him. Despite some research, the individual representative's resolution of how and when to weigh public opinion in his decisions remains largely unknown. The simple alternatives of trustee and·delegate seem sadly incomplete, devoid of subtlety, and probably unrealistic for the problems faced by the representative. Furthermore, the device for assuring representative accountability—public elections—fails to threaten those holding safe seats and those lacking further ambition for public office. While accountability via elections may be generally unfulfilled, the knowledge that elected officials occasionally get defeated may buttress the representative's desire to represent. Similarly, the civicly motivated representative, while uncaring of election defeat, may be offended by an accusation that he misrepresents his constituency, and therefore, also try to weigh opinion into his voting decisions.

But whatever the differences in and motivations of the representative, the opinion he holds as well as those surrounding him may be uncharacteristic of public opinion. Quite possibly, he may not recognize this; but if he should, he faces a difficult task of getting an unbiased measurement of public opinion. When specifically charged to do so, both congressmen and legislators prove able to assess constituency opinions with only modest accuracy. Even more difficult is deciding whose opinion within that public will most affect his level of public support and possibility of reelection. Contributor opinion, attentive voter opinion, and mass opinion may differ greatly. Substantial biases exist in the opinions of those who choose to express their opinions to the representatives and among those to whom the legislators turn for advice, with many of these advisors being active in recruiting candidates.

If elections served as mandates to the representatives for public wants on each program to be faced in the legislative session, the difficult process of the representative's learning constituency opinion would be unnecessary. He would then choose when to reflect public opinion with complete confidence both that he knew it and that it was this opinion that leads to his future support. But the public's votes in elections are the product of many motives besides their support for the positions the winner might have taken in the campaign or in office, if he is the incumbent. Once in office, even the most strongly motivated, responsive representative faces a difficult process in learning his constituency's wishes.

FOOTNOTES FOR CHAPTER 8

[1] Kenneth Prewitt, *The Recruitment of Political Leaders: A Study of Citizen Politicians* (New York: Bobbs-Merrill, 1970), pp. 66.

[2] Ibid., p. 61.

[3] James David Barber, *The Lawmakers* (New Haven: Yale University Press, 1965).

[4] On the social and economic characteristics of American legislators, see Malcolm Jewell and Samuel Patterson, *The Legislative Process in the United States* (New York: Random House, 1966), pp. 106–118; Suzanne Keller, *Beyond the Ruling Class* (New York: Random House, 1963); Prewitt, Chapter 2; and Roger H. Davidson, *The Role of the Congressman* (New York: Pegasus, 1969), pp. 34–71.

[5] Stein Rokkan and Angus Campbell, "Citizen Participation in Political Life: Norway and the United States of America," *International Social Science Journal*, 12 (1960), pp. 69–99.

[6] Leon D. Epstein, *Political Parties in Western Democracies* (New York: Praeger, 1967), pp. 167–200.

[7] For example, 31 percent of the delegates had family incomes of $25,000 or more, in comparison to 5 percent for the nation at large. Source: Haynes Johnson, "A Portrait of Democrats' New Delegates," *Washington Post*, July 8, 1972, p. A-1.

[8] Seymour Martin Lipset, *Agrarian Socialism* (Berkeley: University of California Press, 1950), p. 166.

[9] Within the public, 47 percent of the Democrats and 35 percent of the Republicans favored an increase in "tax on large incomes." Among Convention delegates, only 27 percent of the Democrats and 5 percent of the Republicans did so. Similar breaks were found on the issues of "corporate income tax" and "tax on business." Source: Herbert McClosky, Paul J. Hoffman, and Rosemary O'Hara,

"Issue Conflict and Consensus Among Party Leaders and Followers," *American Political Science Review, 54* (June, 1960), p. 414.

[10] Norman R. Luttbeg, "The Representative Quality of Community Leaders' Policy Preferences: A Study of Prevalent Assumptions, *Research Reports in Social Science, 12,* No. 2 (August, 1969).

[11] V. O. Key, *Public Opinion and American Democracy* (New York: Knopf, 1961), p. 547.

[12] Warren E. Miller and Donald E. Stokes, "Constituency Influence In Congress," *American Political Science Review, 57* (March, 1963), pp. 45–56.

[13] What we call the Parties Model may be the source of these correlations on social welfare issues. As we have seen in earlier chapters, Democratic and Republican voters tend to divide on social welfare issues—Democrats liberal, Republications conservative. As the next chapter shows, the division is intensified for party elites—such as congressional candidates. When congressional voters vote their party line, the liberal (Democratic) districts elect liberal (Democratic) congressmen; thus, the positive correlation between constituency social welfare views and the views of their Congressmen. Liberal (Democratic) districts defeat conservatives (Republicans) while conservative (Republican) districts defeat liberals (Democratic); hence, the negative correlation between district views and those of the typically defeated challengers.

[14] V. O. Key, "Public Opinion and the Decay of Democracy," *Virginia Quarterly Review,* (Autumn, 1961), p. 490.

[15] John C. Wahlke, Heinz Eulau, William Buchanan, and LeRoy C. Ferguson, *The Legislative System* (New York: Wiley, 1962), p. 73.

[16] Davidson, p. 128.

[17] The most germaine study of this relationship is that done by Fisher. William E. Fisher, "Problems in the Application of Generalized Role Theory as a Means of Inquiry into Legislative Behavior," (Unpublished honors thesis, Dartmouth College, 1964). In the area of judicial behavior, studies of the behavioral counterpart to roles have noted what must be called weak consistency. See Henry R. Glick, *Supreme Courts in State Politics* (New York: Basic Books, 1971) and Theodore L. Becker, *Comparative Judicial Politics* (Chicago: Rand McNally, 1970).

[18] This is Barber's theme. See *The Lawmakers, op. cit.*

[19] Donald E. Stokes and Warren E. Miller, "Party Government and the Saliency of Congress," *Public Opinion Quarterly, 26* (Winter, 1962), p. 542.

[20] John W. Kingdon, *Candidates for Office: Beliefs and Strategies* (New York: Random House, 1966), p. 24.

[21] Kingdon, p. 31.

[22] Charles L. Clapp, *The Congressman: His Work as He Sees It* (Garden City: Doubleday, 1963), pp. 111–113.

[23] Clapp, pp. 420–428; See also, Lewis Anthony Dexter, *The Sociology and Politics of Congress* (Chicago: Rand McNally, 1967), Chapter 8.

[24] Key, "Public Opinion and the Decay of Democracy" p. 490.

[25] Joseph Schlesinger, *Ambition and Politics* (Chicago: Rand McNally, 1966), p. 2.

[26] Computed from *Congressional Quarterly* sources.

[27] H. Douglas Price, "The Congressional Career—Then and Now," in Nelson W. Polsby (ed.), *Congressional Behavior* (New York: Random House, 1971), pp. 14–27.

[28] Prewitt, pp. 176–177. Prewitt suggests (p. 201) that the rate of indifference to

reelection among the councilmen studied is in the neighborhood of 50 percent. [29] As far as we know, there exists no compilation of the rate at which state legislators seek reelection. But, of the legislators in four states interviewed by Wahlke et al., only 55 percent reported that they definitely expected to seek re-election. (Recomputed from Table 6.1, p. 122 in Wahlke, et al., The Legislative System). In 1963, about one-third of all state legislators were first-termers, most of whom either replaced a retiree or defeated the incumbent. The percentage in 1950 had been 42 percent. See Duane Lockard, "The State Legislator," Chapter 4 in Alexander Heard (ed.), State Legislatures in American Politics (Englewood Cliffs: Prentice-Hall, 1966), p. 103.

[30] Prewitt. See especially, pp. 175–216.

[31] Prewitt, p. 86.

[32] V. O. Key, Public Opinion and American Democracy, p. 538.

[33] Reports on the frequency of congressional polling can be found in Walter Wilcox, "The Congressional Poll and non-Poll," in Edward C. Dreyer and Walter A. Rosenbaum (eds.) Political Opinion and Behavior, 2nd ed., (Belmont, California: Wadsworth, 1970); tabulation by John E. Saloma III, reported in Donald D. Tacheron and Morris K. Udall, The Job of the Congressman (New York: Bobbs-Merrill, 1966), p. 288; and Lester Markel, What You Don't Know Can Hurt You (Washington: Pacific Affairs Press, 1972), p. 258.

[34] Tacheron and Udall, p. 288.

[35] Richard A. Brody and Edward R. Tufte, "Constituent-Congressional Communication on Fallout Shelters: The Congressional Polls," Journal of Communication, 14 (1964), pp. 34–49.

[36] Carl D. McMurray and Malcolm B. Parsons, "Public Attitudes Toward the Representational Roles of Legislators and Judges," Midwest Journal of Political Science, 9 (May, 1965), p. 170.

[37] Robert L. Crain, Elihu Katz, and Donald B. Rosenthal, The Politics of Community Conflict: The Fluoridation Decision (Indianapolis: Bobbs-Merrill, 1969), p. 138.

[38] For a lively account of McCarthy's rise and fall, see Richard H. Rovere, Senator Joe McCarthy (New York: Meridian Books, 1960).

[39] Nelson W. Polsby, "Toward An Explanation of McCarthyism," Political Studies (October, 1960), pp. 250–271.

[40] Kingdon, pp. 44–81.

[41] For one account of how Congressmen view their mail, see Lewis Anthony Dexter, "What Do Congressmen Hear? The Mail," Public Opinion Quarterly, 20 (Spring, 1956) pp. 16–27.

[42] Leila Sussman, "Mass Political Letter Writing in America: The Growth of an Institution," Public Opinion Quarterly, 23 (1959), pp. 203–212.

[43] Key, Public Opinion and American Democracy, p. 418.

[44] Philip E. Converse, Aage R. Clausen, and Warren E. Miller, "Electoral Myth and Reality: The 1964 Election," American Political Science Review, 59 (June, 1965).

[45] Sidney Verba and Richard Brody, "Participation, Policy Preferences, and the War in Viet Nam," Public Opinion Quarterly, 34 (Fall, 1970), pp. 325–332.

[46] G. R. Boynton, Samuel C. Patterson, and Ronald D. Hedlund, "The Missing Links in Legislative Politics: Attentive Constituents," Journal of Politics, 31 (August, 1969), pp. 700–721.

[47] Ronald D. Hedlund and H. Paul Friesema, "Representatives' Perceptions of

Constituency Opinion," *Journal of Politics 34* (August, 1972).

[48] Computed from *Congressional Quarterly* sources. The frequency with which incumbents seeking to be returned to lower-level offices are successful is largely unknown. Barber (*op. cit.*, p. 8) reports data indicating a return rate (for those who try) of 82 percent in Connecticut—a state known for its strong partisan swings. Among the Bay Area councilmen, the return rate was 80 percent, with considerable variation between cities. (Prewitt, pp. 137–138).

[49] Elections for governor—the second most visible office to most voters after the Presidency—have been the focus of surprisingly little systematic study. Turett has shown that the governor's vote margin generally goes down with each term he survives. See J. Stephen Turett, "The Vulnerability of American Governors, 1900–1969," *Midwest Journal of Political Science, 15* (February, 1971), pp. 108–132. The source of this vulnerability is little understood. Pomper has shown that there is no statistical evidence to bolster the common-sense notion that governors lose votes when they raise state taxes. See Gerald W. Pomper, *Elections in America* (New York: Dodd, Mead, 1969), pp. 126–148.

[51] Stokes and Miller, p. 537.

[52] Following the 1966 election, 44 percent said the Republicans has "elected the most Congressmen"; 21 percent said the Democrats did; the remainder said they did not know. Source: Survey Research Center, 1966 Election Study Codebook, p. 76.

[53] Part of the Miller-Stokes representation study was intended to be an examination of local newspaper coverage of congressional campaigns. But this aspect was dropped when it was found that campaign information was "printed only sporadically and then was usually buried in such a remote section of the paper that the item would go unheeded by all but the most avid readers of political news." See Philip E. Converse, "Information Flow and the Stability of Partisan Attitudes," *Public Opinion Quarterly, 26* (Winter, 1962), p. 587n.

[54] *Gallup Opinion Index,* April 1970, p. 20.

[55] Stokes and Miller, p. 540.

[56] Stokes and Miller, p. 543.

[57] Stokes and Miller, p. 536.

[58] Close inspection of Table 8-7 shows a minority must have been aware of their congressman's SST vote: the perception that one's congressman opposed the SST rose when the congressman actually did so. Still even SST proponents were more often seen by their constituents as opponents than as supporters. Since most voters opposed the SST themselves, they may have "projected" this preference onto their congressman.

[59] Miller and Stokes, p. 54.

[60] Miller and Stokes, p. 55.

[61] *1964 Congressional Quarterly Almanac,* pp. 1014, 2578–80; *Congressional Quarterly,* (June 19, 1964), p. 1216. See also Robert A. Schoenberger, "Campaign Strategy and Party Loyalty: The Electoral Relevance of Candidate Decision Making in the 1964 Congressional Elections," *American Political Science Review, 63* (June, 1969), pp. 515–520.

[62] Miller and Stokes, pp. 51–53.

[63] Miller and Stokes, p. 56.

NINE

POLITICAL LINKAGE: MEDIATING INSTITUTIONS AND IMPLICATIONS

Many theories of political linkage, as we noted in Chapter One, assign an important role to two mediating institutions, political parties and pressure groups. Instead of the representative standing in a one-to-one relationship with his constituency, these theories posit an important role for these institutions in providing information on public opinion to the representative and assuring his accountability. We will first assess the importance of political parties to assuring government policy consistent with public opinion.

POLITICAL PARTIES AND REPRESENTATION

According to the Political Parties Model, party labels clarify the political choices available to the voters. First, each political party would outline the program it would enact if its candidates were elected; thus the candidates' party labels signify what they will do if elected. Second, each voter would make his selection at the polls on the basis of the party that best represented his views. This model simplifies the task of the policy-oriented voter. Instead of monitoring each candidate's campaign statements and hoping that these statements indicate what the candidates would do if elected, the voter would need only to learn the differences between the parties' programs and use party labels as a cue to rational voting.[1]

We have seen, however, that voters do not always behave according to the prescription of the Political Parties Model. In Chapter Three, we found only a modest, though increasing, tendency for Republican and Democratic identifiers to differ from one another on issues. Chapter Seven showed that a voter whose issue stances are incompatible with those of his traditional party's candidate will sometimes vote for the opposition candidate. Nevertheless, it would be incorrect to view Republican and Democratic voters as divided into ideologically opposite camps.

Whether it would be rational for voters to select candidates on the basis of party labels depends on the actual distance between the programs of the two parties. Strong party voting is not meaningful if in fact the policies of the two parties are indistinguishable. But if parties *do* offer different programs, the public has available a valuable guide to voting. Here, we examine the extent to which Republican and Democratic leaders actually differ in their policy preferences and in their behavior in office.

Ideological Differences Between Republican and Democratic Leaders

Do the labels "Democrat" and "Republican" signify anything about the policy preferences of party leaders? Typically, one associates the Republican party with the conservative ideological viewpoint and the Democrats with the liberal viewpoint. Although ideology is not a major source of partisan division between Republican and Democratic *voters,* one might suspect that ideology motivates the party choice of the political activists who become the leaders of their party. On the other hand, to a European, American political parties often appear nonideological. Noting the pragmatism and singular interest in winning office of American political parties as compared with the ideological and often well-disciplined European parties, many observers see American parties as devoid of ideological purpose and program. As we will see, the proper view of the policy option that American political parties offer lies between the two extremes. Although the Republicans and Democrats seldom offer the public a clear set of policy alternatives, the partisan affiliation of a political leader does provide some clues about his personal policy preferences and his behavior.

Perhaps the most complete comparison of the personal beliefs of Republican and Democratic leaders is a study by Herbert McClosky, Paul Hoffman, and Rosemary O'Hara.[2] In 1957 and 1958 they gathered identical data from a public sample of supporters or followers of the political parties and from delegates to the 1956 political party conventions.[3] For each of 24 policy issues the researchers reported the percentages of both leaders and followers preferring an increased government commitment. They took support for expanded government involvement in a policy area as denoting liberalism and compared Republican and Democratic delegates and their supporters within the public on this dimension. Figure 9-1 shows delegates to be ideologically more distinct than their supporters. For example, the first issue noted on the left, concerning the expansion of government ownership of natural resources, reveals little public support either among Democrats (34 percent) or Republicans (31 percent) for this expansion. The delegates greatly amplify this minor distinction among supporters with the Democrats giving a 58 percent approval as compared with only 13 percent among the Republicans. The 45 percent difference among delegates compared with the minor 4 per-

Percent Favoring an Increase

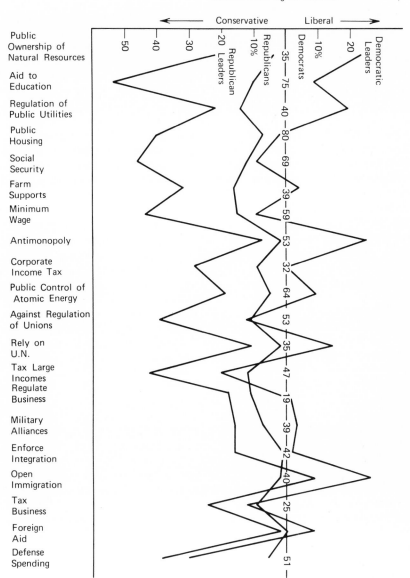

Figure 9-1. Differences in Leaders' and Followers' Opinions.

Source. Adapted from Herbert McClosky, Paul J. Hoffman, and Rosemary O'Hara, "Issue Conflict and Consensus Among Party Leaders and Followers," **American Political Science Review,** 54 (June, 1960).

cent differential among supporters indicates the ideological differences in the two groups. While this and other issues on the left side of the figure most glaringly show the ideological distinctiveness of the delegates, the general pattern persists across the figure.

Four issues are excluded from the figure: tax on small income, tax on middle income, restrictions on credit, and levels on import tariffs. Neither party leaders nor their supporters differed significantly on these issues. The remaining issues shown in Figure 9-1 reveal three patterns. First, in no instance do the Democrat and Republican followers differ as greatly as do the leaders. Second, Republicans prove consistently more conservative than Democrats, both among the public and the delegates.[4] Finally, judging from the gaps in the figure, the ideological difference between leaders and followers is greatest within the Republican party. Indeed, Table 9-1,

TABLE 9-1 **Average Differences Between Leaders' and Followers' Attitudes in the Democratic and Republican Parties**

	Leaders' Attitudes	
Followers' Attitudes	Democratic	Republican
Democratic	10%	22%
Republican	11%	16%

Source. Adapted from Figure 9-1.

comparing the average difference in support between party delegates and supporters for the 24 issues, reveals Democratic leaders represent their supporters better than do Republican leaders by an average of 6 percent. In fact, these average figures also find Democratic leaders actually give better expression to the attitudes of Republican followers than do Republican leaders. As McClosky et al. note, "Republican leaders are separated not only from the Democrats (both leaders and followers) but their own rank and file members as well."[5] The histories of the 1964 and 1972 presidential conventions suggest that similar surveys in those years would have revealed changing patterns of delegate representation.

Delegates to political party national conventions include both elected and influential state officials as well as those who have only earned an invitation by way of their lifelong loyalty and support for their party. McClosky and his associates make no differentiation among the delegates, thus we are left uncertain as to whether those holding public office show the ideological distinctiveness noted of convention delegates. But while one might question the independence of the average delegate because of the state laws which bind his vote to his state's primary winner or because of his subjugation to the influence of party leaders, as a whole the delegates do participate in that important political function of national conventions, the selection of a presidential candidate. The ideological division between Republican and Democratic delegates has significance to actual politics only if delegates show consistency between their attitudes and their political actions.

Among California delegates to the 1960 Democratic Convention, Edmund Constantini finds that those evaluating themselves as liberals do indeed grant more support to liberal candidates.[6] A later study by John Soule and James Clarke of Democrat and Republican delegates to the 1968 presidential conventions finds this pattern within both parties. As shown in Table 9-2, each party's most "liberal" candidate (Rockefeller for the Republicans and McCarthy for the Democrats) received more support from liberal delegates.[7] Democrats continue to be more liberal than Republicans.

TABLE 9-2 **Ideology and Candidate Preference among Democrat and Republican Delegates (in Percent)**

Democrats' Candidate preference		Conservatives $N = 26$	Moderates $N = 44$	Liberals $N = 100$	Total %
Humphrey	$N = 95$	16	38	46	100
McCarthy	$N = 35$	0	3	97	100
Other	$N = 40$	28	18	56	102
Republicans' Candidate preference		Conservatives $N = 67$	Moderates $N = 66$	Liberals $N = 30$	Total %
Nixon	$N = 93$	43	45	12	100
Rockefeller	$N = 35$	26	40	34	100
Reagan	$N = 21$	72	14	14	100
Others	$N = 14$	21	50	29	100

Source. Recomputed from John W. Soule and James W. Clarke, "Issue Conflict and Consensus: A Comparative Study of Democratic and Republican Delegates to the National Conventions," *Journal of Politics, 33* (February, 1971), p. 88.

The impression thus far is one of ideological bias among party leaders affecting their selection of candidates. But apart from Constantini's, none of the studies considers the delegates' different abilities to shape what the party stands for and who its candidates will be. A party's most loyal and devoted supporters may be ideological extremists who threaten the party's appeal to the more moderate voters within the general public. The party leader's dilemma then is, as David Butler states, "to conciliate those who support them with money or with voluntary work, without alienating that large body of moderate voters whose attitudes make them more likely to swing to the other party."[8] Constantini's study of California delegates finds a pattern of increasing moderation as one moves from lower echelon party activists, nominated by their district caucuses but rejected by top leadership, to the highest echelons that include elected officials and delegates chosen to attend the conventions.[9] This would suggest that top leaders hidden among McClosky's delegates would be less ideologically deviant than the more numerous lower echelon delegates. While the greater numbers of these lower echelon, ideologically motivated, delegates make the overall pattern of ideological distinctiveness quite sharp, their lesser influence within the parties allows moderate and electable candidates to be chosen by more moderate, party leaders.[10]

The Voters' Choice: Partisan Differences Between Candidates

John Sullivan and Robert O'Connor demonstrate that the two parties do offer a choice—at least in 1966 elections for the U.S. House of Representatives. They consider the choice available in each congressional district by comparing candidates' attitudes toward the issues of the day. As they argue, "if many candidates do not differ appreciably from one another or if the winners fail to vote in Congress on the basis of the preelection attitudes, there is little reason for voters to become familiarized with the issue positions of the candidates or to vote on the basis of these "positions."[11] A meaningful choice of candidates is essential both to the Political Parties and the Rational-Activist Models as both rely on voters making a choice at the polls.

The candidates in the questionnaire chose among three alternatives for each of eight questions, such as whether they would pursue peace talks, take more decisive military action, or retain the present course of U.S. policy in Vietnam. On the average, opponents answered differently on more than six of the eight issues; and furthermore, their answers showed a liberal or conservative pattern across all issues.[12] But are such differences in opinion significant in terms of the policy implications that would result were one candidate elected rather than the other?

The answer is clearly yes. In Table 9-3 they present alternative Congresses that could have been returned by the voters from among the 813 choices that they had to fill 435 congressional seats.[13] The column labeled "Winners," is the actual elected Congress, which

TABLE 9-3 **Hypothetical Congresses–Domestic Policy Issues**

Score	Winners	Unchallenged and Losers	Most Democratic[a]	Most Republican[a]	Most Liberal	Most Conservative
4 Liberals	79	57	129	7	130	6
5-6 Moderate-liberals	81	105	161	25	160	26
7-9 Moderates	43	85	64	64	67	61
10-11 Moderate-conservatives	70	90	28	132	33	128
12 Conservatives	162	98	53	207	45	214
	435	435	435	435	435	435
Mean	8.7	8.3	6.6	10.5	6.5	10.5
Median	10	8	6	11	6	11

Source. John L. Sullivan and Robert E. O'Connor, "Electoral Choice and Popular Control of Public Policy: The Case of the 1966 House Elections," *American Political Science Review* (December, 1972) p. 1260.
[a] Most Democratic Congress includes Democrats plus unchallenged Republicans; most Republican Congress includes Republicans plus unchallenged Democrats.

proves somewhat conservative in this domestic policy area. But the substitution of all losers would only slightly liberalize Congress. This lack of a difference with complete reversal of election results might be interpreted erroneously to mean that the alternatives afforded the voters lack policy significance, but the last four columns of the table betray the inadequacy of this conclusion. As we see in the last four columns, a hypothetical Congress consisting of all available Democratic candidates or one consisting of the most liberal candidates from each district would differ most significantly from the alternative most Republican or most conservative Congresses. The 290 liberals in the most liberal Congress, for example, could withstand the defection of nearly half of the moderate liberals as shown in the table and still pass desired legislation; whereas the most conservative Congress would find conservatives needing only the support of four moderate conservatives to defeat all liberal legislation. Evidently then a clear policy choice is available to the public.

The other policy areas—civil rights and foreign policy—closely parallel these findings. The most liberal and most conservative Congresses vary only between moderate and conservative in foreign policy and between moderate and liberal in civil rights instead of the full range evident in domestic policy. The parties do structure opinion and present a choice of positions, as the most Democrat Congress varies as much from the most Republican as does the most liberal from the most conservative. The voters, however, show no nationwide pattern of ideological choice as the winners' opinions cannot be distinguished from the losers'. At first blush, this might be taken as an indication that the voters randomly select among liberal and conservative alternative congressmen. This is a conclusion that would strongly condemn the public's ability to make partisan choices. But the proper interpretation is that some districts regularly elect conservatives and others regularly elect liberals—with the result an ideological standoff at the national level.

Sullivan and O'Connor also compare the views of the Republican and Democratic candidates within the same district and find that in only 19 of the 400 competitive races is the Republican more liberal than his Democratic opponent.[14] Moreover, they find that upon entering Congress, the winning candidate generally votes consistently with the values expressed in his earlier questionnaire. Thus, partisan differences appear to extend to actions in office as well as to personal beliefs.

The partisan's choice is clear. "If a voter in 1966 wanted to vote conservatively, he only had to know that the Republican party is generally more conservative than the Democratic party in order to cast his ballot correctly in light of his values."[15] Since Sullivan and

O'Connor note congressmen consistently vote their attitudes, we can conclude that any lack of dramatic change in the policies passed by Congress reflects a lack of dramatic change in party support at the district level.[16]

Because Congressmen are influenced by their constituency as well as by their party, not all Democrats are liberal and not all Republicans are conservative. For example, the two major party candidates in a predominantly conservative district could be a very conservative Republican and a *moderately* conservative Democrat. Both might be less liberal than either major party candidate in a liberal constituency. Thus although the relative positions of the two major party candidates within a given constituency may be distinguishable, both might be either fairly liberal or fairly conservative.

Party Voting in Legislatures

If we examine the roll call behavior of elected Congressmen, we find considerable overlap with many Republicans to the political left of many Democrats. Still, the tendency is that Republican Congressmen hold conservative views and Democrats hold liberal views. This is especially true if we exclude southern Congressmen, as in Figure 9-2.[17] This table shows party differences in liberal ratings by Americans for Democratic Action for the 1970 Congress.

In the day to day procedures in any legislature, many bills are passed with the support of both parties. On divisive issues a representative may judge it inexpedient to vote with the majority of his party because of the particular relevancy of the issue to his constituency. When a party holds a sufficient majority in the legislature, it tolerates such deviations in the interest of assuring the reelection of its representatives. We can assess partisan consistency by noting the percentage of nonunanimous roll call votes on which a majority of the Democrats voted against a majority of the Republicans. This measure, of course, would be independent of any normative judgment of an issue's importance. A high percentage of party votes indicates considerable interparty division and facilitates a public decision as to which party's program it supports.

In a typical Congress some 35 to 50 percent of the votes on which congressmen disagree are party votes.[18] The state senates, on the average, closely parallel this with a 48 percent party vote, but vary greatly between California's low 17 percent and Rhode Island's high 100 percent.[19] Frank Sorauf found an average of 60 percent party votes in the senates and 63 percent in the houses of eight states he studied.[20] It is difficult to set a satisfactory level of party voting to assure political linkage by way of the Political Party Model, but at least in most states the voter could attribute the passage of many

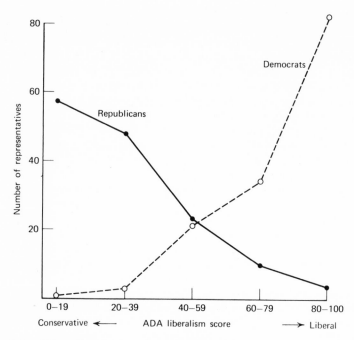

Figure 9-2. Liberalism of Northern Democrats and Northern Republicans in the House of Representatives, 1970.

bills to one of the parties and thereby judge his satisfaction. Party votes most frequently center in areas of narrow party interest (such as election laws and legislative organization), basic administrative and patronage issues (such as appropriations, taxes, and appointments), and social and economic issues basic to liberalism and conservatism (such as the regulation of labor and business and welfare programs).[21] At least the last two types of issues also concern the public. The interparty opposition in the American Congress and in state legislatures permits public monitoring since the differences between them are quite apparent.

The Relevance of Party Platforms

We have noted that while the parties differ ideologically affording the public a clear choice in elections, there is a strong suggestion that the public chooses not to deviate substantially from its regional policy preferences and party loyalties. Having thus dealt with the party before the electorate, we move to a further element in the Political Party Model, the party's ability to implement its policy position by way of controlling its elected members' vote in a representative council. We already noted that each American political party's representatives closely subscribed to the ideology normally attributed to that party and that their votes very substantially reflect this ideology. This would imply that the parties would have little or no difficulty in achieving party control, because frequently the representative would desire to personally vote in the manner consistent with his party's position. Certainly the incidence of party votes varies greatly among the state legislatures and the circumstances affecting the variations do indeed need additional exploration. But in Congress and in most states, the party in power shows a capability to implement its program.

A high incidence of partisan votes would certainly permit the sophisticated observer to evaluate party performance in deciding which party he will support in the forthcoming election, but it is not the only condition necessary for an effective Political Party Model. The model demands that the party vote together in implementing its platform. While critics have long dismissed the party platforms as mere rhetoric, Gerald Pomper's careful study of the implementation of Democratic and Republican national platforms for the period of 1944 through 1964 sharply contradicts this criticism.[22] Table 9-4 presents his evaluation of the content of these 12 platforms. At one extreme, statements in the platforms are platitudes applauding American uniqueness, "The American Free Enterprise System is one of the great achievements of human mind and spirit," or statements about the issues but with quite unclear meanings, "The Anti-Trust Laws must be vigorously enforced."[23] The bottom three categories of statements listed in the table, however, do provide information on the policies the parties intend to implement or have already implemented and thus are consistent with the model. Policy approval statements, for example, include, "In the Nuclear Test Ban Treaty, we have written our commitment to limitations on the arms race," and a detailed policy position is, "The security of the American Trade Unions must be strengthened by repealing section 14B of the Taft-Hartley Act." He notes the Republicans speak of defense and government issues while the Democrats stress labor and welfare issues, but neither party proves deficient in providing a meaningful platform for voter evaluation. Typically the parties' platforms include about 1 statement in 5 which state an evaluation of past policies and about 3 in 10 that offer fairly detailed information on the party's policy intention. Although few voters would read the platforms, popularizations of them by interest groups and in

TABLE 9-4   Content of Party Platforms (in Percentages of Total Platform)

	Dem. 1944	Rep. 1944	Dem. 1948	Rep. 1948	Dem. 1952	Rep. 1952	Dem. 1956	Rep. 1956	Dem. 1960	Rep. 1960	Dem. 1964	Rep. 1964
Unusable in the Parties Model												
General Rhetoric	22	11	12	23	18	9	14	15	20	21	20	11
General Approval	23	3	11	3	11	3	5	15	4	7	14	5
General Criticism	0	7	3	4	1	18	11	4	7	1	1	12
Policy Rhetoric	17	24	17	32	22	20	15	14	20	16	5	16
Usable in the Parties Model												
Policy Approval	13	2	10	8	16	11	9	26	4	13	48	2
Policy Criticism	0	10	8	1	3	14	17	2	11	1	1	25
Fairly Detailed Policy Positions	25	44	39	29	29	25	29	24	33	40	10	28
Percent of Platform Consistent with Model	38	56	57	38	48	50	55	52	48	54	59	55

Source. Data recomputed from Gerald M. Pomper, *Elections in America: Control and Influence in Democratic Politics* (New York: Dodd, Mead, 1968) pp. 159, 164, and 176.

candidate speeches may draw substance from explicit policy platform statements. On the average more than one-half of the parties' platforms are *not* obscure statements and platitudes intended to appeal to all, and thus restricting the voters' ability to judge the parties.

More importantly, Pomper's analysis of the fairly detailed policy positions in the platforms reveals that only one-tenth of these positions are completely ignored in the parties' subsequent actions in Congress.[24] Not unexpectedly, the party holding the presidency experiences much greater success in achieving its platform promises, succeeding 4 out of 5 times as compared with the little better than 50 percent success of the out party. Unfortunately these data are subject to alternative interpretations. The platforms clearly are far from meaningless rhetoric as three-fourths of the policy pledges get fulfilled. But it should be noted that policy pledges constitute only 27 percent of the statements in the platforms and that the parties take alternatives stands on only 10 percent of these pledges meaning fewer than three percent of all platform statements afford the voter a clear choice of alternative partisan positions.[25] Pomper finds a middle ground, rejecting both the conclusion that platforms are irrelevant rhetoric as well as the conclusion that they are "inspired gospel to which the politicians resort for policy guidance."[26]

Pomper argues that the platforms serve as symbolic appeals to the elements of the party's coalition rather than as ideological statements. If the issues on which the parties offered conflicting pledges in their platforms were also those on which they cohesively opposed each other in the legislative arena, platforms could be taken as ideological positions dogmatically adhered to by each party. But Pomper discovers that the parties achieve no greater legislative cohesion in the areas of conflicting pledges—such as in the areas of economy, regulation of labor, and social welfare programs—than in policy areas on which the platforms disagree little. Platforms, he argues, are statements to the groups serving in the party's coalition. Thus the prolabor statements by the Democrats express their continuing commitment to labor in return for its support.

This use of the party platform to facilitate the operation of the political parties runs counter to the purpose of the party platform posited by the Political Party Model. Neither party sees its platform primarily as an inventory listing of specific policies it would enact once elected; thus the policy-directed voter would find little utility in a careful reading of either platform.

The failure of the parties to use their platform as manifestations of their programatic differences need not preclude them from taking distinctive stands on the issues of the day. Pomper finds, however, no instance of platform conflict between the parties in the area of civil rights, as both parties gave pledges to enact civil rights legislation. Lacking this distinction, the civil rights oriented voter would be hindered in voting his intent were this the only information available. But each party has a reputation for being more responsive in differing policy areas as for example the Democrats are normally expected to be the party to enact civil rights legislation. One study bolsters this conclusion with data from the American states.[27] In the north between 1945 and 1964, states enacted civil rights legislation in 24 percent of the instances when the Democrats held control. When legislative control was divided or rested with the Republicans, however, enactment dropped to eight percent.[28] If similar party consistency were found in other policy areas and became part of the popular knowledge about the parties, it might well stand as an imputed platform or orientation on which the policy directed voter might well base his decision.

Conclusion

Many elements of the Political Parties Model are confirmed. Generally, the parties prove ideologically distinct and capable of realizing the programatic difference, if given the reins of government. Furthermore, the task of the party in assuring the elective representatives support for party positions is greatly facilitated by the consistency of opinion among its representatives that makes their action on the basis of their own beliefs quite compatible with party policy. The person with sufficient political motivation to work for a political party or to run for public office usually holds strong political views. The activist will normally choose to work within the political party that best represents his personal beliefs unless there is a compelling reason not to, such as that party being so weak locally that it has little chance for victory. Although candidates generally avoid their party's ideological extreme in order to get elected, their own strong views and those of their ideologue supporters help push their public positions away from the political center. Thus, the Republican and Democratic candidates will ordinarily offer the voter some choice of policies. Probably, party labels would supply voters with a still greater choice if the public shared the ideological commitment of partisan activists and candidates.

The choice presently afforded the voter may be overly restrictive.[29] The typical voter is faced with a choice between a Democrat, whose stands are liberal on foreign and domestic policy and in civil rights, and a Republican typically more conservative in all dimensions. Thus, the voter who favors a "strong" foreign policy and a continuing expansion of domestic programs but no change in civil rights can find no totally satisfactory choice. The trend toward consistency in mass opinion noted in Chapter Three may foretell greater consistency between the choices desired by the voters and the alternatives presented by the parties. Such a development would of course buttress the Political Parties Model.[30] But the failure of the Political Parties Model seems to come more from the public's failing to use the choice offered by the political parties rather than from the parties' failure to satisfy the conditions of the Model.

PRESSURE GROUPS AND POLITICAL LINKAGE

The Pressure Group Model posits groups, instead of individuals, interacting in the political process to form public policy and satisfy the requirements of political linkage. The Model argues that very little individual opinion exists within a modern society, apart from group attitudes. Either groups are the source of all opinions, or all opinions of importance are expressed by groups. In this way, officials indirectly satisfy public opinion when they respond to pressure group opinions. The influence of different pressure groups would be proportional to their number of members and the intensity of member's demands. For example, supposedly the most influential pressure groups would represent the predominant and intense views of the public. Conflicting demands of different pressure groups would result in a compromise with each side getting its way in proportion to the strength of its membership support.

To evaluate the Pressure Group Model, we need to know whether its suppositions are correct. First, to what extent do officeholders respond to pressure group demands? Unless combinations of individuals can influence policy by engaging in pressure group activity, the Model cannot work. Second, to what extent does group opinion represent public opinion? The Model cannot hold if many individuals hold strong political views that are unexpressed by groups. Third, do the leaders of pressure groups know and support the preferences of their members? If there is no linkage between an organization's mass membership's choices and the behavior of its leaders, pressure groups cannot furnish any linkage between public opinion and public policy. Finally, we must examine the assumption that a group's influence ultimately rests on its broad public support. If, as many suspect, certain pressure groups succeed for reasons other than a strong mass following, then it is not public opinion that is being satisfied.

Pressure Group Activity

Compared with the lack of mass political participation, pressure groups pervade the public arena. Jewell and Patterson report that the typical state has 208 registered lobbyists, and even this large number of registered lobbyists probably grossly underestimates the scope and breadth of efforts as many unregistered groups try to influence government policy.[31] But for individual opinion to be summarized by groups seeking to affect legislation, there clearly must be sufficient groups to cover the diversity of public opinion. Thus, the mere 23 registered lobbyists in South Carolina, if exhaustive of the groups seeking to shape policy in that state, might indicate a deficiency of the Pressure Group Model in that state. But this judgment assumes that all significant groups' lobbyists are registered and that opinion within the state has greater diversity than indicated by its few groups. Because state laws requiring lobbyists to register vary greatly, we cannot tell whether the fewer lobbyists in some states reflect less pressure group activity or less rigorous registration law. Moreover admissions of pressure group activity may be more candid in some states than in others.

Harmon Zeigler and Michael Baer studied legislators' and lobbyists' perceptions of the nature of their interaction in four states: Massachusetts, North Carolina, Oregon, and Utah.[32] Table 9-5 shows both variations in the extent of interaction between legislators and lobbyists. North Carolina legislators and lobbyists not only disagree about their contact but lobbyists incorrectly believe that legislators think highly of them.[33] While only a minority of legislators in each state say legislators have occasionally or frequently been influ-

TABLE 9-5 **Mean Interactions per Week as Reported by Legislators and Lobbyists**

	Mean	N
Massachusetts		
Legislators	7.8	244
Lobbyists	10.7	185
North Carolina		
Legislators	8.5	164
Lobbyists	25.9	132
Oregon		
Legislators	34.0	84
Lobbyists	31.0	193
Utah		
Legislators	16.0	90
Lobbyists	18.5	134

Source. Harmon Zeigler and Michael Baer, *Lobbying: Interaction and Influence in American State Legislatures* (Belmont, California: Wadsworth, 1969), p. 147.

TABLE 9-6 **Extent of Influence: Percentages of Legislators and Lobbyists Believing Legislators Have Been "Frequently" or "Occasionally" Influenced**

	Extent of Influence			
	Questioning a Previously Held Opinion (%)	Leaning More Toward the Views of the Lobbyist (%)	Changing From One Position to Another (%)	(N)
Massachusetts				
Legislators	34	31	20	(244)
Lobbyists	51	39	26	(185)
North Carolina				
Legislators	22	20	18	(164)
Lobbyists	76	70	39	(132)
Oregon				
Legislators	45	42	51	(84)
Lobbyists	79	52	41	(193)
Utah				
Legislators	32	38	42	(90)
Lobbyists	77	66	48	(134)

Source. Harmon Zeigler and Michael Baer, *Lobbying: Interaction and Influence in American State Legislatures* (Belmont, California: Wadsworth, 1969), p. 155.

enced by lobbyists to question previously held opinions or to lean toward the views of the lobbyists, Table 9-6 shows substantial numbers of legislators in all states admit to utilizing information provided by pressure groups.[34] Evidently then, at least the information provided by pressure groups, if not their efforts at influence, play an important role in the making of public policy.

Does Group Opinion Equal Public Opinion?

Pressure group activity only satisfies the Model if the opinion of groups corresponds to the opinion of the public. Group opinion could, of course, reflect public opinion without every member of the public being involved in a group as long as those who did choose to be involved in groups and leaders of those groups were a representative selection of the public. Typically, 53 to 62 percent of Americans report they belong to clubs, unions, business organizations, or other voluntary associations.[35] This exceeds the 47 percent figure in the United

Kingdom, 44 percent in Germany, 29 percent in Italy, and 25 percent in Mexico, but hardly suggests we are a nation of joiners. Furthermore, only about 40 percent of group members believe their organization is involved in political affairs meaning, of course, that only about 20 to 25 percent of the American public is involved in politically relevant groups.[36] There is also strong evidence of bias in group membership as in all nations studied group membership, holding an office in the group, and belonging to several groups prove to be more likely among the better educated segment of the population. For example, in the United States 60 percent of those belonging to groups that they believe to be involved in political affairs have a secondary education or better.[37] Thus to the degree that persons of differing education prefer different public policy, group opinion would appear to be biased.

Our analysis of a Florida poll lends additional insights to our understanding of the role of groups in political linkage. Fifty-two percent of a somewhat better educated sample of 318 Floridians claim to belong to one of an extensive list of possible groups.[38] Respondents were asked whether, on local, state, and national issues, they would turn to a group, person, or other source of information and advice that they felt they could trust. Table 9-7 indicates

TABLE 9-7 **Sources of National, State, and Local Advice and Information (in Percent)**

Source	Not Mentioned	Mentioned, Unspecific[a]	Mentioned, Specific
Public persons	55	17	28
Agency of government	63	10	27
Media source	75	22	3
Group	77	7	16
Private person	78	6	16

[a] A specific mention would be to say my senator, instead of an official; the Department of Agriculture, instead of calling city hall; Newsweek, instead of reading about it; UAW instead of seeing how farmers react; and my doctor, instead of seeing how my friend reacts.

that despite this open solicitation to mention groups in answering this question, only 23 percent of the sample were conscious of or admitted to forming their opinion on the advice of groups. Additionally, only 44 percent of the groups mentioned as sources of advice were those to which the individual belonged. In conclusion then, only about 10 percent of this Florida sample concede that they formed their opinions on the basis of advice from groups to which they belonged.

The Model assumes also that each group is homogeneous or relatively so in its members' opinions on germane issues, and that group leaders accurately articulate these opinions to policy makers. Thus the group leaders or lobbyists who serve as the group's voice before decision makers must, if the model is to hold, reflect opinions shared by at least the majority of their group. We sought to assess the distinctiveness of each group's opinions on 20 state issues varying between greater effort to protect alligators and increasing state support to cities for law enforcement.[39] If each group's opinions were totally distinctive, one could predict a person's opinions by knowing his group and its opinions. Technically, this would mean that 100 percent of variation in individual opinion is explained by his group membership. Conversely, were the model totally inaccurate, 0 percent of an individual's opinion would be explained knowing his group. Our findings much more closely parallel the case of groups being irrelevant, since across the 20 different state issues an average of only four percent of the variation in individual opinion is explained knowing group memberships. This evidence might well recommend that legislators should challenge the statement by any group leader that his group consensually stands behind him in his statement of its preferences.[40]

Representation Within Pressure Groups

In their lobbying study, Zeigler and Baer note that both legislators and lobbyists see the strength of a group's impact on public policy as either dependent on its large membership and electoral muscle or on its economic muscle that is capable of having an impact both on the outcome of elections and on the state's economy.[41] Both legislators and lobbyists deny that lobbying skills are vital to this process. This would suggest that, in the case of a lobbyist representing a large membership group, it is essential for the representatives to view his statements of group policy as shared by the group. A 1964 study of the Oregon Educational Association suggests that the group leader has as much difficulty perceiving membership opinion as does the representative knowing his constituency.[42] The administrative leaders in this group were asked to complete a questionnaire broadly assessing their own opinions on various state issues and also how they saw the "average teacher answering." While leaders and members alike accepted the lobbying function of the group and leaders expressed a strong sense of concern with accurately serving their membership, leaders would err were they to assume their personal attitudes represented the group or were they to presume their perceptions matched group opinion.

Leaders would involve the association in more political activities, such as endorsing candidates in school elections and taking stands on issues. And on 11 of 13 political values assessed, leaders are more liberal.[43] But the activist stance of leadership is not as opposed by the membership as the leaders believe nor are the members as conservative on the political values as the leaders think them to be. The Oregon Educational Association leadership is condemned to acting too liberally, should they base their decisions solely on their personal opinions and too conservatively should they try to voice the opinions of their membership. Apparently it is unduly simplistic to conceptualize society as consisting only of group opinion, or to expect no difficulty or biases to be introduced by group leaders representing group opinion before legislative bodies.

We hasten to note that the Oregon findings derive from a group that might be expected to be a great deal more unified and like minded than the typical group to which the public belongs. Very few of the Florida residents claim membership in associations that seem likely to have unified memberships. The task of leaders in less distinctive groups, such as the PTA, for example, might loom even more difficult with even greater membership differences in desired means and ends. The vision of numerous groups unified in their opinions on the issues with their leaders accurately articulating the group opinion seems unrealistic even in the most group oriented society among the modern democracies. It also seems unlikely that representatives sympathetically respond to such group pressures.

Limited other critical evidence is also at hand. When Wahlke and his associates assessed legislative roles they also queried the representatives as to how facilitating they thought they needed to be toward the pressure groups in their state.[44] Typically, only 36 percent of the legislators feel they should facilitate the activities of pressure groups, and 27 percent strongly oppose such activities. Hedlund and Friesema also note that those Iowa representatives who claim they work closely with interest groups prove no more accurate in their perception of the district's opinion.[45] Were groups affording the representatives an accurate assessment of public opinion, we might well have expected the minority of legislators who were receptive to such information would more accurately portray their district's opinion.

Differences in Group Influence

Instead of pressure groups satisfying political linkage as posited by the model, it seems more likely that their activities in the halls of government are contrary to the purpose of achieving a coincidence between public opinion and public policy. As we have seen, many people belong to no group; and many of the groups to which the public does belong are apolitical. Groups lobbying before the legislature would seem, therefore, to be a different ilk than those to which the general public belongs. As we see in Table 9-8, the pre-

TABLE 9-8 **Types of Organizations with Registered Lobbyists (in Percent)**

Type of Organization	Washington, D.C. (1962)	Nebraska (1955)	Oklahoma (1961)	Illinois (1963)	Kentucky (1964)
Business	55	55	42	48	58
Labor	13	16	16	11	19
Farm	7	6	14	3	2
Professional	5	8	7	15	12
Governmental, Citizens	17	10	14	16	9
Other	3	5	7	7	0
Total	100	100	100	100	100
Number	312	86	56	280	57

Sources. Congressional Quarterly Almanac (1962), p. 941; A. C. Breckenridge, *One House for Two: Nebraska's Unicameral Legislature* (Washington, D.C.: Public Affairs Press, 1957), pp. 92–93; the Oklahoma data appear in somewhat different form in S. C. Patterson, "The Role of the Lobbyist: The Case of Oklahoma," *Journal of Politics,* XXV (1963), p. 81. The Illinois and Kentucky data come from unpublished studies by S. C. Patterson and R. Hedlund (Illinois) and M. E. Jewell (Kentucky). Cited in Malcolm E. Jewell and Samuel C. Patterson, *The Legislative Process in the United States* (New York: Random House, 1966), p. 281.

dominant number of organizations with registered lobbyists are business groups.[46] No one has attempted to assess the bias in the opinion pressed on the representative by pressure groups or the success of the groups in their lobbying efforts, although tales of the National Rifle Association's successful efforts to thwart gun registration and the dilatory actions of the American Medical Association on Medicare suggest that pressure groups can successfully *resist* public opinion.

ASSESSING THE IMPACT OF PUBLIC OPINION ON POLICY

In Chapters Seven to Nine, we have discussed five models that have the potential to provide public policy consistent with what the public would prefer. By voting for leaders who share its views, the public can fulfill the basic needs of the Rational Activist Model. If reliable voting cues are furnished by political parties, policy-oriented voters can fulfill the Political Parties Model by choosing the party platform most compatible with their views. Aside from voting, the public can influence policy makers by bringing the policies of the groups to which they belong to bear on officials, thus fulfilling the Pressure Group Model. In addition, linkage between opinions and policy can be furnished by two models that do not demand public coercion of leaders. If policy makers try to follow public opinion because they believe they should and if they perceive that opinion accurately, the Role Playing Model would be fulfilled. Finally, because leaders and followers share many of the same political beliefs, even the Sharing Model provides political linkage in many circumstances.

By itself, each of these sources of political linkage may provide only a small increase in the degree to which officials are responsive to the public. Their total effect may, in fact, be slight, since to show that public opinion can influence policy is not a demonstration that public opinion is followed all or even most of the time. Perhaps the evidence we need is some sort of counting of the frequency with which government policies are in accord with public opinion. A truly definitive study following this design would need information at the national, state, and local levels across a broad range of policies as to whether the process of political linkage results in public policy that is consistent with public opinion. We would want to be able to say which of the linkage models proves most viable and on what issues. Hopefully, we would be able to assess the consequences of linkage failure for the public's opinions about its government, for its participation in political affairs, and ultimately for political stability. Unfortunately such a study does not exist.

Since presently available evidence of the frequency of political linkage is limited, conclusions based on it must be very tentative— perhaps limited to only the specific issues studied, the level of government considered, and the time period involved. Moreover, congruence between majority opinion and government policy may not always be the best indicator of political linkage, since government decisions can be responses to the intense opinions of a minority rather than to the preferences of the majority. Also, as we have seen, "majority" opinion on an issue fluctuates with the exact wording of a survey question. Keeping these cautions in mind, let us see what the evidence shows about the congruence between public opinion and government policy.

Evidence at the National Level: The Case of Medicare

If acts of Congress were determined by the demands of public opinion, then Congress would act whenever public opinion built to majority support or higher behind a proposed program. Because polls do not regularly monitor opinions on specific proposals before Congress, we seldom know how much support the public gives to a policy prior to its enactment. However, polls can offer clues regarding how well Congress serves the broad policy guidelines preferred by the public. One issue on which we can assess this consistency between opinion and policy is Medicare—which became law in 1965. As early as 1935, a presidential commission had proposed a plan for national health insurance that would have covered more people than the present plan. In 1945, President Truman endorsed such a plan. Twenty years later Congress passed a comprehensive health insurance plan, but only for the elderly. Why was there such a delay? One reason was that although most people favored government assistance, they were not insistent. For example, consider the results of an SRC poll in 1956 (when the health care issue was dormant) that asked people whether the government should "help people get doctors and health care at low cost" and also asked for an appraisal of government performance to date (too far, less than it should, about right, or "haven't heard yet what the government is doing"). Although opinion was more than two to one in favor of government participation, only 30 percent said government was doing less than it should. The crystallized opposition who opposed government participation and said the government either was doing about right or going too far made up only 15 percent of the sample.[47] Most people apparently did not have a coherent opinion one way or the other. Even when Medicare became a central issue in the 1960s, few were attentive. According to a 1962 quiz of the public, only 57 percent said they had heard of Medicare and had any understanding of it. In fact, only 7 percent knew the basic facts—that it would be financed by Social Security and limited to people receiving old age insurance.[48]

Perhaps if people had become politically mobilized by their views on medical care, Medicare or something even more extensive would have been enacted much sooner. As things stood, the powerful American Medical Association was able to forestall satisfaction of a feeble-voiced public. In fact, neither Medicare nor its predecessors even emerged from the House Ways and Means Committee in more than very diluted form until the 1964 Democratic landslide tipped the committee's balance in favor of such legislation.

Evidence of Popular Control at the State Level

One popular area of research uses available data on how state and local government vary in expenditures and program quality in the many areas where these governments are involved, such as education, welfare, and highways. Because data are also available for states and cities as to the competitiveness of their political parties, the turnout and direction of their voting, and nonpolitical variables such as the education, wealth, and occupations of their citizens and how concentrated they are within urban areas, we can answer questions as to the relative importance of political versus nonpolitical variables on the quantity and quality of public policy.

While it might seem that this analysis would allow our judging the importance and effectiveness of political linkage to public policy, the data precludes many conclusions. Unfortunately, available political data on cities and states captures few of the important dimensions of representation and linkage. We can note whether political parties are competitive, but not whether uncompetitive cases are the result of the public's strong preference for one party and its program or the result of the public not having a choice. And of course we cannot know whether a party's popularity rests on the popularity of its position on issues or the loyalty of those identifying with it. The main difficulty with this data in general is our lack of information on public opinion.

The early findings in this field stressed that both extensive state and local investment in different policy areas and competitive and participant politics were more characteristic of states and cities with an educated, urban, and industrially employed public.[49] The implication is clear; political variations within the country are the result of differing states of economic development and have little impact on policy. More recent research suggests that the policy influence of economic development has been somewhat overstated, but the restriction of economic resources on policy alternatives seems clear.[50] This restriction has lessened since the turn of the century, and some part of it seems attributable to the routines of decision makers deciding on budgets.[51] Ira Sharkansky, for example, argues that the decision maker's yearly and complex budgetary considerations assume manageable proportions only because of his arbitrary decision to increase all programs only by an increment roughly equal to that available to increase the entire budget. His decision to increase all budgets by five percent, if that is the increase for the total budget, greatly reduces his task.

While these studies alert us to the importance of economic restrictions on public policy, they say nothing about public opinion's impact on policy. Leaders could be ignoring public opinion in voting for what they can afford or following a public mandate to enact public programs when they can be afforded. It is also possible that leaders may wish to act consistently with public opinion but despite their best efforts fail to prevail against the overwhelming restrictions of problems faced and resources available. Because the data do not include directly relevant aspects of political linkage nor any assessment of public opinion, their usefulness to our assessment is limited to the obviously strong impact of resources on policy.

To get an assessment of public opinion in every state with any confidence that the sample is representative of actual opinion would be quite costly. One group of researchers has been trying to estimate state opinion without these costs. The procedure is quite difficult but basically rests on noting differences in opinion among various types of people in available national studies and then estimating the opinions of the states from the percentages of these different types of persons within each state. By comparing these simulated state opinions with policy in the states, it is possible to designate congruent states in which a majority of public opinion is consistent with actual policy, such as when opinion opposes gun regulation and none exists, or opinion favors it and the state has such a law. Sutton uses this rough index to assess the representativeness of each state's policies in 11 broad policy areas, such as civil rights laws and capital punishment laws.[52] Table 9-9 presents his findings of the variation within the states in their success in having at least half of their laws in a given policy area in apparent agreement with state public opinion. More than half of the comparisons between laws and state opinions in New York and Nevada in all but one of the 11 policy areas indicate accurate representation. In only four of the 11 areas do the citizens of Virginia benefit from even this minimal standard of accurate representation. The states vary greatly in the degrees to which public opinion is represented in the laws they enact.

These simulated state public opinions permit the assessment of many provocative questions that before now had only been the subject of speculation. All findings using these data, however, must be viewed as tentative until we have complete assurance that the estimate of a state's opinion validly portrays actual public opinion. First, despite the extensive discussion of the importance of political party competition and voter turnout to the performance of democracy, neither state variations in competition between political parties nor variations in voter turnout seem important to the quality of representation in the states.[53] In fact, New York, the state with the most self-professed liberals, and Idaho, the state with the most self-professed conservatives, are among the most representative states,

TABLE 9-9 **Consistency Between Opinion and Policy in Eleven State Policy Areas**

Number of Policy Areas with More Than 50% Consistency	State Name
10	Nevada and New York
9	Idaho, Iowa, Texas, Utah, and Wyoming
8	Connecticut, Florida, New Hampshire, New Jersey, Tennessee, and Washington
7	Alaska, Georgia, Indiana, Massachusetts, Michigan, Mississippi, Missouri, Montana, North Dakota, Oklahoma, Oregon, Pennsylvania, and West Virginia
6	Arizona, Colorado, Delaware, Illinois, Kansas, Louisiana, Nebraska, Ohio, Rhode Island, South Carolina, and South Dakota
5	Alabama, Arkansas, California, Hawaii, Maine, Minnesota, North Carolina, and Wisconsin
4	Maryland, New Mexico, Vermont, and Virginia
3	Kentucky

Source. Adapted from Richard L. Sutton, "The States and the People: Measuring and Accounting for 'State Representatives,' " *Polity* (Summer, 1973).

while Maryland, the state with a balance between professed liberals and conservatives, is one of the least representative states.[54] Dominant control rather than fear of electoral reprisals may be necessary to achieve representation, as a state with a dominant ideology or political party may get policy compatible with public opinion while an ideologically diverse state with competitive parties may endure only struggles for control, with few desired policy outcomes. This paradox of governments that seem most democratic on one standard (competition) proving least democratic on another (congruence between opinion and policy) is suggested by studies at the local level of government also.[55]

Second, the research finds little importance in the degree of economic development enjoyed by the state and its quality of representation.[56] Education, income, occupational characteristics of the public, and urbanness all prove unrelated to representation. Finally, representation varies with issues. Civil rights and welfare programs seem to reflect public opinion best, while election laws and laws dealing with motor vehicle regulations mirror public opinion most poorly. The variations noted between issues with civil rights and social welfare legislation being most congruent with state public opinion closely parallel the findings of the Miller and Stokes study of Congress discussed in the previous chapter. And these findings suggest that the process of political linkage as future research further

TABLE 9-10 **The Relationship Between the Quality of Educator Representativeness and Public Educational Support**

Sample and Attitude	School Board Electoral Support[a]	Superintendent Electoral Support	Participation and Spending Support	Millage Support[a]
	Dimensions of Public Support			
School Board				
Ban courses[c]				
Shortcomings of Democracy				
Differences in candidates			-35	
Adequate education			-43	
Minorities do as well			-39	-42
Teachers' unions			-61	
Equal education				
Anger at failures			-48	
Busing			-60	-38[b]
Ungraded classes	-49			
Principal				
Ban courses			-54	
Shortcomings of Democracy			-70	
Differences in candidates			-67	
Adequate education			-66	
Minorities do as well			-74[b]	
Teachers' unions			-71[b]	
Equal education			-71	
Anger at failures			-73[b]	
Busing			-72	
Ungraded classes			-72[b]	

Assessing the Impact of Public Opinion on Policy **315**

Superintendent

Ban courses		45
Shortcomings of Democracy		−56[b]
Differences in candidates	−33	
Adequate education		−33
Minorities do as well		
Teachers' unions	−37	
Equal education	−34	
Anger at failures		
Busing		
Ungraded classes	−35	

[a] The signs of the factors have been reversed to correspond with meaning.
[b] Remain statistically significant when controlling for demography.
[c] The wording of the items is:
   Are there any subjects that should not be taught in our schools?
   Open discussion of any shortcomings of democracy in the United States.
   Open discussion of differences among candidates for public office.
   If schools in poorer areas do an adequate job, we should not be greatly concerned that schools in wealthy areas are better equipped and get better teachers.
   Given equal opportunities and education, such minorities will do just as well as other Americans.
   Teachers in your community should be allowed to join unions if they want to.
   More money should be spent on better buildings and teachers and on special catch-up classes to be sure that poor children get as good schooling as others.
   Although our country may have given students much that they should be thankful for, they are right in being angered by its failures.
   Busing students from one school to another as a solution to integration in our schools.
   Grouping children in large classes with many teachers that are then divided into discussion groups, thus allowing children to advance as fast as they can, doing away with the 1st grade, 2nd grade, for example.

delves into it will not find a single process holding across all public issues. Seemingly salient issues, such as civil rights and social welfare, will differ from more technical and professional judgments, such as highways and election laws.

Evidence at the Local Level: School Politics

Also relevant to the estimate of the public's impact on policy are the preliminary findings of a study of the influences on local school policy conducted by one of the authors of this text. The relationship between representation and public support in this study falls short of that predicted by theorists. The three educational decision makers, school board members, superintendents, and principals and the public gave their opinions on issues facing our public schools today.[57] Table 9-10 presents the correlations between the gaps in representation noted on 10 selected issues between each set of decision makers and their constituency and levels of public support for the school noted in those districts.[58]

If the decision makers misrepresent their public, do they lose support? While all but 29 of the possible 120 correlations are negative, showing support decreases with misrepresentation, most of these correlations are quite weak. Notably, the principals rather than either of the elected decision makers have the greatest impact on the level of public support for their schools. Moreover, neither of the support dimensions involving election support for elected officials proves very reactive to the quality of representation. Representation matters, but the public is mostly monitoring the most immediate administrators, the nonelected principals, and expresses itself in the level of voluntary participation it gives to the PTA and in its approval of bond issues. Representative quality at best accounts for little public reaction to government decisions if these educational findings are correct.

The public sample in this study was also asked what they would do were their school system poorly run. Their responses are presented in Table 9-11. Most seem inclined to work out personally the difficulty with school officials, apparently thinking that agreement could be reached among rational men talking out problems. Their next action centered on forming a group to press for solution, and they were strongly repelled by the thought of demonstrating their grievance or even using their legal recourse, the courts.[59] The alternative of defeating or threatening to defeat obstinate officials seldom occurred to the average voter, further buttressing the curious lack of a relationship between returning elected officials to office and being satisfied with their performance.

This analysis of the representation of public opinion by leaders and its impact on the level of public support presupposes the leaders' ability to shape public policy as they desire. Earlier, we noted that congressmen's roll-call voting strongly reflects their personal opinion; but as we have just seen in the analyses of state and local policy, the full range of policy is not available to decision makers. To a very substantial degree, the votes the representatives can cast are defined by the problems existent in their society, by the resources they can muster to cope with these problems, and by the sharing of conventions and proprieties as to what means are accep-

Assessing the Impact of Public Opinion on Policy **317**

TABLE 9-11 **Actions Most Likely, Second Most Likely, and Least Likely if Schools Are Poorly Run (in Percent)**

Response	Most Likely	Second Most Likely	Least Likely
Personally write or talk with school officials	57	19	1
Form a group to take the problem to officials	24	44	3
Work through friends and connections who know school officials	12	20	2
Threaten to not vote for elected officials unless they do something about the problem	2	5	11
Organize a protest demonstration	1	2	57
Go to court	0[a]	4	26
Probably do nothing, too busy	4	5	0
Don't know	0	0	0

[a] Some respondents used this alternative but their response was lost in rounding.

table to cope with problems. It may well be, therefore, that the lack of consistent relationships between attitudinal representativeness and levels of public support mirrors the difficulties the representatives have in forcing even their values and attitudes onto public policy. We turn then to the question of who shapes policy.

Our question here is probably better expressed as who *or what* shapes public policy. Most theorists assume, seemingly without warrant, that if the public does not shape policy by way of enforcing accountability among its representatives, then someone else must be shaping policy, probably the wealthy or the politicians. We do not conceive of the problems as an either/or distinction, but rather assess the impact of both decision makers and the public relative to the impact that they might have.

The Florida education study finds the public having little impact on educational policy. School districts vary in their satisfaction of various educational goals such as having quality faculty and plant, having good financial support, and providing excellent educational training, but variations in district public opinion on a broad range of controversial issues prove largely unrelated to such policy successes.[60] Across 11 issues, public opinion in a school district seems largely irrelevant to school performance, averaging a correlation of only .05. This finding holds little surprise, but the failure of the decision makers to have much more impact (.12) reveals the limits of even their influence. Elected officials charged with making decisions for the school district prove to have no more impact than do nonelected decision makers—the principals—and very little more impact than the largely apathetic public.

Conclusions

The foregoing examples are inconclusive regarding the frequency with which government policy follows public opinion. Sometimes governments appear to do what the public wants; sometimes they do not. These studies need to be evaluated cautiously. The simulated state data, despite careful evaluation and development, may invalidly represent state public opinion. Also, while Florida is a highly diverse state with county education systems running the gamut from large urban counties to rural and predominantly black counties, our findings of little public response to their lack of representation and the only limited public and decision maker influence on policy may not hold elsewhere. This evidence, however, challenges conventional notions about public opinion's role in public policy making, about public responses should there be no political linkage, and about whose opinion shapes policy if the public's does not. At least, at some governmental levels, researchers need to look further to find the substance of democracy.

FOOTNOTES TO CHAPTER 9

[1] This has been a controversial suggestion. See: Committee on Political Parties of the American Political Science Association, "Toward a More Responsible Two-Party System," *American Political Science Review*, 44 (September, 1950), supplement.

[2] Herbert McClosky, Paul J. Hoffman and Rosemary O'Hara, "Issue Conflict and Consensus Among Party Leaders and Followers," *American Political Science Review*, 59 (June, 1960), pp. 406–427.

[3] It should be noted that both samples afford the possibility of sample bias since the return rate on the public mailback questionnaire reached only 51 percent and only 44· percent of the delegates have their opinions included in the analysis. In the case of the public sample, the authors do assert that it, ". . . closely matched the national population on such characteristics as sex, age, region, size of city, and party affiliation . . . though it somewhat oversampled the upper educational levels. . . ."

[4] With the possible exception of the last issue—defense spending—we would expect no argument that the conservative positions on the issues are as we show them.

[5] McClosky, et al., p. 311.

[6] Edmund Constantini, "Intraparty Attitude Conflict: Democratic Party Leadership in California," *Western Political Quarterly*, 25 (1963), 956–72.

[7] John W. Soule and James W. Clarke, "Issue Conflict and Consensus: A Comparative Study of Democratic and Republican Delegates to the 1968 National Conventions," *Journal of Politics*, 33 (February, 1971), p. 88. Liberals in this case are ascribed on the basis of their attitudes rather than being self-professed.

[8] David Butler, "The Paradox of Party Difference," *American Behavioral Scientist*, 4 (November, 1960), pp. 3–5.

[9] Constantini, p. 969.

[10] But for contrary evidence, see Samuel J. Eldersveld, *Political Parties: A Behavioral Analysis* (Chicago: Rand McNally, 1964), p. 188.

[11] John L. Sullivan and Robert E. O'Connor, "Electoral Choice and Popular Control of Public Policy: The Case of the 1966 House Elections," *American Political Science Review* 66 (December, 1972) pp. 1256–1268.

[12] Sullivan and O'Connor report an average item to index correlation of .74, when a liberal-conservative index is created of all eight items.

[13] Sullivan and O'Connor, p. 1258.

[14] Sullivan and O'Connor, p. 1264.

[15] Sullivan and O'Connor, p. 1264.

[16] Sullivan and O'Connor, pp. 1261–1263. These findings are, of course, consistent with those noted by Miller and Stokes and discussed earlier.

[17] V. O. Key, *Public Opinion and American Democracy* (New York: Alfred A. Knopf, 1961), p. 484.

[18] Thomas R. Dye, "State Legislative Politics," in *Politics in the American States*, 2nd ed., Herbert Jacob and Kenneth N. Vines (eds.) (Boston: Little, Brown, 1971), p. 194.

[19] Hugh L. LeBlanc, "Voting in State Senates: Party and Constituency Influences," *Midwest Journal of Political Science*, 13 (February, 1969), p. 36, and recounted by Dye, p. 195.

[20] Frank J. Sorauf, *Party Politics in America* (Boston: Little, Brown, 1968), p. 341.

[21] Malcolm E. Jewell, "Party Voting in American State Legislature," *Midwest Journal of Political Science*, 49 (November, 1955), pp. 773–791. Cited from *Legislative Behavior: A Reader in Theory and Research*, John C. Wahlke and Heinz Eulau (eds.), The Free Press of Glencoe, Illinois (1959), p. 130, and LeBlanc, p. 43.

[22] Gerald M. Pomper, *Elections in America: Control and Influence in Democratic Politics* (New York: Dodd, Mead, 1968), Chapters 7 and 8.

[23] Ibid., p. 156.

[24] Ibid., p. 187.

[25] Ibid., p. 194.

[26] Ibid., p. 201.

[27] Robert S. Erikson, "The Relationship Between Party Control and Civil Rights Legislation in the American States," *Western Political Quarterly*, 24 (March, 1971), pp. 178–82.

[28] Erikson, p. 179.

[29] The literature comparing elite and public orderings of their opinions on public issues finds no instance at the local, state, or national level in which both decision makers and the public share a perspective on issues. See Norman R. Luttbeg, "The Structure of Public Beliefs on State Policies: A Comparison with Local and National Findings," *Public Opinion Quarterly*, 35 (Spring, 1971), pp. 114–116. An extensive analysis of the public attitudes toward public education

compared with school board principals', superintendents' and teachers' attitudes on the same subjects revealed no shared conception of issue patterns. The educational decision makers' conceptions of the issues in public education are not shared by the public. And even though public schools seem to be of concern to the public, their opinions appeared uncrystallized except for issues such as busing for racial integration.

30 Sullivan and O'Connor, p. 1264.

31 Malcolm E. Jewell and Samuel C. Patterson, The Legislative Process in the United States (New York: Random House, 1966), p. 279.

32 Harmon Zeigler and Michael Baer, Lobbying: Interaction and Influence in American State Legislatures (Belmont, California: Wadsworth, 1969).

33 Zeigler and Baer, p. 95.

34 Zeigler and Baer, p. 155.

35 Charles R. Wright and Herbert H. Hyman, "Voluntary Association Membership of American Adults: Evidence from National Sample Surveys," American Sociological Review, 23 (1958) reprinted in American Political Interest Groups: Readings in Theory and Research, Betty H. Zisk (ed.), (Belmont, California: Wadsworth, 1969); Gabriel A. Almond and Sidney Verba, The Civic Culture (Princeton: Princeton University Press, 1963), p. 302; and Sidney Verba and Norman Nie, Participation in Democracy (New York: Harper Row, 1972) p. 41.

36 Almond and Verba, p. 306.

37 Almond and Verba, p. 308.

38 This 1969 study of educational attitudes of 703 Floridians included a drop-off questionnaire that was returned by 318 respondents. While 47 percent of the returnees had an education better than high school, only 37 percent of the total sample had.

39 For a full enumeration of the issues see Norman R. Luttbeg, "The Structure of Public Beliefs on State Policies: A Comparison with Local and National Findings," Public Opinion Quarterly, 31 (Spring, 1971), pp. 114–116.

40 The percentage of explained variance varied between two percent on strengthening state air and water pollution laws, and seven percent on making all church property taxable.

41 Zeigler and Baer, pp. 195–197.

42 Norman R. Luttbeg and Harmon Zeigler, "Attitude Consensus and Conflict in an Interest Group: An Assessment of Cohesion," American Political Science Review, 60 (September 1966), pp. 655–65.

43 Luttbeg and Zeigler, p. 662.

44 Wahlke, p. 327.

45 Hedlund and Friesema, p. 16.

46 Jewell and Patterson, 403.

47 Recomputed from Key, p. 269.

48 Mark V. Nadel, "Public Policy and Public Opinion," in American Democracy: Theory and Reality, by Robert Weisberg and Mark V. Nadel (eds.) (New York: Wiley, 1972), p. 540.

49 Thomas R. Dye, Economics, Politics and the Public: Policy Outcomes in the American States (Chicago: Rand McNally, 1966), pp. 286–87.

50 Ira Sharkansky and Richard I. Hofferbert, "Dimensions of State Policy," in Politics in the American States: A Comparative Analysis, 2nd ed., by Herbert Jacob and Kenneth N. Vines (eds.), (Boston: Little, Brown, 1971), pp. 315–353; James Clarke, "Environment, Process and Policy: A Reconsideration," American

Political Science Review, 62 (December, 1969) pp. 1172–82; and Norman R. Luttbeg, "Classifying the American States: An Empirical Attempt to Identify Internal Variations," *Midwest Journal of Political Science,* 15 (November, 1971) pp. 703–72.

[51] Sharkansky and Hofferbert, pp. 322–23.

[52] Richard L. Sutton, "The States and the People: Measuring and Accounting for 'State Representatives,' " *Polity* (Summer, 1973).

[53] Frank Munger, "Opinions, Elections, Parties, and Policies: A Cross-State Analysis," a paper presented at the American Political Science Association Convention, September 2–6, 1969, New York, p. 30; Sutton, p. 33; and Ronald E. Weber and William R. Shaffer, "Public Opinion and American State Policy-Making," *Midwest Journal of Political Science,* 16 (November, 1972).

[54] Ibid., p. 26.

[55] Robert Presthus, *Men at the Top* (New York: Oxford Univ. Press, 1964), p. 410.

[56] Sutton; and Weber and Shaffer.

[57] This survey completed by the Survey Data Center in 1969 included 62 superintendents and 130 school board members from the state's 67 school districts and sampled 155 principals and 703 citizens within an area random sampling of 27 counties. Interviews with the public were professionally administered and the decision makers completed their own questionnaires.

[58] Representational gap was assessed by noting absolute differences between the means for each decision maker and the mean of the public in that district. The school policy variables are factors found in analyzing 13 measures of public support for their schools in the area of electoral, financial, and voluntary supports. They are:

Superintendent electoral support	—The margin of victory and turnout in superintendent elections
School board electoral support	—The margin and frequency of school board election victories
Participation and willingness to spend	—Private school attendance, school bond victories, and PTA participation

For a complete analysis see Richard W. Griffin, "An Analysis of the Relations Among Attitudes and Values, Public Support, and Public Policies in the County Educational Systems of Florida" an unpublished Dissertation submitted to the Department of Government of Florida State University, August 1970.

[59] Norman R. Luttbeg, "Florida Educational Needs: Public Satisfactions and Dissatisfactions with Their Schools," a final report submitted to the Florida State Department of Education and reprinted by the Institute for Social Research, Florida Sate University.

[60] These opinions are 11 of better than 118 solicited in the study described above. They were selected because they are controversial in school politics within the state and thus might be expected to have implications to performance of the schools.

TEN

MASS PARTICIPATION AND DEMOCRATIC THEORY

According to democratic theory, the health of a democracy depends on the existence of a politically informed and active citizenry. By carefully monitoring government affairs, citizens could develop informed opinions about policies that would represent their interests. By working for and voting for candidates who represent their views, and by making their views known to elected leaders, citizens could collectively translate their various policy preferences into government action. The resulting set of policies that governments would enact would represent a reasonable compromise between competing claims of equally powerful citizens.

INTERPRETING THE PUBLIC'S ROLE IN DEMOCRACY

As this book describes, the public generally does not live up to its prescribed activist role. Moreover, while it is true that public opinion can often influence government policy, in reality public opinion is not the sole determinant of policy outcomes. Why not? Public control of government decisions depends on both the extent to which people actually participate in policies and the equality of peoples' resources for effective participation. The first point is obvious. It seems logical that the more people participate in politics, the more they can influence government decisions. But some people can participate more effectively than others because they command a greater share of the necessary resources such as money, information, articulateness, and access to decision makers. How inequitable one views the distribution of these political resources can determine one's view of how democratic the political system actually is. Some observers see effective political power concentrated in the hands of a "power elite" who control policy outcomes for their own interests. Others more optimistically see the inequality in the distribution of power limited basically to the different political skills that individuals have and their interest in using them.[1] Because this debate over the equality of the distribution of political power is not easily decided by scientific inquiry, we shall not enter it directly here. But, taking into account that the tools of effective political participation are not equally distributed, how can we assess the less than active political role of the public? We shall discuss four different plausible conclusions.

Public Apathy as Mass Political Incompetence

Perhaps the easiest view of the public's limited role in government affairs is that people are simply incapable of doing any better. The frequency with which people fail to hold political opinions, the rarity of the liberal or conservative "ideologue," and the difficulty in locating rational policy-oriented voters may all indicate that people generally lack the skills necessary to make sophisticated judgments about their political leaders and policies. Worse yet, the political views that people do hold may be intolerant, naïve, or simply wrong. Viewed from this perspective, an increase in public participation would only make the situation worse because "bad" public opinion would drive "good" policy makers toward undesirable acts.

If the mass public is viewed as being inherently incapable of playing a useful role, then the remedy of trying to "uplift" public opinion becomes ineffective. Instead, one might have to rely on the proper training or careful recruitment of political leaders as a means of producing desired outcomes. If such desired outcomes include the preservation of the substance of democracy, then one must prescribe both a limited public role and the instillation of a heavy dose of democratic values among political elites. Thomas Dye and Harmon Zeigler, who arrive at this position, call it the "irony of democracy."[2]

Public Apathy as Rational Disengagement

Possibly the reason that most people do not allow politics to intrude far into their lives is that to do so would be irrational. From a strict cost-versus-benefit standpoint, one should not follow public affairs closely, since the investment would get one nowhere. One's vote is useless because it is fantasy to assume that one vote can decide an election's outcome except in the most extraordinary circumstances. Even when one's economic interests are directly at stake in the political arena (which may be rare), organizing like-minded people for collective political pressure is irrational because the costs of organization outweigh the possible benefits one could expect.[3] The cynic might also suggest that increased public knowledge of governmental affairs would only produce greater political withdrawal, as people who learn about their leaders' corruption and unresponsiveness will feel even more helpless at the prospect of changing things.

If this logic is correct, then people who do participate in politics usually are motivated by something other than tangible personal gains. Perhaps they "irrationally" participate in order to gratify a felt obligation or civic duty. If the major determinant of an individuals' sense of obligation to participate is preadult political socialization, then a reformer might hope to increase public participation by improving the "training" of the next generation of citizens. Alternatively, one might hope to eliminate rational withdrawal from politics by somehow increasing the rewards of political participation.

Public Apathy as Elite Manipulation

One can also interpret the public's low participation in politics as the result of manipulation by leaders and their allies. When one observes political docility ·on the part of people who seemingly should have strong reasons for political protest, it is easy to draw the conclusion that the individuals are being misled by propaganda. Whether or not one can support such an interpretation depends on one's convictions that the individuals in question are actually oppressed. A convinced Marxist, for example, can readily view the lack of class consciousness on the part of American workers as a sign of deception by the existing power structure. Similarly, a member of the John Birch Society might attribute the public's lack of concern about what he sees as a pervasive communist conspiracy to be a sign of the effectiveness of that conspiracy.

One does not have to believe in a complex conspiracy in order to view political quiescence as the result of elite manipulation. Because most political events are remote from people's everyday lives, people willingly view these events through the interpretation of their leaders. Also, since people want to believe that their political system is benign rather than corrupt or evil, they readily find reassurance from optimistic interpretations of the existing order and resist the voices that tell them otherwise.[4] This may be why most Americans will deny any immorality to America's role in Vietnam and will support the police in any violent confrontation with political protestors.

If one sees people as unwilling to accept "truth" because they do not want to disturb their cherished beliefs, the obvious remedy would appear to be heavy doses of correct information. But how to make this remedy effective remains unclear.

Public Apathy as Public Contentment

Rather than viewing public apathy as a sign that the classical democratic model does not hold, one can interpret apathy as an indicator of public contentment. If people do not concern themselves with political matters, then they must not have any additional demands to make on their government. Conversely, when many people do participate in politics, it is a distressing signal either that government has ignored public needs or that conflicts between societal groups are no longer being successfully resolved by political leaders.

Interpreting the Public's Role in Democracy **325**

Actually, the view that public apathy means public satisfaction rests on the assumption that the public is rather politically sophisticated. It assumes that people are capable of articulating any grievances they might have, that people feel that their expression of grievances would be effective, and that people are not easily led to ignore their interests. Only if these assumptions are made can one conclude that the lack of political participation indicates that peoples' needs are met by the proper working of a democratic system.

Although they contradict one another, each of these four possible explanations of the public's lack of political participation contains a grain of truth. For example, the public may not be capable of participation in all government decisions, particularly when the decision depends on proper evaluation of advanced technical knowledge. Equally obvious, is that people can take only limited time from their personal affairs to participate in politics. Moreover, people may decide not to participate because they feel (perhaps mistakenly) that they can trust their political leaders. Finally, people may sometimes retire from the political arena because they have no particular grievances.

Simply holding them up to the light of scientific evidence cannot determine which of the explanations of low participation in politics is most valid, since every observer will view the evidence through the filter of his own preconceptions and values. How the observer views such matters as human nature, people's basic interests, and the benevolence of government can shape how strongly he concludes that political inactivity signifies incapability, rational withdrawal, manipulation, or contentment. Similarly, the extent to which the observer sees his own opinions in harmony with majority opinion might influence his view of whether public control of government should increase or decrease.

THE EXPANSION OF POLITICAL PARTICIPATION

Whether increased public political participation is desirable also depends on the type of political participation. Few would applaud the increased mass participation that would result in civil war or mass mobilization in support of an antidemocratic movement. But few would fear an increase in informed, democratic participation—particularly if we ignore possible disagreements over what "informed democratic participation" means. When there is little mass participation, the burden of responsibility falls on the political elites—both to insure the continuation of the democratic rules and also to make policy decisions that are fair and equitable. But if one agrees that the purpose of democracy is to insure that political leaders are held accountable to the people, one can hardly applaud when people do not actively seek to protect their own interests. Are there any ways to increase the number of active participants while at the same time insuring that this participation will be rational and democratic?

Seemingly part of the answer would involve some way of creating a more politically informed public. Since the public can hardly be blamed for its political ignorance when it is given little information on which to make its political judgments, we can favor more thorough political reporting by the news media and the efforts of various "public interest" groups (such as Ralph Nader's organizations and John Gardner's Common Cause) to increase public awareness. Hopes should not be set too high, however, because information campaigns do not always reach the people who are most in need of them. Also, we must recognize the possibility of side effects produced by increased public knowledge, such as greater public cynicism or an intensification of conflict between politically aroused mass groups.

Possibly, an increase in mass political participation could be brought about by the difficult task of creating a culture or climate of opinion that encourages more participation. The place to start would be with children, whose political values and expectations are not yet formed. Since it would be difficult to politicize American families that are not already politically active, the public schools would be a more plausible agent than the family for the encouragement of greater participation—perhaps, as some suggest, by instituting greater student participation in classroom decision making. But even if this would work in principle, it may be politically impossible to implement, since people generally see the proper role of schools as instilling loyalty and respect for authorities rather than permitting premature sharing of classroom authority by pupils. Of course, even more than early schooling, the college experience prepares young people for activist political roles. Thus the trend toward increasing attendance in institutions of higher education may provide some increase in public activism without large-scale reform programs. But events might channel the "idealism" of college youths into cynical withdrawal or violent participation rather than into participation in "normal" political activities.

Simply changing the laws in certain ways may be the most realistic means of bringing about at least modest increases in political participation. For example, the voting rate might increase considerably if obstacles to voter registration are eliminated so that each voter could register automatically rather than having to take the time and effort to do this on his own. Political influence would become more evenly distributed if laws to limit and regulate campaign contributions can effectively weaken the influence of wealthy special interest groups.

Perhaps the existing methods for translating public opinion into government policy are inaccurate relics from a technically primitive time when ballot casting, face-to-face communication, and geographic representation were the only feasible conduits for public expression. A novel but simple way to encourage greater participation would be to increase the number of decisions in which the public can play a greater role. Participation might increase not only from the increase in the public's options to participate but also from a resultant growth in the public's perception that its opinions count. Participation could be encouraged by giving people greater opportunity to participate directly in local decisions, including perhaps more participatory democracy in nongovernmental organizations such as the factory, school, or church. Also the public can play a more direct role by deciding policy questions in referenda instead of letting their elected leaders decide them. There have even been proposals for more direct democracy at the national level, such as by the attachment of electronic devices in every home that would allow the public to pass laws by instantaneous referenda.[5] There is little question that extensive public participation is a desired democratic value. But it is debatable whether additional opportunities to participate would lead to wiser government decisions than elected leaders presently make. While proposals for expanding participation deserve serious consideration, their practicability and desirability remain uncertain.

FOOTNOTES TO CHAPTER 10

[1] The most widely cited representatives of these opposing viewpoints are C. Wright Mills, The Power Elite (New York: Oxford University Press, 1956); and Robert A. Dahl, Who Governs? (New Haven: Yale University Press, 1961).

[2] Thomas R. Dye and Harmon Zeigler, The Irony of Democracy, 2nd ed. (Belmont, California: Wadsworth, 1972).

[3] For the development of this particular point, see Mancur Olson, Jr., The Logic of Collective Action (Cambridge: Harvard University Press, 1965).

[4] For a provocative discussion of opinion manipulation, see Murray Edelman, The Symbolic Uses of Politics (Urbana: University of Illinois Press, 1965).

[5] This proposal may be technically feasible. See Leo Bogart, Silent Politics: Polls and the Awareness of Public Opinion (New York: Wiley, 1972), Ch. 1.

APPENDIX

1968 Survey Research Center Opinion Items

In several places, this book examines the responses to opinion questions asked by the Survey Research Center in its 1968 survey. Because these questions are lengthy, their content is usually presented in the text in an abbreviated form. Below are the complete wordings of these questions. Responses are labeled as (L) for liberal and (C) for conservative according to how these terms are applied to the response alternatives within the text.

Aid to Education

Some people think the government in Washington should help towns and cities provide education for grade and high school children; others think this should be handled by the states and local communities. Have you been interested enough in this to favor one side over the other? (IF YES) Which are you in favor of—

(L)   getting help from the government
or (C)   handling it at the State and local level

Medicare

Some say the government in Washington ought to help people get doctors and hospital care at low cost; others say the government should not get into this. Have you been interested enough in this to favor one side over the other? (IF YES) What is your position? Should the government in Washington—

(L)   help people get doctors and hospital care at low cost
or (C)   stay out of this

Guaranteed Standard of Living

In general, some people feel that the government in Washington should see to it that every person has a job and a good standard of living. Others think the government should just let each person get ahead on his own. Have you been interested enough in this to favor one side over the other? (IF YES) Do you think that the government—

(L)   should see to it that every person has a job and a good standard of living
or (C)   should let each person go ahead on his own

Fair Employment

Some people feel that if Negroes are not getting fair treatment in jobs the government in Washington should see to it that they do. Others feel that this is not the federal government's business. Have you been interested enough in this question to favor one side over the other? (IF YES) How do you feel? Should the government in Washington—

(L) see to it that Negroes get fair treatment in jobs

or (C) leave these matters to the states and local communities

School Integration

Some people say that the government in Washington should see to it that white and Negro children are allowed to go to the same schools. Others claim that this is not the government's business. Have you been concerned enough about this question to favor one side over the other? (IF YES) Do you think the government in Washington should—

(L) see to it that white and Negro children go to the same schools

or (C) stay out of this area as it is none of its business

Public Accommodations

As you may know, Congress passed a bill that says Negroes should have the right to go to any hotel or restaurant they can afford just like anybody else. Some people feel this is something the government in Washington should support; others feel the government should stay out of this matter. Have you been interested enough in this to favor one side over another? (IF YES) Should the government support the right of Negroes—

(L) to go to any hotel or restaurant they can afford

or (C) stay out of this matter

Foreign Aid

Some people think that we should give aid to other countries when they need help, while others think each country should make its own way as best it can. Have you been interested enough in this to favor one side over the other? Which opinion is most like yours?

(L) give aid to other countries

or (C) each country should make its own way

Talk with Communists

Some people think it is all right for our government to sit down and talk to the leaders of the communist countries and try to settle

our differences, while others think we should refuse to have anything to do with them. Have you been interested enough in this to favor one side over the other? (IF YES) What do you think? Should we—
- (L) try to discuss and settle our differences
- or (C) refuse to have anything to do with leaders of communist countries

Trade with Communists

Some people say that our farmers and businesses should be able to do business with communist countries as long as the goods are not used for military purposes; others say that our government should not allow Americans to trade with communist countries. Have you been interested enough in this to favor one side over the other? (IF YES) How do you feel? Should farmers and businessmen be—
- (L) allowed to do business with communist countries
- or (C) forbidden to do business with communist countries

Vietnam Involvement

Do you think we did the right thing in getting into the fighting in Vietnam or should we have stayed out?
- (L) should have stayed out
- or (C) did the right thing

Vietnam Policy

Which of the following do you think we should not do in Vietnam?
- (L) $\begin{cases} \text{pull out of Vietnam entirely} \\ \text{keep our soldiers in Vietnam but try to end the fighting} \end{cases}$
- or (C) take a stronger stand even if it means invading North Vietnam

Lawful Protest

How about taking part in protest meetings or marches that are permitted by the local authorities? Would you approve of doing that, disapprove, or would it depend on the circumstances?
- (L) $\begin{cases} \text{approve} \\ \text{depends} \end{cases}$
- or (C) disapprove

Civil Disobedience

How about refusing to obey a law that one thinks unjust, if the person feels so strongly about it that the person is willing to go to jail rather than obey the law? Would you approve of a person doing that, disapprove, or would it depend on the circumstances?

(L) {approve
depends}

or (C) disapprove

Sit Ins

Suppose all other methods have failed and the person decides to try to stop the government from going about its usual activities with sit ins, mass meetings, demonstrations, and things like that? Would you approve of that, disapprove, or would it depend on the circumstances?

(L) {approve
depends}

or (C) disapprove

Government Power

Some people are afraid the government in Washington is getting too powerful for the good of the country and the individual person. Others feel the government in Washington is not getting too strong for the good of the country. Have you been interested enough to favor one side over the other? (IF YES) What is your feeling, do you think—

(L)   the government is getting too powerful

or (C)   the government has not gotten too strong

AUTHOR INDEX

A

Abelson, Robert P., 165, 249
Adelson, Joseph, 129, 160
Adorno, Theodore W., 117, 121
Alexander, Herbert E., 164, 249
Alford, Robert R., 183, 210
Almond, Gabriel A., 3, 4, 21, 22, 107, 108, 110, 120, 321
Anderson, Ronald E., 95, 96
Anderson, Totten J., 251
Axelrod, Robert, 85, 96

B

Baer, Michael A., 304, 305, 307, 321
Bagdikian, Ben H., 162, 163
Banfield, Edward C., 163, 208
Barber, James David, 254, 285, 286
Barrett, Marvin, 163
Bell, Charles G., 251
Benham, Thomas W., 68, 249
Bennett, Stephen Earl, 95
Berelson, Bernard R., 160, 164, 211
Bogart, Leo, 148, 163, 328
Boyd, Richard W., 251
Boynton, G. R., 287
Brodbeck, Authur J., 251
Brody, Richard A., 227, 250, 251, 276, 287

B (continued)

Bruner, Jerome S., 116, 120, 121
Buchanan, William, 111
Burdick, Eugene, 251
Burnham, Walter Dean, 22, 97, 210, 249, 250, 252
Butler, David, 5, 21, 210, 293, 320

C

Campbell, Angus, 4, 22, 73, 95, 96, 106, 119, 120, 151, 161, 162, 164, 165, 208, 212, 238, 247, 249, 250, 251, 285
Cantril, Albert H., 21
Cantril, Hadley, 21, 43, 44, 57, 61, 62, 68, 69, 70, 95, 111, 113, 120, 180, 191, 211
Cantwell, Frank V., 164
Caspary, William, 63, 96
Cirino, Robert, 162
Clapp, Charles L., 286
Clarke, James W., 293, 320, 322
Clausen, Aage, R., 274, 287
Coleman, James S., 135, 161, 163
Converse, Philip E., 22, 30, 31, 33, 60, 61, 95, 96, 106, 119, 160, 161, 164, 165, 223, 249, 250, 251, 274, 287, 288
Costantine, Edmund, 293, 294, 320
Craig, Robert E., 251

SUBJECT INDEX